'This is a wonderful, and wonder-filled, book. Curry patiently but passionately explores how enchantment returns us to a more elemental relationship with the world through the gifts of art, music, and fiction. Moving seamlessly between theoretical reflection and personal experience, *Art and Enchantment* also serves as a model for a living criticism alert to the necessity of art in a dangerously disenchanted world. We won't heal our earth without finding our way back to it; this book can help.'

Scott Black, Professor of English, University of Utah, USA

'In an era where so many vaunt the subversive, critical and revolutionary potentials of art, Patrick Curry's book is a welcome alternative, a refreshing return to wonder and enchantment. Informed by deep scholarship worn lightly and artistic tradition alike, this work is accessible, thought-provoking, and occasionally even enchanting.'

Tom Boland, Senior Lecturer in Sociology, University College Cork, Ireland

'Patrick Curry's *Art and Enchantment* is one man's journey into the mystery of art: enchantment, being 'in the song'. In his search, Curry discards the enemies of enchantment – the didact, the rationalist, and the one who looks for some quasi-scientific logic – and in doing so compiles a powerful case against modern civilization. His range of references is prodigious. He has read more, seen more and absorbed more than most of us could match. He writes with a disarming modesty and eloquence, and convinces by his pin-point descriptions. This is a book to be savoured.'

John Elsom, PhD, author of Missing the Point: The Rise of High Modernity and the Decline of Everything Else

ART AND ENCHANTMENT

This book concerns the experience of enchantment in art. Considering the essential characteristics, dynamics and conditions of the experience of enchantment in relation to art, including liminality, it offers studies of different kinds of artistic experience and activity, including painting, music, fiction and poetry, before exploring the possibility of a life oriented to enchantment as the activity of art itself. With attention to the complex relationship between wonder in art and the programmatic disenchantment to which it is often subject, the author draws on the thought of a diverse range of philosophers, sociological theorists and artists, to offer an understanding of art through the idea of enchantment, and enchantment through art. An accessible study, richly illustrated with experience – both that of the author and others – Art and Enchantment will appeal to scholars and students of sociology, anthropology, philosophy, and anyone with interests in the nature of aesthetic experience.

Patrick Curry is a tutor in the School of Environment, Archaeology, History and Anthropology at the University of Wales Trinity St David, UK. He is the author of *Ecological Ethics: An Introduction* and *Enchantment: Wonder in Modern Life*, and the editor of *Divination: Perspectives for a New Millennium*. He is also editor-in-chief of the online journal *The Ecological Citizen*.

Contemporary Liminality

Series editor: Arpad Szakolczai, University College Cork, Ireland.
Series advisory board: Agnes Horvath, University College Cork, Ireland; Bjørn Thomassen, Roskilde University, Denmark; and Harald Wydra, University of Cambridge, UK.

This series constitutes a forum for works that make use of concepts such as 'imitation', 'trickster' or 'schismogenesis', but which chiefly deploy the notion of 'liminality', as the basis of a new, anthropologically focused paradigm in social theory. With its versatility and range of possible uses rivalling mainstream concepts such as 'system', 'structure' or 'institution', liminality by now is a new master concept that promises to spark a renewal in social thought.

While charges of Eurocentrism are widely discussed in sociology and anthropology, most theoretical tools in the social sciences continue to rely on approaches developed from within the modern Western intellectual tradition, whilst concepts developed on the basis of extensive anthropological evidence and which challenged commonplaces of modernist thinking, have been either marginalised and ignored, or trivialised. By challenging the taken-for-granted foundations of social theory through incorporating ideas from major thinkers, such as Nietzsche, Dilthey, Weber, Elias, Voegelin, Foucault and Koselleck, as well as perspectives gained through modern social and cultural anthropology and the central concerns of classical philosophical anthropology *Contemporary Liminality* offers a new direction in social thought.

Titles in this series

18. Diseases, Disasters and Political Theory
Reflections of Political Theory from Antiquity to the Age of COVID
Lee Trepanier

19. Political Anthropology as Method
Arpad Szakolczai

20. Art and Enchantment
How Wonder Works
Patrick Curry

For more information about this series, please visit: https://www.routledge.com/Contemporary-Liminality/book-series/ASHSER1435

ART AND ENCHANTMENT

How Wonder Works

Patrick Curry

LONDON AND NEW YORK

Designed cover image: Cover image by Suzanna Saumarez

First published 2023
by Routledge
2 Park Square, Milton Park, Abingdon, Oxon OX14 4RN

and by Routledge
605 Third Avenue, New York, NY 10158

Routledge is an imprint of the Taylor & Francis Group, an informa business

© 2023 Patrick Curry

British Library Cataloguing-in-Publication Data
A catalogue record for this book is available from the British Library

ISBN: 978-1-032-40468-4 (hbk)
ISBN: 978-1-032-40467-7 (pbk)
ISBN: 978-1-003-35322-5 (ebk)

DOI: 10.4324/9781003353225

Typeset in Bembo
by SPi Technologies India Pvt Ltd (Straive)

CONTENTS

Acknowledgements   *viii*

1   Introduction   1

2   What is Enchantment?   8

3   Painting I   48

4   Painting II   92

5   Music I   111

6   Music II   138

7   Fiction I   170

8   Fiction II   203

9   Poetry   223

10 Conclusion   232

Index   *237*

ACKNOWLEDGEMENTS

'Books find their readers', according to Joseph Brodsky. I want to believe that – must believe it – but just as mysteriously, books find their authors. Enchantment has been a lifelong concern for me, consciously so starting more than twenty-five years ago, and I began writing this book more than seven years ago.

Fortunately, authors also find allies and interlocutors. I was extremely lucky in this respect in Arpad Szakolczai, whom I encountered in Cork in early 2020 – a chance meeting, as we say in Middle-Earth – and all the more so that he has honoured this book by welcoming it into his Routledge series. I also appreciate all the help I have received from Neil Jordan at Routledge.

While I was writing, it seemed the world – including the publishing world – was quite content to confirm the negligibility of my project, so I am all the more appreciative of those along the way who indicated that I might be onto something interesting, even important, and were often willing to help with suggestions and critical comments. That doesn't mean any of them agree with everything I've said! Indeed, I doubt if any do. But it does mean that any remaining errors or infelicities are mine alone.

So I am very grateful to Michael Winship, Clay Ramsay and Leslie Van Gelder, and especially, for her unwavering support, Susan Peters. All have read and commented invaluably on all, or significant parts, of earlier drafts. Of the penultimate draft, Mary Attwood read and commented on the chapters on painting, Michael Winship and Jesper Siberg on the chapters on music, and Clay Ramsay on the chapters on fiction; my thanks to them all. I am also appreciative, for insightful exchanges, to Suzanna Saumarez, Liz Greene, Melanie Gold, Elena Bernardini and Fabrizio Manco, on art; Garry Todd, Jesper Siberg, Elan Mehler and Michael and Eleanor Winship, on music; and Andy Barritt and Neil Platts, on fiction. (If I have forgotten anyone, it is only my memory that is at fault.)

I also want to thank the following persons, in addition to those already named, for their kind support: Iain McGilchrist, John Elsom, Sean Kane, Peter Moore, David Abram, Paul Reade, Pico Iyer, Anthony Thorley and Celia Gunn, Beate Süss, Christopher J. Moore, Jan Zwicky, Mark Dickinson, Sue Bayliss, Laurence Coupe, John Parham, Chantal Allison, Stone Fitzgerald, Martine Sandor, Kigen-san Licha, Stephen Fitzpatrick, Garry Phillipson, Michael York and Richard Switzler, Lis McLoughlin, Alf and Natasha Seegert, Scott Black, Nigel Cooper, Naomi Horoiwa, Kathleen Kelley-Lainé, Paulo Palmieri, Walter Weiss, Judy Kravitz and Peter Morgan, Chrissy Philp, Brian Kennedy, Evelien Van Beeck, Chris Beckett and Isao Miura, Joe Gray, Graham Douglas, Lykke Strunk, Karen and Ian Whyte, Petra Stapp, Adam Dickerson, Eileen Crist, Patrick Joyce, Marlene Roeder, Anita Klubjer, Bernard Eccles, Eleanor March, Garey Mills, Daniela Vogt, Nicholas Campion, Alfred Schmidt, Ray Keenoy and my brothers Mark and Steele Curry; also the sadly late Wendy Wheeler, Tim Robinson, Russell Hoban, Mary Midgley, Ursula Le Guin and Stephen Harrod Buhner.

I also remain eternally grateful to Gregory Bateson, from whom I learned to really think. (It would wait until reading Wittgenstein, many years later, to realise what I had been learning.) Not, note, *how* to think, but *to* think. The two are quite different.

Lastly, there is the work of all the poets, storytellers, philosophers, musicians, painters, scholars and critics whom I quote or cite and discuss but didn't know personally. Most are no longer alive. But as Auden ventures, 'works of art are our chief means of breaking bread with the dead, and without communication with the dead a fully human life, I believe, is not possible'. In the course of writing this book I have indeed broken bread and communed with the technically dead, and while I can only hope the result is worthy of them, I know what an honour it's been for me.

INTRODUCTION

One day, in an exhibition, I unexpectedly encountered an old friend whom I was, nonetheless, now seeing clearly for the first time. It was an ancient Chinese landscape painting by Ni Zan, 'Six Gentlemen', which I had only known from reproductions. The gentlemen in question happen to be pine-trees, elegant but tough and aloof, on a tiny island, and they spoke to some ideal I have long held, or which has long held me.

I stood still and stared at it for what was probably quite a while; although it's hard to say, for one of the things that happened was that time radically slowed. Other viewers flickered in and out of my vision around the painting as if in a speeded-up film, while the painting and I communed as if we had all the time in the world. I found myself both outside the painting (obviously enough), looking at it as a whole, and at the same time inside the painting (oddly enough), looking at the scene portrayed from somewhere within it. I was standing alongside the trees in the painting, seeing the distant mountains even as I looked on at them, as if through a window, from a gallery in the Grand Palais.

Like many others, I have also experienced musical transport. As a younger man, for example, I was attending a concert by The Albion Band, and in the course of a folk song with a nautical theme (it might have been 'A Sailor's Life') the oboist played a solo that carried me away. It was the essence of the sea, both its power and its beauty, equally overwhelming. But where did it take me to? I was still in that room in London in the late 1970s, but somehow simultaneously in quite another time and place: a much wilder and saltier place, a long time ago, or perhaps still to come.

Still earlier, I remember vividly reading *Peer Gynt* rapt, wholly gripped, turning the pages in order to find out what would happen to Peer – that is, to me – next. Every reader of a book, says Proust, is actually reading himself, and I just was this eternal teenager, simultaneously in pursuit of and in flight from himself.[1] That was

DOI: 10.4324/9781003353225-1

already true, but I first realised it in something written a hundred years ago by a long-dead Norwegian playwright.

This book celebrates and defends the experience of wonder in art, and of art as enchanting. It explores the characteristics, conditions, and dynamics of artistic creativity and appreciation. But it also concerns the absence of enchantment, and the reasons for that. I don't altogether rule out the possibility of any art enchanting, but I do suggest that some kinds are more likely to than others, and we shall see why.

Every work of art is an amalgam of its own particular properties and their apprehension by a viewer or listener or reader. Their capacities in turn are themselves a mixture of temperament and prior experience. It follows that even the most unlikely art can enchant someone, and that the most enchanting art can fail to do so. However, we are a particular sort of creature, and human nature is not infinitely plastic. So the middle ground of human experience will be much more populated than the extremes, and exceptions do not disqualify generalisations (especially if I can make them explicable).

Enchantment neither exhausts the importance nor the interest of art, nor can it alone determine artistic quality. Fortunately, therefore, we don't need to become involved in debates about what is and isn't art, or what is good and bad art. Our only concerns are whether it is art that enchants – if so, why? – and if not, why not? Any criticisms that I make of some mainstream modern art are thus not a defence of an outdated *ancien régime*, nor of high culture against low. However elusive, enchantment in art is something quite specific which cuts across those debates. Respecting them, I can afford to agree with the elderly cleaner overheard by a friend in a corporate monolith in Johannesburg, whose foyer was graced, so to speak, by a huge, twisted metal sculpture. The cleaner's younger colleague, indicating it with his head, asked in efficiently attenuated English, 'What's?' To which the other replied, out of the side of his mouth, 'Aart.'

Much art is not intended to enchant; the artist is instead keen to emote or arouse or shock or entertain or convince or make a lot of money, or even to disenchant. Even in those cases, though, some works might enchant despite themselves, so to speak, although, on the whole, any such tendency will be dampened if not suppressed. Of course, the artist can set out to enchant, but that by no means guarantees success. As we shall see, true enchantment is wild; it can be invited, but never ordered up, managed or controlled.

There are many instances of art which, it can be universally agreed, are of the first rank of their kind – powerful, stirring, moving – but not enchanting, or only incidentally so. Picasso's 'Guernica', Jimi Hendrix's 'Star-Spangled Banner' of 1969, Margaret Atwood's *The Handmaid's Tale*, Bertold Brecht's *The Threepenny Opera*, and Bob Dylan's early anti-war songs all come to mind. It is no accident that these are all instances, broadly but unmistakeably, of political art.

As John Luther Adams says, 'More often than not, political art fails as politics, and all too often it fails as art.'[2] But even on the occasions when it is exciting, and even effective, agitprop – explicitly and deliberately political art – sacrifices art's potential enchantment. It replaces metaphor, with its almost limitless applicability to the experience of the viewer or listener and their freedom to make connections, with allegory, in which there is only one limited meaning which has already been determined by the artist.

The lack of coincidence between enchanting art and art with an agenda – even if it is progressive – reflects a related point: while art which is use-less, point-less, and price-less is not necessarily enchanting, enchanting art is always all those things. Of course, there may also be an attempt to use, including to make a point; it can be bought and sold, and even make a difference. But that is not why it was created, nor why it is loved.

I may perhaps be accused of conservatism. If so, my accusers will almost certainly be those who conflate it (and not always by sincere error) with reaction. John Ruskin described himself as 'a violent Tory of the old school', but anyone who was an inspiration to William Morris, Mohandas Gandhi and Clement Attlee can hardly be called simply reactionary.[3] To the extent my position is conservative, therefore, it is so in the proper sense of the word: a keen determination to protect the old that is still good, which edges into what Seamus Heaney calls a 'love and trust in the good of the indigenous'.[4] In an epoch of global hyper-capitalism and its culture of permanent revolution, such conservatism is surely an integral part of true opposition. It is those who celebrate modernist-engendered ugliness, brutality, and squalor who are collaborators. As Cyril Connolly says, ultimately 'one cannot serve both power and beauty'.[5]

Indeed, I understand enchantment, in art no less than other forms of life, as precisely indigenous: a fundamental human experience, almost our birth-right. It is, as we shall see, neither pre- nor post-modern, but non-modern. That is why it remains perennially contemporary: at once primordial and completely new each time it happens.

Does this approach deny progress in art? Certainly, there are instances and kinds of progress. But in art these only add to what they move on from. Nor do they form a perfect unity. What I do deny is the legitimacy of an avant-garde for whom art is moving in a single overall direction, so that the value of an artwork can be determined by its position and velocity in relation to that direction, as if art was science, where (in theory, at least) what is new replaces what was true before. As T.S. Eliot notes, artistic change 'is a development which abandons nothing en route, which does not superannuate either Shakespeare, or Homer, or the rock drawing of the Magdalenian draughtsman.'[6]

Unavoidably, my own relationship with art, including its enchantment, is significantly constrained by both my own temperament and my social and historical circumstances, and therefore, of course, by their limits (hip hop and opera, for example, are both closed books to me). So too is my approach in this book. But isn't that true of everyone? In any case, I have chosen to embrace the fact by following the golden thread of enchantment through the art in my life, while drawing on whatever scholarship offers to deepen and refine that connection. I ask forgiveness for the countless fine artists whose work I don't know and therefore can't discuss, as well as for trespassing on the turf of various sensitive experts, but I hope that writing from the heart as well as head, about enchanting art I love and respect, will enable readers to better enjoy and appreciate whatever art has had that effect on them. My book is thus partly premised on an observation by Wallace Stevens: 'It is necessary to any originality to have the courage to be an amateur.'[7]

There is an odd idea that enchantment only happens in art. But the world of a poem or painting or musical motif arises from the primary world, the more-than-human natural world, which it expresses in however unique a way, before returning to it. By the same token, artistic enchantment is part of the enchantment of all life. How could it be otherwise?

Yet we are, as I said, distinct animals, and part of our oddity is that art can enchant while life fails to – even the original, so to speak. C.S. Lewis tells that when he was a child, his brother produced a biscuit tin covered with moss, twigs and flowers. 'What the real garden had failed to do, the toy garden did. It made me aware of nature … as something cool, dewy, fresh, exuberant.'[8]

Let me put down a marker here of a theme that will follow, namely that a key to understanding enchantment is metaphor. Metaphor connects and affirms two truths, even though they are strictly contradictory. Thus, the toy garden both is and is not a 'real' garden. In just such a way a fictional person is and is not a 'real' one, a melodic line both does and doesn't move, and so on. The resulting tensive truths exceed mere knowledge, let alone literary device. As we shall see, they are ontological: a way of *being*.[9]

As such, the dynamics of metaphor are a classic instance of liminality.[10] This is so whether they are considered as logically ambiguous, or in the somewhat deeper sense of a transitional condition between more stable and defined states. In that case, enchantment can involve either a transition from a relatively disenchanted state of normality to a one which has been positively reconstituted by the effects of the enchantment, even though the latter has passed, or there may be a relapse into the former state, perhaps resulting from the experience being denied or misconstrued. But even in that case, the person's new normal will not be completely identical with what was before; it may be defensively strengthened, for example.

In either case, if the original and perhaps succeeding state is the one so memorably associated with modernity by Max Weber – not merely contingently disenchanted, but programmatically so – then the liminal nature of enchantment is further strengthened, which is why I have characterised it as fundamentally non-modern. This is what Weber called 'concrete magic', which is not captured by either of our two competing metaphysical monisms: the material and the spiritual or its secular placeholder, the psychological.[11] The liminal place and moment in which enchantment takes place is a 'third thing'.

This liminal and metaphoric dynamic is as old, and as fresh, as art itself. The extraordinary art in the Chauvet caves, painted around 30,000 years ago, presents the lions, mammoths, horses, bears, rhinos, and aurochs of the time with extraordinary immediacy. They come alive, in all their sheen and stink and jostle. Yet we are also looking at rock, charcoal lines, and daubs of pigment. It is precisely in the metaphorical place of these animals–who-are-not-animals that enchantment flourishes (at least it may for anyone intelligent enough to resist demanding, in the destructive chop logic of our times: well, which are they?). Indeed, such enchantment is sometimes more easily accessible than that of biological animals.

Thus, on the one hand, art doesn't merely represent things 'in the world' which are more real. On the other, artistic things are not wholly different or unrelated to things in the world. How could they be? So art presents things which then join the ranks of what already exists. Its business is not representation but *presence*. And all of it is real. Indeed, sometimes, as Laurence Durrell says, 'A work of art is something which is more like life than life itself.'[12]

Art can accomplish this by adding to, while partaking of, the creative processes of life itself. These are part of nature whose prodigy, to quote Wallace Stevens, 'is not an assembly line but an incessant creation'. And, he adds, 'Because this is so in nature, it is so in metaphor.'[13] We will close the book, then, by reflecting on humans as naturally creative beings, part of whose nature is culture and specifically art, for whom the activity of art itself can form a way of life.

This point offers no hostages to fashionable evolutionary psychology, for ultimately my concern is first-person: what is it like to be or do or feel that? I have no interest in 'explaining' anything. I agree with Ludwig Wittgenstein (and Nietzsche, earlier) that the passion to explain – meaning, in practice, to explain away – is a kind of disease, rooted in neurotic insecurity.[14] In claiming to explain while pretending to understand, the scientism now so prevalent, no less than earlier and continuing supernaturalism, accomplishes neither.

What I seek instead is understanding: a way of thinking about art, or being with it, that respects the phenomena, rather than trying to get at something supposedly more important behind, beneath or above them; that enriches experience, rather than trying to correct it; that acknowledges so-called appearances as all we ever have, which is more than enough. My approach is thus a medley of anthropology, philosophy and aesthetics, but entirely in the spirit of the humanities.

In what follows, the first chapter presents the idea of enchantment as such, followed by some reflections on its relationship with art as a whole. Then there are chapters on visual art – mostly painting, but also photography – music, fiction, and poetry. What I'm after is to see both what these arts can tell us about enchantment and what enchantment can show us about them.

I haven't tried to cover enchantment in all the arts. Indeed, there are serious omissions: theatre, film, opera and dance, for example. And regrettably, a chapter on jazz had to be cut for reasons of space (I shall try to publish it elsewhere). But to try to be truly encyclopaedic would be a hopeless undertaking, and doubtless tedious for the reader. So I have been selective, staying mostly with examples that I know well and have a feeling for, hoping that readers will be able to relate my observations, and those of others whom I quote, to what they themselves have experienced. This is a personal account, then, but not necessarily merely subjective for that.

Finally, it could be asked: in a time of ecocide, toxic politics, mass distraction and pandemic, why does the enchantment of art matter? I will push my luck and suggest that in such times, it may matter more than ever. J.R.R. Tolkien (who knew a thing or two about it) argues that enchantment itself 'is as necessary for the health and complete functioning of the Human as is sunlight for physical life'.[15] Art is an ancient and basic instance of such enchantment.

As we shall see, we cannot set out to be enchanted, and when we are it is by someone or something for their own sake, not for ours. Nonetheless, experiences of enchantment shape our lives, give them meaning, and teach us truths. As Tolkien's sometime student W.H. Auden said, eulogising Louis MacNeice: 'I think he would wish that neither impatience nor despair may ever prevent us from being open at all times to those sudden visitations of joy, those moments of vision … which cannot be commanded or anticipated, but which can only be received by hearts which are open to receive them.'[16]

Inasmuch as enchantment meets a basic human need, then, it seems to do so in a way that pulls art along with it. Art in this capacity is not a dispensable luxury, forever waiting upon the satisfaction of more important needs. Look at any culture where simple survival is a permanent issue (in the Arctic, in the desert) and you will find stories, songs, sculpture. Thus it is not surprising that when communing with art takes place – whether publicly or entirely alone – inessentials like mere time sometimes fall away, to be replaced by a moment, short but deep, of something very like love. This is part of the power of enchantment: to return us to when and where we are just starting out, which is always now and here.

Notes

1 George Stambolian, *Marcel Proust and the Creative Encounter* (Chicago: University of Chicago Press, 1972): 210.
2 John Luther Adams, in the *Barbican Magazine* (Oct. 2018): 10.
3 John Ruskin, *Fors Clavigera*, Letter Ten: 'The Baron's Gate', in Clive Wilmer (ed.), *John Ruskin: Unto This Last and Other Writings* (London: Penguin Books, 1997): 306–307.
4 *Poetry Ireland Review* (2013): 27.
5 Cyril Connolly, *The Unquiet Grave. A Word Cycle by Palinurus*, rev. edn (New York: Persea Books, 1981 [1951]): 55.
6 T.S. Eliot, *Selected Essays 1917–1932* (New York: Harcourt, Brace & Co., 1932): 6.
7 Wallace Stevens, *Collected Poetry and Prose*, ed. Frank Kermode and Joan Richardson (New York: The Library of America, 1997): 908.
8 C.S. Lewis, *Surprised by Joy* (Orlando: Harcourt, 1955): 7. With thanks to Alf Seegert.
9 See Paul Ricoeur, *The Rule of Metaphor*, transl. Robert Czerny (London: Routledge, 2003).
10 On liminality, see Arpad Szakolczai, *Permanent Liminality and Modernity. Analysing the Sacrificial Carnival through Novels* (Abingdon: Routledge, 2017). The classic Anglophone text is Victor W. Turner, 'Betwixt and Between: The Liminal Period in Rites de Passage', in *The Forest of Symbols* (New York: Cornell University Press, 1967).
11 H.H. Gerth and C. Wright Mills (eds.), *From Max Weber: Essays in Sociology* (London: Routledge, 1991): 282.
12 Laurence Durrell, *The Alexandria Quartet* (London: Faber and Faber, 2012): 878.
13 Wallace Stevens, *The Necessary Angel: Essays on Reality and the Imagination* (London: Faber and Faber, 1960): 73.

14 Ludwig Wittgenstein, *Remarks on the Foundations of Mathematics*, transl. G.E.M. Anscombe, ed. G.H. von Wright and Rush Rhees (Oxford: Blackwell, 1956), Part IV, §31. Cf. Ludwig Wittgenstein, *Philosophical Investigations*, transl. G.E.M. Anscombe (Oxford: Blackwell, 2001), 40e.
15 J.R.R. Tolkien, *Smith of Wootton Major*, extended edition, ed. Verlyn Flieger (London: HarperCollins, 2005): 101.
16 Auden on MacNeice: W.H. Auden, *The Complete Works of W.H. Auden, Prose*, Vol. 5, ed. Edward Mendelson (Princeton: Princeton University Press, 2015): 70.

2

WHAT IS ENCHANTMENT?[1]

The heart of enchantment is an experience of wonder. It varies in intensity from charm, through delight, to full-blown joy. The last distinguishes radical or deep enchantment, rare but life changing. That is the kind we shall mainly consider in this chapter, including some of its relevance to art.

Enchantment is not something you do; it's something that happens to you. Its opposite is thus will and all its relations: the will-to-power, power-knowledge, agenda, and programme. When and where you are trying to make something happen, or make someone (including yourself) do something – or when you are the object of those desires – enchantment is absent, and vice versa. But we will complicate this polarity later, in the case of artists in particular.

It is inherently participatory, as the etymology of the word implies: *en chantment*, from the Latin and thence Old French, meaning to be in a song – and by extension, I think, any narrative. If you are merely observing from the outside, enchantment is absent. And you cannot will yourself into it through a 'willing suspension of disbelief', or in any other way.[2] With art, it happens when you find yourself in the picture you're looking at, or the music you're hearing, or the story you're reading. Going deeply into it carries you away to somewhere else, which turns out to be at the heart of where you already were. But a precondition is a selfless love for the work of art itself, not for any use or purpose, nor by an effort of will, but as a result of discovering its true meaning and value.

Enchantment is fundamentally relational. It is wonder *at*, or enchantment *by*, another. It's not power over them, nor being the object of power. And although the extent of reciprocity varies with the degree of intensity, as with any true relationship it is two-way. Apprehending the enchanting other, one is apprehended by them. It also follows that because no one is in charge, enchantment is wild, unbiddable. That inconvenient truth means that although it can be invited, it cannot be created, commanded, or managed.

DOI: 10.4324/9781003353225-2

Enchanted relationship takes place as an encounter, typically across a gap of difference. The boundaries remain, but in being bridged they cease to matter. Thus
enchantment is neither hot orgasmic ecstasy or unity, in which all difference is
obliterated – Dionysian, let's call it – nor the cold hyper-separate control-over of
objectification, domination and manipulation, or Apollonian. The latter doesn't
qualify as a relationship, and in the former case there is no one left to relate or relate
to. Sometimes these two modes act as a pair, with people compensating for one (an
overly regimented life, say) by indulging in the other (risky impulsive behaviour).
The point is that whether moving strongly in either direction, it is possible, even
easy, to pass over enchantment altogether.

What kind of relationship are we talking about, then? Auden says that in true
enchantment, you simply want the enchanting other to flourish, to be well for their
own sake. The mark of false enchantment, in contrast, is 'a desire either to possess
the other or be possessed by them'.[3] Tolkien concurs; enchantment, he writes, is
ultimately 'a love and respect for all things, "animate" and "inanimate", an unpossessive love of them as "other"'. And, he adds, 'This love will produce both *ruth*'
– a word from Middle English meaning pity, empathy, compassion – 'and delight.'[4]

The other party in this process can be anyone or anything: a human being,
another animal, a plant, a place, a sight, sound, smell, taste, texture, or even an
idea. But we are a particular kind of being – not random, infinitely variable or, in
that self-flattering delusion, universal – so enchantment tends to happen in certain
domains: principally love, art, religion, food and drink, learning, sport, humour,
and nature.

A classic instance of enchantment is falling in love, typically an event in which
the human other is apprehended as divine. If they remain narrowly human, any
enchantment is stillborn; but if they become purely divine, that way madness lies.
As I have said, boundaries remain, and remain important, even as they are tran-
scended in connection. When that happens, you are in enchantment's realm: the
more-than-human, which includes but also exceeds the human. However, friend-
ship – less showy than erotic love – can run just as deep, and is often more enduring. And then there's your children, if you have any: so you, and yet so completely
themselves! (Again, it's both.)

What we commonly call love doesn't exhaust enchantment, however. Another
instance is being deeply moved by a religious ritual which connects you with all the
others, however removed in space or time, who have celebrated the same truth. But
enchantment is not always exalted, either. A vital but underestimated kind is sharing
a meal prepared with love and skill, eating and drinking not only the 'physical' food
or drink but the stories it contains of where it was grown and how it was cooked
or made.

Then there is true scholarship: the delight of learning something new for its
own sake – sports: the exhilaration of that impossible return or goal or save or
whatever that someone just made – humour: being literally shaken by something
intensely funny yet so true – and far from least, there is finding yourself both seeing
and being seen, and indeed understood, by a non-human fellow-creature.[5] But the

same thing, if more diffusely, can happen with a living place. In fact, I'm quite sure that all enchantments are ultimately natural, rooted in nature, including ourselves as natural beings. By the same token, enchantment is non-anthropocentric. In other words, it isn't all about me, or us humans. How refreshing!

In this process, whoever or whatever the enchanting other is, they become and are realised to be, in effect and to all intents and purposes, another person: some-one – not something – with a distinct, indeed unique, personality, who is on that account irreplaceable. Or, we could simply say, a *presence*. And if it is a presence-for-you, that tips one into wonder. As Wallace Stevens says, 'In the presence of extraor-dinary actuality, consciousness takes the place of reality.'[6] Ordinary, disenchanted reality, that is. But the new presence doesn't destroy the latter; indeed, as R.W. Hepburn points out, 'it is because we remain aware of the temporally serial ... that we experience delight and astonishment at the partial transcendence.'[7]

William James once asked of a scenario where Jack is deeply in love with Jill, whom everyone else sees as perfectly ordinary: who sees her more as she truly is? He answered, surely it is Jack; he apprehends a truth about Jill which is inaccessible to the rest of us.[8] That is why enchantment doesn't have the qualities of a dream, or a spell, but rather of reality. Indeed, enchanted reality is more real than either ordinary reality or dreams, which are daylight reason's inversion but not its opposite. In this sense, enchantment is our baseline natural condition while, as Stevens says, so-called realism 'is a corruption of reality.'[9]

In the sharpest possible contrast with the boredom, despair and ultimately nihil-ism of serious disenchantment (to which we shall turn in a moment), experiences of enchantment are intensely meaningful. On that account, they are also fateful. As Weber put it, any erotic communion, for example, knows itself 'to be founded ... through a mysterious destination for one another: fate, in the highest sense of the word.'[10] Even refusing the enchantment – difficult, but possible – is fateful, because you always do it too late; you have already been affected, so the refusal too will prove momentous.

Hermes

When one is enchanted, and the world therefore overflows with fateful mean-ing, we could say that one is living mythically. There is a long-standing argument between *logos* and *mūthos*. It was first articulated by Plato, who sided influentially (while partly using myth to do so) with the word and the idea as universal truth, which fed into the idea of One True God alongside the latter's Hebraic provenance. And that, while continuing, eventually morphed in turn into modern system and programme, fatefully construing the world as pure object. Meanwhile myth, identi-fied with ignorance, falsehood, and superstition, was effectively side-lined in dom-inant discourse, or else dragooned into a programme of irrationalism equally alien to its anarchic spirit.

But myth remains. It is the more-than-human world: wild and unmasterable, equally 'inner' and 'outer', overflowing with multiple intrinsic meanings which neither need nor offer uses, in which we are already participating: 'your countless soul', as Judy Kravis puts it.[11] And that world never went away; indeed, it laughs up its sleeve at *logos* and its pretensions. In lived life, as the anthropologist Lucien Lévy-Bruhl says, 'There is nothing further to seek when the myth has spoken.'[12] Reason cannot finally check it, in either sense, unless it is itself mythically powered as per analytical Apollo, or strategic Athena, or cunning Hermes.

The general point at stake is that myth encapsulates and encodes millennia of hard-won wisdom about nature, including human nature, and existential situations – birth and death, love and hate, self and others – that remain as powerful as they ever were. 'Myth does not mean something untrue,' as Doris Lessing says, 'but a concentration of truth'.[13]

However, although all enchantment is mythic, far from all mythic deities are enchanting. In fact, in classical Greek myth only Aphrodite and Hermes embody enchantment as such. And of the two, he has a particular affinity with art, and with the metaphoricity that is its lifeblood. By the same token, as Arpad Szakolczai says, he is 'a god of liminality as such'.[14]

Aphrodite and Hermes share traits as well as mutual fondness, and they were often worshipped together. Both are pre-Olympian with still more ancient origins. A chthonian deity (that is, of the Earth), Hermes first appeared in human culture as herms: heaped-up piles of stones, later statues, often with a prominent phallus, placed at boundaries or crossroads. Sometimes he is accompanied by Aphrodite, in whose company his delight is clearly evident. From the beginning, his association with sexuality as well as liminality is therefore clear. But these are not really two discrete functions. Sexuality is itself an intense meeting across deep difference, and his own sexuality was overtly male but female in its sensibility (hence 'hermaphrodite').

By the same token, Hermes' messages are open to, and often require, interpretation (hence 'hermeneutics'), and his actions slippery, elusive, and logically scandalous. The same qualities are present in his followers, whether consciously or not: thieves, merchants, travellers, and workers in media of all kinds. He is the messenger (*angelus*) and guide (*pompos*) par excellence, moving easily between the realms of gods, ghosts, and humans. He is most often found in liminal places which cross and connect – thresholds, doorways, bridges, stairways, and corridors – and is most himself when ambiguous or paradoxical.

Hermes was thus never a heavyweight like Zeus and his brothers; instead, he is light, fast, and funny, if sometimes intensely so. His interventions are not assertions of power or heroic contestation. Nor are they concerned with theoretical mastery, another kind of power-knowledge, 'rotten with perfection', in the words of Kenneth Burke.[15] Rather Hermes cunningly reframes, seduces, or amuses in order to get his way. And so too artists.

Hermes was born of an adulterous nocturnal love-affair between Zeus and Maia, a nymph with famously fabulous hair. Secrecy, illicit love, beauty, and the night were thus present from the beginning. On the day of his birth, encountering a tortoise, he immediately saw an opportunity, slaughtered it without hesitation, hollowed it out and turned it into a lyre: the first musical instrument, before anything devised by the implacably self-important Apollo. Also significant, therefore, is craft in the service of art, but also craftiness; even ruthlessness, although it's not of the same order as that of the warrior.

To quote Shane Woolridge, a sculptor speaking, I think, for many: 'In all of my work, I want the viewer to be transported into a world of beauty by this very clever thief, a pickpocket, who's taken you and you don't even know you've been taken away. You are simply transported ...'[16] And this is what Russell Hoban says, in words that also have the ring of truth:

> Hermes is not officially the god of artists and the arts but he is for me: in some way there is always the killing of something to make that necessary emptiness from which art comes and in some way the artist is always stealing what he hungers for, stealing cattle of truth and pain, cattle of minutes and hours – often as not simply stealing that part of himself that is somebody else's cattle, stealing it for a secret life of finding and losing and mystery.[17]

More broadly, Hermes' lack of compunction in murdering and disembowelling the tortoise to make a lyre is the mythical archetype of Walter Benjamin's observation that there is no document or other artefact of civilisation 'which is not at the same time a document of barbarism.'[18] But note the qualification, 'at the same time'. As usual with deep truths, the two do not justify or cancel each other out. The barbarism doesn't mean the music isn't beautiful – literally lyrical – and the music doesn't mean the foundational act wasn't morally reprehensible.

Metaphor[19]

Metaphor, Hermes' *modus vivendi*, is essential to enchantment. I don't mean metaphor as merely a literary device or conceptual tool but rather the way enchantment, as part of the world, actually works. Gregory Bateson always insisted that metaphor is both how the natural world thinks, so to speak, and thus evolves, and how we do when we are really thinking rather than just pretending to (often by being strictly logical).[20] Stevens, writing of the fecundity of creativity, comes to the same conclusion: 'Because this is so in nature, it is so in metaphor.'[21]

The word 'metaphor' itself means 'to carry across', to bridge and discover/create common ground between two hitherto unconnected beings, or two aspects of one being. Paul Celan calls poems 'gifts to the attentive'.[22] That perfectly conveys both dimensions of the enchantment of art: you have to pay attention for it to happen, but it remains a gift.

This process takes two principal forms. One is 'X is and is not X'. Thus the actor is and is not the character they portray, just as the character is and is not a 'real' person; the place painted is and is not the 'actual' place, and so on. But it goes deeper than anything we do. It encompasses who we are, because every being is dependent on conditions which, strictly speaking, they themselves are not – I am not the food

I eat, or the air I breathe, and so on – yet those conditions are absolutely integral to who and what I am. So I both am, and am not, myself. The way this truth then plays out in enchantment is the experience, 'I am and am not this other' – person (who may be non-human), or place, or whatever.

The second version is, 'X is also Y', or more precisely, 'X is and is not Y'. Thus, to pick a classical example, 'Achilles is a lion!' (The exclamation-mark is appropriate, as it conveys the quality of a discovery.) Mere simile – he is *like* a lion, or has certain attributes of a lion – doesn't go far enough, because in the very essence of his being, Achilles, while also remaining a man, also just is a lion. Thus in enchantment, this woman, as may be, is a goddess, although she is also still a female human. Broadway, in certain rare cases, may turn out to be *Faërie*, but it also doesn't stop being Broadway. The trick – the necessity, for any sanity – is to handle the ambiguity and allow both ends of the paradox to be. Losing sight of either one is impoverishing or else positively dangerous.

Metaphor is therefore a scandal in terms of standard Aristotelian logic, because the resulting paradoxes offend the so-called laws of identity, non-contradiction, and the excluded middle. And it's true that these have their uses and deserve some respect, even if they are sometimes treated ritualistically. But as Neils Bohr remarks, the opposite of a deep truth is often not a falsehood but another deep truth. And with deep truths, logical impropriety is a small price to pay.[23] The psychoanalyst D.W. Winnicott says that his own contribution to this subject is precisely 'to ask for a paradox to be accepted and tolerated and respected, and for it not to be resolved.'[24] Only that way can it communicate its truth.

Metaphor in Art (or, Minding the Gap)

Three children are looking at a picture of a sailing ship on the wall in a bedroom when it starts to change from static to active, and they are no longer observing it from the outside but taking part in it:

> all three children were staring with open mouths ... The things in the picture were moving... Down went the prow of the ship into the wave and up went a great shock of spray. And then up went the wave behind her, and her stern and her deck became visible .... Lucy felt all her hair whipping round her face as it does on a windy day ... but the wind was blowing out of the picture towards them. And suddenly with the wind came the noises – the swishing of waves and the slap of water against the ship's sides and the creaking and the overall high, steady roar of air and water. But it was the smell, the wild, briny smell, which really convinced Lucy that she was not dreaming.
>
> ... by this time either they had grown much smaller, or the picture had grown bigger. Eustace jumped to try to pull it off the wall and found himself standing on the frame; in front of him was not glass but real sea, and wind and waves rushing up to the frame as they might to a rock. He lost his head and clutched at the other two who had jumped up beside him. There was a

second of struggling and shouting, and just as they thought they had got their balance a great blue roller surged up round them, swept them off their feet, and drew them down into the sea.[25]

The author is C.S. Lewis, of course, and no apology is needed for quoting at length a description of metaphoric enchantment in art whose vigour more than outweighs its broad strokes. What it describes is what happens when any art really enchants: you go into it, and as you do so the inside becomes bigger than the disenchanted outside. Primary reality expands and morphs to include art, and the reverse. But the story also reminds us of the importance of frames, which differentiate and separate. These do not prevent enchantment; they are essential for it.

John Cage influentially defined modern art as art which cannot be disrupted by non-art, and a major impetus in the last century was to eliminate boundaries and structures in all the arts: between performers and audiences, between art and everything else, and between what can be portrayed or played or said and what can't.[26] Witness the move into readymades and on to conceptual art; in music, serial atonalism, and free jazz – both, despite their differences, theory-led – and in theatre, the enforced spontaneity of audience participation. (I think the best performance art, perhaps despite itself, escapes being corralled into this programme.)

To the extent such an effort has been successful, the effect has been to banish enchantment. Wonder, delight, and joy depend upon there being a difference as well as something shared between you and the other. Difference is actually a prerequisite for the exhilaration of transcending it, as enchantment does, without destroying it. So does the tensive truth of deep metaphor, including that of narrative ('finding yourself in a song'). Without any in between, a liminal gap, how can anything or anyone move, cross it, or connect? Jan Zwicky is surely right: 'our intuitions that not everything is a poem' – or story, music, or visual art – 'deserve respect.'[27]

If art has no frame of any kind, there's nothing to go through into enchantment. What matters is that some distinctions obtain, of which a frame serves as an instance and reminder. So, without any difference between art and non-art, not only is the window or door to *Faërie* closed, but there isn't one. Without a distinction between the enchanted world that beckons and the quotidian disenchanted one, there is nowhere to go. And indeed, once the children go through the frame into the picture, and find themselves wholly inside the picture, the distinction between its inside and outside naturally starts to lose its force, and the enchantment of that experience remains only as long as its memory, ever if slowly diminishing.

Once these conditions are in place, metaphor can work its wonder in ways particular to each kind of art, which I intend to trace in the following chapters. But let me jump ahead for a moment to Monet's great watery studies (no less wonderful for being popular), which are metaphoric, and therefore, strictly speaking, non-logical: sometimes triply so, when they show a tree, say – which tree is also a reflection on water – which water is also oil paint on canvas. Yet the tree is still clearly a tree, as the pond remains water. It is all 'real', and all imaginal. In the words of Hoban, 'Everything is metaphor and metaphor is the only actuality'.[28]

Concrete Magic

I have already mentioned Weber's terse but potent definition of enchantment: 'concrete magic'. What he means is that it is both utterly particular – *this* person in *these* precise circumstances – and inexhaustibly mysterious. (A mystery in this context is no mere puzzle which can be cleverly solved; on the contrary, the more ones delves into a true mystery, the deeper it becomes.) Enchantment is thus – as all true lovers know – both embodied, even carnal, and ineffably spiritual.

It follows that it is neither only or even mainly 'subjective' (a state of mind) nor only 'objective' (a condition of the world). As such, it cannot be fully understood either psychologically or neurophysiologically. These twin reductions have already sacrificed living enchantment before they've started, because that experience takes place upstream of the distinction between the two. Wittgenstein captures this point nicely. Life, he writes, is neither psychological nor physiological: 'Life is the world.'[29] And as an especially intense instance of being alive, so is enchantment.

It therefore doesn't fall under the rule of either of our two dominant metaphysical discourses, or what Bateson calls 'two species of superstition': scientific materialism, on the one hand, and supernaturalism (whether spiritual or secularised as psychology) on the other.[30] These two 'competing monisms' indirectly support each other by tacitly agreeing that you can so divide the world up, albeit always hoping to then subsume the other pole into your own.[31]

Asserting a radical split between what is spiritual or mental on the one hand and what is material on the other, and assigning priority to one or the other, has a long history. It begins with Platonism, then taken up, enormously influentially, by Pauline Christianity, and finally adapted for modernity, in a way that is very much still with us, by early modern science. To be sure, pre-Reformation Christianity still left room for sufficient liminality, ambiguity and metaphoric truth to allow some enchantment in practice, and even Protestantism couldn't close that window entirely. As a result, the degree of disenchantment accompanying the ascendency of scientific naturalism and materialism has been unprecedented.

Yet the two monisms remain umbilically connected. As Weber points out, the 'rational cognition and mastery of nature' leaves nature's actual mystery nowhere else to go than a now mystical 'beyond'.[32] Rightly recoiling from a disenchanted world, people then try to *add* mystery and meaning – as the word 'super-natural' implies – in order to re-enchant the world. But that's a futile strategy, because it only reinforces the split that lies at the root of the problem.

Part of the solution is to reject the destructively disenchanting questions which drain the wonder from life: 'Is this (whatever it may be) real, or imaginary?', 'Is it true knowledge, or false belief?', 'Is it physical, or mental?' and so on. In concrete magic, the spiritual dimension ('magic') is not something apart from concrete circumstances, floating above them and perhaps needing to be added to them. In fact, it only exists *in* and *as* the precise situation. In the words of one of its philosophers, Maurice Merleau-Ponty, it is 'not the contrary of the sensible [but] its lining and its depth'.[33] The transcendence of enchantment is therefore immanent. It doesn't take you away from where you are, but further into it.

We can further specify concrete magic as (and not merely in) a unique moment – what the artist Etel Adnan calls 'short but deep' – and a unique place.[34] It doesn't occur as either space or time, which are both disenchanted: immaterial mathematical abstractions, usually measured out in generic, quantitative, identical units for some purpose or other.

Let's take the moment of enchantment first. In the moment of enchantment, the passage of time radically slows. It really does slow right down. But concreteness keeps changing, so the temporal doesn't stop altogether, or forever. Eventually the barely swirling eddy in the pool rejoins the larger swiftly-flowing stream of time, until it is finally swept away. Then it becomes all too easy to question the reality of what happened (although quite unnecessary, and inadvisable).

Enchantment's vulnerability may give rise to the desire to recapture it at will – an utterly doomed enterprise – or at least prolong, perhaps even normalise it. But as Vladimir Jankélévitch points out, the idea of a continual state of enchantment 'is as contradictory as the dream of permanent celebration, which negates the idea of celebration *per se*.'[35] An individual in wonder 24/7 is not enchantment; it is psychosis, senility, or possibly sainthood, but in any case, something less or more than fully human.

Having denied the possibility of permanent enchantment, it is interesting to note Arpad Szakolczai's anatomy of modernity as tending to permanent liminality.[36] But there is no contradiction, I think. In addition to the differing emphases on the individual and the collective, I would say that while enchantment is always liminal, liminality is by no means always enchanting. In other words, the latter is a subset of liminality, and one with its own additional exigencies.

Turning to the place of enchantment, to quote a character in John Crowley's wondertale *Little, Big*: 'The farther in you go, the bigger it gets, until, at the center point, it is infinite. Or at least very, very large.'[37] Chesterton noticed the same thing: 'in everything that matters, the inside is much larger than the outside.'[38] But the difference between infinite and very, very large is important; and once again, the latter is the most concreteness will allow.

Thus enchantment cannot last forever, and despite the fact that it may, in principle, return, we may well be more aware of its passing. The hello of wonder is shadowed by a goodbye from which we hide our eyes; the wonder of childhood is continually becoming grown-up; wild nature is always falling to so-called development; and the Elves are forever passing over the Sea, leaving us behind on the darkening shores of Middle-earth in (god help us) the Age of Men, now known as the Anthropocene.

As a result, enchantment often has a bittersweet, poignant, even melancholy undertow. It can, perhaps perversely, induce pre-emptive nostalgia for something present but whose absence is already palpable. 'Even in Kyoto, hearing the cuckoo's cry,' writes Bashō, 'I long for Kyoto.' How much art is an attempt to freeze the moment of presence and thereby defer that of absence? And doesn't the very success of the few masterpieces which pull this off (Vermeer comes to mind) inadvertently remind us that it is ultimately impossible? Which doesn't stop us trying, of course.

And 'longing' is exactly right. Enchantment is not so much desire, however passionate, as intense longing or yearning: the condition described by the German word *sehnsucht*.

Tolkien's name for enchantment was *Faërie*, which he described 'the realm or state in which fairies have their being.' But, importantly, '*Faërie* contains many things besides elves and fays … it holds the seas, the sun, the moon, the sky; and the earth, and all things that are in it: tree and bird, water and stone, wine and bread, and ourselves… when we are enchanted.'[39] It is thus the place you find yourself when you are enchanted, and it is what the place where you already are becomes – which is also what it is, just then, discovered to be.

The same point holds again, however: we can't live there, only visit, or be visited by it. (In Tolkien's terms, we are not Elves, but humans.) So a healthy relationship with enchantment needs not a weak or diffuse ego but just the opposite: a strong ego, to be able to let go when needs must, not fall into futile grasping or clinging, and to withstand the 'grey and leafless world' that succeeds it. But sometimes, we simply cannot. Then we may find, as Karen Blixen did on the ship leaving her beloved Kenya, that 'It was not I who was going away, I did not have it in my power to leave Africa, but it was the country that was slowly and gravely withdrawing from me, like the sea in ebb-tide.'[40]

For the same reason – the ceaseless change of concrete circumstances – the enchanting other too is at the mercy of change and loss. The contrast with what the great enterprises of (most) religion and (nearly all) science value is striking; their ideal is either spiritual or material truth which is universal, eternal, permanent. But as William James puts it, 'the stagnant felicity of the absolute's own perfection moves me as little as I move it'.[41] Indeed, in enchantment the unique other becomes all the more precious, not less, precisely on account of their vulnerability. Zwicky says it well: 'To abandon classical system is to accept, to comprehend, the inevitability of loss. And at the same time to allow things to bloom into their own radiant specificity.'[42]

I would include enchantment itself in this truth. It is more important, not less, and more to be cherished and attended to, not neglected or despised, just on account of its fragility and ephemerality.

Concrete Magic and Art

The preceding themes have direct relevance for art. There is no prospect of understanding living art as such if it is analytically approached in search of an 'explanation', or in the service of methodolatry, whether as an exercise in psychology or in neurophysiology. The reductionism of the latter, attended by all its inflated claims and broken promises, is obvious, but that of the former hardly less so – as if the experience of artistic enchantment was or ever could be a purely mental phenomenon, an 'inner' with no significant 'outer'.

As for artists, Martin Buber captures the matter perfectly: they are 'faced by something which desires to be made through [them] into a work', and it 'is no offspring of [their] soul but is an appearance which steps up to it and demands of it the effective power.'[43] Thus the fundamental relationality of enchantment holds good in the realm of creation too; or rather, co-creation.

The poet Michael Longley, in what amounts to an artistic précis of concrete magic, observes that 'When you capture something with precision, you also release its mysterious aura. *You don't get the mystery without the precision*.'[44] The mystery ('magic') exceeds the circumstances ('concrete') but doesn't exist apart from them, and depends on their successful evocation. If there's no precision, there's no mystery; and without that, almost no chance of enchantment.

Longley was describing poetry, but his observation is true of all art where enchantment is concerned. It can be developed in various ways. One is summarised in a remark by the theatre director Tyrone Guthrie: 'It is one of the paradoxes of art that a work can only be universal if it is rooted in a part of its creator which is most privately and particularly himself'.[45] This point is important because it includes, within the practice of artistic enchantment, the particular person of the artist – something which radically qualifies the importance of technique and method, since the right means in the wrong hands will invariably produce the wrong result, where anything of importance is concerned. It also suggests that one requirement for consistently inviting enchantment, with at least relative success, is a disciplined intention to work with exactly who one is, as well as whatever the material is: an additional concreteness which releases mystery, allowing it to move further towards greater, even relatively universal, enchantment.

Such universality can only grow out of a particular person or group or culture being thoroughly itself, thus enabling us to recognise therein our own particular selves whose uniqueness we share. Selves being inherently relational, hybridity is not the contrary of such identity, rather essential to it. But programmatic, doctrinaire hybridity is another matter altogether.

In this respect, the unfortunate influence of Peter Brook's dismal later plays such as *Tierno Bokar* provide a salutary lesson.[46] In attempting to be universal as a starting-point, it ends up a facile synthesis of various exoticisms, appropriated from here and there and merged in something almost indistinguishable from a successful global advertising campaign, or the shallow and deracinated 'One World' sentimentality of a pop song. Brook has forgotten, or never heard, that in art the movement is from delight to wisdom, not the other way round.

How can we understand the way the truly universal only grows out of the truly personal? I don't believe it can be explained, only indicated. The Zen master Shunryu Suzuki does so like this: 'There is no way set up for us ... Each of us must make his own true way, and when we do, that way will express the universal way.'[47]

Essensuality

Concrete magic becomes realised in art through the senses. Enchantment is always an embodied experience. Each in its own way, all the senses can activate, and be activated by, the enchantment of art. Or as Laurence Durrell puts it, 'Each of our five senses contains an art.'[48] Smell and taste are perhaps the strongest and least diluted, so it's not surprising that they figure so powerfully in the work of that most sensitive and sophisticated of authors, Marcel Proust. But the sense most implicated in much art is sight, our doorway into the worlds of form and colour. That's not surprising, of course, given its importance in our daily lives. However, although hearing is limited to fewer art-forms, music is one of the most important sources of artistic enchantment, and perhaps the purest.

What sense corresponds to literature, which certainly belongs in such a list but is difficult to place? One must be able to read or hear words, obviously, but more interestingly, reception of the written word is never very far from hearing. In fact, psychic analogues of all the senses can be engaged when reading, and another in addition: the sense (using the word broadly) of self-and-other, in all its variants – self vs. other, self as other, other as self – as it develops through narrative time.

'Sense' here should be understood not as a purely physical capacity (whatever that might be) but as ensouled, alive, an exercise of the subjectivity of the body as defined by William Blake: 'a portion of Soul discern'd by the five Senses'. By implication, it is only when the senses are not informed by their soulfulness that they see a body as purely physical or mechanical – a tree, for example, as 'only a green thing that stands in the way.'[49]

It is this full sense of embodiment that W.B. Yeats (a keen admirer of Blake) splendidly invokes when he writes that 'Art bids us touch and taste and hear and see the world, and shrink from what Blake calls mathematical form, from every abstract thing, from all that is of the brain only, from all that is not a fountain jetting from the entire hopes, memories, and sensations of the body.'[50]

There is a strong parallel here between the concrete magic of an artwork and what is erotically compelling about someone. It is not precisely identical with what the senses can grasp, yet it depends upon them; it is something that lives in the beloved's body, that cannot live apart from it, yet is not quite or just that. The same process is at work in art, where what enchants is something mysterious that isn't completely identical with the concrete words or images or notes but cannot work its 'magic' without them – precisely those ones, together with the person(s) present by whom they are read or seen or heard, in that exact and unrepeatable moment and place.

In other words, what enchants isn't formally identical with the words, images, or notes, because if it was then they would necessarily enchant every time they were read, seen, or heard. On the other hand, it is absolutely inseparable from them just as they were on that unique occasion. It was *that* movement of the fourth Brandenburg Concerto, just as the English Consort, as it then was, played it, in *that* evening's slanting light, there in Holland Park, interspersed with *that* blackbird's song, which transported us. Never before like that, and never again. (Properly speaking even a repetition is altered by the fact of it already having happened once before; in other words, the so-called repetition is different.) Artistic enchantment shares this uniqueness, and therefore its perishability, with that of life itself. There are similar events, of course, but 'never from world's beginning to world's end the same event.'[51]

Perhaps this is why no mechanical reproduction of a work of art in a book or print can replace the original. In 2018, publicity appeared (sounding suspiciously like commercial cheerleading) for new AI techniques for reproducing paintings. The parallel with claims to reproduce primary reality with a neuro-technological simulacrum is obvious. Even setting aside the question, in both cases, of why we should want to do so, I doubt that the bodymind, especially its senses, is so easily fooled.

Nor are the punters; they don't queue up to see original works they know well in reproductions because they have been duped by a mystique of originality – a typically patronising assumption! – but because they know the difference. (With the reproduction of music, though, for reasons I don't understand, this difference doesn't seem to be as much of an issue; there is still a dilution, but perhaps not so much.)

Contra Benjamin

The most influential writer on this topic was probably Walter Benjamin. A committed modernist, he hailed mechanical reproduction as the end of what he attacked as a work of art's 'metaphysical aura': that is, its beauty conceived as a Platonic ladder to 'higher' Truth, and its spiritual inwardness, conceived as mere quietism, which would be replaced by art as a vehicle for revolutionary politics. Note the tacit assumptions – all of which are questionable – that beauty must be Platonic, that quietism is necessarily inferior to activism, and that art can be used for some other end (while remaining art).

Benjamin argued that a work's 'aura' shrinks as a result of technological reproduction because 'In making many copies, it substitutes for its unique incidence a multiplicity of incidences.' He maintained that the 'singularity of the work of art is identical with its embeddedness in the context of tradition', whereas 'its being reproducible by technological means frees the work of art … from its existence as a parasite upon ritual.' And what is that ritual? It is one in which the artwork 'had its original, initial utility value.'[52]

There are many holes in this argument. Is the unique work of art in fact reproducible, *sensu stricto*? No, it isn't. A copy is just that: a copy, which therefore cannot be absolutely identical with the original. It follows that the potential presence of an artwork is quite unaffected by copies, no matter how many are made.

Nor is a work of art reducible to, let alone identical with, the conditions in which it was created; it transcends those conditions, or else it would be incomprehensible to those who don't share them, which is clearly not the case. 'Parasite' is simply a modernist curse aimed at ritual and tradition – a secular version of the Protestant critique of idolatry – while the instrumentalism which underpins his advocacy of art as politics by other means implies that the artwork's main or only value is its utility. No room whatsoever for presence-for-itself here, nor sheer wonder! And as Lesley Chamberlain points out, the resulting shift in aesthetics 'in turn created vast new opportunities for the commercial market to step in, sooner or later, now that art apparently belonged to everyone.'[53]

Benjamin's programme, typical of many Left intellectuals' casual acceptance of brutal philistinism and its consequences, carried straight into that of John Berger. Berger's early modernism in *Ways of Seeing* (1972) was hugely influential among art critics, theorists, and students, but its critique by Peter Fuller in *Theoria* (1988), largely ignored, remains as perceptive as ever. Fuller returned to John Ruskin in order to recover a sense of art that is material but not materialist – that is, material ('concrete') in a way that includes the spiritual ('magic') rather than suppressing it.

Further to the betrayal of materiality by materialism, it seems possible to me that the closer to apparently perfect mimicry an electronic image gets – the visual and aural reproduction on a screen of a living human being, say – the deeper the level of one's animal being that is tacitly disappointed and outraged by the attempted fraud, and the wider the felt gap yawns between the two until it leaves the person who beholds it desolate, and unbearably lonely. Is this part of the reason, at least, why a conversation on the telephone (preferably old-style landline) feels so much more relaxed than one by Zoom, say? Or radio more than TV or video? Or a letter compared to an email? The medium itself makes no inflated claims to be immediate or complete, nor demands that you pretend it is.

Where does all this leave the ever-increasingly disembodied arts of the early twenty-first century – video art, Web-based art, and so on – and the conceptual art that preceded and influenced it? Nothing human can actually be completely disembodied (including out-of-body and near-death experiences). For us, no body means no experience, including enchantment. It is only possible for experiences, on the part of the work or the perceiver or both, to be more or less fully and/or authentically embodied.

Conceptual art, in contrast, holds that all you need is an idea; that you can, after all, have the mystery without the precision, and 'magic' without concreteness. When Mark Twain joked that Wagner's music was better than it sounded, he could never have anticipated that in 2012, a much-fêted sculptor, Anish Kapoor, would defend his giant red squiggle in the London's Olympic Park by maintaining, in all seriousness, that 'It doesn't matter what it looks like'.[54] (Yes, 'process' is important; but to turn it into an ultimate value which justifies anything is itself a travesty of process.)

The following claim, which I recently read, is another instructive piece of nonsense:

> For over 30 years X has been finding ever more economical and elegant ways to separate the art experience from the material means of its conveyance. In a two-part installation, he takes this process a step further, creating a truly non-hierarchical art.

The pop-Platonic assumption that art, or ideas, exist apart from mere materiality, by which they are unaffected and to which they are superior (so much for 'non-hierarchical art') is bad enough, but given that any art with no material means of 'conveyance' will necessarily cease to exist at all for anyone, whether artist or audience, this process can only terminate, short of disappearing altogether, in art that is thinly embodied, not to say emaciated.

For the same sort of reason, I suspect that art which depends on electronic social media starts at a significant disadvantage vis-à-vis genuine enchantment. These media reduce embodiment and the senses to sight, sound, and opposable digits. They are constructed and largely directed by secret algorithms – an acme of will-driven intellectual calculation and therefore disenchantment – while a major part of their job is to close up all gaps, whether of silence, darkness, or reflection – gaps without which enchantment is impossible – and overwhelm users with distraction and misdirection.

The same media, especially as incarnated in a search engine, are the very essence of the primary disenchanting belief, described by Weber, that 'all things can be mastered through calculation'.[55] The instant availability, upon command, of images (including visual art), sounds (including music) and knowledge not only replaces the openness of humility with the arrogance of mastery, but destroys serendipity, good fortune: in a word, giftedness. Since this pair – openness and giftedness – are integral to true enchantment, we are so much the poorer. To be sure, the new media have enabled new platforms for art. But I am concerned here with the conditions for artistic creativity, regardless of what forms it takes; and that is where the problem lies.

Nonetheless, artists are increasingly obliged, in order to get a hearing and even simply survive, to sell themselves to corporate sponsorship, which then turns what they do into another form of advertising. (Did you think companies sponsor the arts because they love them?).

As a result, Jonathan Simons writes, 'the conditions an artist needs in order to develop vision and skill are disappearing'. Without rare strength of character and personal discipline, 'a person never left alone for any length of time, never left to fumble in the dark for their own voice, develops little more than a passion for retweeting the chatter and opinions of others. Art demands interiority.' His conclusion, which I support, is that for both artists and audiences, 'offline culture is indispensable.'[56]

Wildness in Artistic Enchantment

I have said that real enchantment is unbiddable, no less in art than elsewhere. There is plenty of testimony from artists themselves. James Whistler, for example: 'Art happens – no hovel is safe from it, no Prince may depend on it, the vastest intelligence cannot bring it about, and puny efforts to make it universal end in quaint comedy, and coarse farce.'[57] And the adamantine words of Shelley, from 1821:

> Poetry is not like reasoning, a power to be exerted according to the determination of the will. A man cannot say, "I will compose poetry." The greatest poet even cannot say it; for the mind in creation is as a fading coal which some invisible influence, like an inconstant wind, awakens to transitory brightness ... and the conscious portions of our natures are unprophetic either of its approach or its departure.[58]

This truth is continually rediscovered. A modern poet, C. K. Williams, speaking of the inspiration which overlaps with enchantment, puts it this way: 'it's absolutely essential, but you can't schedule it or count on it or be sure it's ever going to happen again or that it will happen at all. In the end, we can only prepare a space, a field, for inspiration to occur. This, of course, is contrary to the way we're taught to believe we should accomplish anything: by deciding to do it, then figuring out how, then making it happen.'[59]

Herein lies something of a paradox, because preparing that space clearly requires an exercise of will, the contrary of wonder, together with effort and skill. Or is it a matter of discipline, something closely related but not quite the same? In any case, the creator or performer will naturally want to affect the audience, to induce in them a certain experience even if it is understood, in an open-ended way, as one of wonder and delight. A similar paradoxical imperative faces art's audiences and participants: to go hoping for but not expecting enchantment, let alone demanding it.

I would say that the possibilities for artists, vis-à-vis enchantment, are broadly twofold. They may desire and work towards bringing about enchantment and, depending on many considerations, largely either succeed or fail. There is nothing automatic about success but with talent, skill, and effort, as well as humility, it is not an unreasonable expectation, and very often happens. Or they may have no concern with that but quite other goals: convincing you of their brilliance, creating nausea and dislocation (which overlaps with disenchantment), shocking and outraging the bourgeoisie or the ruling class, making a political or social point, confirming the truth of a particular theory or simply making a pile of money. In these cases too, enchantment may still happen, but it is much less likely.

There is another paradox, or irony, in being an artist, even one who is dedicated to realising enchantment, because the need for time and energy to do so tends to instrumentalise the rest of your life. You can end up doing other things, or sometimes not doing them, in order to be able to work at your art. That often includes taking the same attitude to relationships, which is what Hoban means, I think, by the artist 'stealing that part of himself that is somebody else's cattle', and what Connolly recommends: 'intelligent selfishness'.[60]

All cultural forms of enchantment, notably art and religion, can help us realise the primary enchantment of life itself, sometimes to a profound extent. But to see that as their point, their use, would undermine their potential to enchant, and therefore their ability to propel that realisation. For artistic enchantment to have any positive effect, it must be valued for its own sake, and its wildness respected.

Many artists and thinkers have realised this truth. 'It is extremely important that art remains absolutely unjustifiable' (Robert Rauschenberg).[61] 'Music is useless, as life is' (George Santayana).[62] 'All art is quite useless' (Oscar Wilde).[63] 'Why is art beautiful? Because it's useless. Why is life ugly? Because it's all aims, objectives and intentions. All of its roads are for going from one point to another' (Fernando Pessoa).[64] André Gide writes that 'If I try to find the quality I most admire in this work' – Proust's *In Search of Lost Time* – 'it is its gratuitousness. I don't know of a more useless work, nor one less anxious to prove something',[65] while at the other end of some scale, the actor Ralph Richardson declares, 'I love fireworks. They are so unnecessary.'[66]

These insights find their deepest meaning in relation to enchantment, including art but not limited to it, insofar as it is concerned with intrinsic value, whereas disenchantment recognises value solely as an instrument or means to something else. That can be something important, although at least as often it is something important to avoid; and everyone understands the necessity of what is strictly necessary. But few seem to understand the necessity of what is unnecessary.[67]

Contrariwise, the problem with modernist art (which, as we shall see, is not the same thing as modern art) is that in Stevens's words, 'It has a reason for everything. Even the lack of reason becomes a reason.'[68] In other words, it has become thoroughly intellectualised – and, inseparably, over-professionalised – and thereby disenchanted. Not as a result of thinking, which can be done well or badly and is no more necessarily disenchanting than dancing or cooking, say, but as a result of a dogmatic attachment to intellectual system and method. But something being useless doesn't make it worthless, or mean that it has no effects.

The 'use' and 'reason' I am problematising includes being enlisted in a progressive and/or transgressive programme of opposition to dominant ideologies. Weber long ago pointed out that campaigns of deliberate irrationalism fail to disrupt modernity's will-to-power and instrumentalism because they themselves are programmatic.[69] (Surrealism, Dada, and punk come to mind.) As for identity politics, consumer capitalism is only too happy to sell you as many identities as you like, and the ease with which it recoups dissent and transgression – Che Guevara t-shirts, punk couturists, Occupy chic – makes investing them with any radical hope a sad joke.

Art is routinely asked to save, purify, educate, elevate, inspire and/or transform us, enabling us to live better, fuller, or more aware lives. But although art can have any or all of these effects, the expectations themselves, especially when enforced, are already disenchanting. That includes, centrally, the modern tyranny of demanding 'relevance', 'impact', and that Trojan Horse for modernist culture, a 'message'. Victoria Thiérrée Chaplin, co-creator of ineffably enchanting performances by the Cirque Imaginaire and Cirque Invisible, states that 'I find that any work of theater – or any work of art for that matter – demands that something in it has to remain undefinable, not talked about, a part that wants to be left alone.' And asked how she would describe her art, replies, 'I wouldn't.'[70] Bob Dylan has, of course, turned evasiveness in defence of his art, deflecting intrusive and often inanely inappropriate questions from journalists, into an art-form in its own right. (When asked about the 'message' of his songs: 'Myself, what I'm going to do is rent Town Hall and put about 30 Western Union boys on the bill. I mean, then there'll *really* be some messages.')[71]

This is the point where woke identity politics tacitly collaborates with the powerfully philistine officialdom in charge of grants, fellowships, and awards. Instrumentalism, whether progressive or bureaucratic, spells the death of enchantment, and the latter's coarse business model of culture can easily accommodate the former's narcissistic sensitivities. You simply have to adapt your advertising (which doesn't cost any more than it already did) and expand marketing to pull in the new kinds of punters.

Art for Art's Sake?

Enchantment flourishes in the midst of simplicity, humility, and purity of spirit, just as sound requires silence to be heard, and light to shine needs darkness. But these commitments must be relatively unselfconscious, undertaken to serve the art itself rather than some other reason. The hint of a programme, like a twig snapping, and enchantment is off and away. For purpose is a hunter.

As ever in this context, the rule of marketing and accountancy – the modern acme of wilful purpose – is a cause of degeneracy, and the corresponding language is its sign. Art can best enchant, and bring whatever good that may do, if it is grace, a gift of the whole, and if its 'creator' disavows subsequent credit or control. You cannot buy, sell or own enchantment. Accordingly, any understanding of enchantment in art must include how it survives or succumbs to the nets and traps of power-knowledge, most consistently in market capitalism, including, most recently, digitalisation.

These often work hand-in-hand with official governmental diktats. In April 2019, the Deputy Chief Executive of Arts and Culture for the Arts Council England, with a special remit for Pompous Posturing and Menacing Manifestoes, declared:

> Relevance is becoming the new litmus test. It will no longer be enough to produce high-quality work. You will need to be able to demonstrate that you are also facing all of your stakeholders and communities in ways that they value.

They didn't specify the fate of those failing the test of 'relevance' but did predict that 'Virtual reality, augmented reality and mixed reality will see significant growth and will become increasingly relevant for the arts.' Since this is the sort of fool in charge of supporting the arts with public money, I guess those who find merely producing high-quality work sufficiently challenging will have to look elsewhere.

The quest for 'relevance' also pulls in the dismayingly fashionable tendency to draw conclusions about the quality of the art from the so-called identity of the artist (already an impoverished conception, limited to race, gender and/or sexual orientation; extraordinarily, class seems to have dropped out of the picture). But you simply cannot get there – the quality of the art – from the person of the artist alone. If art is used or treated as a rhetorical weapon it becomes, if it wasn't already, something else. Milan Kundera has eloquently argued that good art is finally independent of the political, social, and even cultural circumstances of its making; there is something else at work which cannot so be captured, and that is what keeps its enchantment alive.[72]

Is this a pitch for 'Art for Art's Sake'? If the slogan refers to 1890s Aestheticism, in which art was opposed to life or, at least, life in a community, then the answer is no. But that is not the only possible meaning of the phrase, and I am indeed advocating art being valued above all for its own sake rather than for any usefulness, no matter how subtle or elevated. There should be no compromise on this point. Any concession to art's positive 'function', whether socially, politically, or psychologically, clears the way to being evaluated on grounds whose inherent utilitarianism or instrumentalism are fundamentally hostile to its enchantment. As Louis MacNeice puts it, 'art is autotelic [i.e., its own end] in so far as its value (except incidentally) is non–utilitarian ...'.[73]

Some years ago, Suzi Gablik issued an influential condemnation of modernism in art and called for its re-enchantment. But that won't come about as a result of 'a call to arms on behalf of a socially and environmentally engaged artistic practice'. Nor does art exist in order 'to build community through empathic social interaction' (oh, the language!). Nor is the only alternative to activist art what she calls 'autonomous art' and defines as 'art that is cut off from any social or communal definitions'.[74]

Such prescriptions comprise at least three misunderstandings. One is the nature of wonder, especially its immiscibility with will, and a fortiori with agenda. A second is the possibility of art having significant positive effects despite – indeed, partly as a result of – not being dragooned into a programme. Finally, when a ruthless instrumentalism is the very acme of modernist disenchantment (and not only in art but in architecture, agriculture, medicine, education, town planning and so on), what hope is there in calling for a more spiritual, enlightened and/or engaged version? The problematic mode remains untouched, as do its effects.

In short, whatever else it may be art is decidedly not, as she proclaims, 'an instrument'. Not, at least, for those who, like D.H. Lawrence, love its wonder: 'I can never look on art save as a form of delight.'[75]

Crafts

I think the statements quoted earlier about enchanting art's uselessness constitute a truth that survives the most critical analysis. However, they are also partly a modern response to a modern problem, namely trying to protect art, and its possibilities to enchant, from the dead hand of regnant philistinism, materialism, and utilitarianism. Yet crafts of all kinds, by definition, have uses but can certainly still enchant.

The key to resolving this apparent contradiction lies in the difference between an existential usefulness – using a beautiful thing to keep warm, dazzle a mate, cook a meal with or drink from, in which beauty and usefulness co-exist – and modernist usefulness, in which the value of something is determined by its ability to further the goals of the company, government or programme. William Morris's art/craft, which continues to enchant many people despite no longer being hand-produced (so that cannot be an insurmountable problem) as well as subsequent drastic changes of fashion, is useful in the first, non-modern sense, but not in the second. In ecological terms – terms which Morris understood very well – it's the difference between industrial forestry (clear-cutting, often of irreplaceable old-growth forests) and woodsmanship (coppicing, pollarding, and so on).

Embodied, practical skill is not merely cognitive; it engages the whole body-mind, arises out of ongoing particular relationships between the particular crafts-man and the particular material. Neither is merely generic, both are important, and so is the connection between them. 'To carve,' writes David Esterly, 'is to be shaped by the wood even as you're shaping it.'[76] Wood, for example, has its own personality no less than its carver, and when the wheelwright George Surt says that 'it would lend its own subtle virtues to the man who knew how to humour it: with him, as with an understanding friend, it would co-operate', it is no mere figure of speech; he is being precise and accurate. Writing in the early 1920s, Surt says that

> no higher wage, no income, will buy for men that satisfaction which of old – until machinery made drudges of them – streamed into their muscles all day long from close contact with iron, timber, clay, wind and wave, horse-strength. It tingled up in the niceties of touch, sight, scent. The very ears una-wares received it, as when the plane went singing over the wood, or the exact chisel went tapping in (under the mallet) to the hard ash with gentle sound.

He concludes that 'these intimacies are over'.[77] It's some comfort to be able to respond, 'Not quite'. But how much? That could be debated, but what is surely undeniable is that in the words of Laurie Lee, 'the handmade object is one of the last visible defences of humanism left to us', in defiance of 'that hideous and unholy trinity: speed, efficiency, economy.' Craft goods thus entail no regressive urge; rather they 'issue a revolutionary challenge to the mechanistic squalor in which we live.'[78]

By now, however, another qualification is needed. To make impossible demands is neither realistic nor humane, and just as with enchanted love – the unpossessive love of another, in and for their own sake – such radical disinterest by artists in their creations is probably impossible to maintain in a completely pure way, or for very long, unmixed with some self-interest. Maybe, as D.W. Winnicott suggested in regard to parenting, we need a concept of the 'good enough artist' who has learned, as far as possible, to simply let enchantment be.

By the same token, it's a lot to ask of audiences that they enter a theatre or concert-hall or gallery, or open a book, in a state of pure receptivity without any expectations of enchantment. I don't think art can ever fully shake off this ambigu-ity. The purest and often most powerful enchantments are unbidden, unarranged, and unexpected, like grace; yet without the will and work of the artist, and the attendant artificiality of an artistic situation, the particular enchantment that art can offer won't happen. As Tolkien remarks wistfully, 'A story must be told or there'll be no story, yet it is the untold stories that are most moving.'[79]

What remains clear is that enchantment in and as art can indeed have powerfully positive effects, if it is free of any attempt to put it to work. The artist appeals, as Joseph Conrad writes, 'to that in us which is a gift and not an acquisition – and therefore, more permanently enduring. He speaks to our capacity for delight and wonder, to the sense of mystery surrounding our lives ...'[80]

Disenchantment

Enchantment and disenchantment are, of course, a linked pair, so each needs to be understood at least partially in relation to the other. Now there is such a thing as normal and natural disenchantment: 9am on a Monday morning, say. Indeed, I have already mentioned that without such a background, there would be nothing special about enchantment.

However, there is also a powerful programme of disenchantment driven by what I call the Megamachine.[81] It has three principal engines: capital, the state, and techno-science. I have discussed these elsewhere[82] so here will only mention the key point: the Megamachine is the modern incarnation of will, especially the will-to-power and power-knowledge. Its overarching project is the rational mastery of nature, including human nature, and its ideal is 'the system from which all and everything follows'.[83] The way is then clear for the rule of binary code, algorithm, and digitalisation.

This process and its outcome were famously anatomised by Max Weber almost exactly a hundred years ago: 'The fate of our times is characterised by rationalisation and intellectualisation and, above all, by the "disenchantment of the world."' Its key premise is 'the belief' – and the belief suffices, if it is sufficiently strong and widespread – 'that one can, in principle, master all things by calculation.'[84] So the programme consists of turning the world into just such a calculable object, populated by fungible (interchangeable) items, which therefore requires disenchanting it, and them.

In contrast, enchantment, through metaphor, partly reveals and partly creates an existential truth about the other: their unique intrinsic value and meaning, which cannot be calculated and doesn't depend on market value or usefulness. The intrinsic value of the other that enchantment reveals is, in effect, sacred, and whatever is sacred is not for sale. We might say it *is* what is not for sale.

True, even a muddled compromise can keep the door to enchantment ajar. In a market economy money will usually change hands, because the artist must be able to survive, but we know it doesn't reflect the work's true value, because it can't. (One artist I know charges for their work by asking for whatever the buyer earns for the same length of time it took to make the work.) The absolute equation of value with price which now dominates the art world, however, shuts that door. Enchantment is finally only possible with what Jeanette Winterson calls 'a passionate, reckless love of the work in its own right'.[85]

Ruskin, defending art in the bowels of high Victorian materialism, would have concurred: 'Remember that the most beautiful things in the world are the most useless: peacocks and lilies, for instance.'[86] But evolutionary psychology has now claimed even peacocks and lilies for usefulness, via improved reproductive fitness. Here as elsewhere in contemporary culture, we find it working hand-in-glove with capital, penetrating all other values. (I don't say it always succeeds, but it is far too successful for any complacency.) As for the theory of innate adaptive traits, not to mention a so-called 'art instinct', how exactly do we get from art as an attempt to impress potential mates – even unconsciously, manipulated unawares by one's genes – to Monet's *Nymphéas*, say, or Beethoven's late string quartets?

If you can convince yourself that the world is in fact disenchanted – dead, inanimate stuff – then you can do whatever you want to do to it, because it doesn't, precisely, mind. Conversely, if you treat the world that way, the effect is to disenchant it. And once you start, the endpoint is unclear; maybe not only other animals but human beings too are mere stuff, just unusually complicated. Hence the brutality of so much modernism: I'll do this just because I can, I feel like it, and why not?

Being wild, enchantment cannot be controlled; it arrives, as William James says, 'in the manner of a gift or not at all'.[87] And in the experience, as I mentioned earlier, will or the will-to-power is absent. Even when they are entangled, the two remain immiscible, like oil and water. Enchantment is *non*-modern, standing outside the project of modernity. As such, it reminds us of the limits of that project, a reminder which is unwelcome to modernity's countless servants, apparatchiks and apologists. (In this it is very different from magic properly so-called, which – being another exercise in power, even if supposedly 'spiritual' or 'occult', and mastery, even when self-mastery – is easily incorporated into the modern project.)[88]

Enchantment's inconvenient truths are thus an impediment to the rule of capital, the chief engine of modernity, which seeks above all its own free flow. One of commercial and political modernity's principal tools is therefore what I call glamour: a pliant and profitable simulacrum of enchantment which is the stock-in-trade of the billion-pound industries of advertising, marketing, PR, spin and, in the background, commercial surveillance. It's smooth and almost convincing, but if you attend carefully, you can spot the difference. (Start with asking yourself whether you are being manipulated, and if so, why.)

The Megamachine uses glamour to create false enchantment, the desire for possession, which it then offers – for a price – to satisfy. But being devoid of true enchantment, what is bought and sold cannot meet that deep need, so people keep coming back for more. Addiction is built into the business model of those industries, and glamour is their tool. (There is no better example than an expensive new smartphone: sleek, shiny, eager to please – oh, use me! – I can do so much, you're so smart to own me ... and utterly soulless. Who is using whom here, and who owns whom?)

The power of the Megamachine, uniting trillion-pound capital, bottom-line state governance, and morally challenged technoscientific development, is terrifying: 'that vast fortress, armoury, prison, furnace of great power ... biding its time, secure in its pride and its immeasurable strength.'[89] And yet, enchantment is obviously still happening. People are still falling in love, finding deep solace in the natural world and with other animals, sensing divine presence in religious rituals, being inspired by art of all kinds, communing with and through food and drink, exhilarated by a sporting hero, and so on. It seems the disenchantment of the world, undeniable as far as it goes, is a half-truth.

The reason is that although enchantment is indeed vulnerable, it is also finally indestructible. The potential for it is inherent in all embodied, ecological, inter-dependent, analogue, finite Earthlings. Indeed, implicit in all enchantment is an astonished and humbling apprehension of *being* alive. Not coincidentally, that is just what ultra-modernists like the transhumanists want to destroy in exchange for the death-in-life of a spectral, monadic, cyborg Ringwraith, who is not immortal but merely lives endlessly on, terrified of death while craving it.[90] But enchantment reminds us that any such project of total control, predicated on the complete disen-chantment of the world and its replacement by glamour, is finally doomed to fail, although not without wreaking havoc in the attempt.

It also follows (and I have found this to be something that many good people find it hard to accept) that enchantment, or re-enchantment, cannot, upon pain of certain failure or betrayal, be used to further a system, programme, algorithm or app, even when the goal is admirable. Enchantment does not long survive an agenda, no matter what type.

There are things you can do, however. First and foremost is to practise what Freya Stark calls 'fearless receptivity'.[91] This is where the will comes into its own, in a good way, because you can intend and make the effort to pay attention, keep the door to wonder open, and invite it in.

That means engaging in John Keats's famous 'negative capability': the capacity to be 'in uncertainties, mysteries, doubts, without any irritable reaching after fact and reason'.[92] As part of the same discipline, we can refuse to engage in modern-ist self-policing, retrospectively second-guessing enchantment as something that 'seemed' or 'appeared' to be, was merely 'projected', was merely a 'subjective' state of mind and so on. As Wittgenstein asserts, 'If everything behaves as though a sign had meaning, then it does have meaning.'[93] And *cui bono?* Who benefits from its denial? Not the enchanted person, if they were truly so.

If you are an artist, you can work to create the right conditions for enchantment, starting with what T.W. Adorno calls 'the capacity for being voluntarily involun-tary'.[94] In fact, since enchantment is at no one's beck and call, that is an essential thing to do, and doing it will take all the will and skill you can muster. Then, if enchantment does attend, learn what you can and try to work with it, carefully and respectfully. In this way, it can become a leitmotif which embraces both personal and artistic life. Yet sometimes, even in what seem to be all the right conditions (a great story/script/cast/team/funding etc.), enchantment fails to attend.

Imagination is key. I don't mean mere fantasising but rather imaginatively engag-ing with the 'lining and depth' which I mentioned earlier: the inner meaning of the concrete present place and moment. We tend to assume that to be fully present or 'mindful', the imagination must be suppressed, whereas very nearly the opposite is true. The senses must be engaged, but without creative imagination as well you cannot truly be here and now. 'Reality,' to borrow the title of a poem by Wallace Stevens, 'is an activity of the most august imagination'.

The imagination in this sense is an organ of perception: 'an ontological organ', Merleau-Ponty calls it, because it enables us to grasp (and be grasped by) what he calls 'wild being'.[95] That is also what enables works of art to enchant in a relational encounter, whereby an artefact is apprehended by the beholder's imagination as an agent in a story in which they too are participating. Then the work becomes what it always potentially was: a subject, with whom a relationship is therefore possible.

Is it frivolous, in our times, to defend enchantment, artistic or otherwise? I have already suggested it is not a luxury but something which can make life worth living, and even be life changing. Additionally, in such deeply disenchanted times, why should we try to take away what wonder remains? Remember too that Tolkien defined it as ultimately 'a love and respect for all things, "animate" and "inanimate", an unpossessive love of them as "other".[96] Don't we need that in our lives more than ever? Dare we forget that such a thing is possible?

Modernism

I will be associating 'modernism' and 'modernists' throughout this book with programmatic hostility to enchantment, in art and elsewhere. Especially since those terms are often used in other and varying ways, let me explain why.[97]

I understand modernism to be a sensibility, sometimes hardening into an ideology, which includes but exceeds any movements bearing the name. That sensibility is revolutionary, and therefore positively oriented to a hypothetical future but negatively to the historical past; alternately self-confident, including un-self-critical, and insecure; either puritanical, even prudish, or licentious, with very little in between; and impulsively iconoclastic. Modernism therefore needs icons to smash, and enemies, both past and present, to smite. In this, as in many other ways, it resembles the Protestant impulse which provided its principal historical provenance. (As so often, being secular makes little difference to the mode.)

Of course, everyone alive now is modern in the sensible if banal sense of living in the present, which is modern in relation to the times that preceded it. But beginning in the nineteenth century, in the West (and to some extent, Japan), some people started to consider themselves modern. This self-consciousness entailed, among many other things, a newly relaxed attitude to tradition in virtually all aspects: religious, political, social and cultural, including artistic. They felt freer to disregard traditional strictures and to innovate and experiment.

Towards the end of the century, however, in a further step, modernism as an ideology – or, if you prefer, a faith – appeared on the scene, and continued to gather strength throughout the next forty years or so after the devastation of World War I. And its adherents didn't just happen to *be* modern, they *believed* in it; hence, 'modernists', rather than simply moderns. As Richard Taruskin says, 'Modernism is not just a condition but a commitment.'[98] And as part of that belief, they identified tradition with oppression, ignorance and superstition: in short, secular heresy. So the goal was no longer to simply ignore tradition but to destroy it, and replace it with endless progress, or what Trotsky, and later Mao, called 'permanent revolution': a prescription as inhumane as that of permanent repression.

Modernist ideology is based on faith in secularism, materialism, and rationality. Mind, and thence psychology, replaces spirit or soul, and even when the rational mind is perceived as something that needs supplementing or correcting, it must come from the sub- or unconscious mind – in effect, a human-centred solipsism. This belief coalesces with a narrative of salvation through zealous progress (which borrows heavily from Christian eschatology) and smiting one's enemies, chief among them superstition, which is a result of popular ignorance and thus calls for re-education.

The term 'superstition' originally meant religious heterodoxy, based on ignorance and/or fear. It was used by Protestants to attack Catholicism and associate it with paganism. Modern science then redefined it as secular ignorance, and modernism in turn as simply tradition. Hence modernism's iconoclasm: if you smash all the idols, the thinking goes, you will be left with the Truth (itself God in secular drag). Hence too the wafer-thin partition between modernism and nihilism – because why stop there? – and the resulting lack of resistance to big money. When nothing any longer has any intrinsic value, there is no compelling reason not put anything on the market and make a killing.

All these things are part of the mental furniture of most moderns, but modernists actually believe in them. And they still do, because it's far from over. In both visual art and music, modernism lost some of its authority in the 1980s with some return to traditional figuration in the former and tonality in the latter. But the epigones of pure abstraction and readymades, atonal dissonance and 'experimental' fiction haven't vanished, and postmodernist irony merely left a leaner, fitter, more up-to-date modernism in place, while the reduction of aesthetic to market value gallops on apace. And doubtless something with a strong family resemblance will carry on under another name. Ultimately, at the heart of what I am calling modernism is an attitude, a stance, a way of being, to which the movements of that name gave particular expression, emphasis and scope but did not exhaust; so it continues.

Now there's no doubt that modernism was originally experienced by some as tremendously liberating and exciting, nor that it resulted in some good and occasionally great art, along with a lot of rubbish. But wonder, delight, and joy in art are things that modernists largely reject. Actually, they are sometimes slightly more nuanced, asserting that as a matter of 'fact' the world is now disenchanted, so the only way to be in accord with contemporary reality is to be disenchanted too. In the impeccably logical but mad words of Jay Bernstein, 'Authenticity without cruelty is no longer possible.'[99] Which again leaves enchantment as apparently regressive or reactionary. Modernists' pronouncements are not a disinterested description, however, but an intervention intended to *make* things so, and thereby be proved right. But reality remains an ongoing and stubbornly messy amalgam of enchantment and disenchantment – 'incorrigibly plural', in Louis MacNeice's words – so their conclusion falls too.[100]

Such a set of values and views is hardly new, of course. One of modernism's high priests, Le Corbusier, described the poorer citizens of Paris as a 'dead weight on the city, an obstacle, a black clot of misery, of failure, of human garbage'. He extolled, in contrast, the Plan. The correct, realistic, exact plan, the one that will provide your solution … This plan has been drawn up well away from the frenzy in the mayor's office or the town hall, from the cries of the electorate or the laments of society's victims. It has been drawn up by serene and lucid minds … It is a biological creation destined for human beings and capable of realization by modern techniques.[101]

It is impossible not to hear in this authoritarian peroration echoes of the embittered late Plato, admirer of the Spartan police-state and hater of the vulgar mob (*demos*), with their ignorant opinions (*doxa*) as opposed to true knowledge (*epistēmē*). And to be sure, the Church in earlier centuries was powerfully controlling, and tried to stamp out unlicensed wonder. But God as the ultimate mystery at least reserves a place for 'magic', even the concrete kind. With the ascendency of scientific natural-ism and materialism as supreme template, that last bulwark was removed. The prom-ise of complete and total mastery – be it ever so unfulfillable in practice – entices, and for those who like this sort of thing it is hard to resist. Hence modernists' hatred of enchantment, upon which they turn dogmatic assertion, destructive analysis, contempt, and scorn. Even humour, in this context, is not funny but weaponised. By the same token, as Adam Zagajewski says, 'When it occupies the central place in someone's thought, irony becomes a rather perverse form of certainty.'[102]

Modernism returns us to the disenchantment, so succinctly analysed by Weber, which results from the belief that the concrete magic of life can be divided into matter and idea, and that for most modernists, the latter can be reduced to the former. This is the sharp end of disenchantment, compared to which religion con-tinues to harbour a place, erratically policed, for enchantment. And I say 'most' modernists because there has long been a minor magical modernism, Theosophical in provenance and supernaturalist or idealist in metaphysics. As we shall see, it is evident in the informing beliefs of Kandinsky, Mondrian and several other major artists.

However, since Romantic supernaturalism concedes the fundamentally disen-chanting splitting of life into either material or spiritual – the two competing mon-isms I mentioned earlier – and favours the latter, it leaves the rule of materialism intact. Ultimately, therefore, in either variant the project of modernity remains hostile to enchantment and to its sources in the living body, the female, and the Earth. No wonder Kundera – an insider, as it were – asserts that 'To be absolutely modern means to be the ally of one's gravediggers.'[103]

Inasmuch as enchantment is wonder at, and by, a particular incarnation or instance of life, and involves an intensification and appreciation of being alive, to be anti-wonder is to be anti-life. It's almost that simple. (Part of the complexity of life is that some things are simple.) Positively, it is therefore necessary to insist that the body is subject as much as object; that the female, properly understood, includes, as well as complements, the masculine; that the Earth is as much culture as nature, just not only human culture. Indeed, I see the struggle to understand and live these truths as incumbent on anyone who wants to be truly progressive.

Berger, mulling over the enchantment of a deceptively simple white wooden bird, wonders aloud that 'One is looking at a piece of wood that has become a bird. One is looking at a bird that is somehow more than a bird.'[104] We humans have been doing this sort of thing for a very long time, and its persistence is encouraging. As the twenty-first century begins to unfold, and the damaging illusions of modernism, although still powerful in the marketplace, become ever more apparent, may we not hope that enchanting art will be renewed? Perhaps, but it won't happen unless the renewal is radical (literally, a return to the roots), which requires abandoning the cult of always and only the new.

Modernism in Art[105]

The difference between moderns and modernists is clear enough if you compare modern artists – Claude Debussy, Henri Matisse, Barbara Hepworth, David Hockney, Joseph Conrad or Wallace Stevens, say – with modernist artists like Arnold Schoenberg, Marcel Duchamp, John Cage, James Joyce or Ezra Pound. (In jazz, it would be Thelonious Monk, Sonny Rollins or Bill Evans, as against Charlie Parker, Cecil Taylor or John Coltrane.)

The former artists were all indisputably modern, and as such they boldly experimented in relation to the traditions they inherited – perhaps the single most striking characteristic of modern art. They don't qualify as modernists, however, because their innovations were a way of extending, and thus honouring, the traditions in which they worked. None had that programmatic quality, driven by transgressive fervour, a burning desire for immortality, and/or coldly theoretical intellectualisation that marks the true modernist. And the art of all of them is powerfully enchanting.

Of course, it is impossible to posit a formal criterion for distinguishing modern from modernist: a point at which innovation becomes iconoclasm and there is no longer any interest in honouring while revising the relevant tradition, but rather in declaring a Year Zero. And there are ambiguous cases aplenty: Pablo Picasso, who strenuously resisted abstraction in art, and Virginia Woolf, whose genteel dismay at Joyce's *Ulysses* marked the limits of her own modernism. That does not mean there is no difference between the two kinds, however. The artists I have termed modernist tried to undermine, even destroy their traditions, and replace them.

But why does their iconoclasm make an enemy of enchantment? Because they subscribe to the modernist programme of mastery, whereas enchantment is wild and cannot be controlled or managed. It reveals tensive truths which have not been vetted and approved, its mode is dark *mūthos*, not bright *logos*, and its concrete magic subverts the convenient division of metaphysical labour between spiritual and material authorities. For these believers, it is therefore not merely suspect but deeply offensive. (With almost comical extravagance, Bertolt Brecht denounced theatre audiences for looking 'at the stage as if in a trance, an expression which comes from the Middle Ages, the days of witches and priests.')[106]

Modernist ideology became highly influential; as we shall see, some of the most iconic artists of the last century were believers. At the same time, I don't want to exaggerate its importance, because although modernism changed the face of art in the twentieth century, it also failed to uproot people's desire for enchantment and their willingness to look for it beyond what critics applaud.

Not surprisingly, I find many critics of modernism more acute than its adherents. One such was Philip Larkin. (The fact that Larkin was famously curmudgeonly doesn't mean he was stupid or necessarily wrong.) He trenchantly summarised modernism as Parker in music, Picasso in painting, and Pound in poetry, and although that is somewhat unfair to Picasso, we shall return to them and their influence in later chapters, along with related attempts at pure abstraction and 'readymades' in art, atonalism in classical music, and anarrativity in literature.

A theme runs through this scenario. 'The terms and the arguments vary with circumstances,' Larkin writes, 'but basically the message is: don't trust your eyes, or ears, or understanding. They'll tell you this is ridiculous, or ugly, or meaningless. Don't believe them. You've got to work at this: after all, you don't expect to understand anything as important as art straight off, do you?'[107] But as the artist Isao Miura asks, 'if a food looks and smells foul, you don't eat it, nor do you try to convince yourself that it really is good for you. Why do we do this with art?'[108] If you succeed in convincing yourself, you're halfway to agreeing with the art critic Sarah Kent, for example, extolling an exhibition of life-size castrated and mutilated dummies: 'They satisfy your blood-lust, they seduce, and they make you sick. Brilliant.'[109]

Being intimidated by 'experts', submitting to over-intellectualisation, not trusting your own feelings or your senses – these undercut enchantment from the start. Of course, those feelings or senses might tell you, 'There's something new going on here, something important you don't yet understand', and that's a perfectly good place to start. But Eugenio Montale is right: 'Art destined to live has the aspect of a truth of nature, not of some coldly worked-out experimental discovery.'[110]

I found a tiny but telling example of what enchantment in art is up against just before finishing this book. The reviews editor of *Harper's Magazine* (April 2022) quotes approvingly a critic, Gary Indiana, commenting on an artist that

> You don't have to read Lacan to appreciate this work, but Lacan is helpful if you want to take the work in without miring yourself in direct, frontal relation to what it's saying at the moment you're looking at it.

Let's set aside that Lacan's metapsychology is an inflated and fatuous fraud. What's really striking is the fear of direct encounter with art (not to mention life) unmediated, indeed uncontrolled, by theoretical correctness – 'miring', for all love! – especially if, as sometimes happens (if you are lucky) in moments of enchantment, it is saying something to you. Here is theory as a weapon, both defensive and offensive.

Central to modernism is the idea of a privileged intellectual elite, one of paranormal perspicacity and alarming self-confidence which knows the way art as a whole is heading and leads the way. This preposterous proposition depends on there actually being a single overall direction in which all art is moving, and therefore comprehensive progress towards a single goal, or else backsliding.

Yet to argue, as I will, for the greater potential for enchantment of the penta-tonic do-re-mi over the modern diachronic scale, or the desirability of retaining figuration in visual art or story in literature, is not to advocate what is ancient or 'traditional' for its own sake. It is simply to recognise their rootedness in embod-ied, embedded and ecological life, and to respect that fact. We could also call it 'human nature' – something which, over the past few decades, has been banished from polite intellectual discourse for fear of falling into 'essentialism'. But this is to throw out the baby with the bathwater, because to all intents and purposes there are indeed certain essentials.

To say that human nature changed on or around December 1910, as Woolf did, is to make a bold and interesting if ultimately implausible claim. But to say that there is no such thing as human nature – that actually, or even only potentially, the human animal is universal, unlimited, infinitely plastic – is absurd at best, and at worst, menacing: Promethean, hubristic, androcentric, nature-hating and tech-nology-worshipping. As such, it plays into the hands of the programme to destroy life on Earth and replace it with a robotic playground for its overgrown adolescent purveyors which, being apparently totally secure, is totally sterile. There is no room for unplanned encounter or surprise, let alone enchantment.

I have described the experience of enchantment as fundamentally non-modern. In that short but deep moment of delight and rapt attention, all the issues that so concern modernists, the abstractions they venerate – mastery, freedom, truth – fall away in an instant. By the same token, as time slows into moment and time gives way to place, history and geography too lose their grip. As Michael Oakeshott says, images in contemplation are simply present: 'they provoke neither speculation nor inquiry about the occasion or conditions of their appearing but only delight in their having appeared.'[111] So if the viewer, listener or reader is receptive, art speaks not according to when or how it was created but only insofar as it succeeds as enchanting art.

But this prospect is appalling for modernists, so they portray wonder and valu-ing wonder as anti-intellectual, anti-progress, and so on. They would never accept Oakeshott's further observation that 'Of course, from one point of view, [art] is an "escape" ... from the considerabilities of practical enterprise. But there is noth-ing sacrosanct about practical enterprise, moral endeavour, or scientific inquiry that "escape" from them is to be deplored.'[112] It's not difficult to imagine what an arch-modernist like Edmund Wilson, for example – once described as obsessed with being the Adult in the Room, and, not coincidentally, a bitter critic of Tolkien – would have had to say.

But to be positively anti-intellectual is to take a side in a debate one thereby accepts, and thus to indirectly support the importance of intellectualism. As Ursula Le Guin says, 'To oppose something is to maintain it. To be sure, if you turn your back on Mishnory and walk away from it, you are still on the Mishnory road. You must go somewhere else; you must have another goal; then you walk a different road.'[113] Enchantment walks a different road. In this case, it is simply non-intellectual, or non-analytical. Artistic enchantment, like other kinds, can slip Hermes-like through all the nets and snares set for it, whether by stratospherically high theory or abysmally low and vulgar commerce. It shows up in the humblest as well as grandest places.

Cave Art

Let me return to the subject of cave paintings, because they have much to show us about all art, not only visual. Let's start with the obvious: they are indisputably great art, no matter how you define it, and if your definition excludes them, then it fails. Zbigniew Herbert recalls that after visiting Lascaux, 'I did not emerge from an alien world. Never before had I felt a stronger or more reassuring conviction: I am a citizen of the Earth … The road opened to the Greek temples and the Gothic cathedrals.'[114] Even Picasso, in a rare moment of humility after visiting the caves there, is supposed to have remarked that 'We have learned nothing in twelve thousand years.' And their continuing power to so powerfully enchant is integral to that greatness.

It is noteworthy that although the artists portrayed a few figures either human or theriomorphic (part human and part other-animal), they did so much less frequently and with markedly less passion and precision than they drew their fellow-creatures from the wider natural world. There is no trace of human-centred narcissism, and their interest appears to have been the creatures for own sakes, not their usefulness. In other words, the artists were enchanted by them. Attempts to reduce the paintings to self-interest and utility – 'they conferred magical power over prey' and so on – are implausible. Almost none of the animals portrayed supplied the human Palæolithic diet, and they do not show hunting scenes.

There is also a theory that these artists were shamans. There may have been some truth to this theory, although it seems suspiciously flexible, and I doubt it's the whole story. Traditional shamans are noteworthy for two things. One, they have the hard-won and dangerous ability, as per Hermes, to enter and occupy the perspectives of other beings, animal or divine, before returning with what they have learned. (A sharp distinction between divinity, human and other-animal is a very recent, not to say decadent, idea.) Two, they negotiate with those others on behalf of their own communities. It's not much of a stretch to see those activities as true of art, too. So whether or not Palæolithic shamans were also artists, perhaps artists have become our shamans. Or perhaps I should say, real artists; not the entrepreneurial purveyors of what Brian Sewell memorably terms 'shiny shit'.[115]

It certainly seems that although we now distinguish, quite sharply, between religious ritual, theatre, and art – and within the last, between variously music, painting, poetry, and so on – they share common roots, and were understood and practised that way as late as classical Greek times. In Palæolithic caves, some (but not all) paintings tend to cluster where resonance is amplified (although that is also where surfaces are less porous and therefore good for painting), and bone flutes found in Southern Germany – one from 35,000 years ago – date from the same long period, and were located not far away. At Chauvet, some paintings have been dated to 36,000 years before the present, and others to between 17,500 and 20,000. It seems highly improbable that their painting or music, whether singing or instrumental, wouldn't have had a religious, that is, sacred dimension. That doesn't mean, as we moderns would tend to assume, that they were always solemn. Enchanting art is upstream of the distinction between the two, and the opposite of serious isn't funny; it's not serious.

On the face of it, nothing could be odder and perhaps sadder than the way we have recreated groves of trees in columns of stone, the land in landscape paintings, and other animals in two and three dimensions while nodding through the destruction of the originals. Be that as it may, the durability of art confirms its power, and the power of metaphor to enchant is part of the reason. The lions, bears and horses on the wall both are (thanks to the skill of the artists) and are not 'real' animals, and in the liminal place between those two truths – precisely the 'excluded middle' or third thing (*tertium quid*) forbidden by deductive logic – they assume enchanted life.

It's worth adding that as Leslie Van Gelder points out, the artists and their contemporaries would only have seen the animals in the light of flame, which, moving, co-creates motion and depth (from shadows).[116] But it is striking that we moderns can see the animals moving even in the static light of an overly bright single beam of light! So vividly do the animals come to life, in fact, that it raises the awkward question we touched on earlier: when presented with sufficient skill, are they more enchanting than 'actual' animals? Can art replace life, so to speak?

There is a trap to be skirted in that question, and if we think that art is an 'idea' and life the actual or material 'reality', we fall straight into it. Ideas are fully real and include a material dimension, just as embodied life is fully ideational or spiritual. The question of whether painted horses can be more enchanting than biological ones remains, however. I would say, of course they can. But they need not be, because when fully and properly apprehended, the real horses are themselves metaphorical. (It would be tiresome to have to continually put scare-quotes around 'real'; it is always meant here in a non-exclusive way. 'Whatever is, is real', as one of Russell Hoban's characters says.)[117]

On the one hand, each kind of being is completely and uniquely itself. Horses are intensely horsey and thus different from any other kind; plus, of course, no two horses are exactly alike. The cosmos runs to personality. On the other hand, all beings are completely dependent upon the relationships that comprise their so-called environment, both 'internal' (genes, proteins, cells, organs and so on) and 'external' (sun, earth, rain, grass, other animals, other horses). More than that, those relationships comprise us; ultimately, we are them. So each being both is and is not. Such metaphorical space is home to enchantment, whether in 'life' or 'art'. That is also why the world is its own magic, and needs neither God nor a human surrogate to enchant it.[118]

However, I did say 'when properly apprehended'. While most children naturally do so, given half a chance – which is why we associate childhood with a state of wonder – most adults have learned not to see things that way, or forgotten how to. So most of us need to re-learn to grasp the wonder of living beings, and of being alive; and to the extent we succeed, we open to the enchantment of what is. I think this is what Nietzsche meant when he urged us to rediscover 'the seriousness one had as a child, at play.'[119]

But 'succeed' implies that it is also possible to fail. And there are degrees. For some, life as art might be easier to access than life 'itself'. That doesn't make it inferior; we are talking about two different kinds of life, not life plus an imitation or substitute, and both can enchant. Personally, I sympathise with those for whom direct experience, so to speak, is sometimes either not enough or too much, and I would reject any demand that we must all be Supermen. That is inhuman, and therefore inhumane. Nietzsche himself, who first argued it, spoke truer when he encountered a cruelly whipped horse in a street in Turin and put his arms around its neck, broke down and wept.[120]

Widening Participation

I was once upbraided by a friend for mentioning that Wagner's operas left me cold. Didn't I realise, she asked me severely, that the Ring cycle was Feuerbach set to music, so to speak, just as *Tristan and Isolde* was Schopenhauer? Now this person happens to know not only operatic music but the work of dead white male German philosophers, as she affectionately calls them, very well. So knowledge enables her to participate in what she is hearing is in place, while leaving someone such as me looking, or listening, more from the outside. And the outside is always a disenchanted space.

Of course, the reasons why someone finds this rather than that particular work of art enchanting are complex and subtle. I only want to emphasise that with enough comprehension and the right temperament, most works will probably enchant at least someone. But the work itself – its nature, the methods its creator used, and even the intentions – also determines what happens. Without going into the character of Wagner's operas in any detail, they certainly evoke my dislike of the spectacular, the monumental and the grand. But my friend is evidently not thus averse; perhaps quite the opposite.

Does that mean that my 'definition' of enchantment as wonder, delight and joy, with its emphasis on relationship and, by implication, intimacy and subtlety rather than orgiastic, orgasmic or oceanic union, fails? No, because I believe that what happens when she is enchanted in a performance of *The Ring of the Nibelungen*, say, is that it speaks directly to her. In other words, however epic it may appear to myself, a disenchanted observer, to her it has become intimately personal. Enchantment, even by one of his own operas, is not Wagnerian. Conversely, if an experience has a Wagnerian character, it is something very different from enchantment, such as the sublime: majestic, terrible, awful, and possibly annihilating. Or in a word, Dionysian.

This story has another implication. Wagner's repellent personal beliefs and the way they were taken up, along with his music, by some extremely repugnant people in the middle of the last century, supply those who dislike his work with plenty of reasons to justify their position. Those who are enchanted by it – including descendants of the very people who suffered so from his powerful admirers – have to work pretty hard on that score. Nonetheless, I support the latter, because potentially, at least, any deeply felt experience of enchantment leaves those it affects on the cusp of understanding that despite the terrible things that have happened and still do, this world can be an inherently meaningful and precious place.

From the example I've just given and others, it is clear that on the 'perceiver' side of art, more knowledge of an art-form – its history and present context, say – extends the range of its enchanting possibilities. Education, including (or especially) self-education, can indeed expand the range of what enchants, as long as it is led by delight, inspiring a desire to know more in order to appreciate more. If it is led instead by programme – what Foucault calls a 'regime of truth', whose main concern is correctness as a weapon in a struggle of power-relations – then it can only close down enchantment.

But there is another dynamic, verging on a requirement, which is almost the contrary: openness to new experience. If you know it all already, if you've seen, heard, or felt it all before, you cannot apprehend the concrete uniqueness of what you are experiencing and thence its mystery. Enchantment is shut out.

As a result, there is a spectrum of the appreciation of art, with ignorance at one end and over-knowingness at the other. Both extremes inhibit enchantment. It's not quite symmetrical, though, because some art requires almost no prior knowledge; or to put it another way, almost no one is so lacking in knowledge that they cannot be enchanted by any art at all.

Some Other Arts

The complex dance between enchantment and power-knowledge is played out in every corner of every art. In what follows we shall consider it in visual arts, music, and literature, but it's also clear in film from the struggle between the Hollywood machine of industrial entertainment and independent, culturally local filmmakers: the former continually dominating or appropriating the latter, whose freshness and creativity nonetheless continue to evade a profit-driven, market-research-led formulae.

Forgive me for barely touching on this subject, but as examples of filmic enchantment I cannot not mention Edgar Reitz's extraordinary trilogy, *Heimat* (1984), *The Second Heimat* (Leaving Home) (1992) and *Heimat 3* (2004). Rightly described by Karl Miller as 'one of the most important events in the history of the cinema', one of its models was Proust's novel, which it approaches in sublimity.[121] There is also Richard Linklater's trilogy of *Before Sunrise* (1995), *Before Sunset* (2004) and *Before Midnight* (2013). In his long sequences, writes David Denby, 'Linklater has given the moment, and the moment after that, as substantial an existence as anyone has in American movies'.[122] But wonderfilms cannot be confined to the indie genre. Did you know, for example, that Frank Capra's *It's a Wonderful Life* was his riposte to Leni Riefenstahl's tribute to Nazism, *Triumph of the Will*? Perhaps that is what impels it past the ordinary enchantment of simply a good film.

Let's take a slightly more manageable topic, animated films. Who could deny that *Spirited Away* and other animation feature films by Hayao Miyazaki are enchanting? Or Sylvain Chomet's *The Illusionist*, itself an elegy for artistry which proves that it's not dead yet? Or Tomm Moore's *Song of the Sea*, which celebrates wildness? Yet they certainly depend, in part, on advanced technology (although I would add that Miyazaki is well-known for hand-drawing and colouring his images). Why doesn't that result in disenchantment?

To answer that question, let's contrast his creations with Hironobu Sakaguchi's *Final Fantasy: The Spirits Within*, a film adapted from a video game, which stars a completely computerised cast. The heroine flourishes a head of hair whose sheen comes from the individually programmed placing of each of its 60,000 hairs. She's pretty. The problem is, she's also pretty lifeless. It seems that technology cannot replace character and narrative. Which won't stop the cultural industries from trying, of course, because unlike enchantment, technological glamour can be profitably arranged.

The difference, it seems to me, is that animators like Sakaguchi are so glamourised by technology that it becomes the master and assumes centre-stage, whereas animators like Miyazaki use it to serve the story. (This is another instance of the legitimate place for will in the artistic process.) Of course, it is quite possible for advanced digital media to be used sensitively even without the involvement of a Miyazaki. *Up* is a good example. But there are major temptations making that harder and less likely: the false promise of complete control and hence profit, and the way technology, driven by capital, tends to become an end in itself.

A second contrast is irresistible, namely with Disney's industrial fantasy. Maybe that's not how it started; the early cartoons had a vigour and anarchic humour that was enchanting, and that quality lasted as late as *The Jungle Book*. But rigid stereotypes, overlaid with the sentimentality that so often accompanies imperialism, were evident as early as the reworked fairy tales, beginning with *Snow White and the Seven Dwarfs*. A double dose, in fact: Disney's corporate dominance of the entertainment industry, and the global dominance of the modern American empire, of which Disney – a union-busting, borderline-fascist pal of J. Edgar Hoover who informed on his employees – was a keen supporter. These two goals unite perfectly in the secular religion, disguised as mere business, of global consumerism. And I'm afraid that Disney's recent incorporation of political correctness is just another carefully market-based calculation. True, that might be a good thing anyway; but what other messages, thus lubricated, are slipping down more easily?[123]

Finally, let's consider Guillermo del Toro's *Pan's Labyrinth* (2006). It serves as a helpful reminder not to identify enchantment with fantasy as such, in any of the arts. *Pan's Labyrinth* fails as enchantment for two reasons. First, its central concern, of which it virtually makes a fetish, is deliberate cruelty – an exact opposite of enchantment, combining terror with the boredom of bureaucratic procedure. Second, the film suggests that the enchanted world is essentially one of delusion, compensation and escape from the 'real' world. This radically undercuts enchantment as an experience, value and place or world in its own right, one which is not a whit less real or important than the disenchanted world, and which owes the latter no tribute.

In other corners of the field, more worlds: circus, mime, and puppetry, for example. Compared to expensive galleries and concert-halls it is plebeian art, but no less powerfully enchanting for that. The dance with power is happening here too, though. For example, Cirque du Soleil (whose founder is now worth an estimated $2.5 billion at least) keeps more than twenty shows going at any one time. Accompanied by blandly positive sentiments about 'humanity', they are remarkable for spectacular sets, costumes, and physical prowess. Yet over-professionalism, hyper-control and 'mission' disenchant. To quote a comment by my daughter (then eight years old), delivered during a show in a stage whisper, 'These people should realise that it would be more interesting if they made a few mistakes.'

The relevant contrast is with Le Cirque Invisible – formerly Le Cirque Imaginaire and before that, Le Cirque Bonjour – of Victoria Chaplin and Jean-Baptiste Thiérrée, who kept their shows to the small scale that encourages enchantment, working extraordinary transformations that invoke the ancient trinity of human, other-animal, and god, turning from one into the other, as in our common ancestral matrix.

Turning to puppetry, I hope to be forgiven for passing over countless enchanting small-scale and local productions in favour of the biggest of them all, *War Horse*. Based on a novel by Michael Morpurgo and realised by the Handspring Puppet Company, it premiered in London in 2007 and by 2011, it had been seen in theatres by one million people. Notwithstanding this relatively grand scale and status, though, the wonder of its puppets has been irresistible for adults and children alike.

On the face of it, this is puzzling. The horse-puppets, although life-sized, were clearly just that, with no effort to make them look 'exactly' like horses, and they were carried around and manipulated by people who were clearly visible; yet within minutes, they just were horses, alive and utterly equine – a vivid lesson in animism in action! A committed secularist-modernist might possibly have been able to resist by spending the whole play telling himself, 'It's okay, they're not really horses. They just seem like it because my mind – and thank God it is still my mind (damn, I just thanked God) – can't help projecting aliveness into what is just…' But more likely, even he would have had to wait until after the play to resume being the Adult in the Room. It is simply more honest, parsimonious and elegant to admit that while it's happening, those simply *are* horses up there, whatever else they are, and the problem actually lies with our constipated ideological/technical concept of 'alive'.

Whence the enchantment, though? It's not so hard to understand. A puppet-horse can be even more enchanting than a biological horse, because we can too easily mistaken the latter as literal, just a horse and nothing else; no gaps, no relations, nothing happening. (People who love and understand horses don't see them that way, of course.) Whereas a puppet – both a thing of metal, wood and wire, and a horse, with both realities simultaneously indubitable – creates its own metaphoric gap, crossed by the tensive truth of horse-and-not-horse, that is one of enchantment's essential dynamics. Add the fact that the puppets leave work for the imagination to do which literal representations foreclose, and it's no surprise that the 'real' horses in Spielberg's film version failed to enchant to anything like the same extent. (Contrast that with his *E.T.*, the wonder of whose central character, a puppet, cannot sensibly be doubted.)

The enchantment of puppetry was summed up by a consummate insider, Kermit the Frog. When he was interviewed by Seth Meyers on 'Saturday Night Live', Meyers called him 'a puppet'. Kermit responded, 'I'm not a puppet, I'm a muppet.' Surprised, Meyers asked, 'Oh, what's the difference?' 'Well, a puppet is actually controlled by a person,' replied Kermit, 'whereas I am an actual talking frog.'[124]

Notes

1 On the question posed by the title of this chapter, see also my essays 'From Enlightenment to Enchantment: Changing the Question', pp. 106–118 in Ruth Thomas-Pellicer, Vito de Lucia and Sian Sullivan (eds), *Contributions to Law, Philosophy and Ecology: Exploring Re-embodiments* (London: Routledge, 2016), and 'The Experience of Enchantment and the Sense of Wonder,' *Green Letters: Studies in Ecocriticism* 25:2 (2021) 115–29.

2 Tolkien makes this point in 'On Fairy-Stories', pp. 9–73 in *Tree and Leaf* (London: Unwin Hyman, 1988 [1964]): 37. For a recent edition, see Verlyn Flieger and Douglas A. Anderson (eds), *Tolkien on Fairy-stories*, expanded edition, with commentary and notes (London: HarperCollins, 2008): 32.

3 W.H. Auden, *A Certain World: A Commonplace Book* (London: Faber & Faber, 1971): 149.

4 Tolkien, *Smith*, 101.

5 As I write, 'My Octopus Teacher' has just won an Academy Award; and deservedly so.

6 Stevens, *Collected*, 905.

7 R.W. Hepburn, *'Wonder' and Other Essays* (Edinburgh: Edinburgh University Press, 1984): 113. Although neglected, Hepburn is possibly the best philosopher of enchantment, certainly in terms of aesthetics.

8 William James, *Pragmatism and Other Essays* (New York: Penguin, 2000): 286–87. See also William James, *The Heart of William James*, ed. Robert Richardson (Cambridge MA: Harvard University Press, 2010): 165–66.

9 Stevens, *Collected*: 906.

10 *From Max Weber*: 348.

11 Judy Kravis, *these women* (Garravaugh: A Boreen Book, 2018), 'sea spinach' (n.p.).

12 Lucien Lévy-Bruhl, *The Notebooks on Primitive Mentality*, transl. Peter Rivière (Harper & Row, 1975): 109.

13 Interview on BBC 1 TV (27.5.2008).

14 Agnes Horvath and Arpad Szakolczai, *The Political Sociology and Anthropology of Evil: Tricksterology* (Abingdon: Routledge, 2020): 49.

15 Kenneth Burke, *Language as Symbolic Action: Essays on Life, Literature, and Method* (Berkeley: University of California Press, 1966): 16.

16 Shane Woolridge: from an interview with Leslie Van Gelder in February 2016 in New Zealand, where they live; with thanks to them both.

17 Russell Hoban, *The Moment Under the Moment. Stories, a Libretto, Essays and Sketches* (London: Jonathan Cape, 1992): 163–64.

18 Walter Benjamin, *Illuminations*, transl. Hannah Arendt (New York: Schocken Books, 1968), 'Theses on the Philosophy of History' VII.

19 The *locus classicus* (and rightly so) is Ricoeur, *Rule*. See also Patrick Curry, 'Radical Metaphor' (accessible at http://www.patrickcurry.co.uk/papers/Patrick%20Curry%20 EarthLines%206.pdf) and *Defending the Humanities: Metaphor, Nature and Science* (accessible at https://roundedglobe.com/books/d85e8601-391b-4755-8c7e-fc5e157c8427/ Defending%20the%20Humanities:%20Metaphor,%20Nature%20and%20Science/)

20 *Mind and Nature: A Necessary Unity* (New York: E.P. Dutton, 1979).

21 Stevens, *Necessary*: 73.

22 Mark Glanville, 'The man who wrote poetry after Auschwitz', TLS (20.11.2020) 19–20: 19.

23 Quoted by Hans Bohr in Stefan Rozental (ed.), *Niels Bohr: His Life and Work* (New York: Wiley, 1967): 328. See also Philip Wheelwright, *Metaphor and Reality* (Bloomington: Indian University Press, 1962).

24 D.W. Winnicott, *Playing and Reality* (London: Routledge, 2005): 7.

25 C.S. Lewis, *The Voyage of the Dawn Treader* (London: Geoffrey Bles, 1952): 13–15.

26 I believe this remark is in his (unindexed) *Silence: Lectures and Writings* (London: Marion Boyars, 1968).

27 Jan Zwicky, *The Experience of Meaning* (Montreal: McGill-Queen's University Press, 2019): 40.

28 Russell Hoban, *The Medusa Frequency* (London: Jonathan Cape, 1987): 85.

29 Ludwig Wittgenstein, *Notebooks 1914–1916*, ed. G. H. von Wright and G. E. M. Anscombe, transl., by G.E.M. Anscombe, rev. edn (Oxford: Basil Blackwell 1979): 77e.

30 Gregory Bateson and Mary Catherine Bateson, *Angels Fear. An Investigation into the Nature and Meaning of the Sacred* (London: Rider, 1987): 51.

31 Hans Jonas, of *The Phenomenon of Life* (Chicago: University of Chicago Press, 1982): 16.

32 *From Max Weber*. 282.

33 Maurice Merleau-Ponty, *The Visible and the Invisible*, ed. Claude Lefort and transl. Alphonso Lingis (Evanston: Northwestern University Press, 1968): 149.

34 I read this on a notice beside one of her paintings in an exhibition in Basle.

35 Vladimir Jankélévitch, *Music and the Ineffable*, transl. Carolyn Abbate (Princeton: Princeton University Press, 2003): 127.

36 Arpad Szakolczai, *Permanent Liminality and Modernity: Analysing the Sacrificial Carnival through Novels* (Abingdon: Routledge, 2017).

37 John Crowley, *Little, Big* (London: Victor Gollancz, 1982): 43.

38 Simon Leys, *The Hall of Uselessness: Collected Essays* (New York: NYRB, 2013): 104.

39 Tolkien, *OFS*: 14.

40 Karen Blixen, *Out of Africa* (New York: Random House, 1970 [1937]): 381.

41 William James, *A Pluralistic Universe* (Cambridge MA: Harvard University Press, 1977 [1909]): 27.

42 Jan Zwicky, Lyric Philosophy (Toronto: University of Toronto Press, 1992): 8. Since re-published in a revised and corrected 2nd edn by Brush Education, Edmonton, in 2014.

43 Seamus Heaney, *The Government of the Tongue* (London: Faber and Faber, 1988): 117.

44 *The Irish Times* (11.1.92) (my emphasis).

45 Reginald Gibbons (ed.), *The Poet's Work* (Boston: Houghton Mifflin, 1979): 227.

46 On Brook's plays, see the excellent commentary by Mark Beeson, 'The particulars of acting', *TLS* (26.4.96).

47 Shunryu Suzuki, *Zen Mind, Beginner's Mind* (New York: Weatherhill, 1970): 111.

48 Laurence Durrell, *The Alexandria Quartet* (London: Faber and Faber, 2012): 285.

49 William Blake, *Complete Writings*, ed. Geoffrey Keynes (London: Oxford University Press, 1972): 149, 793.

50 Louis MacNeice, *The Poetry of W.B. Yeats* (London: Faber and Faber, 1967 [1941]): 91.

51 Tolkien, *OFS*: 53.

52 Walter Benjamin, 'The Work of Art in the Age of Mechanical Reproduction' [1936], pp. 228–59 in *One-Way Street and Other Writings*, transl. J.A. Underwood (London: Penguin, 2009): 233, 237, 236.

53 Lesley Chamberlain, 'Sacrificing beauty', *TLS* (18.4.2014) 14–15: 15.

54 'Giant red squiggle': I have borrowed this description from Hugo Williams, *TLS* (6.7.12): 16. The quote from Kapoor comes from an interview here: http://www.bbc. co.uk/programmes/p00tqbln

55 *From Max Weber*, 139.

56 Jonathan Simons, 'The Revolution Will Not Be Digitized', *Analog Sea Review* 3 (2020) 1–3: 1.

57 John Julius Norwich (ed.), *Christmas Crackers* (Harmondsworth: Penguin Books, 1980): 204.

58 Percy Bysshe Shelley, *Shelley's Prose*, ed. David Lee Clark (London: Fourth Estate, 1988): 294.

59 C.K. Williams, *All at Once* (New York: Farrar Strauss Giroux, 2014): 120.

60 Cyril Connolly, *Enemies of Promise*, rev. edn (New York: Persea Books, 1983 [1948]): 137.

61 *RA magazine* 83 (2004): 47.

62 George Santayana, *Life of Reason* (1905), vol. 4, Ch. 4.

63 In his Preface to *The Picture of Dorian Gray*.

64 Fernando Pessoa, *The Book of Disquiet*, transl. Richard Zenith (London: Penguin, 2002): 278.

65 John Bayley, *The Power of Delight. A Lifetime in Literature: Essays 1962–2002* (London: Duckworth, 2005): 449.

66 Quoted in Peter Hall's diary (entry for 16.3.76).

67 Inspired by Zhuang Zi's observation that many people understand the use of what is useful, but few the use of what is useless.

68 Stevens, *Necessary*: 167.

69 See Nicholas Gane, *Max Weber and Postmodern Theory* (Basingstoke: Palgrave Macmillan, 2004).

70 Victoria Thiérée Chaplin, interview (19.6.2012): https://aureliathierree.com/blog/ life-defined

71 Jonathan Cott (ed.), *Bob Dylan: the Essential Interviews* (New York: Wenner Books, 2006) 100. (With thanks to Clay Ramsay.)

72 Milan Kundera, *Testaments Betrayed* (London: HarperCollins, 1995).

73 MacNeice, Poetry: 194.

74 Suzi Gablik, *Has Modernism Failed?* rev. edn (London: Thames and Hudson, 2004): 18.

75 D.H. Lawrence, *Assorted Articles* (London: Martin Secker, 1932): 171.

76 David Esterly: quoted in the *TLS* (10.4.15): 8. On craft, see his *The Lost Carving. A Journey to the Heart of Making* (London: Duckworth, 2015); also Richard Sennett, *The Craftsman* (New Haven: Yale University Press, 2009); and Peter Korn, *Why We Make Things and Why It Matters* (London: Square Peg, 2015).

77 George Surt, first as quoted in Hubert Dreyfuss and Sean Dorrance Kelly: *All Things Shining: Reading the Western Classics to Find Meaning in a Secular Age* (New York: Free Press, 2011): 209; then George Surt, *The Wheelwright's Shop* (Cambridge: The University Press, 1958 [1923]): 201–2.

78 Laurie Lee, *Village Christmas and Other Notes on the English Year* (London: Penguin Books, 2015): 135, 1.

79 J.R.R. Tolkien, *The Letters of J.R.R. Tolkien*, ed. Humphrey Carpenter and Christopher Tolkien (London: HarperCollins, 2006): 110.

80 Joseph Conrad: *The Nigger of the Narcissus* (New York: Doubleday, Page & Co., 1926): xii. I owe this quotation to Lewis Hyde, *The Gift. How the Creative Spirit Transforms the World* (Edinburgh: Canongate, 2006) 155.

81 'Megamachine' is borrowed from Lewis Mumford, *The Myth of the Machine*, 2 vols. (New York: Harcourt Brace Jovanovitch, 1967, 1970).

82 Curry, *Enchantment*, Chapters 9 and 10.

83 Max Horkheimer and Theodor W. Adorno, *The Dialectic of Enlightenment*, transl. Edmund Jephcott, ed. Gunzelin Schmid Noerr (Stanford: Stanford University Press, 2002 [1947]): 4. 'Mastery of nature' comes from Val Plumwood, *Feminism and the Mastery of Nature* (London: Routledge, 1993).

84 *From Max Weber.* 155, 139.

85 Jeanette Winterson, 'The secret life of us', *The Guardian* (25.11.02).

86 John Ruskin, *The Stones of Venice* (1853), Chapter 2, paragraph 17.

87 William James, *The Will to Believe and Other Essays in Popular Philosophy* (London: Longman, 1897): 154.

88 See my 'Magic vs. Enchantment', *Journal of Contemporary Religion* 14:3 (October 1999) 401–412 (accessible at http://www.patrickcurry.co.uk/papers/Magic%20vs%20 Enchantment.pdf).

89 J.R.R. Tolkien, *The Lord of the Rings* (London: HarperCollins, 2012 [single pb edn]): 555.

90 See my 'Fantasy in transhumanism and Tolkien', *The Ecological Citizen* 4:1 23–24.

91 'Fearless receptivity': Freya Stark, *Perseus in the Wind* (London: I.B. Tauris. 2013 [1948]): 107.

92 Letter to Fanny Keats (September 1817); J.L.C. Peerless (ed.), *The Sayings of John Keats* (London: Gerald Duckworth and Co., 1995): 49.

93 Wittgenstein, *Tractatus Logico-Philosophicus*, transl. D.F. Pears and B.F. McGuiness (London: Routledge, 2001 [1921]): 3.328, p. 19.

94 T.W. Adorno, *Minima Moralia: Reflections from a Damaged Life*, transl. E.F.N. Jephcott (London: Verso, 2015): 222.

95 Merleau-Ponty, *Visible*: 203.

96 Tolkien, *Smith*: 101.

97 See, e.g., James C. Scott, *Seeing Like a State* (New Haven: Yale University Press, 1998) and Stephen Toulmin, *Cosmopolis: The Hidden Agenda of Modernity* (Chicago: University of Chicago Press, 1990); and in relation to art, Julian Spalding, *The Eclipse of Art* (London: Prestel, 2003); Marc Fumaroli, *Paris-New York et Retour* (Paris: Fayard, 2009); John Elsom, *Missing the Point. The Rise of Modernity and the Decline of Everything Else* (Cambridge: The Lutterworth Press, 2007).

98 Richard Taruskin, *Music in the Early Twentieth Century* (Oxford: Oxford University Press, 2010): 1.

99 Jay Bernstein, 'The death of sensuous particulars: Adorno and abstract expressionism', *Radical Philosophy* 76 (1996) 7–18: 16.

100 From his poem 'Snow'.

101 Scott, *Seeing*: 116, 112.

102 Adam Zagajewski, *A Defense of Ardor*, transl. Clare Cavanagh (Farrar, Straus and Giroux, 2004): 13.

103 Kundera, *Immortality*, transl. Peter Kussi (London: Faber & Faber, 1991): 159.

104 John Berger, *Why Look at Animals?* (London: Penguin, 2009).

105 On modernism in art, see, e.g., Spalding, Eclipse; Fumaroli, Paris; Gabriel Jocipovici, *What Ever Happened to Modernism?* (New Haven: Yale University Press, 2010; and late writings by Robert Hughes.

106 Rita Felski, *Uses of Literature* (Oxford: Blackwell, 2008): 56.

107 Philip Larkin, *All What Jazz* (London: Faber & Faber, 1985): 23.

108 Personal communication.

109 Sarah Kent, in *Time Out* (5–12.10.1994). Or try this: 'A clock made of movie clips, a severed head vomiting into a bucket, a man on a burning bench … Adrian Searle is thrilled by the best British Art Show ever' (*The Guardian* [26.10.10]).

110 Clive James, *Cultural Amnesia. Notes in the Margin of my Time* (London: Picador, 2007): 493.

111 Michael Oakeshott, 'The Voice of Poetry in the Conversation of Mankind', pp. 488–541 in in *Rationalism in Politics and Other Essays* (Indianapolis: Liberty Fund, 1991): 509–510.

112 Ibid, 535.

113 Le Guin, *The Left Hand of Darkness* (London: Futura, 1981): 132.

114 Heaney, *Government*: 59.

115 Brian Sewell, describing an exhibition by Damien Hirst in London exhibition, in *The Evening Standard* (5.4.12): 50.

116 Leslie Van Gelder, personal communication. Together with colleagues from the University of Otago, she has developed a hand-held battery-powered lamp which almost exactly reproduces the light from the wick-and-tallow lamps of the artists.

117 Hoban, *Medusa*: 85.

118 This point has no bearing either way on the question of whether there *is* a God or not, of course.

119 Friedrich Nietzsche, *Beyond Good and Evil* (Harmondsworth: Penguin, 1973): 94.

120 See Lesley Chamberlain, *Nietzsche in Turin: The End of the Future* (London: Quartet Books, 1996).

121 Karl Miller, 'Diary', *LRB* (9.10.1986).

122 David Denby, in *The New Yorker* (27.5.13): 87; and on Frank Capra, Denby in *The New Yorker* (17.3.14).

123 See Ariel Dorfman and Armand Mattelart, *How to Read Donald Duck*, transl. David Kunzle, 2nd edn (London: International General, 1991), and Henry A. Giroux, *The Mouse That Roared: Disney and the End of Innocence* (Cumnor Hill: Rowman and Littlefield, 2000). (Did I mention that Snow White and the Seven Dwarfs was apparently Hitler's favourite film?)

124 19 Nov. 2011.

3
PAINTING I

This chapter and the next address enchantment in visual art, mainly the kind I know and love best: paintings. For me, just to think about them is already to leave the dusty world behind and begin to move into broad, sunlit uplands.

I started this book by describing an experience of enchantment I had with a Chinese landscape painting. It seems this sort of encounter is not uncommon. Ali Smith records something similar with an Impressionist painting: 'The gallery falls away, leaves nothing but leaves and striplings in a landscape where the curve of the tree is the curve of the eye is the curve of the surface of the piece of gristle inside the chest that happens to be keeping me breathing. What just happened?'[1]

Again, Adam Zagazewski was having a bad day in New York City when

> I came across a museum, the Frick Collection, and there, in front of Vermeer's Girl Interrupted at Her Music, all of a sudden, I felt how reality stopped for an instant and froze in harmonious motionlessness ... Before me, a girl is having music lessons, wrapped in a light as soft and blue as the ocean's interior. Suddenly there is tranquillity, in me and in all of New York.[2]

Clive James too recalls encountering the paintings of Toulouse-Lautrec in Sydney in 1957. 'He had died in Paris in 1901, but suddenly, and with overwhelming enchantment, he was alive again for me'.[3]

Sometimes, as James implies, the experience is startlingly timeless. In the Pitti Palace, Annibale Caracci's *Testa Virile* (Manly Head) looked back at me, amused and quizzical – looked into my eyes, as I was looking into his – across 400 years as if they were nothing. The *Madonna dei Francescanni* in Siena was painted in about 1290, but Hisham Matar, writing in 2019, 'felt the painting was painted specifically for me'.[4]

In these instances and many others, I would like to see if we can find out something about what happened, and how. I'm not after a tightly structured argument;

DOI: 10.4324/9781003353225-3

although there are arguments along the way, the goal is rather to explore and discover enchantment in visual art. And any exploration must take a particular path, so both here and in the following chapters on music and literature, I shall proceed mainly by concentrating on a few exemplars. This not only makes the task manageable but also seems a promising approach. Enchantment in art, both its creation and appreciation, transcends individuals but also depends upon them. I would add that most of the artists discussed here are modern, meaning no disrespect to the art of earlier times; I am simply not competent to discuss most of it.

There is art that is enchanting where the artist has tried to depict or convey enchantment. Naturally, that is no guarantee that the work actually succeeds, but it would be odd if the intention didn't increase its chances. In any case, I am more concerned with the enchantment of the viewer by the work, than of the artist.

To say that an artwork is enchanting means that it is so for some people, often many people (although not, of course, everyone), and that its enchantment is more readily accessible than other work by other artists, or even by the same artist. These generalisations are unavoidable. But I can at least give reasons, in terms of the dynamics of enchantment.

First, though, a point that seems so obvious, as well as so important, as to hardly be worth mentioning but which, like so much these days, is just what is in danger of being forgotten. How long do we actually spend looking at any picture in a gallery or museum, on average? A minute or a few, at most? But any picture worth looking at all is worth taking an hour over, say, and repeatedly so. In fact, it's very hard to look at a really good painting for too long, and it's very easy not to really see it at all. Millions of people, merely glancing or snapping a photo, do that all the time.

Monet

Claude Monet was the leading Impressionist painter, itself probably the most successful movement in modern art – 'successful' being some mixture of publicly popular and artistically consequential, and 'modern' meaning coterminous with the late nineteenth and entire twentieth century. Monet's *Impression, Sunrise* was derided by contemporary critics as a mere rough sketch when it was shown in Paris in 1874, and a hostile review gave rise to the name for the movement that this act of naming helped create. By the end of his life, though, Monet's work had developed to the point where it is doubtful whether he could still be meaningfully classed as a member of any group. To call Monet an Impressionist would be like describing Bob Dylan as a folksinger, or *Moby-Dick* a novel about a whale.

Monet's fate is to have become almost invisible as a result, almost as an index, of his popularity. His paintings are among the most viewed and loved in the history of art, but many people can no longer see them because they 'know' them, while many critics, congenitally suspicious of popularity, ignore them. So ignore the snobs in turn, and fight your way past the queues – his exhibitions regularly generate record attendances – and endless merchandising with indifferent reproductions – mouse pads, napkins, tablecloths, T-shirts, jewellery, T-shirts, scarves, and of course, postcards and posters – because as Robert Graves once said of Shakespeare, the remarkable thing is in spite of all the people who say that he is very good, Monet really is very good. In particular, his popularity should not be allowed to obscure the astonishing *Nymphéas* cycle that he painted late in life: a high point in Western art comparable to, say, Beethoven's final string quartets. (Oddly, Monet painted it while struggling with increasing blindness, while Beethoven was already deaf.)

Monet didn't need Max Weber's warning about the disenchanting effects of intellectualisation. In a letter in 1912, he wrote, 'I only know that I do what I think best to express what I experience in front of nature' and repeated this assertion almost verbatim in 1926: 'I've always had a horror of theories, and finally the only merit I have is to have painted directly from nature with the aim of conveying my impressions in front of the most fugitive effects ...'[5] He used the terms *sentir* (to feel) or *éprouver* (to experience), only rarely *voir* (to see). Matisse later did the same. Monet didn't share, and was unaffected by, the contemporary scientific theorising about optics which Georges Seurat and Paul Signac incorporated in their pointillism. Typically, leading critics at the time hailed their 'scientific rigour' as against the Impressionists' romanticism.[6] Seurat's *Sunday Afternoon on the Island of La Grande Jatte* (1884–86) shows the result: a uniformly hard, brassy light on everything, and in every scene. Monet's desire was to reveal common times and places, each one, as extraordinary and unique.

In 1890–91, Monet started working on a radically innovative series of paintings of the same scene in different seasons and times of the day. The first series was of grain stacks, almost thirty. In a letter, he writes:

> I'm grinding away, struggling stubbornly with a series of effects (stacks) but at this time of the year the Sun sinks so fast I can't keep up with it. I'm beginning to work so slowly that I despair, but the longer I go on, the more I see that it is necessary to work a great deal in order to succeed in rendering what I seek – instantaneity, above all the 'envelope' ...[7]

Note the artist's paradox: the will and effort required over time to communicate a timeless and gratuitous moment of enchantment. 'Envelope' means the precise ambient luminosity that interacts with the particularities of the objects it envelopes to create the concrete magic of that moment and place. Monet was the most non-Platonic of painters, concerned above all with effects, not supposed causes, and the appearances, not 'underlying realities', which speak to bodied minds and mindful or ensouled bodies, living fully in this world. Nor are these appearances taken to imply an underlying reality we cannot have; they are all we can have, or need. And he painted their sensuous particulars so skilfully that we can perceive their essential mystery, their otherwise invisible lining and depth.

His next extended series, in 1892–95, comprised portraits of Rouen Cathedral. They 'naturalise' the Cathedral just as his more usual subjects 'spiritualise' non-human nature. By now, Monet was able to work longer in the studio than *en plein air* without the result losing any freshness. Another series painted in 1896–97 showed the Seine outside Paris in early morning. (The delicacy of these paintings, both in form and colour, don't reproduce well.)[8] These were followed by the London, mainly Westminster, fog pictures in 1900–05.

From 1904, aged 64, Monet was preoccupied with the gardens at Giverny: the pond and its watery reflective surface, trees, especially willows, and flowers, including the famous waterlilies. Finally, at the age of 76, sometimes working within earshot of the guns of the Western front and with his eyesight steadily deteriorating, Monet started his great cycle of paintings of waterlilies, the *Nymphéas*.[9] He worked on them until his death ten years later. (In 1922, Monet finally agreed to have his cataracts removed: a serious operation at the time. He was left seeing everything too blue, and had to wear special, yellow-tinted glasses.)

These last paintings show only the most elemental things in our lives, things we completely depend upon, even though so many of us have forgotten it: earth, water, plants and sky. They bring to life Monet's beloved water-lily ponds at Giverny at all times of the day, from dawn to dusk. Writhing with spiritual fire, Monet's water-lilies are just that but equally a force of nature, incarnate in and as vegetable forms, about to burst their bonds. (One contemporary critic accused Monet of abandoning the Western man-centred worldview in favour of 'oriental self-effacement'. This was apparently a bad thing.)[10]

By now, however, even they are not the principal subject. The watery surfaces in which the lilies float, and what those surfaces mirror, have become the entire painting. Monet himself remarked that 'The water flowers are far from being the whole scene; really, they are just the accompaniment. The essence of the motif is the mirror of water…' And he praised 'this mobile, constantly changing stuff that water is…which renews itself and shows itself in an important light at every moment.'[11]

In 1927, after many vicissitudes, Monet's *Nymphéas* finally ended up in a public place, in effect a chapel dedicated to art, L'Orangerie, in Paris. The enormous canvases occupy all the walls of two large oval-shaped rooms where, in a visual equivalent of enchantment in the semantic sense – *enpeinturement*, perhaps, or *entableaument* – one is, in effect, walking among them, looking at the flowers, trees, water, sky, and reflections from inside the paintings, not merely looking at but walking in, and through, a complete day.

That participation in a narrative is one way they enchant. More subtly, there is their metaphoric truth. Any recognisably figurative painting doesn't simply represent something. It both is and is not its subject. On the one hand, what you see is necessarily related in some integral way to what one recognises in it, something which (usually) has depth; yet what you are seeing is also a two-dimensional painted surface. As a variation on that process, when a painting prominently and convincingly shows a surface of any kind, such as Monet's watery surfaces, then the painting invites you to go deeper, past its own literal surface and into it.

The motif of reflections on water adds yet another potent dimension. A reflection on 'real' water is already metaphorical, since it both is and isn't what is reflected. Monet then doubles that effect by painting the reflection. In the process, his water-lilies – 'blossoms in the middle of the sky', Proust called them[12] – remind you that you are seeing real but reflected waterlilies; and since Monet shows you slightly abstract 'impressions' of waterlilies, not hyper-realistic ones, they remind you that you are also seeing a (painted) reflection of a (watery) reflection.[13] In all ways, then, the waterlilies embody tensive truth.

In yet another twist, as with mirror-images, everything is reversed, so the reality of this world, while remaining real – a tree, or cloud, or figure – is inverted into another reality, that of 'the other world' sometimes known as *Faërie*.

> Shadows of the trees
> on the water, with lights – source
> unseen. Who lives there?

Monet's watery surfaces thus open a door onto another world, like but unlike ours. They invite us to go through the looking-glass and into it. And since the normal, quotidian world in which most of us pass most of our time is disenchanted, this other one irresistibly presents itself as its contrary – the one we know, but transfigured.

Matisse

Henri Matisse is another exemplar of a modern artist, possessed of a prodigious talent, who consciously chose to work with enchantment. In this he both resembled and differed from his great rival and friend Picasso. (Picasso's nickname for Matisse was 'the Magician'. The latter's for Picasso was, slyly, 'the Boss'.) Nearly thirty years younger than Monet, Matisse first encountered his work in 1897, and visited the elder man at Giverny in 1917. They were not themselves close, although Pierre Bonnard, whom we shall discuss later, was close to both. But Matisse worked at a time when the cultural tide, driven by modernism, was increasingly running against enchantment. For this reason, he offers a fascinating study of artistic enchantment surviving, even flourishing, in hostile times.

For Matisse, as for Monet, light was a primary concern. Picking out one of his paintings as characteristic (*My Room at Beau Rivage*, 1918), Elaine Scarry says that in it, there is a 'place where light pools and then spills outward in all directions'.[14] I hope I may be forgiven a digression here on what light does when it and you are enchanted, because Tolkien noticed the same thing. In his mythic cosmogony, there are two radiant trees, one white and the other golden, and the radiance of their flowers as they wax and wane in differing cycles, in mingled silver and gold, is the source of light. (Eventually, one fruit of each would become the Moon and the Sun respectively.) What seals their enchanted nature, however, is that this light falls onto the ground, whence some of it is taken up into the air, some sinks into the earth, and some is collected in wells of light from which it overflows, sometimes rising and other times falling, through a 'Light Cleft' into and over the land. In other words, the light acts as radiant water.[15]

And not only light. Fleeing Cambridge in 1948, Wittgenstein settled on the west coast of Ireland. He remarked to a friend, 'I can only think clearly in the dark, and in Connemara I have found one of the last pools of darkness in Europe.'[16] On the other side of the globe, Jun'ichirō Tanizaki talks about how, in sharp contrast to electric light, candle and lamplight run through a room, 'collecting in little pools here and there', and darkness too 'gathers' at certain places.[17]

Matisse was first classed as a Fauve, and his lifelong affair with light did indeed begin with their uncompromisingly bright colours. But significantly, as the Fauves' influence began to scatter and wane, Matisse declined to join the general drift to Cézanne, turning instead to Renoir for inspiration. (This was also when he visited Monet.) Around 1930, after a series of notably enchanting paintings partly inspired by the quality of the light in Provence and Morocco, his visual imagination changed again, returning to a more personal kind of Fauvism. In the 1940s, after surviving near-fatal surgery, Matisse began experimenting with coloured paper cut-outs. His first book of paper cut-outs, *Jazz*, appeared in 1947. 'True jazz', he explained, 'has a number of excellent qualities: the gift of improvisation, of life, of harmony with the listening audience.'[18]

Matisse also remarks in *Jazz* that 'Cutting directly into colour reminds me of a sculptor's carving into stone'.[19] He certainly would have been aware of the 'direct carving' by Eric Gill and Jacob Epstein in early twentieth-century England, which was a reaction against machine-produced sculpture, that is, industrially produced using machines and assistants in which the artist's role was limited to making the initial model. Gill in particular was trying to resist the modern sharp distinction between art and craft. Later, in her fine work, Barbara Hepworth embraced the same practice.

Direct carving was thus a revival of the practice and ethos of earlier carvers, ancient and medieval, but principally the work of Michelangelo. His Pietà in the Vatican is powerfully enchanting if devastating, but the effect is concentrated in the face and hands of the Madonna, sculpted as he remembered those of his mother, who had died when he was a boy. There is nothing generic about them, which is why they achieve effective universality. Michelangelo was to accomplish the same thing again in his late and uncompleted Pietà of Joseph, whose distinctive face is a self-portrait.[20] Concrete magic indeed.

Given these examples, including that of Matisse, I am tempted to suggest that any art which doesn't require the direct participation of the whole artist, not just her or his 'mind', is already well on its way to disenchantment. The teams Bridget Riley uses to paint (in a technical sense) her Op-art come to mind. (Interestingly, Riley was influenced by another programmatic artist, Georges Seurat.) As usual, however, Hirst provides the ultimate *reductio ad absurdum*, using assistants to make his random spot paintings because 'I couldn't be fucking arsed to do it'.

After *Jazz*, partly in gratitude to Sister Jacques-Marie, who had nursed him back to health after some serious operations in 1942–43, Matisse devoted several years' work to the Chapel of the Rosary in Vence. He was rebuked for doing so by the severely anticlerical Picasso, but a chapel is not inappropriate. To quote Scarry again, 'beautiful things, as Matisse shows, always carry greetings from other worlds within them.'[21] His stained-glass windows, affirming earthly life as offering the only true heaven, show the Tree of Life in flowing forms of yellow, blue, and green, whose colours, he says,

> compose a light within the chapel which is not strictly speaking any of the colors used, but is the living product of their harmony, their mutual relationships ... It is in this sense, it seems to me, that art may be said to imitate nature: by the quality of life that creative work confers upon the work of art. The work will then appear as fertile and as possessed ... of that same resplendent beauty, that we find in the products of nature.[22]

Matisse devoted the remainder of his life to the paper cut-outs which make up his final bequest, a glorious marriage of form and colour that I hope the reader has had the pleasure of seeing.[23] Delicate yet exuberant, they emerged in a death-defying burst of creativity during what he called his 'second life', after surviving an operation at the age of 71.[24] They do indeed radiate the irrepressible return of life (again and again, amen) but their wonder is deepened still more, I think, by the way they communicate a life lived in its praise.

In common with Monet, Matisse distrusted theoretically driven art. In a letter to Bonnard he remarks that theory is 'something a little sterile and limiting', and he strongly disliked Surrealism, saying 'They're the kind of people who force themselves to see things in a certain way.'[25] Unlike his peers Kandinsky, Mondrian, or Klee, Matisse avoided systematic metaphysics and overt theoretical statements, preferring to discuss (in Jack Flam's words) 'the actual activity of being an artist'.[26] 'To sum up,' he writes, 'I work without theory. I am conscious only of the forces that I use, and I am driven by an idea that I only really grasp as it grows with the picture.'[27]

As we have seen, metaphor, so often at the heart of enchantment, discovers as it creates and creates as it discovers, and that is exactly how Matisse worked. It was his only 'method'. As part of that approach, he refused to wilfully impose himself or any preconceived ideas on materials, or to treat them as inert and secondary.

There is, of course, a theoretical or philosophical dimension to this position. As Proust says, 'if intellect only ranks second in the hierarchy of virtues, intellect alone is able to proclaim that the first place must be given to instinct.'[28] But in Matisse's lifelong quest for self- and world-discovery through art, he had found that when theory led, rather than followed, it interfered with that process. To put it another way, it is not intellect but intellectualisation – the wilful pursuit of an intellectual system, programme, or method – that disenchants, and thus destroys what for an artist like Matisse is both the means of discovery and, in the specific forms that eventuate, its end.

In 1947, with the ascendancy of abstract art in mind, Matisse wrote, 'I sense a need to be free of all compulsion and all theoretical ideas, to express myself fully, beyond this fashionable distinction between the representational and the non-representational.' His solution was thus 'abstraction rooted in reality'.[29] The importance of this statement cannot be overstated. As we shall see, it offers a key to enchantment in modern art, not only his own but more widely.

Matisse complained that 'It makes for a life of torment … when an acute sensibility keeps you from leaning on a method for support', and he once remarked, with reserve but also with feeling, that 'this happiness, this light, this dispassionate wisdom which seem to be mine, are sometimes well-deserved'. The price of realising enchantment as a way of life can indeed be high. It requires constantly eschewing methodology for discovery. Often, as was the case for Matisse, the 'lack of a theoretical programme,' as Flam says, 'is mistaken for a lack of intellectual rigor, even for a lack of artistic ambition or significance.' Matisse warned young artists against relying too much on technique alone, on borrowing too freely other artists' motifs, and on trying to 'possess nature'. And he 'resolutely refused to tell his viewers what his pictures were supposed to "mean".' Quite so! You cannot learn to see without looking, and only by looking can you see. Both for artist and audience, however, the rewards of that effort can be great.[30]

Matisse didn't object to abstract art – or more precisely, non-figurative art, since, as he himself points out, every art involves a degree of abstraction – on theoretical grounds. His objection was rooted in the practice of art, and in particular, as Flam notes, 'a dislike of what he felt to be a loss of contact with nature.'[31] Even his work that is apparently completely non-figurative, such as *The Snail* (1953), is an instance of some definite thing in and of the world. Here is how Matisse describes the process of making it:

> First of all, I drew the snail from nature, holding it between two fingers; drew and redrew. I became aware of an unfolding; I formed in my mind a purified sign for a snail. Then I took the scissors. It was important that 'the end should be contained in the beginning.' Further, I had to establish the connection between the object observed and its observer …

An artist must at some point forget about what he is painting, he said, but

> deep within himself, he must have a real memory of the object and of the reactions it produces in his mind … As for the so-called abstract painters of today, it seems to me that too many of them depart from a void. They are gratuitous, they have no power, no inspiration, no feeling, they defend a non-existent point of view: they imitate abstraction.[32]

Why non-existent? Because no artist starts from nothing, and the world is already present in everything the self undertakes. Conversely, every undertaking by the artist entails a kind and degree of abstraction. Hence to turn abstraction into a mere theory – and one that inauthentically denies its own provenance by pretending to start from a blank – leaves the artist imitating abstraction. This is a devastating criticism.

I don't know whether anyone else has noticed this, but Matisse was practising Goethean phenomenology. I don't mean he was 'applying' something he'd read about, whether in Goethe or elsewhere – an approach which itself contradicts phenomenology, because it is not aware of either the subject who is painting or the one being painted so much as 'the method'. I mean he spontaneously rediscovered for himself what Goethe had for himself, and Ruskin after him, and so on. Mike Glier, a contemporary artist working in this way, sums it up as 'abstract painting based in direct observation of nature'. (Glier adds that 'Improvisation is the key' – a musical and especially jazz metaphor explicitly shared by Matisse.)[33]

Goethe's *Urpflanz* or 'archetypal plant', for example – being led by the senses and realised through the concentrated imagination – is no abstractly universal Idea. Goethe records that 'When I closed my eyes and lowered my head, I could imagine a flower in the centre of my visual sense. Its original form never stayed for a moment; it unfolded, and from within it new flowers continuously developed ... I do not rest until I have found a pregnant point, from which much can be deduced, or rather, that freely brings forth much out of itself and bears it towards me ...'[34] In the process, any sharp distinction between abstraction and figuration becomes unsustainable, along with the possibility of either as 'pure'; although not identical, each is impossible without the other. So too, for the same reason, does any radical difference between imagination and observation.

Matisse held that 'In art, what is most important is the relationship between things.' Even colour, he averred, 'exists only through relationships'.[35] I am reminded of Gregory Bateson, who used to ask students where the difference is between any two objects, a glass and a book, say. It's not in either one or the other, and it's not in the space between them. The answer, of course, is to realise the inaptness of the question: difference, being a relation, is precisely not a thing, so it's 'in' the liminal in between which makes metaphor possible, and where enchantment lives. Yet without the completely 'concrete' subject-objects, both difference and connection are impossible.

David Hockney spoke recently of a Matisse exhibition he had been to see. His interviewer pointed out that 'Critics can be dismissive of art that makes people feel good – as they have been at times of Hockney's. Sod'em, he said. "That Matisse show was unbelievable. It was pure joy. Pure joy. And joy is a great thing to give to people."'[36]

The In Between

The liminal place 'between abstraction and figuration' is so potentially enchanting because it offers the greatest possible freedom for the active imagination short of collapsing into random meaninglessness. With pure abstraction, imaginal connections with 'the world' are no longer possible; with pure figuration, the work is largely already done for you (which is boring, as so many dull early eighteenth-century paintings attest). In the small but deep place between the two, it can realise, in a moment in which nothing has happened but everything changes, that, say, these interlacing lines and cool colours are a tree! (I am thinking of Piet Mondrian's semi-abstract *Tree* (1912).)

The art of Monet and Matisse, among many others, confirms that there is a place between fully or 'realistically' figurative art on the one hand, and fully abstract on the other, where enchantment can flourish. This was the tensive point where both artists stopped short of full abstraction – or struggled to remain, as Gabriel Josipovici says[37] – and with good reason, if I am right. In the deceptively simple words of the artist Ian Fairweather, painting 'is something of a tightrope act; it is between representation and the other thing – whatever that is. It is difficult to keep one's balance.'[38]

The work of Piet Mondrian and Wassily Kandinsky, which we shall consider properly in the next chapter, supports this suggestion. Their early figurative work is largely unremarkable, while their final, completely abstract work seems relatively lifeless; but their work at the point where it was passing through the overlap, in which the figures or objects are still recognisable as such but are no longer treated literally, so to speak, is, for myself and others in my unscientific sample, wholly enchanting.

Why so? I suggest it is because those paintings are tensely true; the images are and are not their referents. Both poles are needed. The earlier paintings are too literally figurative, so there is little left for the imagination to do, while the later are utterly non-figurative, so there is little for the visual sense, informed and structured by natural phenomena, to engage with. In both cases, the viewer's participation is discouraged because there is almost no metaphoricity in play whereby this is-and-is-not a tree, say; and the imagination needs that ambiguous place to enchant.[39]

It follows that to the extent it succeeds, any attempt to eliminate the boundaries and structures in art – between performer and audience, between the work of art and the rest of the world, between what can be played or said and what can't be – tends to destroy enchantment. A close parallel in music is so-called free music or free jazz. Enchantment needs boundaries, differences, and limits. It lives in the gaps between them, waiting to be brought to life by the imagination and senses working together.

D.W. Winnicott was a pioneering theorist of liminal intermediate spaces, and he argued that being 'inherent in art and religion', their implications extended beyond childhood into adult life.[40] They apply directly to enchantment. For example, Winnicott draws attention to the paradox involved in the enchantment of children by what he calls 'the transitional object': an item such as a soft toy or piece of material, which both is and is not the child's self, and intensely so. 'By flight to split-off intellectual functioning it is possible to resolve the paradox, but the price of this is the loss of the value of the paradox itself.' Which is to say, you lose the metaphor's tensive truth, and with it, enchantment. It is therefore 'a matter of agreement between us and the baby that we will never ask the question: "Did you conceive of this ['subjective'] or was it presented to you from without ['objective']?" The important point is that no decision on this point is expected. The question is not to be formulated.'[41]

Compare this resolve with the asinine commentary on an ice-age carving of a female figure in an exhibition at the British Museum: 'Was this a real goddess or a spiritual one?' Quite apart from the assumption that 'spiritual' isn't 'real' (and that a real goddess isn't spiritual!), the enchantment of the figure depends on it being both.

'At this point,' Winnicott continues, 'my subject widens out into that of play, and of artistic creativity and appreciation ... play is in fact neither a matter of inner psychic reality nor a matter of external reality ... if play is neither inside nor outside, where is it?'[42] For an answer, *Faërie* – the liminal place where we and the world are enchanted – seems as good as any.

Why then do some abstract paintings enchant more readily than others? I think at least part of the answer lies in the extent to which the forms invoke natural forms, along with associated colours. There are many patterns in nature which could be described as abstract: those made by freely running water, certain formations of clouds, and organic forms, from branches, bark, leaves, and flowers to seashells and coral to animals' coats, both fur and feathers, to pick only a few. We are animals ourselves, still growing up in continuous contact (if greatly varying) with the natural world, and a part of it, so it would be very odd if we didn't recognise and respond to such forms.[43] In which case, even 'purely' abstract art of this kind could still work metaphorically, in the same way as paintings I have described as midway between abstract and figurative. The painting would still be, and not be, the natural forms it reveals.

For an example of a semi-abstract artwork – which, if I am right, is the best as well as most one should aspire to – let's return to Matisse's *The Snail*. An instance of his own dictum, 'abstraction rooted in reality', it is at once an irregular collage of pieces of highly coloured paper and, mysteriously but clearly, a snail. And with the metaphoric power of that gap between the two, which it crosses with such grace and humour, enchanting.

In that case, what kind of abstract art would preclude metaphor and with it, for most observers, at least, enchantment? In a word, it would be what Matisse called 'imitating abstraction': contrived, self-conscious striving to avoid any reference to anything whatsoever recognisable. That is difficult to accomplish. (Try to produce a random string of numbers or words and before long, patterns start to emerge.) Nonetheless, to the extent someone succeeds, 'success' will consist of tending towards complete disenchantment.

In practice, much abstract art becomes sensuously significant, sometimes despite itself, through forms, especially organic forms, to which we can relate on deep levels. Since the artists share those levels, it is as difficult for them to avoid painting meaningful forms as it is for viewers to avoid seeing them. Picasso's criticism of abstract painting, that all things do in fact appear to us as figures, says just this. I suppose it is just possible, on the part of either artist or audience, to avoid them altogether; after all, a bear might be trained to ride a bicycle. But who benefits? (Not the bear!)

The more purely abstract the painting, then, the less there is anything for the sense of sight to apprehend – to see *as*, which is the only way we can see anything at all, let alone anything meaningful, and further establish a relationship. And that loss is a radical impoverishment. With it goes the inner idea, the 'lining' of the sensible, which only the viewer's imagination can awaken. And without the precision, you lose the mystery.

Bonnard

Pierre Bonnard is one of the great modern painters of enchantment and among the most enchanting of modern painters. In this respect he belongs with Monet and Matisse, whom he worked alongside, as it were, but he repays particular attention in his own right. I want to consider the aspects of his personality and practice that contributed to such an outcome, paying particular attention to the dynamics of enchantment at work in his paintings.

There can be no doubt that Bonnard was keenly aware of the matter. He speaks of 'the enchantment that makes a painting', and describes the work of art as 'stopping time'.[44] Of one painting he admired he says, 'everything sparkles and the whole painting vibrates.'[45] In his hands, the simplest setting – a picnic table in the garden, a child and a dog by a window – is no longer just a setting; it radiates intrinsic meaning and value. The intimate becomes inexhaustible and the domestic cosmic; his paintings reveal, even release, the enchantment at the heart of the ordinary. As Proust put it, and Bonnard shows, 'The real act of discovery consists not in finding new lands, but in seeing with new eyes.'[46] It is thus not too much to say that Bonnard is the twentieth century's Vermeer. His domain too is the domestic (to use Zwicky's term) as a way of life that mediates between instrumental use-values, on the one hand, and lyric enchantment on the other. In so doing – recalling that we cannot live completely or forever in enchantment – the domestic keeps open its possibility.

Early in his career Bonnard was one of the Nabis, a small group of painters whose best-known other member was Édouard Vuillard, and like them, he admired Gauguin's bold forms and colours. In time, though, although he retained *intimisme*, Bonnard outgrew decorative mannerism. He described van Gogh as 'a great artist I admire' and was respectful of Symbolists such as Gustave Moreau (one of Matisse's teachers) and Odilon Redon, but he followed the Impressionists in rejecting overtly esoteric and religious symbolism, limited to a cognoscenti, in favour of paying passionately close attention to the visible natural world that is our common home.[47]

Bonnard was obviously close in spirit to Impressionism, and personally to both Renoir and Monet. Before moving south he lived at Veronnet, very near Monet at Giverny, where he was a regular visitor, and he was a pallbearer at Monet's funeral. Bonnard shared two of Monet's primary commitments: to art as bearing witness to the beauty of nature, including people as natural beings, and to life as light and light as colour. However, he evolved his own version. 'It's not a matter of painting life,' he wrote (as Monet would have said), 'it's a matter of making paint live'.[48] And his taste was eclectic. On the wall of his *atelier* in Cannet were photographs by Cartier-Bresson and Brassaï and reproductions of a nude by Renoir, a seascape and a *Nymphéas* by Monet, *Bathers at Asnières* by Seurat, *Seated Woman* by Picasso, Gauguin's *Vision after the Sermon*, and *A Street in Delft* by Vermeer.[49]

Bonnard's lifelong model, muse, and wife called herself Marthe de Méligny. She appears in more than 300 of his paintings, and the crowning glory of Bonnard's work is his *Baignoires*, the late series of Marthe bathing. In *Nude in the Bath* (1936–39), for example she reclines in a bath in a room such that, if Heaven has bathrooms, this is one. It glows with a deliquescent golden light flecked with indigo and peach, while a section of sky appears to have slipped down to where a wall was. The light is liquid and the bath-water lucent, effecting an alchemical transmutation of Marthe's body as it dissolves and transforms into something like one of Mondrian's ethereally corporeal lilies. I hardly need add that Aphrodite is an honoured presence.

John Elderfield puts it this way (with my emphases to remind us of the visual dynamics of enchantment): 'The bathroom tiles form a screen that reflects and projects an aquatic array, a liquid wavy surface where light and shade interchange rapidly in both directions, and *oscillates* in an *iridescence* that is *glittering, sparkling, brilliant*.'[50] Echoing the point made about enchanted light made by Matisse, Nicholas Watkins points out that 'The nude, rather than the window, is the principal light source. Light from her body bathes the back wall and *spills like water* on to the blue-tiled floor, gelling into solidified blobs of gold.'[51] If this is charm it is high-voltage charm, as close to the edge of figurative art, in its way, as Monet's final work.

I once saw a photograph of the same room in Bonnard's house in Le Bosquet; it was a plain provincial French bathroom, drab and functional. I suppose one could ask which is a lie: the disenchanted one mechanically reproduced, or the enchanted one as transformed by the artist's hand and eye? William James would have plumped for the latter. But we might also say (having unwisely permitted the question) that both are truths, albeit of a different kind, the latter no less than the former and maybe more so. When a conjuring magician's trick is successful, it acts not as an illusion but just the opposite, because that incomprehensible moment of wonder opens up onto the nature of reality. Doesn't all art partake of this? Bonnard defined painting as 'many little lies to create a great truth'.[52] But to call them lies offers too easy a hostage to the literal-minded guardians of truth, with their single vision. So let's say instead: many little truths to make a great one. And that truth, as René Magritte points out, is an insoluble mystery.

There are other dynamics of enchantment in Bonnard's paintings, notably lots of open windows and doors. Since the paintings themselves are a window or a door, opening onto what they show, they offer a double invitation to find yourself there, participating in the enchantment shown. And the kind of tensive truth we identified in Monet, a painting which is and isn't a place, is also at work here. Of course, it helps to be drawn in if you actually like the place and people or things shown. Those who have a problem with the pleasure of enchantment, and the enchantment of simpler pleasures, will tend to stay outside, disenchanted, while those who actively dislike them – a small but vocal group, who always seem to turn up where enchantment is to be found – will attack.

The principal mode of enchantment in Bonnard is colour. Already in 1890, he wrote, 'I understood that it was possible to translate light, shape and character by colour alone …'[53] This insight grew into his entire artistic practice: 'The principal subject is the surface and its colour, its laws, over and above its objects.'[54] It was by the apparently materialist practice of giving priority to the precise surface of the painting that Bonnard was able to release the mysterious aura of what that surface portrayed. There is no contradiction here. He had grasped that seen without modernist spectacles, the material world is (to quote the ecofeminist Val Plumwood) 'already full of form, spirit, story, agency, and glory'.[55]

Bonnard once observed of *Asia* by Matisse that evening light brings out its red, whereas 'By day it's the blue that plays the major role. What an intense and changeable life colours live in different lights!'[56] This awareness of colour as relational was something he shared with Matisse. Bonnard was particularly fond of the light of late evening, that liminal moment between day and night which he called '*l'heure bleue*'.[57]

Bonnard's final painting, *Almond Tree in Flower* (1946–47), shows the tree, visible from his bedroom, exploding into blossom. This tree is rooted in *Faërie*; it couldn't be in, or of, anywhere else. Yet equally clearly, the dark lowest branches are arms, and with the trunk they form a cross. Both the primal enchantment of life and its promise, and the sadness of its painful ephemerality, are present. And at the heart of the tree is a gap through which its transcendent heart shows: the sky, as resonant in its blueness as his yellows.

In January 1947, days before he died and too weak to paint, he asked his nephew Charles Terrasse to retouch the green on the lower left on the picture with yellow, saying, 'It's a question of yellow …' In his account, Terrasse adds, 'that is to say, gold.'[58] In Bonnard's opinion, 'You can't have too much yellow'.[59] That should be no surprise, given the associations with Aphrodite (gold, sunlight, honey, sexual fluids).[60] From *Daffodils in a Green Pot* (c. 1887) and the stunning *Studio with Mimosa* (1939–46) to the golden light streaming from and around Marthe in the bath, he remained a lifelong devotee. That colour exemplifies Bonnard's sunny reputation, especially among those who don't know his pictures well. His reputation is captured in the popular punning association of his name with '*bonheur*': pleasure, delight, good fortune.

Yet an inexpungable awareness of transience attends enchantment. To the very extent its moments overflow with timeless meaning, they also evoke the transience which is their inescapable double. We should therefore not be surprised to discover an undertow of deep sadness in Bonnard's work. A note in Bonnard's diary from 17 January 1944 says, 'Those who sing are not always happy', and sorrow is indeed present in his paintings even while they sing.[61] It is evident in his luscious still-life fruit which, as Whitfield says, often 'verges on over-ripeness', about to tip into decay;[62] in the sexually-charged but darkly melancholy nudes of Marthe in the 1890s; and again in the elegiac bathing portraits of Marthe, some painted after her death. They remind us that the moment of enchantment is a razor's edge, separating the fullness of life and its passing. The combination, so characteristic of much enchantment, is bitter-sweet. As Josipovici says, 'This, the picture says, is all life is. But at the same time it says: what a miracle it is, to be alive, to be here, now.'[63]

A sadness without self-pity, at once personal and existential, is evident in Bonnard's late self-portraits. Always unsparing, after the deaths of Vuillard, then his brother Charles and, soon afterwards in 1942, Marthe, they show a man who, even when surrounded by the colours of beauty, looks back at you from the depths of despair, all resistance gone, his eyes lightless black holes of disenchantment.

Proust is unavoidable in this connection. Not only are all paradises 'paradises we have lost' but what grants entry to them, in all his work, are those unbiddable moments of enchantment when the remembered and re-imagined past of lost time and the sensuous present of a particular concrete circumstance meet. Did Bonnard ever really paint anything else? We know that he read *In Search of Lost Time* before 1925 and again after 1940, but Proust can have done no more than articulate and support Bonnard's own experience. With the initial conception of a picture, he wrote, 'The emotion surges up: the shock is instantaneous, often unforeseen.'[64]

This affinity is surely also the reason, or part of it, why Henri Cartier-Bresson, photographer of 'the decisive moment', felt that 'For me, before all others, there is Bonnard and only Bonnard'. He stressed the latter's happy/sad ambiguity – 'There is a sensuality and a doubt at the same time, that's very important' – and added perceptively that 'Bonnard has something of a monk about him' (something that is clear in his self-portrait of 1945). 'He is perpetually on the edge of an equilibrium. In Buddhism also, it is the equilibrium which comes first ...'[65]

Remember the criticism of Monet's 'Oriental' treason? Something similar is happening here, except that Cartier-Bresson approves. And despite the un-oriental centrality of the figure to both Western art and Bonnard's, it's true. His human figures concentrate and elaborate the mystery of life, of being alive, and that mystery is equally evident in the other presences in his paintings, as well as in his animals and landscapes. They do not exhaust all mystery, rendering everything else a mere setting. In this respect too, Bonnard belongs with not only Matisse but Vermeer, whose figures are human without being exclusively human-centred.

Anti-Bonnard

Bonnard is an artist quietly loved by many but noisily disliked by a few. His luminous fruit baskets, breakfast tables in early afternoon light and nudes in the bath have engendered a surprising rancour which goes well beyond mere unfashionability. Picasso famously loathed Bonnard's work, and in one recorded conversation went on about him at revealing length:

> Don't talk to me about Bonnard! That's not painting, what he does ... Painting isn't a question of sensibility. It's a question of seizing power, taking over from nature, not expecting her to supply you with information and good advice ... He's not really a modern painter.[66]

It would be hard to invent a more telling encapsulation of the modernist attitude, and consequently its problem with enchantment in art in general and Bonnard in particular. It needs no elaboration, except perhaps to add that Picasso hadn't misunderstood Bonnard's art or sensibility; he perceived it accurately, and disliked what he saw. Cartier-Bresson observes that unlike Bonnard, Picasso had no tenderness.[67] Indeed, and part of the reason for Picasso's lack of tenderness, even hostility to it, was surely his ideological as well as temperamental modernism.

In striking contrast, Matisse and Bonnard were friends and mutual admirers all their adult lives. Matisse said Bonnard's paintings gave one a sense of 'being confronted with something passionate and alive.'[68] In October 1947, a large post-humous exhibition of Bonnard's work took place at the Musée de l'Orangerie. A major journal, *Cahiers d'Art*, featured a review by Christian Zervos, a camp-follower of Picasso, entitled 'Pierre Bonnard – est-il un grand peintre?' Answering his own question in the negative, Zervos described him as weak, unoriginal and facile. This was no more than the standard avant-garde line at the time but when Matisse saw it, he became incensed, and scrawled in a large hand on the front-page, 'Yes! I certify that Bonnard is a great artist for our time and certainly for the future. Henri Matisse, Jan. 1948'.[69]

Clement Greenberg, champion and part-creator of the American modernist avant-garde in art after the war, condemned Bonnard because he 'never abandons the object...nor does he violate it as Picasso has done'.[70] Quite so! Bonnard refused to take the step of abandoning it or wilfully, let alone masterfully, imposing his ego on the living natural world and its concrete particulars. Greenberg once unleashed a tirade in the presence of the writer Nuala O'Faolain: 'a rant,' she recalls, against people 'who had no edge, who weren't in the game, who were unimportant, who were soft and melancholy and depressed instead of out there in the bright, hard world, fighting toward success.'[71]

Closer to our own time, in response to an exhibition in New York in 1998, Linda Nochlin, a professor of modern art at New York University, found Bonnard's paintings 'abject and sinister', and was so 'repelled by the melting of flesh-and-blood model into the molten object of desire of the male painter' that she fantasised about attacking it with a knife.[72] This reaction contrasts in an interesting way with that of Michel Serres, for whom Bonnard's 'immensely tactful and tactile art does not turn the skin into a vulgar object to be seen, but rather into a feeling subject, a subject always active beneath the surface.'[73] One finds Marthe has been turned into an object, the other a subject!

Most damningly for Nochlin, however, Bonnard's paintings apparently involve 'a retreat from the public world'.[74] Peter Schjeldahl weighed in too, describing them as 'masturbatory', 'eye candy' and 'art that is on its last legs as a culture-changing enterprise'.[75] The last charge is the most significant, because it supplies the judgement, and probably the animus, of the others. And in the disenchanted perspective of these Adults in the Room, 'Whoever is not with me is against me', so anyone who fails to sign up to Progress is condemned as an escapist at best, and at worst a deserter. But Bonnard was resigned to neglect and incomprehension, perhaps even hostility: 'it's because people have no idea how to look that they hardly ever understand.'[76] (These are the same people whom Matisse describes as forcing themselves to see things in a certain way.)

It's a relief to turn to another artist's assessment of Bonnard. On 8 May 1998 at the Tate Gallery, the artist Ken Kiff talked with Colin Wiggins and a receptive audience on Bonnard's art. He asked rhetorically, 'Is modern art a march towards abstraction? No', and stressed that 'Bonnard is not just coming out of Impressionism

... A late Bonnard is more like a Klee or a Miró than a Vuillard, because the signs are coming at us in a twentieth century way.' He described those signs as bits – lumps or strokes – radiating meaning, 'a kind of rich, untranslatable thing coming at you, rather like a piece of music', asking, and asking us to ask, 'What is that yellow doing?' (It's busy enchanting, of course.) Finally, he said, Bonnard 'is respecting painting, and that runs incredibly deep.'[77]

One of the last notes in Bonnard's diary concerns the future of his work: 'I hope my painting will endure without craquelure [cracking]. I should like to present myself to the young painters of the year 2000 with the wings of a butterfly.'[78] Not 9,000 dead butterflies, as in one of Damien Hirst's exhibitions, but one living one. And not as an investment, but a gift.

Colour

Because it is so important for the enchantment of painting, colour deserves its own discussion. But first let me note that in the absence of colour, forms and structures more easily become clear. Think of bones or a skeleton, or the naked branches of a tree in winter. Ink painting and black-and-white photography thus have particular potential to reveal the structural dimension of their subjects. An analogy might be a piece of wood which is unremarkable until staining – the artist's intervention – reveals its grain, and with it the 'idea' of the wood.

The photographer Daido Moriyama puts it this way: 'Monochrome has stronger elements of abstraction or symbolism. Perhaps there is an element of taking you to another place. Black and white has that physical effect on me ... Colour is something more vulgar.'[79]

What about this? Colour is more often vulgar in photography than in painting, I think. Nonetheless, Moriyama gets something important right here, because it is actually a deeper truth. The desire of life for life, in all its irrepressibility, redundancy, and promiscuity, is indeed vulgar – gloriously so. Colours are the joys and sufferings not so much of light, as Goethe averred, as of life expressed in light. And that's enchantment, too. The immanent ideas whose discovery enchants can be either deep, cool and 'inner' or surface, hot or 'outer', either more structural or more emotional, either form or colour. Their common opposite, against which they are sisters under the skin, is the grey meaninglessness of disenchantment.

Colour as light is not identical with colour as pigment. Their so-called primary colours differ somewhat: as light, they are red, blue, and green, while as pigment they're red, blue, and yellow. Furthermore, running all colours together as pigments results in black; but considered as light, black is the absence of colour. Nevertheless, the distinction is less obvious than it may seem, because light as such is invisible.[80] The colour of everything we see is an amalgam, so to speak, of coloured light – differing according to the air, atmospheric conditions, time of day, location in relation to the Sun and so on – and the pigment of what is illuminated.

The demand on the artist who wants to enchant, then, is to turn light-plus-pigment into pure pigment on the canvas in a way that re-appears as light-plus-pigment for the observer. The careless or inept painter falls like a stone into this gap which the skilful and/or talented one crosses like a high-wire artist. Bonnard was well aware of the challenge. He wanted, he said, to 'reconcile colour with light based on sensations and feelings', and added that 'the moment pigment becomes colour the problems begin. In the process of metamorphosis colour became light and light colour.'[81]

Goethe published his theory of colour in 1810. By then it was too late to shake the dominant understanding of science from the mechanistic-mystical Newtonian model he was criticising, with its disenchanted starting-point.[82] We can be glad he set out his phenomenological stall, though, for the colours of enchantment are Goethean, not Newtonian. Their physical properties, together with human physiological responses, may be fascinating but they are at a remove, one that takes inquiry in a very different direction. In enchantment, what matters is not what colours 'are' in any abstract or technical sense but how we experience them. In this process, self and world are distinguishable but interdependent. So colour is an aspect of both; it is never only subjective ('psychological') or only objective ('physiological'), nor can one be derived wholly from the other.

This is something to stress because it is being forgotten. Take a popular contemporary treatment, Kassia St Clair's *The Secret Lives of Colour*: 'What we are really seeing when we look at, say, a ripe tomato or green paint, is light being reflected off the surface of that object and into our eyes.'[83] Now there are interpretations which serve our understanding of an experience by respecting the latter and then deepening the former, and there are others which simply and summarily occupy both. This statement is one of the latter, and the telltale sign is the 'really'.

Its matter-of-factness obscures the point that when we are looking at a tomato, whatever else is going on we are indeed looking at a tomato – and a particular tomato, not a generic one, let alone any other kind of fruit, or indeed anything else whatsoever. And in that primary fact is the fundamental starting-point of the experience of looking, which entails an observer, an observed, and the relationship between them, and therefore constitutes the very possibility of visual wonder. So to batten onto and divert it into a discursive world of electromagnetic wavelengths, light-sensitive cells and neurophysiology – and cap it all by calling that experience more real! – is practically criminal, and the fact that it is now commonplace does not make it any less so.

The same goes for the enchantment of which colour, when concretely realised, is the occasion. Incarnate as pigments, colours are made from earth and mud, minerals, charcoal, fruits and vegetables, sea-creatures and who knows what else. No one, not Penelope herself, could unpick the cultural from the natural. In the hands of the painter, pigments are an armoury of enchantment. Each one can open its own particular door to the greetings from other worlds that, as Scarry said of Matisse's paintings, beautiful things convey to us. *The Artist's Handbook* lists 74 pigments (including three blacks and three whites) that are available to contemporary painters.[84] Their very names are poetry. From there and elsewhere, here are a few:

Reds: Rose Madder, Crimson, Scarlet, Carmine, Ruby Red, Vermillion, Crimson Lake, Alizarin, Magenta, Cinnabar, Kermes, Ruddle or Ruddy, Venetian Red, Fuchsine or Rosaniline, Solferino, Blood Red, Poppy Red, Carnelian Red, Cadmium Red, Cardinal, Salmon Pink, Hot/ Deep/ Shocking Pink.

Greens: Teal, Chartreuse, Midnight Green, Cyan (between blue and green), Viridian, Cobalt Green, Emerald Green, Paris Green, Verde-Antique, Malachite.

Yellows: Gamboge, Naples Yellow, Lemon Yellow, Cadmium Yellow, Indian Yellow, Chrome Yellow, Orpiment, Xanthin, Weld, Yellow Ochre, Amber, Golden, Tawny.

Blues: Azure, Cerulean Blue, Robin Egg Blue, Ultramarine, Cobalt, Indigo, Aquamarine, Turquoise, Kingfisher Blue, Bice, Verditer, Chartres Blue.

Surely every colour carries within it its own particular enchantment. Perhaps, though, as with the classical pantheon of divinities, some colours are more closely or integrally related to enchantment as such, so to speak. Let's consider two candidates, yellow and blue.

Yellow, as golden, is Aphrodite's colour, and figures strongly in Bonnard's work, as we have seen. But he was not the only the artist under the spell of what Wallace Stevens calls 'the first colour'.[85] Van Gogh describes yellow as 'a colour capable of charming God.'[86] An episode in Proust's *In Search of Lost Time* concerns the 'little patch of yellow wall', in Vermeer's *View of Delft*, which the eminent novelist Bergotte, sick and suffering, feels impelled to seek out in Paris, where it is on exhibition.[87]

Absorbed in it, on the very edge of death, he finds himself measuring his entire lifework against that little patch of yellow wall, and he cannot convince himself that the former outweighs the latter. Fittingly, as if to safeguard us against any literal-mindedness, it is not clear exactly what Proust is referring to in that painting, since there is a patch of yellow, but it is not a wall, and there is a wall, but it is not yellow! Yet it's clearly important; Proust was still making corrections to this story the night before his own death.

Curiously, it seems that no ancient language had a word that corresponds to our sense of blue, and apparently in all languages, words for colours emerged in the same order: first black and white, then red, then yellow followed by green (or sometimes the other way round), and lastly blue.[88] As if making up for lost time, however, blue has assumed a rich array of meanings, ones which at first seem to vary widely. To take a few, by the twelfth century, it had become the colour of the Virgin Mary's cloak and a key ingredient, as cobalt, in the stained-glass windows of the great Gothic cathedrals.

By the sixteenth century, blue had taken over from gold as the colour of heaven, its association with divinity and the sky given a new lease by the increased availability of ultramarine pigment, made from Indian lapis lazuli. But since the photograph taken from Apollo 8's orbit of the Moon in 1968, we have realised that blue is also the colour of the Earth: a tantalising reversal of our customary idea of heaven.[89]

In modern times, blue became deeply entwined with melancholy. It is ubiquitous in popular music as the blues, of course, and indirectly, but massively, in its influence on other kinds of music. And there are gradations. According to the great jazz singer Nina Simone, you've never been blue 'Till you've had that mood indigo'. A little thought shows what links these meanings. Blue is the coolest colour and heaven (as we in the West have come to think of it), the sea, melancholia and sad songs, are all cool. Light passing through snow or ice becomes a particularly beautiful blue, on any scale from a hole poked in a snowbank to, most enchantingly, the interior of a glacier.

In a red and overheated world, blue is balm, as is quiet in a noisy one. As a teenager unprepared for impending exams, I once forced myself to stay awake studying for 48 hours. About midday on the third day I fell asleep over my books, yet somehow, I remained conscious for a few moments even as I was already asleep, so to speak. What I experienced was falling slowly, ever more deeply, away from the violent reds and yellows of the surface glare into a deliciously cool and healing sea of swirling blues, from azure to indigo mixed with aquamarine, growing ever darker as I slowly descended until losing consciousness.

The work of painters, not least the most enchanting, is, of course, almost unimaginable without blue. Matisse mentions a blue butterfly's wing that 'pierced my heart'.[90] Yves Klein, who devised a hue he made famous as International Klein Blue, speaks of its 'enchanting emptiness'.[91] If I understand him aright, he was describing the way blue can transform absence as a mere lack into a presence, which thereby enables a relationship with it, one which, furthermore, can enchant. But let's give the final word to Kiff: 'Blue is devastating, it's a colossal space inside you, it's ablaze with emotion.'[92] It is fitting, then, that in several cultures, from Japan and India to Central America, indigo, the natural dye for textiles, has – or rather, is – its own god.[93]

Beauty

Beauty cannot be ignored, being so obviously important in enchantment, yet I cannot afford to address it in its own right; that would take another whole book. So I shall try to stick to visual art. We shan't go far wrong if we start with a typically clear and concise observation by Oakeshott. Beauty, he writes,

> is not a word like "truth"; it behaves in a different manner. It is a word the use of which is to describe a poetic image which we are compelled to admire, not as we admire (with approval) a noble action, nor as we admire a thing well done (such as a mathematical demonstration), but on account of the pre-eminent delight it plants in the contemplative spectator.[94]

In other words – *pace*, reluctantly, Keats – beauty is decidedly not truth, nor is the reverse the case. And both are distinct from goodness.

But cultural, social and intellectual contexts are important too. Here, Simon Leys aptly sums up beauty's modern reception, albeit with ancient antecedents:

> True Philistines are not people who are incapable of recognising beauty; they recognise it all too well; they detect its presence anywhere, immediately, and with a flair as infallible as that of the most sensitive aesthete – but for them, it is in order to be able better to pounce upon it at once and to destroy it before it can gain a foothold in their universal empire of ugliness.[95]

Barnett Newman, the American abstract expressionist, observed in 1948 that 'The impulse of modern art was to destroy beauty.'[96] And 'modern art' – or rather, what I am calling modernist – takes in both the art itself and art criticism. Critical opinion has swung from romantic pastoralism – that nature must be portrayed as charming and beautiful, thus promising comfort if not compensation for raw urban industrialism – to its opposite: that only the ugly and shocking are acceptable. And there, to a remarkable extent, it has stayed. James Putnam, with the work of the land artist Andy Goldsworthy in mind, notes that

> In contemporary art circles a work that has an outward appearance of beauty tends to be regarded with great suspicion, even contempt, while a critical prejudice prevails that art needs to be generated in an urban environment in order for it to have a serious, credible 'edge'.[97]

Elaine Scarry discusses the banishing of beauty as a legitimate subject of discussion from both art and the humanities, in the 1980s and 1990s especially, and she unpicks the lazy and questionable assumptions involved.[98] For example, much modern discourse about art is really about politics, imposing a kind of single vision that silences other perspectives and values, not least enchantment. Jacques Derrida, no less, points out that 'All that is political, but it is not only political.' ('All that' being 'quite simply everything'.)[99]

The basis for the modernist antipathy to aesthetic beauty seems to be the assumption that admiring the beauty of persons somehow harms them, or others, and this idea is then extended to all instances of natural and artistic beauty. John Cage, for example, held that 'the highest responsibility of the artist is to hide beauty'. Presumably (this is the only way I can make sense of it) he thought that beauty in art somehow obscured beauty in the rest of life, or in daily life, so refusing the former would encourage the latter. But why should it? One is at least equally likely to end up without any beauty at all. And by Cage's logic, outright ugliness in art would actually encourage appreciation of beauty in life – an idea whose silliness reminds me of the theory, briefly popular in the 1970s, that a repressive right-wing government was a good thing because it would inevitably provoke the Revolution.

It has also apparently been proposed that painting is bad because brushes are phallic. The same logic dictates that refraining from painting, or even looking at paintings, will strike a blow against sexism … If only it was that easy! A related charge is that comparing the female body to landscape and the reverse, seeing the Earth, in whole or part, as feminine, objectifies women: that is, turns them into sexual objects. Well, it could, if you assume that the land itself is – can only be – an object, and that that way of regarding it is therefore unproblematic.

A related objection to much painting is 'the male gaze': basically, the idea that men are free to look with sexual desire at women, in art or life, while women are not free to do so in return. Thus, in art, the female nude is an object of male views, which thereby expresses and reinforces an unequal power-relationship between the two genders. There is certainly some truth to this. At the same time, however, it can be overplayed in the interest of politics rather than art.

We should be careful to distinguish between situations in which the women, whether living or as portrayed, did and did not have real choice, for these have very different consequences. If choice did exist and the woman exercised hers, she cannot be or become purely the object of a gaze. Even if she freely chose to be object-like, that result carries within it the ineliminable trace of her choice as a subject.[100] Furthermore, in some of those situations the gazer is at least as vulnerable as the one seen, although in a different way. As Scarry rightly points out, in many accounts 'it is precisely the perceiver who is imperilled, overpowered, by crossing paths with someone beautiful.'[101] Even in the relatively controlled situation of a male artist working with a female model, the latter is employed by the former but very often she is necessary to him in a way, or to an extent, that he is not to her.[102]

Sometimes this is plainly evident in the paintings themselves, beginning, perhaps, with Francisco Goya's *The Nude Maja*, whose look back at the viewer is at least that of an equal. Modigliani's models too are no victims of a male gaze. They 'own' their own selves, agency, and sexuality, and not coincidentally, they glow with life. Then compare their flesh with Lucien Freud's or Jenny Saville's dead meat, objectified and uglified. But neither is more 'realistic'. One is enchanted reality, the other disenchanted.

The nude is central to the European tradition of art from the Greeks to the present. In this context, François Jullien registers an important distinction between 'nude' and 'naked'. 'Nakedness implies a diminished state, being stripped, laid bare', whereas the state evoked by the nude 'is one of plenitude; the nude is total presence, offering itself for contemplation.' In the process, 'this only becomes all.'[103] The resonance of presence here with the presence of enchantment, displacing mere listable attributes, is significant; so too is the agency of the nude which Jullien invokes. And at the risk of stating the blindingly obvious, this is the domain of Aphrodite, one of the two classical divinities with an elective affinity with enchantment as such (along with Hermes, with whom she was and remains often entwined).

Thus Botticelli's Venus, for example, 'does not open onto a "transcendent" beyond, as would be expected from a religious or spiritual revelation; here it is the visible itself which, in this nude, becomes simultaneously the locus and the object of the revelation.'[104] But this truth cannot be kept within safely classical limits. In Sylvie Lancrenon's photographs of her, for example, Emmanuelle Béart manifests neither as primarily sexual nor even primarily vital but as intensely herself, and thus effectively universal.[105] Béart is without either *pudeur* (that odd mixture – French, or simply Catholic? – of shame and modesty) or its opposite, lascivious exhibitionism; she neither uses her beauty to seduce nor denies its power to do so.

A Bar at the Folies-Bergère is Édouard Manet's last composition, painted the year before he died. On a trip to the Courtauld Galleries, Raymond Mason found it hanging opposite a row of Cézannes, 'each of good quality'.[106] He was struck by the barmaid's stare, 'looking you straight in the eyes,' and her agency. As I see it,

> The barmaid in the mirror
> is attending to another punter,
> but the one centre-stage
> is looking directly at us, wholly
> without illusions, amid the
> opulence and hypocrisy of an
> advanced civilization.
> 'Go on,' her looks says.
> 'Surprise me.'

'If you walk backwards from the painting and look at it from the opposite wall,' Mason continues, 'it expands and moves towards you, flooding the room with vivacity and life and light.' Turning to the Cézannes now, the 'opposite occurs: they withdraw into the wall.' Mason adduces their vertical construction, their relative lack of light, but above all 'their uniformity. Cézanne pursued a problem that he considered he never solved. Since the problem never changed, all his paintings look much the same ... *A Bar at the Folies-Bergère*, on the other hand, is unique.'[107]

Gerhard Richter is also fascinating in this context. One reason is his ongoing struggle to overcome his own virtuosity – potentially a great enemy of enchantment, encouraging as it does both egoism and careerism. (This effort is exemplified in the stunning series *Annunciation After Titian*, for example.) The second reason is a keen awareness of enchanting beauty as an artistic issue. In his painting of his daughter, *Betty*, her presence is qualified by the act of facing pointedly away from the viewer. Richter described it as 'an idealisation, since its essence is a longing for culture, for the beauty in art which we no longer have, which is why she turns away.'[108] It is also no coincidence that Betty's body is in the same position as that of *The Girl with a Pearl Earring*.[109]

Clearly as intelligent as he is a great artist, and mindful of enchantment, Richter rejects a critical theoretical framing of his work: 'The reason I don't argue in "socio-political" terms is that I want to produce a picture and not an ideology.'[110] His insistence carries all the more weight coming from the creator of a harrowing series of portraits of members of the Baader-Meinhof gang, both as perpetrators of violence and its victims.

This rejection is part of a larger or longer perspective which many critics will dislike but which I hail, which casts doubt on analysis as potentially exhaustive in understanding or appreciating art, or even necessarily helpful. About Vermeer, one of his exemplars, Richter says:

The fact that his paintings are good, better than most others, has nothing to do with his special way of painting. It's connected with another quality entirely, a mysterious something. It's not about skill, the so-called craft, that's a given, and virtuosity alone has nothing to do with art. I don't know how I can describe the quality … it's just there, and it endures.[111]

In a way that looks back to Piero della Francesca and Raphael, as well as forward to Richter and Bonnard, a painting by Vermeer glows as luminously now as it did when it was painted more than three centuries ago. It's no wonder that Proust described *View of Delft* as 'the most beautiful picture in the world.'[112] Painted by Vermeer, a particular and therefore limited room in mid-seventeenth-century Delft becomes the Room of Rooms; and this truth does not depend on an essence but is metaphoric, as the copula signifies: this (room) *is* that (Room).

As we remarked of Bonnard – another painter of light, like Richter and Vermeer – the last artist's interiors show perfectly ordinary items and events of daily life – loaves of bread, someone pouring milk from a pitcher, rugs, a cracked window, a woman reading a letter, another one weighing what looks like two drops of light in a scale – transfigured into something deeply mysterious. (A modern practitioner, who largely confined himself to still-lives of ceramics, was Giorgio Morandi. The purity and intensity of his forms and colours remind me of those of Mondrian, in which, however, enchantment has not been sacrificed.)

Bonnard's paintings do not show scenes constrained by time and space; indeed, they are not really 'of' anything. Seen with the eyes of enchantment, which they invite, they are themselves those moments-and-places, which now include the viewer. As per the etymology of 'enchantment', as Josipovici says of *Dining-room in the Country*, 'we move round it as we would if we were in the room ourselves.'[113]

By the same token, as Bonnard said of art when it enchants, Vermeer's paintings stop time (or rather, slow its passing to imperceptibility), because the moment portrayed is still happening. And being enchanted, their insides are almost infinitely roomy and practically eternal, as they resist dissolution into the mere time and space raging outside, as they did for Adam Zagajewski in the opening story of this chapter … For a time. (Vilhelm Hammershøi's paintings, superficially so like those of Vermeer, are almost the reverse: studies in melancholy, attended by a dim, faint enchantment, like distant bells.)

Actually, Vermeer's paintings present something of a challenge to my argument that enchantment flourishes best in the interstices between fully figurative and fully abstract art, because they are the former, yet they certainly enchant. They remain liminal, in between, however, in that they present our visual sense with three dimensions through only two, and a flat surface whose forms and colours were painstakingly built up, layer by layer, leaving virtually no texture but which has nonetheless clearly been painted – that is, created, not simply 'taken' like a photograph – while simultaneously looking entirely real. Real, that is, in the way that a place looks when it and you are enchanted: glowing with inner light, pregnant with meaning.

As Richter says, virtuosity alone is radically insufficient to make art that enchants – a point which holds in all the arts, not only painting. That should not mislead us into taking skill or craft for granted, however. Whatever art enchants does indeed exceed skill, but skill is needed for it to be born. In the words of the eleventh-century Chinese poet and painter Su Shih, 'If one has Dao' (which term will suffice for something essential but mysterious) 'but not skill, then although things have been formed in one's mind, they will not take shape through one's hands'.[114]

Sadly, though, even that doesn't guarantee enchantment. It's true that as François Cheng writes, 'all beauty collaborates precisely with the uniqueness of the moment.'[115] But a downside of concrete magic is that the moment may not be right for enchantment. When I first walked into the large upstairs room of Botticelli's paintings in the Uffizi Gallery, I entered an antechamber of Heaven, literally, if ineffably, glowing with light and colour. Thirty years later, upsettingly, it was dead to me and I to it; the paintings had become little more than objects of pigment, oil, canvas, and wood. I still have no idea why.

Klee

Paul Klee is another modern artist whose work, figurative but strongly imaginative, stays open to enchantment. One of Klee's dicta, resonating with those of Matisse and Bonnard, say, is that 'art does not reproduce the visible; it makes visible.'[116] His art respected wild otherness – 'Nothing can be rushed. It must grow, it should grow of itself'[117] – and his self-effacement stands in striking contrast to macho modernism:

> The artist, standing between the root of a tree in nature and its crown in art, does nothing other than garner and pass on what rises from the depths. He neither serves nor commands – he transmits. His position is humble. And the beauty at the crown is not his own; it has merely passed through him.[118]

Klee was a deep and subtle colourist, but I would like to develop a hint from his famous description of drawing as taking 'an active line on a walk, moving freely, without goal. A walk for walk's sake.'[119] A better invitation to enchantment could hardly be imagined, although the other half of the story is that the line then takes *you* – in different but overlapping ways, both the artist and the audience – for a walk. Indeed, if it doesn't, enchantment has probably failed. Why? Because insofar as enchantment is relational, it is not under the control of our conscious will; so if you're in charge of the walk, it's still all just about you. When it enchants, the line in art takes you out of yourself to somewhere else which you had forgotten, or didn't realise it when you were there, or perhaps have never been to before.

By now it should come as no surprise that Klee too has been largely side-lined by modernism as a *petit-maître*. Clement Greenberg, for example: 'Klee's irony is never bitter.'[120] This is meant as a damning criticism; for modernists, irony normally must be present for the work to be taken seriously, and ideally it should be bitter. Compare it with an observation by Adam Zagajewski, who isn't afraid of enchantment: 'Sometimes in museums the paintings speak to me/ and irony suddenly vanishes.'[121]

Another contemporary artist, Brian Clarke, has developed the practice described by Klee further:

> What I'm trying to achieve … is to use the figurative idea – the tube of paint, the fleur-de-lis, or the cross before that: it doesn't really matter – but it provides you with some kind of curious road-map, and then you use that as the springboard from which to leap into the air with your line. Having made that springboard, I feel we're getting near to a place now where we can allow the line to take its own route.[122]

This perspective takes the enchantment that attends the meeting of figurative and abstract – 'abstraction rooted in reality', as Matisse put it – which we found in the 'transitional' work of Kandinsky and Mondrian, and connects it with Klee's walking line. Clarke advocates retaining the figurative but moving beyond it, or rather, allowing oneself to be moved beyond it.

Such lines, not incidentally, are almost always curved and flowing, as organic as those of living organisms or water or clouds. They are everywhere in the Arts and Crafts movement, the architecture of Antoní Gaudi, and Art Nouveau (all roughly in the same period, the last two decades of the nineteenth century and first of the twentieth), as well as the psychedelic art of the late 1960s produced by artists who had studied Art Nouveau. Both times, briefly but unmistakably, enchantment left its usual underground course for the cultural bright lights. Then the first died on the killing fields of World War I, and the second was broken on the wheel of the Reagan–Thatcher 1980s.

To repeat the Viennese artist, Hundertwasser, 'The straight line is godless.' Yet even I can see that that is a bit simple-minded, for nature contains straight lines too (geological strata, tree-trunks, fruit segments and so on). I guess the straight line only becomes destructive of enchantment in art when it is allowed to dominate, as if we could dispense altogether with curves, or the Earth, or the feminine. Franz Marc, just before his tragic death at Verdun, experimented with full abstraction, and his *Forms at Play* (1914) shows lines both straight and curved, playing joyfully.

Other Contemporary Painters Working with Enchantment

Let's look at a few other visual artists working with enchantment, most of them recent and some living. They constitute a kind of counter-lineage and counter-community to the modernism that has dominated modern art, especially insofar as painting itself has declined in fashionableness (not least because it's so difficult to do well). Such painters now must have the strength of character, and either relative success or independence of means, to say to hell with critical fashion. But they're not just about resistance; they have wonders to show us.

Alexander Calder is often critically disregarded as another *petit-maître* because his work resists being drafted into the grand narrative of modernist art, with its teleologically-driven cast of heroes in the cause of Progress. His mini-circus performances were not just playful, they were play itself, and the same enchanting quality pervades his early mobiles and stabiles before he succumbed to the lure of commissions for clunky metal behemoths in public plazas.

The artists comprising so-called psychedelic art, mainly in America and England from the mid-1960s until the early 70s, belong here too. (They flourished on the West Coast in particular, for obvious reasons, but my own favourite is the English artist, John Hurford.)[123] Their work positively revels in enchantment, not to say simply love of life. But as Titus O'Brien explains,

> Art history has no place for psychedelic art. Probably because it broke so many aesthetic and compositional rules and referenced such out-of-fashion art movements as late nineteenth-century romanticism, art nouveau, *Jugendstil*, and the Pre-Raphaelite painters, psychedelic art is hard to fit within a modernist sensibility.

He adds that 'psychedelic artists rejected modernism's mania for clarity but also academic postmodernism's Duchampian critical detachment', as well as the contemporary cold-hearted commercialism of Warhol on the East Coast.[124]

I have already mentioned Brian Clarke in connection with Klee and the line. He is an artist working with enchantment in both stained glass and paint, and his art is equally craft. He speaks of having had 'a glimpse into paradise' – 'They're not frequent, such experiences, but by constantly producing art, day after day, in a routine, you are always trying to get close to that experience again' – and he contrasts that way of life and work with the dominant one:

> I think artists today are mostly businessmen, pretending to be inspired, and they work in such tandem with art dealers and museums and collectors that it becomes an entirely bland and colourless business mechanism, designed to fulfil a market need at the expense of innovation, originality, and honesty. And I think that I exist in a kind of parallel world to the art world … So long as I remember the power of liberating oneself through the imagination and through the subjective interpretation of the world, I feel I can go anywhere.[125]

David Hockney is another thoroughly modern artist who has worked with photography and recently an iPad, alongside painting 'traditional' portraits and landscapes in oils and acrylic and hailing Matisse and Monet. Derided by a spokesman for the so-called Britpack artists as a 'strange old loony figure',[126] Hockney's exhibitions at the Royal Academy of Arts in 2012 and 2020, and elsewhere in Europe, showed beyond any doubt that the enchantment of the natural world in figurative painting, to say nothing of the pure love of life, still has a large and enthusiastic audience.

He recently observed that 'At art school you can teach the craft; it's the poetry you can't teach. But now they're trying to teach the poetry and not the craft', which neatly captures the point that without the craft of precision, you don't get the mystery.[127] Not only can't you teach that directly, but you also can't jump straight to it in artistic practice either.

Hughie O'Donoghue has been well-described as a painter's painter. 'I'm interested in the alchemy of paint. I don't have technique because I believe that technique is the enemy of good painting.' (He means what I have called a 'method' that one 'applies'.) O'Donoghue's twisted torsos have all undergone some sea-change, and his lambent land- and sea-scapes, rich and strange, evoke memories of somewhere you have never been; at least, not in your waking hours. His works engage, he says, 'with the idea of remembrance as opposed to memory ... Remembrance is a creative act and you have to work at it.' More generally, 'what I'm trying to achieve [is] a unity of the painting of an object with the Renaissance idea of the painting as a window. So window and object are held in a tension, in which the painting has an independent existence.'[128]

Speaking of windows, Howard Hodgkinson is another superb colourist, to an extent that seems to render further comment superfluous.[129] Just look at the paintings! I want to point out a couple of things, though. One is his creative use of 'window' frames. His paintings' frames serve to put that necessary distance between what is and isn't the artwork: a space crossing which permits enchantment. But most of his frames are painted, so they are also (but not only) part of the painting itself. Just as the painting thereby reaches out beyond itself, the world, including us onlookers, is reciprocally invited into it.

The other thing to notice is the work that the titles of his paintings do. Hodgkin's paintings are strongly abstract, yet the carefully chosen titles allow the viewer to engage in a double process whereby one looks for and finds the figurative dimension that is 'there', no matter how elusive, but at the same time one's imagination co-creates that figuration. Since finding what one creates and creating what one finds is at the heart of metaphor, another way opens.

Ken Kiff has already figured in this chapter in his interview and on the colour blue, for Kiff's colours are alive in a way that coheres with his landscapes, where everything – the Sun or Moon, a hill or tree, all kinds of persons, only some of them human – is a living presence, addressing you. Kiff's worlds are not only animist but deeply mythic. Transformation is a hallmark of myth, and his figures are always somewhere between human, other-animal, and god or goddess, with none simply one or the other. By the same token, they are inherently narrative, although we may not be sure what the exact story is. Andrew Lambirth notes that 'The gradual unfolding, the journey within a painting, which is characteristic of Chinese art, made a deep appeal to Kiff'.[130] It is also similar to the approach taken by one of Kiff's exemplars, Paul Klee.

Kiff cast his net wide, however. Bearing in mind the lineage lines of enchantment in art, consider the postcards and reproductions in his studio: a Klee, a Renoir nude, Bonnard's *Almond Tree in Blossom*, a medieval manuscript page, van Gogh's *Self-Portrait with Pipe and Straw Hat*, a tree by Claude, a Miró woodcut, a willow-tree by Monet, and four Chinese paintings.[131] Chinese landscape painting has been a minor but significant note throughout this account, admired by Monet, Matisse, and Bonnard as well as Kiff.

The work of one of my favourite living artists, Isao Miura, isn't particularly fashionable (so it doesn't date), nor is it publicly funded (so it is independent). Nor are the severely mystical landscapes of Delia Woodman, the dream-portraiture of John Winship, or the living lines of Bettina Fung. They sell their work in exhibitions and a few galleries, and to those who know or find them.

Miura was a student of Kiff. His paintings seamlessly combine glorious Impressionist and post-Impressionist colours with a Far Eastern sense of natural form, and his figures, whether human or other animal, don't merely occupy or dominate the places shown but embody the personalities of those places. That seamlessness takes will and skill, of course (as Fred Astaire once remarked, 'If it doesn't look easy, you're not trying hard enough'). But it is wholly in the service of the idea in and as the picture, so enchantment is made welcome. Ironically, a lazy approach to a medium, a method employed to save effort and obviate the need for real application, and an idea which hasn't been passed through the artist's soul, result in something that looks laboured. (Random dots come to mind.)

Miura describes himself as 'a figurative painter but not at all interested in realism … Therefore the shapes and colours in my painting are neither purely figurative nor abstract, but a sort of symbolism': the natural habitat of enchantment, as we have seen. His own lineage looks back to Bonnard, Matisse, Chagall, Nolde and, later, Hodgkin and Kiff:

> One of the main reasons that I entered the Royal College of Art was in order to learn about colour from Ken Kiff, a painter I truly admire. I learned a lot about colour from him, especially about the infinite shades of yellow. Ken Kiff himself was interested in Bonnard, another great colourist, and both of them were interested in *ukiyoe* (Japanese woodblock prints) and oriental scroll paintings, for their technical concepts (e.g. lack of shadows, unusual angles and composition) and the treatment of man and nature.[132]

Photography

I am going to risk a foray into photography, which became a major visual art in the twentieth century, because it is interesting both for the dynamics of enchantment it shares with painting and for its own particular emphases. One problem with photography (which applies equally to video art) is that in technical terms, it's too easy. As a result, the temptation to proceed automatically or mechanically, and superficially, is often overwhelming. As David Bailey puts it, 'Anything that's that easy to do is really difficult to excel at.'[133]

Another obstacle to enchantment is that we are more easily fooled into believing that a photograph straightforwardly reproduces its subject. With a painting, there is a bigger, more obvious gap between the 'reality' and its artistic recreation; so if and when that gap is crossed, the charge is greater. That's why black-and-white photographs sometimes enchant more readily; they enable one to dispense with the afore-mentioned illusion. As Joseph Brodsky says, 'one is grateful to a black-and-white photograph, for it unleashes one's fantasy, one's intuition, so that viewing becomes an act of complicity: like reading.'[134]

By virtually unanimous agreement, a photographer who excelled in enchanting images was Henri Cartier-Bresson, whose admiration in turn for Bonnard I have mentioned. He was famous for his artistic philosophy of 'the decisive moment'.[135] He describes it in a book of that title in 1952: 'To me, photography is the simultaneous recognition, [in] the fraction of a second, of the significance of an event as well as of a precise organisation of forms which give the event its proper expression.' In our terms, the decisive moment occurs at that charged liminal point where three things meet: the precise concrete form of someone or something, its mysterious idea, and the participation of the artist.

Not surprisingly for a photographer, Cartier-Bresson emphasises the moment aspect of concrete magic, rather than the place aspect; but moment and place are intimately linked.

> There is nothing in the world that does not have its decisive moment, and the masterpiece of good conduct is to recognize and seize the moment. If you miss it … you run the risk of not finding it again or of not perceiving it.

One of his best-known photographs – a man jumping over a puddle in the Gare St-Lazare, in a never-to-be-repeated moment in 1932 – is a miracle of timing. But the unarranged visual felicities of the exact place are equally striking.

Raymond Mason recounts that Cartier-Bresson and Yves Bonnefoy 'were crossing a sunlit and rather sleepy village square together when the poet saw Henri make a movement with his hand while talking. We later saw what he had captured by firing from the hip like the hero in a Western: an arcaded vantage-point with some young people and a few animals, all distributed in significant poses, and, above all, with all the pillars of the building perfectly vertical …'[136]

Photography is unlike painting in that it depends even more on the concrete moment: 'sometimes the pictures disappear and there is nothing you can do. You can't tell the person, "Oh, please smile again. Do that gesture again." Life is once, forever.'[137] Cartier-Bresson shared this emphasis with many others, including one of his own mentors, André Kertész, his friend the Czech photographer Josef Koudelka, and many members of subsequent generations of photographers.

The British photographer Terry O'Neil identified the lesson he learned from Cartier-Bresson as the fact that 'you don't stage a great photograph' – an act of will and control – 'you wait for it': one of relation, negotiation, cooperation. 'Fearless receptivity', in short. His own most famous 'decisive moment' resulted in his portrait of a wind-whipped Brigitte Bardot smoking on a Spanish beach in 1971, the very image of female sexual self-possession; it was taken with the last frame left on the film, just as the wind gusted. 'I just wanted the wind to blow once more – and it did. Then everyone started pushing and shoving and I lost the place – but I knew I had that frame. It was a picture in a million.'[138]

Cartier-Bresson famously used a handheld Leica, refused telephoto lenses or light reflectors, very rarely cropped his pictures, and hated flash photography: 'The flash destroys the secret network of relations that naturally exist between the attentive photographer and his subject'. In short, his gift for brilliant simplicity was matched by a distrust of complex technological paraphernalia, acting as an extension and, by implication, imposition of the photographer's will. Bill Cunningham, the New York City street fashion photographer, would have agreed: 'I let the street speak to me'.[139] (Not, à la Picasso, 'I tell the street what to say'.)

But let's turn to a very different photographer, Sally Mann. She uses an 8x10 inch view-camera which needs to be stationary and requires long exposure-times, yet her photographs of her family are among the most powerfully enchanting I've ever seen. So wonder in photography cannot be simply reduced to issues of equipment or its lack.

The attitude of the photographer, the third of the three vectors I identified as meeting in the decisive moment, is integral to its success; and that of Mann is indistinguishable from Cartier-Bresson's, although I'm sure she worked it out for herself. Photographs, she writes, are 'gifts that come in a moment as fleeting as the touch of an angel's wing. I pray to that angel to come to us when I set the camera up, knowing that there is not one good picture in five hot acres. We put ourselves in a state of grace we hope is deserving of reward …'[140] Hope, not know. More recently, she has described waiting for 'the angel of uncertainty', a muse who grants a great photograph, as a moment 'of transcendence; it's the ecstatic time: better than sex. The parallels are all too obvious and can only be understood, I maintain, by a woman.'[141] (I'm not going to argue.)

I am reminded in this connection of the sculptor David Nash, who works sculptural wonders with natural materials, especially wood, and who speaks openly of the spiritual aspect of art, albeit as one that is 'immensely practical and physical'. Nash too describes himself as 'a responding artist … rather than putting my will into something, although obviously there's a willing involved; I will the response.'[142] More specifically, 'I try to be responsive to my material and follow what the wood is suggesting.'[143] Now Nash sometimes uses a chainsaw – not exactly a tool associated with eco-sensitivity – in much of his large-scale work. That use is guided by years of practice with hand tools, however, after which 'I found that all that I had learnt from the use of hand tools I could do with this chainsaw … I knew wood by then, I knew how to cut and work with it, I had ten years' deep experiences behind me …'[144]

Nevertheless, technology is not innocent. Its neutrality is overplayed by those with an interest in pushing it; a bomb is not a bicycle. And there is indeed a problem with the rampant technological development of contemporary photography. As Robert Musil once remarked, 'Progress would be wonderful, if only it would stop.' The problem is the set of temptations I have already identified, and what is lost by those who succumb: not everyone, nor all the time, but too many and too often.

Digital photography, including that of smartphones, discourages enchantment through making it too easy to overcontrol and indulge in neurotic micromanagement. The facility too of recording many images in a tight serial row hasn't destroyed the truth of the decisive moment, but it has devalued the idea and made it much more difficult to practise. The result has been over-hyped, too, as is perhaps beginning to be recognised. 'Real photos from digital media!' proclaims a notice in a shop near me. As for the ubiquitous solo selfie, it is the photographic equivalent of masturbation. The equivalence is rather exact, and I guess that's okay; but let's be honest about it.

Reflecting on his career in photography, Brian Duffy said 'I loved it. But it was only enjoyable because it was mysterious. The revelation came after – when I'd go, "Christ, that's interesting!"'[145] No one who has worked with film – least of all those for whom that included developing it – will forget the enchantment of images alchemically appearing out of nowhere, after they had been taken and then disappeared again. The interval was crucial, as if the very lack of human control it involved allowed the cosmos, God, or whatever name you prefer for ultimate mystery to intervene and have its say.

With the hyper-control and instant gratification of digital photography that has pretty much gone; and if we can't admit that the loss is real, even grievous, then we are every bit as much prisoners of mind-forged manacles as those who are mocked for nostalgia. As Tacita Dean, curator of a moving elegy to 35mm film at the Tate Modern in 2011, puts it: 'Digital relies on post-production. No longer do you rely on the moment, and you lose a certain vitality of the moment.'[146]

We have already encountered another epic street photographer, Daido Moriyama, some of whose work was taken with a small camera held at arm's length and simply aimed at the subject. (According to some accounts – his own is ambiguous – Cartier-Bresson also took the iconic 'Behind the Gare Saint-Lazare' without looking through the viewfinder.) Moriyama was influenced by haiku poets, especially Bāsho, the wanderer, and the tea master Sen no Rikyu, whose maxim was *Ichigo ichie*: 'one instance, one encounter'.[147] Again, the resonance with Cartier-Bresson, despite their different epochs and cultures, is unmistakable. But let's give Moriyama the last word on the determining attitude, the intention, that can make technology a friend of enchantment rather than its enemy:

> My friends or critics are often surprised and ask me why I never get bored after walking around for more than fifty years, but I never get bored. I often hear it said that people, even photographers, do their best work when they are in their 20s and 30s. I'm 73 now, but I could never see the city with an old man's eyes, or as if I understood everything … that way of thinking or speaking is nonsense to me.[148]

Chinese Landscape Painting

Of the two greatest traditions of visual art, one, in the West, focuses principally on the human form and face, and the other, in the Far East, on landscape. The second is committed to painting the natural world in ways that open us up to its wonder and suggest that ultimately, nature itself is the source of artistic enchantment.

In both traditions the subjects are bodies, in the fullest sense of the word, but there is a fundamental difference which contributes to both their respective triumphs and their limitations. Western art is very largely human-centred. This is obviously true in its glorious evocations of the human body, perhaps particularly the female nude, but also in its religious art, through which emotional pathos, tenderness, and suffering, often transcending dogma, speak across ages. The glories of Western art thus result, in large part, from its fascination with the human. It holds up a mirror in which we can see ourselves, in all our variety. And it offers deep and near-universal enchantment through its intense concentration on the concrete magic of the particular body or face portrayed.

That enchantment is bounded, however, by the fact that the human form occupies centre-stage, and even when it doesn't fill the canvas, everything else is usually drafted into a supporting role. Even when modern Western artists have rebelled against this provenance, they have often done so by torturing the images, like Bacon, or escaping into an abstraction whose rigorous impersonality – whether like Apollonian, like Mondrian's, or Dionysian, like Rothko's – serves only to confirm the preoccupation.

There are exceptions, of course, and we have discussed a few. Nevertheless, this is a limitation of the tradition as a whole which Chinese landscape painting throws into sharp relief, and renders its potential downside clear: an anthropocentric self-obsession with the flattering message that it's all about you. Egoism and ultimately narcissism, whether individual or collective, drives out enchantment. Once one has become aware of nature in its fullest and most comprehensive measure, any assumption that the human figure and face exhausts true art appears childish, even absurd. I should add, though, that Western classical humanism (as exemplified by Montaigne) also refuses any notion that humanity exhausts all value, reminding us that it is possible to value who and what we are while leaving the way open to enchantment by others.

In sharp contrast, Chinese art, together with its Korean and Japanese offspring, tends to be ecocentric and animist, honouring the more-than-human natural world. Landscape painting – known generically as *shan shui*, literally mountains and rivers – has been its principal preoccupation for a thousand years, and human figures very often appear in their proper scale, ecologically speaking: tiny. Dwarfed by the mountains and rivers though which they wander, they are not the centre of attention. Self-importance thus becomes harder to sustain.[149] As Stark puts it, in the desert what becomes clear is 'the greater size of the world: and no amount of civilisation is worth the loss of this fundamental sense of proportion between the universe and man.'[150] Conversely, the land in this art has never been drained of its life in favour of the human spirit, soul, or mind alone.

This is reason enough to include some consideration of Chinese painting, especially from the centuries of its greatest flowering in the dynasties of the Song (960–1279) and Yüan (1271–1368). The former was its golden age; as Michael Sullivan says, 'In the hundred years between 950 and 1050 a galaxy of great names' – Li Cheng, Dong Yuan, Fan Kuan, Guo Xi – 'succeed one another in what must be looked upon as the supreme moment in classical Chinese landscape painting.'[151]

Without altogether rejecting that work, the literati movement of the Yüan Dynasty marked a retreat from epic and overtly ambitious landscapes to more subtle, carefully casual ones. 'Bland', meaning unassertive, humble and pure, became a term of high praise.[152] Its four great masters, proud amateurs, were Huang Gongwang, Ni Zan, Wu Zhen, and Wang Meng. The experience of wonder I began this book with took place before one of Ni Zan's austere landscapes, *The Six Gentlemen*.

In another contrast with Western art, where colour holds pride of place, Chinese painting is mostly and best done in ink. We are thus alerted to a different kind of enchantment, cooler and more structural. (Its greatest practitioners would have completely concurred with Moriyama and Cartier-Bresson that colour is vulgar.)

A striking absence, from the Western point of view, is that in Far Eastern culture there is no hard-and-fast distinction between 'high' art and 'low' craft. Two parts snobbery and one part lazy thinking, that distinction undermines our ability to recognise the necessary element of craft in good art and of art in good craft. It also discourages enchantment which, as concrete magic, requires both.

Although there were precedents in sixteenth-century Germany, seventeenth-century Holland, and early to mid-nineteenth-century France and Britain – of the former, most obviously Corot and Daubigny, and of the latter Turner and Constable – Impressionism was the first major movement in Western art to consider largely natural landscape as a worthy principal subject in itself. Despite its success, that is still a minority view in critical opinion, as witness the relative marginalisation of another, more recent movement in visual art to break away from its baseline anthropocentrism, the 'land art' of such artists (even allowing for their differences) as Richard Long, Andy Goldsworthy, herman de vries, Chris Drury, Nikolaus Lang, and Giuseppe Penone.[153]

Long affirms that

> in spite of living in the world of the internet and high technology and super science and everything, water is still more important than technology. The most important themes in my work are water or space, night and day, the tides, or just the wind … the most important fundamental things.[154]

And Goldsworthy describes his art as

> a way of learning, in which instincts guide best. It is also very physical – I need the shock of touch, the resistance of place, materials, and weather, the earth as my source. It is a collaboration, a meeting-point between my own and earth's nature.[155]

This truth would have been instantly recognisable to a Song Dynasty painter or poet.

It seems to me that the enchantment of art is ultimately rooted in nature, regardless of whether the natural dimension of bodies, faces, places and so on is the subject, or non-human nature. Chinese landscape painting accomplishes this in at least three ways.

First, the most fundamental, is by presenting a non-human nature that is alive. With the realisation that nature, as a whole and in all its parts, is material in a way that allows it to be an agent, a character, so relationship with it and its avatars becomes possible.

Second, in these paintings, human figures are almost always relatively small, encouraging viewers to find themselves situated within the larger narrative of nature. That route to enchantment is often closed off in Western art, where human figures usually occupy, in every sense, nearly all of the available space. But Chinese landscape painting is practically all about being in the painting, especially going for a walk in it. As Michael Sullivan writes of a painting that occupies a place of highest honour in the tradition, *Travelling amid Mountains and Streams* (c. 1020), by Fan Kuan: 'This is not a picture to stand back from, grand as it is, but to lose oneself in … until, as we gaze on it, the sounds of the world about us fade away, and we hear the wind in the trees, the thunder of the waterfall, the clatter of hooves on the stony path.'[156] Another great artist of the same time, Guo Xi, writes that 'It is generally accepted opinion that in landscapes there are those through which you may travel, those in which you may sightsee, those through which you may wander, and those in which you may live.'[157]

At a less exalted level, members of the civil service in the world's oldest state bureaucracy, when taking a break from work, would escape the disenchantment of what they called 'the dusty world' by going for a metaphoric walk in a landscape scroll, almost all of which show a path that can be followed among the mountains or hills, lakes and streams, and forests. Then, when it was time to return to work, they would roll up the scroll at the point where their walk ended, so that it could be resumed at the same point next time. Thus, as Guo Xi says, 'Without leaving your room you may sit to your heart's content among streams and valleys.'[158] In this process, the human perceiver finds him- or herself in and as the land, while the land realises itself in and as the human. The result is no grand unity, a oneness in which differences disappear, but something much more valuable: mutual transformation.

Third, without gaps of some kind between them, there are no relatively distinct entities. In other words, space between entities is a prerequisite for relations, thus metaphor, and thence enchantment. In a great deal of Chinese landscape painting, such space is itself the subject, or part of it, of the painting. Often taking the form of fog and mist (which also fascinated Monet), it is decidedly not an empty void, a simple absence, but rather fecund, the originary maternal matrix that gives birth to all beings and enables relationships between them, figured in the *Daodejing* as 'the dark female'.[159] Then that gap in turn – between emptiness and fullness, each in secret sympathy with the other – opens a liminal place for wonder.

Traditional Chinese culture possesses a profound awareness of the Dao, the unmasterable ultimate source of all things. In painting, the form it takes is both mysterious, an illimitable potentiality, and doubly concrete: mist or fog or cloud, and the white paper which surrounding details in ink reveal to be those things. In these paintings, the 'void' is thus triply tensive: it is a metaphysical emptiness, and mist, and paper.

Still, it does take *some* form – there are perceptible marks on the surface, if only around it – and that is important. A story completely untold, a note completely unplayed, a brushstroke completely withheld: these do not convey blandness because they cannot convey anything at all, whether presence or absence or something beyond either. They do not even constitute a *via negativa*. As Zwicky maintains, someone or something blooming in its 'own radiant specificity' is the only way universality can actually be apprehended.[160]

It follows that consistent and thorough-going blandness is self-defeating. All the more reason, then, to be grateful to these artists for their extraordinarily sensitive, skilful and powerful concrete invocation of blandness as an experience in defiance of blandness as an ideology.

However unlikely the source, the remark by Tolkien quoted earlier summarises the issue: 'it is the untold stories' – what Jullien extolls as pure, undifferentiated, unmanifest potentiality – 'that are the most moving'. Yet 'A story must be told or there'll be no story …' – including the story of that potentiality. Neither point invalidates the other; both are true.

I am also taken with an observation by the painter-critic Gong Xian (1619– 89): 'Compositions need both strangeness and stability. Strangeness without stability is immature; stability without strangeness is commonplace.'[161] Read 'figuration' for 'stability' and for 'strangeness' read 'abstraction', and you have a good summary of my earlier association of enchantment with semi-abstract figuration.

Another way the Chinese tradition differs from the Western is in largely ignoring linear perspective, which has dominated the latter since the fifteenth century, in favour of moving or continuous perspective. The difference is significant, and it does not lie in the objective superiority of one or the other. In linear perspective, the feeling of three dimensions is maintained by adopting a single perspective within the two-dimensional picture, which is identified with the position of the person observing the picture. There is only one correct point of view, the one the viewer is given to occupy by the artist, with its implicit egoism (always you) and anthropocentrism (always a human viewer), and nothing in the picture is allowed to escape that imperious vision. Unless, of course, it is deliberately twisted or distorted, as in Cubism and some Surrealism – another rebellion that confirms the original rule.

Continuous perspective ignores this convention, preferring instead a different artifice with an implicitly democratic or anarchic principle of multiple perspectives, as if the observer was moving through, and thus within, the picture. (This is especially true, for obvious reasons, of scroll paintings.) Continuous perspective thus unfolds as the viewer walks along, so to speak, providing a new perspective with each step and remaining open to the possibility of other undetermined viewers.

Historically, it is clear that although Chinese artists became aware of the Western model in the seventeenth century, most of them resisted adopting it.[162] They knew what they were doing. As Bonnard too realised, 'The eye of the painter gives to objects a human value and reproduces things as the human eye sees them. And this vision is mutable, and this vision is mobile …'[163] More recently, Hockney has incorporated multiple perspectives into his work, explaining that 'If you look, the eye is always moving … This means there are hundreds of vanishing points, not just one.'[164] The tyranny of a single correct perspective – 'single vision', in Blake's term – depends on immobility, both of the viewer and their gaze.

The central place of metaphorically imaginative vision, as against literal-mindedness, runs deep in the Chinese tradition. It's not simply about copying or representing nature but evoking, re-presenting and ultimately embodying nature, in the person of the artist and the artistic co-creation that ensues. The activity of the artist then participates in the continuous narrative of natural transformation, which opens the door to the enchantment of finding oneself in a story, perhaps the ultimate story: that of being, together with other beings, in the greater world that is itself a metaphoric being. Thus, as early as the Tang Dynasty, a critic was stressing the importance of 'the image beyond the image',[165] and a later inscription advises the painter and, by implication, viewer, that 'One must move from capturing its resemblance to embodying its essence, in order to transmit its spirit through form.'[166]

This statement raises at least two questions. First, what is the nature of that essence? It is certainly no Idea. In words by Jullien with which I wholeheartedly concur, 'It is not a world separate from the one we have here, but the same one (the only one) cleansed of its opacity, liberated from its realism, and returned to its original state of freshness.' By the same token, since it does not take us away to another world but carries us deeper into this one, it offers an 'experience of transcendence reconciled with nature – and divested of faith.'[167]

How does that transmission occur? Here it matters that the connections between calligraphy and ink painting run deep. And with calligraphy, as anyone who has done it or seen it being done can confirm, there is nowhere to hide. There is no safety net; a mistake cannot be corrected. In this respect it must be the absolute opposite of Photoshop, in which nothing is final and irrevocable because it can always be eliminated or revised. Do I need to add how jejune and impoverished, in a distinctively modern way, the latter seems in comparison?

So there is a 'decisive moment' here too, and it is when the artist's brush encounters the paper. The ink is the agent which links them, as well as the trace of each specific and unique encounter. In that trace, as François Cheng says, 'the carnal relationship between the feeling body of the artist and the felt body of the landscape is formed.'[168] Look at the best calligraphy (that of Carolyn Carlson, for example) and you will see what he means.[169] These are not merely shapes, nor representations; the figures are themselves clearly bodies. Just as are the mountains and rivers portrayed, and ultimately the creative processes which produce both them and the artwork are the same. As I have already quoted Wallace Stevens, nature is an incessant creation, and 'Because this is so in nature, it is so in metaphor.' In other words, what these artists do is essentially the same as what they are painting is doing.

What Cheng calls 'true beauty' in Chinese art is very close to what I mean by enchantment. He defines it as

> beauty that occurs and is revealed, that just suddenly appears to touch the soul of the one who perceives it, [and says that it] results from the encounter between two beings or between the human spirit and the living universe. And the work of beauty, always arising from a 'between', is a third thing that, springing from the interaction of the two, allows the two to surpass themselves. If there is transcendence, it lies in this surpassing.[170]

Zao Wou-Ki

I am going to close with the work of Zao Wou-Ki, a Chinese painter but long-time resident in France. Its success as enchanting art owes something to both traditions, which he negotiates in his own distinctive way. That distinctiveness is the key to a corresponding degree of universality.

Zao is heir to both Chinese and European traditions in two ways: in terms of their respective sensibilities, and in terms of specific painting practices, black-and-white ink painting emphasising form on the one hand, and oil painting with colour on the other. In that double in between, enchantment might have foundered. Instead, it has triumphed. His large-scale abstracts crackle with the energy of Song Dynasty dragon paintings, birthing forms from the void, while their swirling colours (often reminiscent of Turner) are integral to that process. They are powerful but not crushing, and tender without being precious.

But as Jonathan Haye says, 'Abstraction is somewhat misleading as a description of Zao's paintings; it would be more accurate to say that their image field hovers between nature and abstraction'.[171] We have said much the same of Matisse's 'abstraction rooted in reality' and Isao Miura's 'neither figurative nor abstract but a sort of symbolism'. This is a consistent thread running throughout enchanting art. Zao's forms evoke the spirit, the qualities, of mountains, rivers and trees without over-explicitly referencing them. To be able to do so without sacrificing the precision required for enchantment is art of the highest order.

Zao's influences are legion, but in each case, he has turned them to his own good account. For example, 'more than the Chinese landscape it was Chinese space that interested me.' We have seen the vital importance of such space, gaps and voids for enchantment. 'What's more,' he adds, 'nature is more important than landscape, because landscape may be limited.'[172] He's right, of course – there can be nature without landscape but not the reverse – and a living nature is the fount of his art.

From the Western side, Klee for Zao 'was a short cut to contemplating nature in a different way. It is by looking that you become a different painter. Klee opened up the path that led me to look at nature in my own way.'[173] (That is true teaching.)

In his *Homage to Matisse*, with its colours opening onto a luminous black, Zao explicitly references Matisse's *French-Window at Coullioure*. More fundamentally, he remarks that 'when you make the tiniest change it may influence the entire composition. That means you have to go back to the beginning' – just what Picasso noticed about Matisse's paintings.[174] And Zao's *Homage to Monet* succeeds in evoking the master without the slightest imitation.

Recently interviewed in the course of a ramble through the Louvre, his interlocutor noted that like Zao, Bonnard too conveys delight in painting. Zao concurred, adding that 'You can see it in Matisse as well.' And standing before a landscape by Poussin, he exclaimed, 'What enchantment! There is the joy of painting …'[175]

Notes

1 *The Guardian* (18.9.10) 17. The painting in this case was Cézanne's 'Etang des Soeurs, Osny, près de Pontoise'.
2 Adam Zagazewski, *Solidarity, Solitude*, transl. Lillian Vallee (New York: The Ecco Press, 1990): 162–63.
3 Clive James, *Amnesia*: 392.
4 Hisham Matar, *A Month in Siena* (London: Viking, 2019): 81.
5 John House, *Monet: Nature into Art* (New Haven: Yale University Press, 1986): 217; then in Richard Kendall (ed.), *Monet by Himself* (London: Little, Brown, 1995): 265; and see p. 224.
6 Carla Rachman, *Monet* (London: Phaidon, 1997): 197, 189.
7 Rachman, *Monet*: 244.
8 See Rachman, *Monet*: 268.
9 See Michael Hoog, *Musée de l'Orangerie: The Nymphéas of Claude Monet* (Paris: Adago, 2006).
10 Rachman, *Monet*: 292.
11 House, *Monet*: 221.
12 *The TLS* (30.10.09): 18.
13 On the power of reflections to enchant, see Yasunari Kawabata, *Snow Country*, transl. Edward G. Seidensticker (London: Penguin Books, 2011): 7.
14 Scarry, *Beauty*: 36.
15 J.R.R. Tolkien, *The Silmarillion*, ed. Christopher Tolkien (London: George Allen & Unwin, 1977): 38–39. See Patrick Curry, 'The Two Trees, p. 682 in Michael D.C. Drout (ed.), *J.R.R. Tolkien Encyclopedia. Scholarship and Critical Assessment* (London: Routledge, 2007).
16 Tim Robinson, *Connemara: The Last Pool of Darkness* (Dublin: Penguin Ireland, 2008): 1.
17 Tanizaki, *Praise*: 14, 20.
18 Volkmar Essers, *Matisse* (Köln: Taschen, 1987): 80.
19 Essers, *Matisse*: 18. There is a slightly different translation in John Elderfield, *The Cut-Outs of Matisse* (New York: George Braziller, 1978): 7.
20 With thanks to Susan Peters for pointing this out to me.
21 Scarry, *Beauty*: 47.
22 Jack Flam, *Matisse on Art*, rev. edn (Berkeley: University of California Press, 1995): 219.
23 See Jean Guichard-Meili (ed.), *Matisse: Paper Cut-outs*, transl. David Macey (New York: Thames and Hudson, 1984).
24 See Alistair Sooke, *Henri Matisse: A Second Life* (London: Penguin, 2014).
25 Nicholas Watkins, *Bonnard: Colour and Light* (London: Tate Gallery Publishing, 1998): 44; Essers, *Matisse*, 12.

26 Flam, *Matisse*: 13.

27 Flam, *Matisse*: 19.

28 *Marcel Proust on Art and Literature 1896–1919*, transl. Sylvia Townsend Warner, 2nd edn (New York: Carroll and Graf, 1997): 25–26.

29 Essers, *Matisse*: 90.

30 Quotations in this paragraph from Flam, *Matisse*: 11, 19, 21, 22.

31 Flam, *Matisse*, 210.

32 Flam, *Matisse*, 214, 217.

33 Mike Glier, personal communication to a mutual friend. See his *along a long line* (Lenox: Hard Press Editions, 2009).

34 See Henri Bortoft, *Taking Appearance Seriously. The Dynamic Way of Seeing in Goethe and European Thought* (Edinburgh: Floris Books, 2012) e.g. 83, 104.

35 Flam, *Matisse*: 89, 211.

36 *The Guardian Magazine* (9.5.15).

37 Josipovici, *Modernism*, 187.

38 In an interview by Hazel de Berg in 1963; Hazel de Berg collection, National Library of Australia, tape no. deB 1.

39 On participation, see Dario Gamboni, *Potential Images: Ambiguity and Indeterminacy in Modern Art* (London: Reaktion Books, 2002) on pictures that depend on the participation of the viewer to 'come fully into being' (p. 9).

40 Winnicott: 'Transitional Objects and Transitional Phenomena: A Study of the First Not-Me Possession', *International Journal of Psycho-analysis* XXXIV/2 (1953) 89–97: 90.

41 D.W. Winnicott, *Playing and Reality* (London: Routledge, 2005): xvi, 17.

42 Ibid, 7, 129.

43 See Rebecca Burrill, 'Art as Ecology: A mutual nod', *The Ecological Citizen* 5:2 (2022) 178–85.

44 Nicholas Watkins, *Bonnard* (London: Phaidon Press, 1994) 104; Suzanne Page (ed.), *Pierre Bonnard: l'oevre d'art, un arrêt du temps* (Paris: Musées/ Ludion, 2006): 279.

45 Sarah Whitfield and John Elderfield, *Bonnard* (London: Tate Gallery Publishing, 1998): 43.

46 This quotation comes from the chapter 'The Captive' in Proust's *In Search of Lost Time*, but I'm afraid I cannot now find the exact page.

47 Van Gogh reference: Timothy Hyman, *Bonnard* (London: Thames and Hudson, 1998): 156.

48 Page, *Bonnard*: 31. ('Il ne s'agit pas de peindre la vie, il s'agit de rendre vivante la peinture'.)

49 Page, *Bonnard*, 85, and Whitfield and Elderfield, *Bonnard*, 43.

50 Whitfield and Elderfield, *Bonnard*: 43. ('Brilliant' is italicised in the original.)

51 Nicholas Watkins, *Bonnard: Colour and Light* (London: Tate Gallery Publishing, 1998): 208. (My emphasis.)

52 Hyman, *Bonnard*: 193.

53 Watkins, *Bonnard*: 35.

54 Whitfield and Elderfield, *Bonnard*: 31.

55 Val Plumwood, *Environmental Culture* (London: Routledge: 2002): 226.

56 See Hilary Spurling, *Matisse: The Life* (London: Penguin, 2009): 519.

57 Watkins, *Bonnard*: 140.

58 Whitfield and Elderfield, *Bonnard*: 284.

59 Whitfield and Elderfield, *Bonnard*: 38.

60 See my *Enchantment: Wonder in Modern Life* (Edinburgh: Floris, 2017): 30–33.

61 Watkins, *Bonnard*: 10.

62 Whitfield and Elderfield, *Bonnard*, 29.

63 Gabriel Josipovici, 'To be here, now', reviewing 'Pierre Bonnard: The colour of memory' at the Tate Modern, *TLS* (15.2.2019).

64 Hyman, *Bonnard*, 141. See pp. 141–42 for an excellent discussion.

65 Page, *Bonnard*: 269.
66 Hyman, *Bonnard*: 211. (I have very slightly altered the translation.) Also in F. Gilot and C. Lake, *Life with Picasso* (Harmondsworth: Penguin, 1966): 263.
67 Michael Kimmelman, *New York Times* (19.6.98) 'A Dream World of Painting, Yielding its Secrets Slowly': http://www.nytimes.com/1998/06/19/arts/a-dream-world-of-painting-yielding-its-secrets-slowly.html?pagewanted=all&src=pm (accessed 10.3.13).
68 Spurling, *Matisse*: 519.
69 Albert Kostenevitch, *Bonnard and the Nabis* (New York: Parkstone Press, 2005): 7 (my translation).
70 Mario Naves, writing in *Style* (http://www.observer.com/2009/style/20th-centurys-vermeer-or-masturbatory-hack) (accessed 10.3.13).
71 Nuala O'Faolain, *Are You Somebody? A Memoir* (Dublin: New Line, 2008): 148.
72 Nochlin writing in *Art in America* (July 1998). See the excellent piece by Hilton Kramer, 'Bonnard and "the stupidities"', *New Criterion* (Oct. 1998). https://www.newcriterion.com/articles.cfm/Bonnard-and--ldquo-the-stupidities-rdquo--2989 (accessed 10.3.13).
73 Michel Serres, *The Five Senses: A Philosophy of Mingled Bodies* (London: Bloomsbury, 2016): 30.
74 Nochlin, *Art*.
75 Schjeldahl writing in *The Village Voice* (29.7.98).
76 Whitfield and Elderfield, *Bonnard*: 17.
77 Ken Kiff, conversation at the Tate Gallery: Lib. Call no. 1) TAV 1972A.
78 http://nga.gov.au/bonnard/Default.cfm?MnuID=4 (accessed 8.2.13).
79 Daido Moriyama, *In Pictures* (2012): http://www.tate.org.uk/context-comment/video/daido-moriyama-pictures (accessed 3.1.13).
80 I found Ueli Seiler-Hugova, *Colour: Seeing, Experiencing, Understanding* (Forest Row: Temple Lodge Publishing, 2011) helpful.
81 Watkins, *Bonnard*: 31 (emphasis in the original) and 208.
82 'Mechanistic-mystical': for Newton, gravity was either God's action or was itself God. Subsequent modern science unavoidably reaches an equivalent point where it too cannot be rationally or materially grounded without bootstrapping or question-begging.
83 Kassia St Clair, *The Secret Lives of Colour* (London: John Murray, 2016): 13.
84 Ray Smith, *The Artist's Handbook*, rev. edn (London: Dorling Kindersley, 2003): 16–28. (See also www.farrow-ball.com).
85 Andrew Lambirth, *Ken Kiff* (London: Thames and Hudson, 2001): 70.
86 Ibid.
87 See Eric Karples, *Paintings in Proust* (London: Thames & Hudson, 2008): 234.
88 Guy Deutscher, *Through the Language Glass: How Words Colour Your World* (London: William Heinnemann, 2010).
89 James Fox, 'Blue' BBC 4 TV, broadcast 13.1.13; thanks to Suzanna Saumarez for pointing this out.
90 Hilary Spurling, *Matisse: The Life* (London: Penguin, 2009): 330.
91 Richard Williams, *The Blue Moment: Miles Davis's Kind of Blue and the Remaking of Modern Music* (London: Faber and Faber, 2009): 34.
92 Lambirth, *Ken Kiff*: 207.
93 See the excellent documentary on DVD *Blue Alchemy: Stories of Indigo*, by Mary Lance.
94 Oakeshott, *Poetry*: 527.
95 Leys, *Hall*: 42.
96 Alexander Nehamas, *Only a Promise of Happiness: The Place of Beauty in a World of Art* (Princeton: Princeton University Press, 2007): 13.
97 Andy Goldsworthy, *Enclosure* (London: Thames & Hudson, 2007): from the Introduction by James Putnam: 10.
98 Scarry, *Beauty*: e.g. 57, 62–63.
99 Jacques Derrida: *Limited Inc* (Evanston: Northwestern University Press, 1988): 136.
100 As Nehamas asserts of Manet's *Olympia in Promise*.

101 Scarry, *Beauty*: 73.
102 A point made respecting Matisse by Liam Hudson and Bernadine Jacot, *The Way Men Think: Intellect, Intimacy and the Erotic Imagination* (New Haven: Yale University Press, 1991): 145.
103 François Jullien, *The Impossible Nude. Chinese Art and Western Aesthetics*, transl. Maev de la Guardia (Chicago: University of Chicago Press, 2007): vii, 4, 126.
104 Jullien, *Impossible*: 25.
105 Sylvie Lancrenon, *Cuba Libre* (Munich: Schirmer/ Mosel, 2008); also see the work of Ellen von Unwerth.
106 Raymond Mason, *At Work in Paris: Raymond Mason on Art and Artists* (London: Thames and Hudson, 2003): 154.
107 Ibid, 154.
108 Achim Borchardt-Hume, '"Dreh Dich Nicht Um": Don't Turn Around. Richter's Paintings of the Late 1980s', pp. 163–198 in Mark Godfrey and Nicholas Serota (eds), *Gerhard Richter: Panorama* (London: Tate Publishing, 2011): 164–65.
109 See Craig Raine, 'The beauty of the blur', *TLS* (21.10.11).
110 'Painting History', Peter Schjeldahl, *The New Yorker* (16.3.2020).
111 Ed Vulliamy, *The Guardian* (18.11.1995).
112 Ibid.
113 Gabriel Josipovici, 'To be here'.
114 Su Shih quoted in Susan Bush and Hsio-yen Shih, *Early Chinese Texts on Painting* (Cambridge MA: Harvard University Press, 1985): 207. (An invaluable collection.)
115 François Cheng: *The Way of Beauty: Five Meditations for Spiritual Transformation*, transl. Jody Gladding (Rochester: Inner Traditions, 2006): 15.
116 Klee quoted in Gamboni, *Potential*: 216. See also Arfin Bø-Rygg, 'Thinking with Klee', pp. 84–100 in In *Paul Klee's Enchanted Garden* (Ostfildern: Hatje Cantz Verlag, 2008).
117 Lambirth, *Ken Kiff*: 70.
118 Gamboni, *Potential*: 186.
119 From the Pedagogical Sketchbook (1925).
120 The *LRB* (9.1.14).
121 Adam Zagajewski, *Without End. New and Selected Poems*, transl. C. Cavanagh and R. Gorcznski, B. Ivry and C.K. Williams (New York: Farrar, Straus and Giroux, 2002): 243.
122 Quotations from the BBC documentary 'Colouring Light: Brian Clarke – An Artist Apart' (2011).
123 See Jonathan Hill (ed.), *Johnny. The Work of Psychedelic Artist John Hurford* (Exeter: Sunrise Press, 2006).
124 Titus O'Brien, *Dreams Unreal: The Genesis of the Psychedelic Rock Poster* (Albuquerque: University of New Mexico Press, 2020): xvii, 126. See also Gayle Lemke and Jaaeber Kastor, *The Art of the Fillmore 1966–1971* (Petaluma: Acid Test Productions, 1997).
125 Clarke, BBC.
126 Quoted in Spalding, *Eclipse*: 107.
127 Hockney, *The Guardian*.
128 All quotations from *RA Magazine* (Autumn 2012): 53.
129 See Julia Marciari Alexander and David Scrase (eds), *Howard Hodgkin: Paintings 1992–2007* (New Haven: Yale University Press, 2007).
130 Lambirth, *Ken Kiff*, 203.
131 Ibid, 144.
132 All quotations by Isao Miura from http://www.isaomiura.com/ (accessed 31.3.13).
133 *The Guardian* (26. 2.99).
134 Joseph Brodsky, *On Grief and Reason: Essays* (London: Penguin, 1995): 237.
135 The following quotations by Henri Cartier-Bresson from Pierre Assouline, *Henri Cartier-Bresson: A Biography*, transl. David Wilson (London: Thames and Hudson, 2005): 181, 245–46. On Cartier-Bresson's attitude to equipment, see also Philippe L. Gross and S.I. Shapiro, *The Tao of Photography: Seeing Beyond Seeing* (Berkeley: Ten Speed Press, 2011): 93.

136 Mason, *At Work*: 129.

137 Gross and Shapiro, *Tao*: 123.

138 Terry O'Neil in http://www.culturecompass.co.uk/2012/11/06/henri-cartier-bresson-his-influence-on-five-photographers/ (accessed 27.3.13) and *The Guardian* (18.12.2008).

139 Quoted in the documentary 'The Times of Bill Cunningham' (2018).

140 Sally Mann, *Immediate Family* (London: Phaidon Press, 1992): n.p.

141 The *TLS* (9.10.2015).

142 David Nash, *Forms into Time* (London: Academy Group Ltd., 1996), incl. Marina Warner, 'Through the Narrow Door: Forms into Time', pp. 8–24: 24, 20.

143 Quoted in *RA Magazine* (Summer 2012): 17.

144 Interview with David Nash, with Tom Raines, *New View* (Winter 2012/13) 13–21: 17.

145 *The Guardian* (13.1.10).

146 *The Guardian* (11.10.11).

147 Daido Moriyama, *The World through My Eyes*, ed. Filippo Maggia (Milano: Skira, 2010): 18.

148 Moriyama, *In Pictures* (2012) http://www.tate.org.uk/context-comment/video/daido-moriyama-pictures

149 For an excellent discussion see Jullien, *Impossible*.

150 Freya Stark, *The Journey's Echo. Selected Travel Writings* (New York: The Ecco Press, 1988): 170.

151 Michael Sullivan, *The Arts of China*, 4th edn (Berkeley: University of California Press, 1999): 165. (I have also drawn upon the work of James Cahill.)

152 See François Jullien, *In Praise of Blandness: Proceeding from Chinese Thought and Aesthetics*, transl. Paula M. Varsano (New York: Zone Books, 2004).

153 Do not confuse this art with the masculinist and monumental environmental installations of Robert Smithson, Michael Heizer and others, mainly in America, which are all about imposing human will on 'dirt': eco-modernism, in a word (with thanks to Fabrizio Manco). See Gablik, *Re-enchantment*: 140, and especially Mel Gooding with William Furlong, *Song of the Earth: European Artists and the Landscape* (London: Thames and Hudson, 2002).

154 Gooding, *Song*, 142.

155 Andy Goldsworthy, *Hand to Earth. Sculpture 1976–1990* (The Henry Moore Centre for the Study of Sculpture, 1990): 161.

156 Michael Sullivan, *Symbols of Eternity. The Art of Landscape Painting in China* (Oxford: Clarendon Press, 1979): 69.

157 Bush and Shih, *Texts*: 151.

158 Ibid.

159 Roger T. Ames and David L. Hall (eds), *Dao de Jing. A Philosophical Translation* (New York: Ballantine Books, 2003): 85–86.

160 Zwicky, *Lyric*: 536.

161 Regrettably, I cannot recall the source for this quotation.

162 See Sullivan, *Symbols*: 74, 166–68.

163 Hyman, *Bonnard*: 159–60.

164 *The Guardian* (18.4.15).

165 Sullivan, *Arts*: 168.

166 Xiao Yuncong (1591–1668), inscription on painting 'Ink Plum' (1669).

167 Jullien, *Blandness*, 115, 144.

168 Cheng, *Way*: 110.

169 Carolyn Carlson: e.g. *Traces d'Encre* (Paris: Actes Sud, 2013).

170 Cheng, *Way*, 105.

171 Jonathan Hay: http://www.asianart.com/exhibitions/zao/essay.html (accessed 22.2.13). I wish there had been space to discuss another remarkable artist working within and extending both Western and Far Eastern paradigms, Yoshida Kenji.

172 José Frèches, *Zao Wou-ki: Works, Writings, Interviews* (Barcelona: Ediciones Polígrafa, 2007): 102.
173 Ibid.
174 Ibid, 117.
175 Ibid, 117, 129.

4

PAINTING II

Picasso

Especially given the pairing in life and art of Matisse and Pablo Picasso, some consideration of the latter is in order. As we shall see, the contrast is not entirely straightforward or symmetrical.

One consequence of Matisse painting 'the difference between things' is that 'Wherever you look,' as Flam puts it, 'you should also be looking somewhere else at the same time.'[1] Picasso noticed the same thing. 'The fact that in one of my paintings,' he says,

> there is a certain spot of red isn't the essential part of the painting. The painting was done independently of that. You could take the red away and there would always be the painting; but with Matisse it is unthinkable that one could suppress a spot of red, however small, without having the painting immediately fall apart.[2]

One wonders if Picasso appreciated the implications for his own work.

I don't see how it could sensibly be denied that all things considered, Picasso was a great artist – earlier, I mentioned his Guernica in this connection – but that's not really our concern. More to the point, he certainly appears to qualify as a modernist in the sense I am using the term. Picasso's art is restlessly intellectual, with the peculiar quality, both fiery and cold, which often goes with that. By the same token, it is often deliberately violent and shocking. 'In my case, a picture is a sum of destructions.'[3]

Equally significantly, he maintained, as a point of principle, that the artist should dominate and impose himself on both nature and women. In all these respects, the contrast with the art of Matisse – emotional even if harmoniously expressed, pacific, and deeply respectful of women and the Earth – could not be clearer. But

DOI: 10.4324/9781003353225-4

I am speaking primarily of Picasso's painting here. His decisive line drawings and playful ceramics, perhaps with less to prove, are a rather different matter.

However, it should not be overlooked that Picasso never painted a purely abstract picture. Indeed, he dismissed the concept of abstract art *en tout*, because 'everything appears to us in the guise of a figure', and he maintained that 'Nonfigurative painting is never subversive'.[4] And Picasso's Cubist paintings are still figurative, so they can potentially partake of the enchantment that semi-abstraction (such as that of Monet's late water-lilies) enables.

To be sure, the Cubism that Picasso and Georges Braque invented in 1907 – significantly influenced by Cézanne, that great geometrician – was analytical and theory-driven, and as such, a step towards disenchantment. Picasso's own strictures notwithstanding, Cubism also made possible the next step that followed in the same direction, full abstraction. That is not surprising if you consider the implications of Picasso's attempt to see all sides of a figure from all possible perspectives. When you look at someone, there is always some aspect you cannot see. It will vary, depending on your and their positions, but it is ineliminable. (Even if a mirror is employed, you are only looking at a fractured composite of the other person.) In its metaphysical aspect, this resistance to being wholly seen all at once could be considered a sign of everyone's right, as it were, to a degree of privacy and mystery. The unseeable aspect says that I cannot be wholly comprehended and mastered by you, nor you by me – nor, for that matter, either of us by ourselves.

Cubism attempted to overcome this 'limitation' (an interpretation that is already revealing) by showing all aspects of a figure, from all points of view, at once. If there was ever a perfect artistic instance of the buzzword 'totalising' this is it; and as with all totalising enterprises, it is implicitly totalitarian. The artist is in control, and the model really is reduced to an object.

Wendy Woon, a director at the Museum of Modern Art, described the 'enchantment' (her word) of Picasso's *Demoiselles d'Avignon* in this way: 'It's a struggle. It's a drama. It's problem-solving. It's a painting about working through new ideas. The surface is a battleground of forces ...'[5] It should be clear that what is being described here, including her response to it, concerns heroic struggle, the evolution of ideas about painting, and so on. From that perspective, *Demoiselles* is indeed admirable. It's just not enchanting.

In sum, Picasso is too complicated a figure to be drafted into pure modernism. He did indeed dislike, even hate, enchantment (witness his diatribe against Bonnard), but he was nonetheless, in Gabriel Josipovici's words, one of the 'artists who have struggled to remain at the crossroads of figuration and abstraction, such as Bonnard or Bacon': a provocative but astute pairing. And as Josipovici adds, 'only an art which recognises the pitfalls inherent in both realism and abstraction will be really alive.'[6]

Abstract Art

I touched on abstraction in the previous chapter, but let's look into it in more depth. The prime mover behind abstract art was Paul Cézanne. Almost an exact contemporary of Monet, Cézanne's influence among younger generations of painters, and on subsequent schools and movements, was greater. The difference between the two is neatly encapsulated in his back-handed compliment to Monet's work: 'He's only an eye, but what an eye!'[7] The 'only' makes clear what Cézanne thought was missing: an intellect.

He and Monet shared a devotion to working before and with nature – what they called 'sensation', which in French usage includes a greater degree of emotion than in English – but for Cézanne what became paramount was not so much colour and light or surfaces as form, structure and geometry: 'I see planes bestriding each other … [and] the meeting of planes.'[8] As a result, emotion became tensely contained and controlled by an intellectual vision, even programme, that was Pythagorean in its emphasis on fundamental forms, planes and solids, and in its search for underlying structures. (Perhaps the sharpest contrast is between Cézanne and the painfully open emotion and radical innocence of Vincent van Gogh.)

The effect of such an effort cannot but be disenchanting. Yet enchantment keeps breaking through – as witness Ali Smith's opening story of her encounter with *L'Etang des Soeurs, Osny* – in Cézanne's water, trees, and in particular Mont Sainte-Victoire, 'his' mountain. The upshot is painting strangely at war with itself, alternating without any resolution between the two.

Cézanne's restless intellectual energy and quest for universals deeply impressed Picasso, leading him, along with Braque, into the rupture of Cubism (so named, derisively, by Matisse).[9] Cubism was still figurative, but it licensed breaking and remaking visible patterns in a way that was idiosyncratic while still laying claim to universal truths. As the Cubist Robert Delaunay phrased it, in classically Platonic terms, the quest was for a 'universal reality' concealed beneath 'contingent and obvious' appearances.[10] Although not itself fully abstract, then, the disenchantment of Cubism made possible pure abstraction as a further step in the same direction.

Along with Cubism, Cézanne's work also impelled both Mondrian and Malevitch into full abstraction, as well as Kandinsky and his version of the same. (Historically speaking, they were preceded by another painter seeking the truth underlying or overarching 'mere' appearances, Hilma af Klint.)

From them the torch passed to America and the Abstract Expressionism of Pollock, Rothko, Rauschenberg, and others. We shall turn to Mondrian and Kandinsky later. In the meantime, note the proclamation in 1916 of Kazimir Malevich, whose *Black Square* (which was just that) of 1915 just preceded Mondrian's first abstracts and was still being copied by Robert Rauschenberg (in white) in 1951 and Yves Klein (in blue) in 1954: 'in our era of Cubism the artist has destroyed objects together with their meaning, essence and purpose…. Our world of art has become new, non-objective, pure'. Indeed, he claimed grandiosely that 'I destroyed the ring of the horizon and escaped from the circle of things, from the horizon ring that confines the artists and forms of nature'.[11]

The implications for enchantment are clear enough, because that can only arise as a result not by attempting to destroy the things of this world but by going deeply into them and engaging with the immanent 'idea' (to repeat Merleau-Ponty) that is their 'lining and depth'. There is nothing, for us, outside the circle of things and forms of nature – indeed, they have no 'outside'! – so such disembodied purity is a philosophy of death.[12] Its provenance is the philosophical idealism beginning (and continuing) in Platonism, where the mind, originally spirit, is regarded as something that can, even should, 'escape' from the 'confines' of the body and, by extension, the Earth; and that is placed higher, as superior, and therefore valued more. The disenchantment that results is very convenient for materialist capital, of course, because nothing (no thing) is left with any inherent meaning, let alone dignity; so its value can all the more easily be taken over and defined by market forces.

The same considerations were abundantly at work in Abstract Expressionism in the 1950s and 60s. At the risk of being tactless, I wonder if the connections between the tragic lives and their art of Jackson Pollock and Mark Rothko, two of its leading members, are fortuitous. They both seem to share the quality of a dead-end. Pollock innovatively dripped and poured paint in seeking 'pure painting' that swirls with energy, at least; but in the year before he died in a drunken car crash, he did none, while he was under vile pressure to prove himself America's greatest artist in order to eclipse Paris and establish a 'blue-chip' contemporary art market in New York.

In the previous chapter, I mentioned two opposing (but sometimes conspiring) modes which are equally non-relational and therefore hostile to enchantment. One is Dionysian – hot, consuming, tending towards orgasmic union, and thence dissolution – while the other is Apollonian: cold, distancing, and objectifying control-over. For the reasons I have been discussing, the 'purer' abstraction becomes the more it tends to disenchantment. That is not to say, however, that all purely abstract art is of the same kind; it can differ as widely as these two ways of being do. Thus, the volcanic emotionality of Pollock's canvasses are strikingly different from the hyper-controlled work of Mondrian.

I would add, necessarily briefly, that the work of Milton Avery and Helen Frankenthaler are good examples of abstract art that could not really be called anything else, but which succeeds, thanks to retaining an affinity with organic forms and natural colours, in escaping the Apollonian/ Dionysian problematic and affirming life.

Mark Rothko further complicates my narrative without compromising it, combining Apollonian control – always a very small number of swatches – with powerful Dionysian feeling to make rectangles of two or three colours, adjacent or partly superimposed, which glow with burnished colours that are oddly compelling, and sometimes enchanting. In his long descent into depression and eventual suicide, however, they darkened. Finally, even dark purple and maroon were too colourful; only black would do, and that of a certain kind.

It is instructive to compare the deeply opaque black of Rothko's final canvasses with what the visionary painter Odilon Redon called 'the deep health of the black', which in his case tended to be velvety. One is the black of despair; the other, of rest and renewal … Ostensibly the same colour, it's not. Another potent comparison would be with the black in Matisse's *French-Window at Coullioure* (1914), which is different again. I experience it as inviting me in, or out through the window. Rothko's black, in sharp contrast, is a blank block in both directions. If you are already inside it there is no way out, and if you are not there is no way in.

William Boyd, a writer sympathetic to Rothko, describes the subject of his paintings as 'the despair at the heart of the human condition, doom, entropy, the void and oblivion.'[13] Another critic (again, one sympathetic to modernism) describes Rothko's final works as 'unremitting, sullen, remorseless'. His paintings, even the best, 'sort of eat you up'.[14] False enchantment, if you remember, lies in wanting to consume or be consumed. Thus another door to true enchantment in Rothko's late paintings closes. Yet despite their imperious narcissism and overwhelming self-pity, enchantment sometimes leaks out, like the delicate washes of their borders – testament to its tenacity, and their complexity.

Mondrian

In the second decade of the twentieth century, together with Malevich, Piet Mondrian pioneered pure geometric abstraction in painting. After a series of semi-abstract tree studies that lasted from 1908 until 1912, Mondrian's abstraction emerged between 1912 and 1921 and continued till his death. This work consisted solely of vertical or horizontal straight lines and a few blocks of primary colours – red, blue, or yellow only – against geometric grids of black lines and white spaces. 'This new idea,' he wrote, 'will ignore the particulars of appearance; that is to say, natural form and colour; on the contrary, it should find its expression in the abstraction of form and colour.'[15] In relation to enchantment, this manifesto expresses exactly the problem (in addition to the programmicity of a manifesto as such).

Mondrian admitted his debt to Cubism and Cézanne. Portraying and imposing grids, he shared the intellectualism of both, as well as Picasso's emphasis on wilful mastery. A philosopher who influenced Mondrian, M.H.J. Schoenmaekers, wrote that 'we want to penetrate nature in such a way that the inner construction of reality is revealed to us.'[16] Note the misogynistic language so reminiscent of Francis Bacon – not the painter but one of the fathers of modern science, who also advised us to 'penetrate' and 'pierce' nature and 'put [her] to the question', in order to force her to reveal her secrets. Impelling him in the same direction was the fear of uncontrolled passion Mondrian shared with Cézanne.

These imperatives Mondrian combined in an ascetic geometry. In his view, which he developed in programmatic theoretical statements, 'The emotion of beauty is always hindered by the particular appearance of an "object"; the object must therefore be abstracted from any figurative representation.'[17] (This was just Wittgenstein's sardonic description of Plato's idea of pure beauty as 'unadulterated by anything that is beautiful'.) Mondrian goes on to say that 'As a pure expression of the human mind, art will express itself in an aesthetically purified, that is to say, abstract form … in the straight line and the clearly defined primary colour.'[18]

Obviously, these goals are hostile to the conditions needed for enchantment. But Mondrian seems to have wanted to actively discourage it. A contemporary painter and critic, Fairfield Porter, detected a puritanical repression in Mondrian's abstracts, comparing their black lines to prison bars and perceptively noting his fear of 'the dangerous mystery of fact'.[19] The enthusiastic support for Mondrian by Clement Greenberg, the ultra-modernist critic, rather confirms the point. Equally important, Mondrian's artistic practice was not painting which then may or may not be theorised: it was disenchanted theory, which is then expressed visually, just as was the case with Schoenberg's music.

When I gave a talk on this point, a friend objected afterwards that he found Mondrian's abstract paintings thoroughly enchanting. This was bound to happen, of course. You will remember a similar episode involving the music of Wagner. Do such examples, which could be multiplied, invalidate my argument? I don't think so. I have already made the point that the temperament and knowledge of the viewer, listener, or reader of art can open or close doors to its enchantment, if any. In this case, my friend has a grasp and appreciation of mathematics and geometry with obvious implications for his ability to respond to Mondrian's paintings as enchanting structures.

He was also a visual artist and intimately acquainted with the development of modern abstract art, which he found realised one day upon entering the room of Mondrian's work in the Metropolitan Museum of Art. In other words, his knowledge of that story – together with his own particular self-story – opened a door to the enchanted potential of those paintings: a door that in their absence remains closed to many people; myself included.

It might still be asked, where is the in between, liminal, metaphoric space in Mondrian's abstracts that enchantment needs? As I remarked in the opening chapter, there are various doors to enchantment, not one overarching one. This person was enchanted by abstract art, for example, despite its lack of tensive truth – one door – because his grasp of the development of Western art enabled him to find himself participating in that narrative: another, different one ... although not entirely different. If you find yourself in the story you are reading, picture you are seeing, etc., you are also sitting reading, or standing looking, and not in it at the same time. So metaphor is at work here, too.

We still need to keep in mind, though, that enchantment lies in the work itself too, and all works of art are far from equally enchanting. Some indeed cannot conceivably be considered enchanting, no matter how generously defined. (Witness, if you need convincing, Hirst's rotting, fly-blown cow's head. Other examples abound.) And however complex and subtle the process, the intentions of the artist have some effect on that.

As a modernist, Mondrian himself was not concerned in his art with enchantment. He sought rather to represent the spiritual reality underlying 'mere' appearances; hence the straight lines and primary colours. Such an enterprise is of Platonic and Pythagorean provenance, obviously, and like those philosophies, one of its goals is disenchantment, construed as manly freedom from a bewitchment or *ensorcellement* which is firmly gendered as female.

Mondrian wouldn't have been impressed by van Gogh's speculation that 'Life is probably round.'[20] Nor would he have been bothered by Hundertwasser's belief that the straight line is godless, since the gods must be sacrificed anyway in order to gain God, or His secular placeholder. ('All gods and qualities must be destroyed', said Horkheimer and Adorno of the programme of the Enlightenment.)[21] Similarly, it is reasonable to assume that Mondrian limited himself to primary colours precisely because they lack the blended, ambiguous colours which provide the gaps and hence crossings that enchantment needs.[22]

It is important to add that Mondrian was a committed Theosophist. There is no contradiction here with his modernism. Spiritualism – placing spirit and its placeholder the intellect (implicitly male) as 'higher', more important and morally superior to body or matter – is a species of philosophical idealism. As a philosophy, Theosophy was basically neo-Platonic Hermeticism, with some Vedanta and largely misunderstood Buddhism thrown in, reworked for modern times. It retained those traditions' spiritual reductionism, as well as their problem with beauty. Mondrian's Theosophy was modulated by Hegelianism, but that hardly helps, Hegel's philosophy being perhaps the supreme nineteenth-century example of spiritual idealism and intellectualism.[23]

Modernist truth too has no room for mere appearance or adornment, even – or, because it is considered so seductive and misleading, especially – beauty. These two discourses thus share a powerful impulse to purify and universalise – really, to 'save' through purifying and universalising – so it is hardly surprising that their confluence turns Aphrodite's sensual beauty into a shameful secret. In dismissing what the senses can perceive as mere appearances, however, the profound mystery of life that only carnal experience can disclose is also lost. And since we are embodied beings, who cannot live forever on some plane of 'pure', universal, self-identical, and therefore non-metaphorical truth, Plan B for the zealous is some version thereof which is, in effect, a particular god, and therefore in some sense or other an embodied one, but swathed in clouds of deception, not least self-deception.

Thus Mondrian, having expelled enchantment from his public and programmatic paintings, or imprisoned it within the bars of his horizontal and vertical bars, with just a bit of pure primary colour allowed, seems to have found that he couldn't live without it. It is well-known now that for over thirty years – secretly, as if they were pornographic – he painted exquisitely sensual, alchemically mysterious flowers. He kept them on a special wall that only close friends were permitted to see, and sold few. Meanwhile, he told friends that he hated meadows and fled trees. The single tulip in his atelier was artificial, and he told a reporter that even its leaves were whitewashed in order to avoid 'the hideous green of nature'. In one of his guarded comments on his single-flower studies, he said (out of the side of his mouth, one imagines), 'Naturalistic flowers are for children and the feminine spirit.'[24]

Nonetheless, for all that, just look at his chrysanthemums (1908–9 and early 1920s), amaryllises (1907–9), blue lilies (1908), lily (after 1921) and roses (1908–10, and after 1921): sensuous, carnal, even erotic. (Interestingly, though, they are not explicitly sexual in the way that Georgia O'Keefe's flowers are. Mondrian's almost make hers feel like they have been used to make a point.) It is virtually impossible to see Mondrian's flowers and not be reminded of the human body, not as a symbol but in terms of what all bodies, human and flower alike, share: coming into being, growing and flourishing, then ageing, decaying, and dying. Yet at the same time, as per the true lineaments of enchantment, they are undeniably, delicately, inwardly spiritual.

There is a Symbolist element in these paintings, but corrected by the empiricist's adherence to observable material forms. Likewise, there is an empiricism, but supplemented by the Symbolist's loyalty to the spiritual meanings inherent in form. In this work Mondrian understood the principle whereby, in the words of the writer Yasunari Kawabata, 'The single flower contains more brightness than a hundred flowers.'[25] (Which, incidentally, is why his flower studies are more enchanting than Klimt's meadows, charming though the latter may be.)

As William Empson once remarked, 'Life involves maintaining oneself between contradictions', and this was Mondrian's solution to the contradiction in which he evidently was caught. I throw no stones. But the dynamics of that solution precisely and invaluably illustrate the collective contradiction of enchantment and modern art, particularly in relation to modernism. As David Shapiro, their chronicler and collector, writes:

> The flowers of Mondrian have been triply neglected, by the artist, by his critics, by the public. No one who knows them is not entranced by them, but all reject them as minor, fragile, or sentimental when they are seen through the mediating blinders of theory and ideology. The flowers themselves survive.[26]

Kandinsky

Wassily Kandinsky arrived at his version of abstraction by a somewhat different route. Despite the shared commitment to increasingly nonfigurative painting, Kandinsky was not strongly influenced by Cubism. He identified his sources rather as 'Cézanne's paintings and late Fauvism, particularly the work of Matisse.'[27] Deeply impressed by one of Monet's glowing grain stacks when he saw it in Moscow in 1896, he was also inspired by Arnold Schoenberg, whom he praised as 'almost alone in abandoning conventional beauty and in sanctioning every means of expression'.[28] One of his last partly figurative pictures was *Impression III (Concert)* in 1911, the concert being one by Schoenberg.

Kandinsky was a founder member of the influential Blue Rider group, along with Franz Marc. He invited Matisse to contribute to the group's almanac for 1912 but the latter refused, saying that he was not a writer. (The unspoken rebuke is unmistakable.) Kandinsky himself never shied away from large theoretical statements, most notably *On the Spiritual in Art* (1911). Like that of Mondrian, Kandinsky's art cannot be understood without reference to his Theosophy, together with the implications as he saw them for art.

Not surprisingly, with this idealist provenance, Kandinsky sought a pure and universal art which showed 'the inner essence of things' and required 'a rejection of the external, the accidental.'[29] In a modernising Platonism that is by now familiar, form is merely 'the outer expression of the inner content', and 'the soul of the object can be heard at its strongest through [i.e. without] its shell because tasteful outer beauty can no longer be a distraction.'[30]

Kandinsky's spiritualism thus functioned in the same way as Mondrian's, impelling him towards a disembodied and disembedded abstraction. We see again that the search for abstract universal principles disenchants, whether they are underlying and material or overarching and spiritual. Reduction 'up' is still reductive, disrespecting the precise integrity of lived life. *A fortiori*, such a demand destroys the enchanted moments/ place when life is lived most intensely, which is to say, in liminal terms: that which is in between, neither altogether one nor the other, or both.

Kandinsky's most enchanting paintings date from 1908–12 when he was living in Murnau, especially the 'Improvisation' series. They emanate meaning, with radiant colours and forms sufficiently definite to recognise as such but sufficiently undefined by context as to invite in the imagination. (Those that portray another world, with mysterious but obviously angelic figures, remind me of Doris Lessing's strange but compelling Shikasta novels.) In comparison, the abstracts after about 1915 feel self-conscious, arbitrary items of little inherent interest, and the glowing colours too have diminished.

Kandinsky differed from Mondrian and Malevitch in remaining a kind of romantic idealist, a quality which resurfaced in the emotional dramas of Abstract Expressionism. By the same token, even his nonfigurative paintings retain a kind of life, motion and energy that Mondrian denied to his own, and are thus not unlike Pollock's. His abstracts offer little purchase to the senses, however, and their quasi-organic forms aren't enough to overcome the feeling of being conscripted into an artistic theory. That applies equally to a couple of closely related movements in art at the same time, Dada and Surrealism.

Surrealism and Magritte

Dada began in Zurich in 1916, soon spreading to other European capitals. Marcel Duchamp was one of its initial movers. In Paris, it fed into Surrealism, where André Breton became the latter's chief spokesperson, Salvador Dalí its most famous artist, and Georges Bataille its subconscious mind – an important role, for Surrealism was strongly influenced by Freudian psychoanalysis. It could even be described as a cult of the subconscious.

In hindsight, Dada and Surrealism failed to have the impact (for better or worse) of those who either radicalised artistic conventions, such as Picasso, or abandoned them altogether, such as Mondrian. They didn't produce much enchanting art, either. As Weber points out, a programme to systematically cultivate irrationality through art is still a programme, and as such it extends intellectualisation even when the goal is creative madness.[31]

As Wallace Stevens puts it, 'The essential fault of Surrealism is that it invents without discovering.' Metaphor invents as it discovers and discovers what it invents. 'To make a clam play the accordion,' he adds, 'is to invent not to discover.'[32] Salvador

Dalí's paintings are a good example of deliberate irrationalism, abetted by raging egotism. The result is as far from enchantment as the driest rationalism. (Interestingly, Dalí is a hero to Jeff Koons, the emperor of orgiastic commercial kitsch.)[33]

There were exceptions to this truth about Surrealism: Leonora Carrington, splendidly, Max Ernst, erratically, and René Magritte, especially. Magritte deliberately mixed the possible and the impossible, the real and the fantastical, in order to open a gap between them and invite enchantment in. To that end he discovered for himself the same principle as Monet had in his reflections and doubled reflections of other worlds, metaphorically connecting what in the disenchanted world are contraries, in such paintings as the series from the 1950s, entitled *The Empire of Lights*, of a night-time landscape under a daytime sky.

His practice thus deliberately accomplished a phenomenon described by Oakeshott, namely that usual images which are encountered out of their normal context, or have been rendered ambiguous, are thereby potentially enchanting. 'Indeed, any practical image which, from the unfamiliar circumstances of its appearance, induces wonder may open a door upon the world of contemplation, so long as wonder does not pass into curiosity (*scientia*).'[34]

That Magritte himself understood and highly valued enchantment is perfectly clear. Only someone who did could have remarked that 'The only painting worth looking at has the same raison d'etre as the raison d'etre of the world – mystery.'[35] Furthermore, mystery 'is not to be confused with a sort of problem, however hard to solve', adding that 'The world and its mystery are inseparable.'[36] (Every disenchantment starts with the belief that the two can – indeed, must – be separated.) Therefore, 'Progress is a preposterous notion.'[37] And in further evidence of Magritte's distance from modernism, he asserts that

> our minds have been warped: we think that if life is seen in a tragic light, it is seen more clearly, and that we are then in touch with the mystery of existence. We even believe that we can reach this objectivity ... The greater the terror, the greater the objectivity. This notion is the result of philosophies (materialist or idealist) that claim that the real world is knowable ...[38]

Magritte thus rejects scientific determinism, 'but I don't believe in chance either. It serves as still another "explanation" of the world.'[39]

He also denies a central tenet of the Surrealism with which he is sometimes lazily identified: 'I have never dreamt of pictures to be painted ... I cannot "see" a picture unless I am fully awake, and have, moreover, perfect presence of mind. I do not have that presence of mind when I am asleep.'[40] W.H. Auden would have agreed: 'Whatever useful functions it may perform, nothing could be less like a work of art than a dream.'[41]

Duchamp: Into the Abyss

The contrast between enchanting art and much of the other modern art on offer makes some discussion of it unavoidable. Faced with a factory-line reproduction of a portrait of a film star or mass murderer, a self-portrait of the artist mugging in expensive *flagrante delicto*, a mutilated mannikin, a life-sized pickled shark, or a painting of a flayed torso, does anyone actually find these enchanting? I don't mean falsely enchanting (the desire to possess it, or possibly be possessed by it), but truly? And not only moving – the realisation of imagined horror, perhaps – but wondrous, delightful, joyous? Perhaps; it's a funny old world. Given the nature of the work, however, it is more likely they are having some other kind of experience.

Conceptual art is incontestably modernist. To quote one of its practitioners, Michael Craig-Martin, it seeks 'to create the nexus of art in the idea, in effect proposing the dematerialization [of] the object.'[42] (So much for concrete magic.) But we do have a first-hand account of such art apparently enchanting someone. When Peter Schjeldahl, an art critic, encountered some bricks lying on the floor of a New York gallery in 1966, a thought halted him in his tracks: 'What if it is art?'

> Scarcely daring to hope for anything so wonderful (I may have held my breath), I asked a person in the gallery and was assured that, yes, this was a show of sculpture by Carl Andre. I was ecstatic. I perused the bricks with a feeling of triumph … With them at my feet as I walked around the gallery, accumulating views, I felt my awkward self-consciousness, physical and psychological, being valorised … here, at last, was the purely and cleanly existing heart of the matter.[43]

These bricks are indistinguishable from, although not identical to, those purchased by the Tate Gallery in 1976 and shown under the pretentious title 'Equivalent VIII'. The resulting controversy (possibly combined with an atavistic English fondness for bricks inherited from the Victorians) led to gratifying levels of publicity and numbers of bemused visitors.

Schjeldahl is a likable and perceptive critic. Upon closer examination, though, it is clear that he was not experiencing enchantment, with its wildness and recursive relationality and the humility they engender. He was not moved by the bricks themselves, nor did they present themselves to him; he had to be told what they were ('a work of art'), and what he found moving was not their sensuous or mysterious reality but the idea of art (largely Marcel Duchamp's) that they passively represented. As a result he felt triumphant, vindicated in his theoretical view of art, with his self-consciousness not disappearing but 'valorised', that is, with his ego reinforced.

The bricks business, and much else, can be traced back to Marcel Duchamp. If I describe him as modern art's evil genius, I don't deny the validity of the last term. The scabrous contempt for art expressed in his 'readymade art' culminated with Fountain, an inverted urinal, which he devised and exhibited in New York in 1917. On the deadening effect of programmatic intellectualism on art I have said enough, but it is worth mentioning that Duchamp wanted to restore art to 'the service of the mind', instead of 'something that appealed to the eye', thus aptly invoking the ghost of Cézanne rebuking Monet. He described his own mind (with satisfaction) as 'Cartesian', and called tradition a 'prison'.[44]

Revealingly, when asked (in 1922) for his views on photography, Duchamp replied that 'I would like to see it make people despise painting until something else will make photography unbearable.'[45] Isn't this hatred of art straightforward nihilism, fed by the Gnostic/ Platonic fear of, and contempt for, embodied life?

The cheek of Duchamp's *Fountain* is admirable but the joke long ago became stale, along with the tiresome desire to shock. The underlying message of readymades – that everything is art, if the artist says it is (and anyone can call themselves an artist, by the same logic) – is inseparable from the accompanying message that nothing is, and no one really is. And without concrete precision there is no mystery, just as without distinctions there are no relationships; so both prerequisites for enchantment are eliminated. In other words, readymade art is inherently disenchanted. And being therefore biddable, that suits the art market very well. The high theorisation of art both facilitates and sanctifies its gross commodification.

Readymades also inspired conceptual art, which aspires to the bloodless purity of the idea alone, together with some installation art, and their tendency to disdain the integrity of materials and the practices of craftsmanship, painting included. As I mentioned earlier, there is a quiet creative enchantment in woodturning, furniture-making, spinning and weaving, pottery, engraving, calligraphy, jewellery, quilting, bookbinding and couture that is equally to be found in the best art, but that the expensive and pretentious vulgarity of much of today's high art will never know.

But let me clarify a point. My argument is that Duchamp (along with his acolyte John Cage) was a bitter and brilliant enemy of art *tout court*. That includes abstract art, whether that of Mondrian and Kandinsky or Pollock (whose raw emotionality repelled him). Artists such as Picasso and Bacon, however, although they shared Duchamp's modernist hostility to enchantment, were not. Duchamp took arbitrariness to its ultimate conclusion and thereby opened the door to the now regnant art market, but as Josipovici says, Picasso drew back and asserted his right, as a great individual artist, to overcome arbitrariness.[46] That Picasso ended his artistic life imitating himself is, in this context, neither here nor there.

One of Duchamp's offspring was the avowedly commercial art of Andy Warhol, produced in his studio he named The Factory (motto: 'good business is the best art'). Indeed, it is no exaggeration to say that Warholism is neoliberalism as a theory of art.[47] Warhol, who started as a commercial artist working in advertising, commodified everything he could, starting with himself. He was fascinated by, and encouraged, the process whereby someone's image first occupied and then consumed the living person, like a caterpillar by parasitoid wasp hatchlings. Combining the worst of both elite high art and vulgar populist art – something he facilitated by destroying the difference – the result was very profitably marketed. It still is. Thanks to the monetarised art market he himself did so much to create, Warhol's *Silver Car Crash* sold in 2013 for $104.5 million. But what exactly does that measure? I can think of a few things, but enchantment isn't one of them.

Warhol in turn, together with Duchamp and Bacon, strongly influenced and paved the way for Damien Hirst.[48] And the effects of Duchamp's patrician populism continue. Will Gompertz recently described Hirst as 'one of the greatest exponents of creative thinking today.'[49] When asked why he replied, 'because of the way he's responded to the art market. He's definitely entrepreneurial.' In the same interview, he also delivered this fatuous aperçu: 'We are all artists. We just have to believe it.' That takes some believing alright, so let's work up to it by trying to believe that the BBC made Gompertz its Arts Editor.

Of course, if Hirst didn't exist, he would have had to have been invented. A foul-mouthed brutalist whose grotesque self-pity has survived extravagant wealth (c. $384 million) – the reward of an art world run by business – he draws on Warhol's corporate nihilism and Bacon's cruelty and self-loathing, with some of Picasso's macho swagger but none of his talent. With his rotting fly-blown cadavers and diamond-encrusted platinum skull, Hirst is surely the ultimate modernist magician of art. Inseparably, he is also indeed its most successful entrepreneur. His career was kick-started by Charles Saatchi, the charming author of *Be the Worst You Can Be: Life's Too Long for Patience and Virtue* (2012), who made a fortune in the advertising industry and used it to promote the 'Young British Artists' throughout the 1990s. Old hat now, you might think, but they are now among the grandees of British art, and no new movement – certainly none that contradicts their values – has since arisen.

By 2008, to quote *The Guardian*'s sycophantically admiring report, 'A month on from that £111m auction at Sotheby's, Damien Hirst and Science, his own production and marketing company, have made it to the top slot in the new ArtReview Power 100'. Hirst's themes pretty much exhaust the disenchanted possibilities: power, money (a form of power), the body as pure object, and death as necessarily nullity, thus impelling nihilism.

The permanently adolescent desire to shock exemplified by Gilbert and George emerged from the same nihilistic stable. If nothing is in fact sacred, then iconoclasm becomes a crypto-sacred duty. Hence *Naked Shit Pictures*, and so predictably on.

Schjeldahl has said of Jeff Koons, the master of porno-kitsch, that 'His majestic baubles are carefully empty-minded monuments of and to the global impunity of sheer wealth. To dismiss them, you'd need to get into a time machine and redirect the course of present history.'[50] But that's exactly, not what enchantment is – it's more an anti-time … what's the opposite of a machine? Angel, perhaps, or god – but that is what enchantment does! For as long as it lasts, enchantment suspends time and with it, history. If you stand before a painting transfixed, then its historical development and context, what the artist was trying to do or reacting against, the various movements beginning with capital letters, all the reasons why painting is now of negligible importance or, for that matter, why it isn't – in short, everything beloved of critical intellectuals – vanishes. That includes any knowledge that has helped you into the frame, so to speak.

Thus the mega-rich modernists may have divided up the artistic spoils, and painting itself may have long been superseded, but at that moment you find yourself in a tiny painting by Samuel Palmer, say, that glows with a sourceless inner light, coming home from church under a huge Moon. And there's plenty of room in there.[51]

Modernism has led to the disenchantment of visual art in another crucial way. The process was already underway in the nineteenth century, but by desacralising art more radically than ever before, modernists directly contributed to its make-over as a commodity, a product in an turbo-charged art market that increasingly resembles the private equity market of the 1980s and hedge funds in the '90s.[52] As the relations between corporate donors, museum curators, gallery owners, wealthy collectors, art dealers, auction-house directors, celebrity artists and modernist critics have become increasingly cosy, enchantment – wild wonder, not power, and intrinsic value, not market price – has almost vanished from the mainstream of the art world, and is increasingly to be found only on the margins.

In 2003, Dinos Chapman was asked what the artistic justification was for defacing and then selling some etchings by Goya. His reply says everything you need to know about the disenchantment of art in the modern art market: 'You can't vandalize something by making it more expensive.'[53] So vandalism is okay as long as it pays, and you think money is the ultimate arbiter of value. But maybe it was ever thus. On the other hand, it is implausible that the ratio of enchantment to disenchantment never varies. Overall, I think the latter has definitely increased over the past hundred years, not only in the visual arts but all of them, with enchantment accordingly more fugitive, elusive, and invaluable.

In sum, then, modernist art, which has dominated much of the art since the early twentieth century, is not incidentally disenchanted but systematically so. Being about, as well as based on, power-knowledge and the supremacy of the human and particularly male will, it is actively hostile to enchantment and its roots. Especially its mystery, which they cannot control or abide. And money being today's most potent form of power, unless you are among society's 1% and therefore a potential buyer, its servants really don't care what you think.

I Remember Looking

John Ruskin was a great defender of artistic enchantment, from the beauty of curved lines as against straight to the value of ornament – bitterly attacked by Otto Wagner, Adolf Loos, Le Corbusier, and other leading modernists – as that part of labour which resisted reduction to practical necessity, and therefore the demands of economics.[54] How much more oppositional than the Marxists' admiration for the capitalism they hoped to build on and exceed!

Ruskin also eulogised seeing. 'The greatest thing a human soul ever does in this world is to see something, and tell what it saw in a plain way. Hundreds of people can talk for one who can think, but thousands think for one who can see. To see clearly is poetry, prophecy, and religion, all in one.'[55]

To see one must first look. He would have liked Wittgenstein's advice for how to get something out of an exhibition: 'Walk into a room, select one picture which attracts you, look at it for as long as you want to, then come away and don't look at anything else. If you try to see everything you will see nothing.'[56]

In recent years, doing this has become steadily more difficult. One reason is egregious overcrowding as a result of galleries' greed in packing in punters, rather than limiting access and enabling people to be viewers, and indeed participants. Another is the audio guides telling you what you are looking at in details that completely fill the available mental space, thereby cutting off at the knees any possibility of a direct encounter.

A third reason is the licence smartphones apparently give people to snap – usually that acme of contemporary egoism, a selfie, with the painting as background, if you please – and move on without really looking, let alone seeing. In the context of a museum or art gallery, why do they bother going? The images are all online, after all. So is it some kind of unconscious admission that the artefact in question has a presence 'in the flesh' which cannot be replaced by a pixelated reproduction? If so, they immediately betray that truth.

On 13 June 2015, I was looking at Van Eyck's *Arnolfini Wedding* in The National Gallery in London, standing slightly off-centre so as not to hog the painting. After about ten minutes, a security guard came over and told me to get out of the way of visitors who wished to take a photograph of it, as I was obstructing them and had been standing there long enough. I enquired of the management whether it was now their official policy to allow (if not encourage) taking photographs of the paintings to take precedence over actually looking at them.

The reply from a 'Visitor Engagement Assistant' (VEA, doubtless) denied there was a time limit for how long someone is able to view a painting and explained that 'The decision to relax the rule on photography was taken so that we are able to accommodate the new ways in which our visitors wish to interact [sic] with the collection.' But couldn't there be some attempt to remind members of the public that in concentrating on what they can see on their little electronic screens, they are sacrificing a precious opportunity to engage now with the sole original? And for what? A mechanical reproduction, viewed later, which is inferior in every way and which they can obtain and look at almost anywhere else. In other words, a souvenir of something they didn't really see in the first place.

As it is, the supposed guardians of art are collaborating with the process of converting it from potential unique subjects, with whom a relationship and therefore enchantment is possible, into a series of essentially identical objects. 'Betrayal' doesn't seem too strong a word.

Enchantment, Fate, and Modernity in a Bridge

Ivon Hitchins found the elusive middle ground of figurative abstraction early on in life, and he spent his career deepening and developing it. He shared significant common ground with the better-known Continental painters defending enchantment. Like Monet and Matisse, for example, Hitchins believed that 'theorizing is very dangerous for creative artists', and insisted that 'It is a painter's job to paint ideas about what he sees, not to paint ideas about ideas.' He linked his pictures rather with the experience of music: they are 'painted to be listened to' as they unfold visually, followed as they flow through the viewer's time, just as they did through the painter's.[57]

On 14 September 2019, I took a day trip from London to Chichester to see an exhibition of paintings by Hitchins. I had a persistent feeling that there was something waiting for me, and sure enough, as I turned the corner into one of the rooms, there it was: *Iron Bridge Over the Rother* (1966). It reached out and pulled me in, even while I remained in a room in a provincial (but excellent) art gallery. Time instantly slowed, and tears started. I'm sure Hitchins's bridge bears the same relationship to the 'real' iron bridge as Bonnard's paradisiacal portal does to a provincial French bathroom.

So what happened? Surely the artist imaginatively apprehended the 'lining and depth' of that place, and had the will and skill to present it to us transformed into what it could be. Note too that in grasping that enchanted reality, the viewer engages in the same process as did the artist, perceiving not only the daubs and swirls of paint on canvas but *their* lining and depth; and that takes the viewer of the painting into the same place and moment the artist was in when painting it.

Afterwards, I was aware of not being quite the same person I had been. Add the distinct feeling of being called to that gallery by the painting, and the fatefulness of radical enchantment is evident. I can't 'explain' that, but isn't explanation so much whistling in the dark anyway, as Nietzsche saw? And the common concept of fate, which inspires such unease, is a misunderstanding in any case. Fate is not what moderns imagine: a blind and pitiless determinism imposed by external forces. Rather, as Heraclitus (in one translation) puts it, character is fate. What one does with one's character is not altogether captured by that character, so what actually eventuates is the result of an ongoing negotiation with your fate. And in that relationship, fate often makes suggestions, as it did that day. (It can also make you an offer that is very difficult to refuse.)

A.E. Housman, in a letter quoted by Auden, tells this story of a bravura performance, during a public lecture, by John Ruskin in 1877:

> This afternoon Ruskin gave us a great outburst against modern times. He had got a picture of Turner's, framed and glassed, representing Leicester and the Abbey in the distance at sunset, over a river … Then he said, 'You, if you like, may go to Leicester to see what it is like now. I never shall. But I can make a pretty good guess.' Then he caught up a paintbrush. 'These stepping-stones have of course been done away with, and are replaced by a be–au–ti–ful iron bridge.' Then he dashed in the iron bridge on the glass of the picture. 'The colour of the stream is supplied on one side by the indigo factory.' Forthwith one side of the stream became indigo. 'On the other side by the soap factory.' Soap dashed in. 'They mix in the middle – like curds,' he said, working them together with a sort of malicious deliberation. 'This field, over which you see the sun setting by the Abbey, is now occupied in a proper manner.' Then there went a flame of scarlet across the picture, which developed itself into windows and roofs and red brick, and rushed up into a chimney. 'The

atmosphere is supplied – thus!' A puff and cloud of smoke all over Turner's sky: and then the brush thrown down, and Ruskin confronting modern civilisation amidst a tempest of applause.[58]

But Turner himself was, of course, enchanted by many modern artefacts, including both steam trains and railway bridges. And I was enchanted by a painting of one of the iron bridges Ruskin hated – and not without reason – as a mechanical artefact of industrial modernity!

Of course, it's good to be reminded that what is modern can enchant – although even then, one is having a thoroughly non-modern experience (wonder, not will or mastery; stopped in one's tracks, not matter in ever faster motion; and so on). But there is another reason to tread carefully when drawing conclusions, because Ruskin wasn't altogether wrong. Retrieving wonder from the wreck of the world as it is made over by the modern Megamachine is consoling, but it is no reason to celebrate that process uncritically, as modernists are wont to do. Of course, we should value much of the progress in medicine, hygiene, dentistry, and so on, which has accompanied industrialisation. But as Carl Jung points out, in a disturbing *aperçu*, 'Everything new worth having is paid for by the loss of something worth keeping.' And too often, that loss is of a source of deep enchantment.

But I take heart, and others might, from the fact that enchantment remains, in the words of Etel Adnan, 'vulnerable and indestructible'.[59] As George Mackay Brown realised in the Orkney Islands, 'The ancient magical ceremonial quality of art makes it profoundly suspect to all puritans, hedonists, humanists, democrats, pragmatists, rationalists, progressives; and nowadays nearly everyone fits into one or other of these categories.' In music, dance, and poetry, no less than in their bread and ale, the islanders 'recognised that they were in the presence of a mystery and that they themselves were part of it.'[60]

Notes

1 Flam, *Matisse*: 9.
2 Flam, *Matisse*: 260.
3 Ben Lerner, 'Damage Control: The modern art world's tyranny of price', *Harper's Magazine* (Dec. 2013) pp. 43–49: 43.
4 Gamboni, *Potential*: 214.
5 Wendy Woon: 'Behind the Frame: Picasso, Barack and Me' (18.1.10): http://www.moma.org/explore/inside_out/2010/01/18/behind-the-frame-picasso-barack-and-me (accessed 19.4.13).
6 Josipovici, *Modernism*: 187.
7 Rachman, *Monet*: 293.
8 Stevens, *Necessary*: 174.
9 Spalding, *Eclipse*: 63.
10 Ross King, *Defiant Spirits: The Modernist Revolution of the Group of Seven* (Vancouver: Douglas & McIntyre, 2010): 72.
11 Charles Harrison, *Modernism* (London: Tate Publishing, 1997): 49–50.
12 See my *Enchantment*: 112–118.
13 William Boyd: 'The mean reds', *The Guardian* (12.12.09): 12.

14 Adrian Searle, *The Guardian* (9.1.01): 12.
15 Derek Mahon, *Olympia and the Internet* (Loughcrew: Gallery Press, 2017): 78.
16 Herbert Read, *A Concise History of Modern Painting*, 2nd edn (London: Thames and Hudson, 1968): 198–200.
17 Susanne Deicher, *Mondrian 1987–1944: Structures in Space* (Köln: Taschen, 2010): epigraph.
18 *RA Magazine* (Winter 2011): 29.
19 David Shapiro, *Mondrian: Flowers* (New York: Harry N. Abrams, 1991): 28.
20 Gaston Bachelard, *The Poetics of Space*, transl. Maria Jolas (Boston: Beacon Press, 1969): 232.
21 Horkheimer and Adorno, *Dialectic*: 5.
22 A point I owe to Liz Greene, with thanks.
23 See Harry Cooper, 'Mondrian, Hegel, Boogie', *October 84* (Spring, 1998), pp. 118–142; with thanks to Stone Fitzgerald.
24 Shapiro, *Flowers*: 13, 25, 13.
25 Kawabata: Nobel Prize address, 12.12.68.
26 Shapiro, *Flowers*: 10.
27 Hajo Düchting, *Wassily Kandinsky 1866–1944: A Revolution in Painting* (Köln: 1991): 86.
28 Read, *History*: 171.
29 Harrison, *Modernism*: 48.
30 Wassily Kandinsky and Franz Marc (eds), *The Blaue Reiter Almanac*, ed. Klaus Lankheit (London: Thames and Hudson, 1974 [1912]): 149, 161–62.
31 See Gane, *Weber*.
32 Stevens, *Collected Poetry*: 919.
33 *The Guardian* (30.6.09): G2, p.9.
34 Oakeshott, *Poetry*: 515.
35 René Magritte, "Letter to Alphonse Waelhens" (28.4.62), in Galen A. Johnson (ed.), *The Merleau-Ponty Aesthetics Reader* (Evanston: Northwestern University Press, 1993): 336.
36 René Magritte, *Selected Writings*, ed. K. Rooney and E. Plattner and tranl. J. Levy (Richmind: Alma Books, 2017): 204.
37 Harry Torczyner, *Magritte: Ideas and Images* (New York: Harry N. Abrams, 1977): 25.
38 Magritte, *Selected*, 202.
39 John Berger, *Selected Essays*, ed. Geoff Dyer (London: Bloomsbury, 2001): 347.
40 Magritte, *Selected*, 202.
41 Auden, *Prose* vol. 6, 578.
42 Michael Craig-Martin, *On Being an Artist* (London: Art Books Publ. Ltd., 2015): n.p.
43 Spalding, *Eclipse*: 67.
44 Calvin Tomkins, *Marcel Duchamp: The Afternoon Interviews* (Brooklyn: Badlands Unlimited, 2013): 13, 64, 83.
45 Josipovici, *Modernism*: 138.
46 Josipovici, *Modernism*: 119–21.
47 'Neoliberalism is simply Warholism as a theory of governance': Stephen Metcalf, 'Warhol's Bleak Prophecy', 122–24 in *Analog Sea Review* 2 (2019) 122.
48 On Hirst, see excellent pieces by Hari Kunzru, 'The value of banality', *The Guardian* (17.3.12) and Peter Schjeldahl, 'Spot On', *The New Yorker* (23.1.12): 84–85.
49 *The Evening Standard* (15.7.15): 20.
50 Peter Schjeldahl, 'Going Pop', *The New Yorker* (24.10.12): 95.
51 The painting I am thinking of is 'Coming from Evening Church' (1830).
52 On the art market, see Robin Pogrebin and Kevin Flynn, 'As Art Values Rise, So Do Concerns about Market's Oversight', *New York Times* (27.1.13), with thanks to Clay Ramsay for this reference; and Felix Salmon, 'Occupy Art' (19.11.12), http://blogs. reuters.com/felix-salmon/2012/11/19/occupy-art/
53 Ben Lerner, 'Damage Control: The modern art world's tyranny of price', *Harper's Magazine* (Dec. 2013) pp. 43–49: 48.

54 See P.D. Anthony, *John Ruskin's Labour: A study of Ruskin's social theory* (Cambridge: Cambridge University Press, 1984); and in relation to art, Peter Fuller, *Theoria. Art, and the Absence of Grace* (London: Chatto & Windus, 1988).

55 John Ruskin, *Modern Painters* (1856), Vol. 3, Part 4, chapter 12.

56 Rush Rhees, *Recollections of Wittgenstein* (Oxford University Press, 1984): 118.

57 Peter Khoroche, *Ivon Hitchins* (Farnham: Lund Humphries, 2009): 78, 165, 161.

58 Henry Maas, *The Letters of A.E. Houseman* (Harvard University Press, 1972), quoted in Auden, Prose, vol. 6: 498.

59 From a notice next to one of her paintings in an exhibition in Basle in 2017.

60 George Mackay Brown, *An Orkney Tapestry* (London: Victor Gollancz, 1972): 142, 143.

5
MUSIC I

Let's start with a story. Here is an account, by Laura Barton, of musical enchantment:

> … we sat there a long while, talking and drinking, and listening to the music of the street – to the shouts in the night and the chatter of the bugs and the bursts of distant car radios and, from somewhere up above, the sound of Django Reinhardt playing 'I'll See You in My Dreams' … And whenever I think of it now, it seems wound up in the song I was playing a lot, and that drifted out of the open window and up into the warm Oregon air … It offers not a giddy, tumbling happiness, but that glorious feeling that rises up after rain, a serene kind of happiness that is also somehow in possession of a peculiar near-sadness …
>
> I listen to this record, and I know precisely where I am – I can see the soft blue-green colour of that porch, the number of steps it took to get there from the sidewalk, the sweetness of the peach-flesh and the scent of the trees; I can even hear the lyrics I knew were absent from Django Reinhardt's version of 'I'll See You in My Dreams' …[1]

A perfect, dangerously ripe happiness that is attended by near-sadness, which is what the song that is playing articulates; the entanglement of the song with the place; the full engagement of the senses – sound, colours, smell, taste – with something ineffable that transcends them … even peaches, one of Aphrodite's fruits: it's all here.

But there are other kinds of musical enchantment. The pianist Jeremy Denk tells of when he was wrestling with how to play Charles Ives's *Piano Trio*:

> One afternoon, the violinist of the group and I were driving off campus and happened to cross the Connecticut River. Looking out of the window, he

DOI: 10.4324/9781003353225-5

said, 'You should play it like that.' From the bridge the river seemed impossibly wide, and instead of a single current there seemed to be a million intersecting currents – urgent and lazy rivers within the river, magical pockets of no motion at all. The late-afternoon light colored the water pink and orange and gold. It was the most beautiful, patient, meandering multiplicity. Instantly, I knew how to play the piece.[2]

This description too resonates with almost every dynamic of enchantment: multiplicity, motion, relationality and, these being all under the aegis of Hermes, mythicity, plus the visual effects of light playing on water, the arrestedness of enchantment ('magic pockets of no motion') and this time the colours of Aphrodite. Marvellously, there is also animist agency: the enchanted place itself, in an act of spontaneous divination, instructs the person who is looking for help. That too can happen.

As the pianist Susan Tomes, puts it: 'music is a gift, even for the giver.'[3] That is something it shares with all forms of genuine enchantment. Jordi Savall, who resurrected the viol, a Renaissance stringed instrument, says that 'When I started to play the viol, there was no model for me to learn from – the tradition has been dead for over two hundred years.' So how did he proceed? 'Instead of learning from other players, I learned how to play the instrument from the music itself, from the viol repertoire. Slowly the music told me what to do.'[4]

Tools for Understanding

The starting point for this enquiry into enchantment in music is a double acknowledgement. First, there is the impossibility, to which Wittgenstein plaintively alludes, of capturing music in words: 'It is impossible for me to say in my book one word about all that music has meant to me in my life; how then can I possibly make myself understood?'[5]

But we have already encountered this stricture concerning enchantment in general. ('*Faërie* cannot be caught in a net of words; for it is one of its qualities to be indescribable, though not imperceptible', as Tolkien says.)[6] So it is not unique to music, although it might be doubly so for enchanting music. But thoroughly understanding and accepting this warning can actually be liberating, because then we can discuss it without any illusions of owning or exhausting it.

The second thing that needs to be acknowledged lies in the question: is life without music actually worth living? Whether the answer is yes or no, the question itself is entirely valid. Many people feel as Anthony Storr does, that 'Music has incomparably enriched my life. It is an irreplaceable, undeserved, transcendental blessing.'[7] Or a character from a novel by Vikram Seth: 'It is enough, it is to be blessed enough, to live from day-to-day and to hear such music – not too much, or the soul could not sustain it – from time to time.'[8] Quite so, and if we combine these two points into an awareness of the impossibility of capturing in words or concepts one of the things that arguably makes life worth living, we are probably safe to start.

The violinist Christian Tetzlaff said, 'I find that music is humans' most advanced achievement, more so than painting and writing, because it's more mysterious, more magical, and it acts in such a direct way.'[9] And although the arts are not a competition, I suspect he's right. This is presumably what Walter Pater meant by his famous remark that 'All art constantly aspires towards the condition of music.' But in order to understand the enchantment of music there are certain things about music that we need to know first.

Music is both ancient and ubiquitous. A bone flute discovered in the Swabian Jura is approximately 40,000 years old, and song, although we have no way of knowing for sure, is probably much older. There are no known human societies without it. However deep and dark its roots, though, and however distinctive it is, music is certainly one of the arts. That may seem blindingly obvious but as we shall see, there have been attempts to define music as merely one kind of sound, or 'sound effect', with no distinction allowed between musical tones and noise except their subjective apprehension. That, I shall argue, is a good way to destroy what is unique to music while leaving noise untouched.

It is significant, by the way, that the flute's holes are clearly arranged in a pentatonic scale. As the musicologist Bob Fink observes, 'This is powerful evidence that the do–re–mi scale has a natural foundation' – rooted in both the human body and in acoustics – 'and is not just an arbitrary set of notes constructed by composers.'[10]

Another obvious point that nonetheless needs stating is that just as the first demand of a picture is 'Look!', that of music is 'Listen!'[11] I mean open up to it, give yourself over to it, suspend everything else for now. It is remarkable how many people don't. Or, depending on how you look at it, how many people still do.

Music is a temporal art. Duration in time is essential to it, even if it is insufficient in itself, and even if it works in ways that cannot be identified with time as it is measured. So too, as we shall see, is motion – although again, not in any way that be quantified or directly observed. For whatever else it does, music moves. But what else is indispensable for understanding musical enchantment? We are not engaged in music theory, nor acoustics, nor psychology, nor even aesthetics, but certain concepts are helpful: melody, harmony, and timbre in particular.

There is another more general issue at stake: what is the place of theory at all? Wittgenstein, for example, is not altogether encouraging: 'When a theme, a phrase, suddenly says something to you, you don't have to be able to explain it to yourself. Suddenly this gesture too is accessible to you …'[12] Certainly you do not need to know any of the disciplines I just mentioned in order to be enchanted by a piece of music. We might want to think about it, though, or discuss it, and it is surely possible to do so in ways that respect the integrity of the experience.

In what follows, I am going to explore the dynamics of enchantment that seem to be specific to music, or at least emphasised, before considering disenchanted music. As usual, the contrast is revealing. I shall concentrate on specific genres of music in the following chapter, and since this book is a personal account, not encyclopaedic, I will only discuss those with which I am relatively familiar. The absence of your favourite genre or musician therefore does not necessarily imply a negative value-judgement ('What, nothing on post-acid-house techno-paganism?').[13]

Of the resulting absences, maybe the most obvious is opera. I recognise that opera is deeply enchanting for some, even if it often strays rather into the Dionysian. (Wagner is surely the ultimate musical Dionysus.) I am temperamentally averse to spectacle, however, so to me most opera is a closed book.

By the same token, I prefer, and find more enchanting, chamber music than orchestral. And that isn't merely a subjective preference, although it is a personal one. As Wittgenstein points out, 'You could play a minuet once and get a lot out of it, and play the same minuet another time and get nothing out of it. But it doesn't follow that what you get out of it is then independent of the minuet.'[14]

Like all works of art, musical compositions and performances thus have their own qualities and characteristics, albeit waiting to be apprehended to become fully real. For example, taking Chopin's work as emblematic of what later French chamber music developed to perfection, Richard Taruskin hails its intimate and sensitive scale as a strategy whose success 'explains why in Schumann, Schubert, Dvorak, Brahms, the pieces of lesser size, lesser sonority, seem more alive, more beautiful (often very beautiful), than the symphonies and concertos.'[15]

I also prefer instrumental music to choral. I can't seem to hear the saving more-than-human note in the human voice; instead, I feel confined to *only* the human. On the disenchanting effect of spoken words mixed with music (less so lyrics, because they are at least integrated with the music), the subjects of Eliot's *Prufrock* poem linger with 'sea-girls wreathed with seaweed red and brown/ Till human voices wake us, and we drown'. Drowning here is the blow of disenchantment. But this is a failing, in all likelihood. So I am not arguing that instrumental music is inherently more enchanting than choral, just trying to understand the potential enchantment of instrumental music in particular. The twelfth-century Saint Hildegard is quoted in an inscription on Leonardo Da Vinci's viola organista: 'Holy prophets and scholars immersed in the sea of arts both human and divine dreamt up a multitude of instruments to delight the soul.' Amen to that!

The Uniqueness of Musical Enchantment

Visual and aural arts have a vital difference based on how they are received: you can close your eyes or look away, but you cannot do so with your ears. Thus there is a directness to music, an instant intimacy (whether welcome or not), and its effect is uniquely powerful.

The body is essential to both music's making and its hearing: the auditory apparatus, which includes not only the ear, in all its intricate complexity, but the entire nervous system via the vestibular apparatus, and in addition, for music makers, the hands, arms and so on, until you arrive again at the whole body. All of which is inseparable from sound waves, vibration and movement, part of what is aptly called acoustic ecology. And part of that is the physics of tonality and frequencies with musical instruments.

But understanding music must include – cannot avoid – how it is received and apprehended, so it will not stay in an objectivist box. Music belongs neither wholly to the 'external' world which physicists and biologists study nor wholly to the 'internal' world that is the province of psychology.

One of the most striking things about music is that it clearly comes from without, but it is encountered, from the very first moment, within. Yet even when one is remembering or imagining music, the source strikes one as somehow 'out there'. However, there is also music's ineffability and intangibility. It is not 'there' like a painting or sculpture, or even a book. Each moment of music has no sooner emerged from the void than it is already disappearing back into it.

Music is thus both natural and cultural, corporeal and mental or spiritual, all at once, and its enchantment is an elusive but vital *tertium quid*, a third thing, neither purely physical nor purely mental. Except, of course, that it is precisely not a thing but a relation across the gap between things.

It is surely the amalgam of physicality with intangibility or ineffability that most distinguishes music from other arts. And just that mingling of object and subject, as concrete magic, is one of the fundamental keys to enchantment, so with music we are already on its home ground. Evoking its liminality, the philosopher of music Victor Zuckerkandl puts it unimprovably well. Music, he says,

> rejects the claim which either world makes [on] it, the physical world and the world of the psyche; thus it extends beyond both of them in the same fashion. Music makes us aware, unmistakably and inescapably, that 'beyond the world of things and places' is not, as common belief has it, identical with the world of the psyche; nor is 'beyond the world of the psyche' identical with the world of things and places. A third stage must exist which is neither ...[16]

In this vein, a modern composer working with enchantment, to whom we shall return, was Tōru Takemitsu. He described one of his pieces, *Dream/Window*, as facing both inwards and outwards, since 'To make the inner and the outer resound simultaneously is the prime object of the music.'[17] When such an intention succeeds in the experience of a listener, the result is a realisation of enchantment as concrete magic.

These considerations resonate with D. W. Winnicott's emphasis on the liminal third place or stage, between inner and outer, as essential not only to play but all creativity.[18] In the same vein, Antonio Machado describes art as 'pure and intense play, so it is like pure and intense life.'[19] Play, like art, is a serious business. In play, the child has to be able to be and simultaneously not be a superhero or whoever, while in religion the devotee has to be able to wholeheartedly partake of divinity without succumbing to inflation, that is, while remaining fully human. Slightly more loosely, the artist too has to be able to handle both creating the work while at the same time acting as its vehicle, its instrument.

Winnicott argues that this process needs to be protected by resisting a flight to intellectualism – the same intellectualism that Weber identifies as the engine of disenchantment, and that we found Monet, Matisse, and Bonnard refusing. Instead, he says, one must accept paradox and refrain from forcing the participant, whether oneself or another, to choose between 'subjective' or 'objective', 'inner' or 'outer', 'spiritual' or 'material'. Iain McGilchrist also affirms the importance of taking 'proper trouble *not* to pin down the meaning too closely, so as to let it live – the proper rigour of ambiguity.'[20]

I had a musical experience once which seems relevant to this issue; I heard divine music. The circumstances were these. Aged 19, I was living in a house in the Palo Alto hills, and I had a rash from poison oak all over my body. (Once the oil is on your hands, it spreads by contact.) It was so painful to the touch that I couldn't wear clothes and I couldn't lie down, so I spent two days in the house upright, naked, and slathered in Calamine lotion. At dawn on the third day, perched on the end of a chair, I was playing an acoustic guitar very quietly, so as not to awaken my girlfriend, asleep in the next room, when I heard …

Well, what I still recall, more than fifty years later, is the sound of two guitars, both coming from somewhere above me, one closer, above my left ear, the other further off, above my right (and notice the quasi-spatial locatedness) whose purity of tone, and the beauty of whose interweaving lines, were beyond comprehension, let alone description. Although Proust (who else?) comes very close, when he says that the sonata overheard by Swann communicated 'an ineffable joy which seemed to come from paradise.'[21] The pioneering electronica composer Iasos was similarly inspired by what he described as 'paradise music' or 'heavenly music'.[22]

Certainly, after 48 hours without sleep I was in an altered state of consciousness, but that doesn't say anything very interesting. And no, no drugs were involved. I still don't know what it 'meant', in the way that term is usually used. I do know that there is one question, though – the obvious one – that I would refuse to answer. It's the same one Winnicott rejected: 'But Pat, did you really hear that music? Or did you just imagine it?' That is a pseudo-choice. Either of the two answers on offer would betray the experience itself, in which no such disjunction, even for a moment or to the slightest degree, was in play. And what a lot of disenchanting work is performed by that 'really', as opposed to the implied 'imaginary'!

There is quasi-repeatable music that sometimes comes close to what I heard, by the way. Mozart, obviously, as well as J.S. Bach in one of his lighter moods. And on a good night, Jerry Garcia.

'Just a Little Phrase'

An enchanting tune also haunts Charles Swann in the first volume of Proust's *In Search of Lost Time*: a 'little phrase' of just five notes from the andante of the sonata for piano and violin by his fictional composer, Vinteuil.[23] Proust's model was probably the slow movement of Gabriel Fauré's *Piano Quintet in D Minor*, and/or the second part of Camille Saint-Saëns's *Violin Sonata in D minor*. (Gabriel Pierné's *Sonata for Violin and Piano* has also been suggested.) In any case, by keeping the identity of the music fictional Proust intelligently refused the reassuring but misleading closure that would have resulted from being able to identify what it was is 'real life'. Only in that way can its potential universality be saved from being put in a precisely-delimited historical box, 'known' and then forgotten.

It is one of those musical motifs that are 'recognised only by the particular kind of pleasure which they instil, impossible to describe, to recollect, to name, ineffable'. Swann has heard it at a concert without really paying attention, but when he unexpectedly encounters the motif again, 'it was so peculiarly itself, it had so individual, so irreplaceable a charm, that Swann felt as though he had met, in a friend's drawing room, a woman whom he had seen and admired in the street and had despaired of ever seeing again. Finally the phrase receded …'[24] I don't expect to ever hear my angelic motif again, sad to say, but there doesn't seem to be a radical difference between Swann's experience and mine.

The 'little phrase' actually has three lives: first, as music heard by Proust; next, literary, embedded in the story of Swann; and finally, philosophical, as interpreted by Merleau-Ponty. Each are equally rich in their own way. Merleau-Ponty avers that 'No one has gone further than Proust in fixing the relations between the visible and the invisible, in describing an idea that is not the contrary of the sensible, that is its lining and its depth.' Ideas that enchant, he said, live 'behind the sounds or between them, behind the lights or between them'. They are (and he quotes Proust here) '"perfectly distinct from one another, unequal among themselves in value and in significance"' – never generic, mere instances, nor necessarily enchanting, let alone all equally so.

He continues, relating Proust's insight specifically to music:

> We do not possess the musical or sensible ideas, precisely because they are negativity or absence … they possess us. The performer is no longer producing or reproducing the sonata: he feels himself, and the others feel him to be, at the service of the sonata; the sonata sings through him or cries out so suddenly that he must 'dash on his bow' to follow it.[25]

This description certainly fits my own experience of music, and it accords with what we know of enchantment: finding the musical idea already in one's personal inner citadel – the humility required to be in its service rather than the performer's own – and its unbiddability. I would only add that chasing the tune need not be a highbrow phenomenon. I have heard the fiddler Dave Swarbrick trying to keep up with *Swaggering Boney*, and Martin Hayes, dashing on his bow as he followed every twist and turn of *The Crooked Road*.

Hayes is a master interpreter and transmitter of Irish traditional music. In addition to his skill, one reason is his humility; the music comes first. Less important, but helpful for my purposes, is an unusually articulate awareness of what he's doing. On the unbiddability of enchantment, for example, he says that 'to get to the essence of music, I more often spend time talking about it and hoping for it than achieving it.' (Many would dispute that but never mind.) But, he continues,

It's when I finally accept that I've completely missed the point, and that I don't really get it, that I have this moment when I get it. And of course I want to put my arms around it, I want to put it in a bottle, I want to keep it, I want to store it, I love it, and I can't. And I have to let go of it again.[26]

(Like love, then.)

The Dynamics of Musical Enchantment

There are a few terms that are especially helpful in thinking about musical enchantment. The one that seems to come closest to identifying that unmistakable but elusive spark of concrete magic is 'timbre'. Timbre is what enables us to distinguish between two notes of identical pitch, loudness, and duration – one kind of instrument from another, say – but it extends further, to that unique quality and feel that makes certain artists immediately recognisable the moment you hear them, which we also describe as 'style'. Timbre realised in a unique style announces someone in particular, not just anyone. It is thus presence, with its precision without which, as Michael Longley says, you don't get the mystery. And appropriately, timbre defies precise technical analysis. It is 'everything about a sound that is not loudness or pitch', as Daniel Levitin puts it.[27]

Another key to enchantment, relationality, is also inherent in music. It is the foundation of two essentials in Western music: melody – the relationships between successive tones – and harmony, the relationships between simultaneous tones. (That doesn't establish all such music as enchanting, of course, but only as potentially enchanting, in principle.)

One of the most distinctive things about music, which I have described as its intangibility and ineffability, is the way it has no sooner come into being than it vanishes. But notes hang in the air before dissolving; they don't disappear before finding some kind of relationship with the ones preceding and replacing them, and so on. In that sense, they are no longer there but also don't entirely disappear, remaining as a trace 'behind the sounds or between them'. It is a musical version of absent presence.

The process of succession, whether of melodic tones or in harmonic chords, is inseparable from another vital characteristic of music, namely motion. There is no question that we hear music, especially melodies, rising or falling, moving fast or slow, speeding up or lingering, coming closer or receding. Yet there is equally no question that such musical motion does not exist as physical space or its temporal equivalent. In those terms, there is nothing in music that can move. And not only doesn't it move in any literal sense, there literally is no thing there at all. Furthermore, in what sense can a tone be said to move from one pitch to another? A 'C' that becomes an 'E' is no longer a 'C', so how is it the same tone, let alone the same line of melody, that moves?

That puzzle is tied to a parallel one concerning musical narrative. As Philip Ball says, in music 'there are no characters, no dialogue, no events.' Although the imaginative apprehension of music, like that of a narrative journey, takes clock-time, it unfolds in felt time, so to speak. The latter cannot be understood through time as measured, so what is happening? Or even (as a science-ridden age might ask), how is such an experience possible at all?

The answer to this apparent riddle is that we make, apprehend and appreciate music metaphorically. It moves as if it was a living body of some kind, moving in time and space, and is none the less real, not 'merely' metaphoric. This is why musical experience cannot be reduced to sound, vibrations, and physiology and neurology, although it depends on them. That essential metaphoricity includes the creation of music. As Susan Tomes observes,

> whereas a technical adjustment to playing would sound insanely complicated if you tried to analyse it … if you ask a good musician to imagine that, for example, the notes are falling like snow, or that the sound is paper-thin, or that the music is getting dark as they play, they respond with instinctive alteration of their touch and weight on the keyboard.[28]

It follows that the is-and-is-not of metaphor, which we found at the very heart of enchantment, is also at the heart of music. No wonder music can be so powerfully, insistently, and sometimes instantly enchanting!

Enchantment and *Charme*

Vladamir Jankélévitch deserves his own section because his philosophy highly values musical enchantment, which he calls *Charme*, above all else; yet in the end, he fails to understand it. He contrasts it with 'every definite thing' as 'the poetic influx through which beauty…will enter in a transitive relationship with the human'.[29] In the words of Carolyn Abbate, his translator:

> Enchantment – the state engendered by Charm – is a state of continence and, often, delight, at an opposite pole to bewitchment (*envoutement*) in which one is involuntarily transfixed and spiritually immobilized by "black magic" (*sortilège*) … The experience of this 'Charm' … is equivalent to the power of love, caritas and eros – the love of another or for an Other …[30]

This working definition corresponds, note for note, with that of true as against false enchantment, its character as delight, its essential relationality, and its apotheosis (mentioned in Chapter 2) as an unpossessive love of the other *as* other. Jankélévitch's defence of Charm against the scientism that has infected so much of the humanities' work on the arts is also admirable.[31]

Despite this promising start, however, he asserts that 'Melodic lines ascend and descend – on staff paper, but not in the world of sound, which has neither "up" nor "down"'.[32] But unless interpreted by the same scientism (not to say outright positivism), there is indeed up and down in musical experience, and a great deal more besides, the reality of which only the generous tensive truth of ontological metaphor can accommodate.

Again, we find that 'A sonata is like a précis of the human adventure that is bordered by death and birth – but is not itself this adventure.' But thanks to the tensive truth-function of metaphor, the sonata (say) both is and isn't the adventure – and precisely in that combination, which resonates with the nature of our deepest self and the world which mingle at that point, is to be found music's enchantment. So Jankélévitch's failure to understand metaphor means every use of 'metaphorical' is sabotaged by a 'merely'; Fauré's *Tendresse* 'which imitates dialogues does so only metaphorically', and 'The horn sonorities at the beginning of his Pelléas are not calling me personally'. But that is precisely what art does when it enchants! In the end, all Jankélévitch is left with is the pallid and pliant domesticity of simile and analogy ('like'), which touches neither the soul nor the world. It is a bizarre denial of the very *Charme* he champions.[33]

That blind spot also means that he is not a reliable guide to transcendence, which he identifies wholly with a Platonic 'Beyond', thus overlooking its immanence (as described by Merleau-Ponty, for example) in enchantment. By the same token, his advocacy of 'music itself, in itself … and not music in relation to something else', while correct about analytical abuses of music in order to advance agenda, misses the deeper truth that no such thing, no *noumenon*, can have any reality or meaning for us.[34] We see only *as*, and indeed *live* only as – that is, by metaphor – and an 'in itself' can only exist, for us, in and as a result of relationship.[35]

The meta-lesson is that not all theorisation amounts to the 'technical analysis' that Jankélévitch so strenuously resisted – and rightly so, when it is 'simply a means of not sympathizing, not being touched by the Charm, of sundering the covenant made with innocence and naïveté upon which all enchantment depends …'[36] There is such an activity as thinking about art sensitively and respectfully, which seeks not to 'explain' its subject but rather, with humility, to understand it, and to imaginatively describe it in a way that deepens appreciation. That is what Jankélévitch often does in spite of himself, certainly what Merleau-Ponty does, and what I am trying to do.[37]

Sound and Place

Not only do melodies metaphorically move but, if you are fortunate, they take you with them. In this respect a melodic line corresponds to a line in visual art 'taking you for a walk'. Sometimes a melody takes you unawares; other times it seems to occur in response to your paying attention and trying to stay with it, to follow it. The resulting enchantment is one of the most moving experiences music can offer. (I mentioned one that happened to me, courtesy The Albion Band, at the start of the first chapter.)

Certainly music includes a strong sense of place. When Nick Coleman, a music critic, was afflicted by 'sudden neurosensory hearing loss', he could no longer hear beloved works of music in the same way: 'I used to inhabit all of them, as they inhabited me, in three-dimensional space. Now I only look in.'[38] (Looking in or on, rather than inhabiting and being inhabited by, is a sure sign of disenchantment.) Again, such places must be understood as metaphorically real.

I puzzled long over where one goes when musically transported. Finally I realised that the problem was my assumption that to be taken somewhere means to be taken somewhere else. But this transport is not an away but an into. You are carried into the heart of where you already are – which is the same place (so you haven't left it), but is also not exactly the place it was when you were not enchanted (so you have). As Paul Eluard puts it, '*Il y'a un autre monde, mais il est dans celui-ci*' (There is another world, but it is in this one). Much later, I read Zuckerkandl's elegant summary: music involves 'an internal transcendence; it does not lead away from the phenomenon but into it, to its core.'[39]

Enchantment thus reveals the heart of where you are to be a larger, richer, deeper place than you had realised. In the case of the experience I had, the song, in particular as voiced by the oboe-player, opened a door into what it was about, and I passed through it even while I otherwise remained in the room. After all, song or tune is a part – a big part – of the place where and when you hear it.

Nothing illustrates this sense of music as place better than the Penguin Café Orchestra, founded by the English musician Simon Jeffes. A series of dreams while he was ill in the summer of 1972 culminated in a message from someone identifying themself as the proprietor of the Penguin Café. This personage told Jeffes that, in the latter's words, 'randomness, spontaneity, surprise, unexpectedness and irrationality in our lives is a very precious thing' – all non-willed, non-instrumental, enchantment-friendly modes, if the temptation to put them to work is resisted – 'and if you suppress that to have a nice orderly life, you kill off what's most important. Whereas in the Penguin Café your unconscious can just be...'[40]

So the quietly passionate, subtly emotional music developed by Jeffes and his fellow musicians, variously described by him as 'imaginary folklore' and 'modern semi-acoustic chamber music', became the music he had heard being played in an imaginal place, the Penguin Café. ('Imaginal' denotes anything not perceptible to the usual senses but nevertheless real, as against 'imaginary'.)[41] The Penguin Café is thus the place where the music that the PCO plays comes from, has its fullest being, and takes you to when you hear it.

Jeffes's son Arthur describes 'the dark wood of its walls', candle-lit in the early evening, the wine always red but the atmosphere 'not wildly Mediterranean, but slightly other. It's a gently magical place.' Helen Liebmann, cellist in the PCO and Jeffes's partner, remembers 'our concerts overflowing with emotion.'[42] (So do I.) In short, if there is a café in *Faërie* – and why not? – it's the Penguin Café.

Improvisation

Although this must remain an impression impossible to confirm empirically, it seems to me that transport by a melody happens frequently and strongly when it is improvised. Improvisation is a more elusive concept than it appears, but at its broadest it means creating music in a way that is sensitive to the limits which constrain while enabling it but also open to the moment, which includes but extends beyond those limits. This is music that can travel to where it wants to go, which is not necessarily where the performer was intending or expecting it to go.

In parallel with painting, it is a combination of familiarity (aural figurativity) and uncertainty or surprise (aural abstraction), where either one alone offers less fertile ground for enchantment. The best improvisation happens on the liminal edge of control, neither too far in – secure but lifeless – nor too far out: mere chaos. It demands, as Carolyn Abbate puts it, 'an alliance between courage and humility'.[43]

Improvisation also gives performers the most scope to sing or play in their own unique style. Savall's successful revival of a repertory for the viol demonstrates this point. 'The music I was playing,' he comments, 'by Diego Ortiz [a sixteenth-century Spanish composer], wasn't so much a collection of pieces as a book that showed you how to improvise and compose yourself'.[44] As Tom Service comments, 'That's the heart of Savall's musical philosophy – by learning to improvise, he was able to make the instrument and its music speak to audiences today, not just be a relic...'[45]

In a real sense, of course, a composer is improvising in the act of composing. For performers too, the line between improvising and interpreting is not always clear. There is often great enchantment in performing, with subtle variations, already composed and notated music. I think what is crucial is the players' ability to enter into the piece so fully that they are recreating it in the same spirit, the same metaphorical place where it was originally composed. As Eleanor Winship says, 'It's as if you enter the same stream the composer was in, and its current carries you along.'[46] Then listeners can participate too.

There is significant common ground between playing music, especially improvising or recreating it, and playing a game. Not a game in the sense of a board game or mechanical electronic toy; I mean a full-blown game, with a few rules (maybe themselves changeable subject to meta-rules), in which the imagination is in charge and outcomes are unpredictable and essentially unlimited. Such play, being rigorously non-goal-directed, is almost always enchanting for its participants, both players and listeners (an overlapping set). And there is a deep seriousness to it which should remind us that wilfully accomplishing preset goals is not the only option. Conversely, how revealing it is to consider play as necessarily frivolous! As Jankélévitch rightly says,

> if the magical half-hour whose name is Sonata resembles an enchanted oasis or a hidden garden in the desert expanse of working days and business hours – an 'isle heureuse' in the quotidian ocean – this same half-hour, in that it becomes an eternal present, a universe apart and whole, is absolutely, utterly serious.[47]

Gaps

Gaps are a prerequisite for relations, and thence metaphoric truth, in enchantment. In music, these take a specific form as the intervals between musical tones, both harmonically and melodically, and each one comes with its own peculiar mood. But more generally, there can be no enchantment in music without gaps between the tones, without pauses for the perceptible items to be themselves against or in relation to each other. Indeed, as Merleau-Ponty suggests, it's in the liminal gaps that enchantment lives. (Note how producers of mass-market music, videos and films leave as few and as small gaps as possible, relentlessly hurrying you on. Doing so increases their mastery over the product and you, while reducing the enchantment which, since it is wild, they can't control.)

Enchantment lives even in the cracks, in the sense of imperfections, within the notes – one reason why I think acoustic instruments, improvised music, and live performances have the greatest potential for enchantment.

Thus a line of music which incorporates significant differences (pitch, loudness, phrasing, and so on) has more potential to enchant than the same note held for so long that others start to fade from awareness; so too does music which allows places where little or nothing is played, compared to where the different notes are played so fast that they leave little room for perceptible gaps. The visual parallel is contrasts, either of shade or colour, which lend themselves to enchantment more than swathes of the same colour or shade. So the fewer and smaller the gaps between notes, the fewer and weaker relations between them, and the more enchantment diminishes. Charlie Parker's saxophone playing and John McLaughlin's electric guitar-playing, amid countless other possibilities, will serve as instances where any possibility is severely reduced by too many notes, too close together. (You can enjoy the effect for other reasons, of course. I trust I don't need to keep saying that.)

As usual, however, there is an opposite condition with the same effect of discouraging musical enchantment. It is perfectly illustrated by John Cage's famous 4 minutes and 33 seconds of silence, which is nothing but space; the whole thing is a gap. But anything one hears in that gap – a car horn, air conditioning, a distant pneumatic drill or, if you're lucky, birdsong – is random. In other words, unlike music that is improvised in relation to a structure, such sounds share no internal relationship or consistency, either with each other or with the gap itself. Enchantment therefore can fail to flourish from too much space as well as too little.

Between those two ultimately suffocating extremes lies music which suggests, or states suggestively. As François Jullien says,

> The most intensive sound is not the most intense: by overwhelming the senses, by manifesting itself exclusively and fully as a sensual phenomenon, sound delivered to its fullest extent leaves us with nothing to anticipate … In contrast, the least fully rendered sounds are the most promising, in that they have not been fully expressed.

The result is a 'lingering' effect which is also 'full of promise', both the past and the future, respectively – not as serial abstract time, but as deepened resonances of the experience of the present moment.[48] These resonances are accessible (as I have argued elsewhere) by the imagination, acting as an organ of perception of what is implicit in, but not exhausted by, what is immediately or completely given, especially the past of the present moment and its future.[49]

Enchanting Sound

Clearly, sounds that are not music can enchant, sometimes profoundly. Think of the final sentence of James Joyce's short story *The Dead*: 'His soul swooned slowly as he heard snow falling faintly through the universe and faintly falling, like the descent of their last end, upon all the living and the dead.' (Not the sound of snow landing, note, but falling.) Or a remark by a character in Yasunari Kawabata's *Snow Country*: 'The sound of rain and the sound of raindrops aren't the same.'[50]

A skilful composer working with 'found sounds', like Bill Fontana, can sometimes also succeed in enchanting, and his comments show that he knows what he's doing. 'I try not to get in the way too much. I feel as if I am bringing something alive, and the less of me, and the more of it, the better.'[51]

Now the enchantments of this other art of sound are easier to acknowledge and appreciate if one is not obliged to defend music against its false friends. Its original inventor/discoverer, Pierre Schaeffer, is absolutely right: '*Musique concrète*, in its work of assembling sound, produces sound-works, sound-structures, but not music. We have to not call music things which are simply sound structures.'[52]

Perhaps the most interesting and often enchanting composer working today in the ambiguous ground between music and sound effects is John Luther Adams. For example, his installation in Fairbanks, Alaska, *The Place Where You Go to Listen* (a translation of a local Inuit placename), turned seismological, meteorological, and geomagnetic information into sound and light. Here's is Alex Ross's description:

> What you notice first is a dense, organlike sonority, which Adams has named the Day Choir. Its notes follow the contour of the natural harmonic series – the rainbow of overtones that emanate from a vibrating string – and have the brightness of music in a major key. In overcast weather, the harmonies are relatively narrow in range; when the sun comes out, they stretch across four octaves. After the sun goes down, a darker, moodier set of chords, the Night Choir, moves to the forefront. The moon is audible as a narrow sliver of noise. Pulsating patterns in the bass, which Adams calls Earth Drums, are activated by small earthquakes and other seismic events around Alaska. And shimmering sounds in the extreme registers – the Aurora Bells – are tied to the fluctuations in the magnetic field that cause the Northern Lights.[53]

Adams's performances often succeed, I believe, not only because he is working with enchantment, but also from the way he does so. As it grows out of his work, he becomes conscious of it and reflects on it, which reflections then feed back into that work. This organic process is very different from imposing a largely preconceived theory. It's only a slight and forgivable exaggeration to say, as he does, that 'The work has a life of its own, and I'm just along for the ride.'[54]

Adams is engaging with some of enchantment's strongest and most durable roots in the concrete magic of place and nature. His

> original conception for "The Place" was grandiose. I thought that it might be a piece that could be realised at any location on the earth … That idea – tuning the whole world – stayed with me for a long time. But at some point, I realised that I was tuning it so that this place, this room, on this hill, looking out over the Alaska Range, was the sweetest-sounding spot on earth.

Thus his music has gone, as he says, 'from being about place to becoming place.'[55] In doing so, it has fulfilled his wish in the semantic meaning of enchantment, 'to be in a song': 'I no longer want to be outside the music, listening to it as an object apart. I want to inhabit the music, to be fully present and listening …'[56]

In a further twist of the enchanted gyre, at once mysterious and unsurprising, Adams remarks that 'My life's work has always been haunted by a sense of longing – longing for the natural world as it once was, longing for the human world as it might be. But now my work seems to have led me to a new sense of longing – longing to experience the magical fullness of each moment just as it is, here and now.'[57] (Even in Kyōto, I long for Kyōto.)

In his book *Winter Music*, Adams writes that 'Much of Alaska is still filled with silence, and one of the most persuasive arguments for the preservation of the original landscape here may be its spiritual value as a reservoir of silence.' Note the echo of Connemara as 'the last pool of darkness in Europe', now well on its way to being floodlit. Even deep in Alaska, you will now sometimes hear a snow-mobile or plane. Thus, 'A piece like "In the White Silence" is almost – I didn't realise this at the time – an elegy for a place that has disappeared.'[58]

Silence and Noise

Without darkness, there can be no meaningful let alone enchanting light, and the same is true of silence and sound, including music. And the enemy of silence is, of course, noise. We are such a numerous, demanding, and decibellous species. The fact is that in the developing and the over-developed world alike, there is now less silence, for fewer people, all the time. It's appalling, a kind of plague at once physical, psychosocial, and cultural.

Whatever its 'progressive' intellectual credentials might be, noise especially afflicts those too poor to buy silence and those pursuits least valued by muscular modernists, like reflection and sleep. It is also well-established that being exposed to excessive noise has various damaging medical consequences, both physiological and psychological, including hypertension, aggression, insomnia, high stress levels, tinnitus and hearing loss; and these can lead to further chronic disease.[59] (What shall we tell these people: that they should listen harder, or longer? That if they think about it, they will realise that there is no reason why the noise afflicting them isn't actually music? Maybe they need to be 're-educated'.)

There is one kind of noise, responsible for most of these ills, which is now inescapable in all cities and often the countryside too. It is machines: engines of all kinds, motorised vehicles, airplanes and helicopters, jet skis, chainsaws, angle-grinders, pile-drivers, sirens, alarms and, god help us, leaf-blowers: a roaring, growling, snarling, whining, wailing, moaning cacophony. And the quality it expresses above all else is moronic will-power. Mechanical noise, including electronic, is the anti-music of modernity, an obscene liturgy for sacrifices upon the alter of the anthropocentrically Useful and Convenient and, within its purview, the death of enchantment.

Jankélévitch terms the noise that destroys silence 'the Sirens' music'. It is, he writes, 'more than distracting noise, more than noise that diverts or dissipates, preventing reflective thought: it is a fraudulent art of pleasing.'[60] Indeed, to judge by the relative lack of resistance to junk sound, whether public or at home – piped muzak, the plastic pop and inane chatter of most radio, and the mind-numbing banality of most television – many people actively fear silence and are willing to sacrifice aural enchantment in order to avoid it.

The modernist *Manifesto of Futurism*, issued by the fascist Filippo Marinetti in 1909, identified noise, the louder the better, as worthy of worship, along with speed, machines, men (but contempt for women), strong leaders, violence, the 'hygiene' of war, and death. Unsurprisingly, he worshipped Wagner. C.S. Lewis may have had this example in mind when, in *The Screwtape Letters*, his senior demon in the bureaucracy of Hell exclaims, 'Music and silence – how I detest them both! … Noise, the grand dynamism, the audible expression of all that is exultant, ruthless and virile … We will make the whole universe a noise in the end.'[61]

Rich, deep, vibrant silence – not merely the absence of audible sound – is something rare and precious. It is full of promise, like a young life full of possibilities before it has begun to take a more particular form. Of course, just as promise and possibility sour if they are neurotically extended in order to avoid commitment, silence too must be savoured and then released, again and again. But where sounds and music are concerned, it is a precondition of their being, and being heard, at all. Thus silence is indispensable for aural enchantment too, including that of music, not only as a background but as the gaps between sounds or tones. As András Schiff says, 'To begin with there is silence, and music comes out of silence. Then comes the miracle of highly varied, progressive forms growing out of sounds and structures. After that, the silence returns.'[62]

In her book on silence, Sara Maitland notes that its experience tends to have some quite specific things in common which resonate with enchantment: for example, 'a sense of "givenness" – that this experience comes from "outside" the normal self and cannot be commanded or controlled', and 'ineffability – the experience is not only very hard to speak about, it is actually very hard to recall, remember, to reconstruct emotionally'. There is also 'an interior dimension to silence, a sort of stillness of heart and mind which is not … [a] lack or absence, but a positive presence'.[63] In that case, of course, silence itself can enchant.

While silence properly so-called is a technical or social phenomenon characterised by negativity, a lack of something, however, quiet is a positive condition.[64] David Toop quotes a sound recordist, Chris Watson:

> Quietness is the key. In an undisturbed place where there is a layer, a reference, an atmosphere which we can rest our ears upon. These are usually harmonically complex and with a significant, noise free, low level, low frequency content. Other single sounds can impinge upon this layer, but if the dynamics are too great, i.e. loud, the effect is cancelled.[65]

Ruskin would certainly have agreed. 'No air is sweet that is silent,' he writes, 'it is only sweet when full of low currents of undersound – triplets of birds, and murmur and chirp of insects ...'[66] But note that none of Ruskin's sounds are made by humans. And he's right; low currents of drills, motors of any kind and even voices are, it seems to me, distinctly less enchanting and more disturbing. The nonhuman sounds are refreshingly other, self-directed, not more of the same self-important man-made racket you can always get at home – indeed, cannot escape even at home, unless perhaps you are a hermit in what remains of wilderness.

Music and Nature

The subject of enchanting sounds bring us to the natural world, as intimated in the work of such composers as Olivier Messiaen and Tōru Takemitsu, as well as John Luther Adams. Unexpectedly, as we shall see, nature also returns us to music. Just as with sound, all music is natural, in the fullest sense of the word, but not all nature is musical, by any means. So what kind is?

Michel Serres describes a kind of music as:

> great, exceedingly rare, [that] vibrates in order to express the tension of bodies, the sea breeze, the feminine trembling of the ice in the snowmelt season, the interlacing of universal relations, and the background noise of the world ... [But] Emitted by inexhaustible chatterboxes, the cries of politics – noises of conflicts, carnage, jealousies – keep us from hearing the world's song. A keen ear and silence give us over to its enchantment ... And some, never hearing the song of the world with their hardened ears, devoted to the human sciences and thus deafened by the noise of the collectivity, even believe that the universe is disenchanted.[67]

I also concur with David Rothenberg that there is 'music in nature and nature in music', that there are 'real powers out there inside a birdsong or a thunderclap', and that we 'have too much of everything we have made and not enough of the source material from which we and all other life emerge.'[68] Rothenberg has jammed with whales, a natural choice given that whales sing songs that are shaped, to quote another musician on this point, 'like any good musical composition, with themes, phrases, climaxes, resolution, and dying away.'[69] These songs evolve over time, with new aspects (frequency, length, rhythm and patterns) continually appearing and being adopted by different pods in different parts of the ocean, to be picked up and repeated, as they pass through hundreds of miles of deep sea, by other whales, who introduce their own changes.

Another candidate for natural music, smaller, sharper and closer to home, are those virtuosos of birdsong, members of the thrush family. In North America, these include the hermit, song and wood thrushes, the veery and the American robin. I used to listen to these as a boy, both the robin's comforting suburban refrain and the hermit thrush's call, so liquid you could almost drink it, echoing in the mosquito-ridden boreal woods at dusk. In Britain, I am moved to wonder by the singing of the blackbird, and song and mistle thrushes (the last so named for its fondness for mistletoe berries).

My bird book describes the blackbird's song as 'a deliberate, loud, and melodious warbling, easily distinguished from thrushes' by its 'purer, fluty notes, lack of repetitive habit, and characteristic "collapse" into weak, unmusical ending'.[70] (Critics, eh?) In more detail, concerning a close relative, here is the composer and writer Eric Salzman:

> Any music is hard to describe, but I will try to give an impression of the hermit thrush song. Our earth-colored bird has a glinting, ethereal melody that begins with a single pure note followed, in a very calm, measured cadence, by ascending silvery trills. These trills are actually quite complex. More than one pitch is sounded simultaneously, and these chords (for that is what they are) are quickly alternated or trilled with other tones or chords; each sound is itself a reedy, shimmering harmony. The ascent is not in a straight line but rather appears to climb in a series of steps or spirals.[71]

It is commonplace to dismiss birdsong as mere biological mechanics: territorial sparring or sexual advertising for mates. However, for a superlative put-down, keeping the nonhuman natives in their place, try Roger Scruton: 'although we can hear music in the songs of birds, whales and bonobos, they themselves are deaf to it.'[72]

But a human cannot finally or certainly know what it is like to be a bird. (Thomas Nagel established that in a famous essay entitled 'What is it Like to be a Bat?') So no one who isn't a bird can know that a bird doesn't hear music in its own song, or in another bird's song. No human can say that they definitely do, either, for the same reason, but at least the question remains open; it must be argued on the balance of probabilities and plausibility. And the ornithologist Charles Hartshorne points out that birds often persist in singing even when there is no evident need or reward for doing so; so it must, to some extent, be self-rewarding. On those grounds, Scruton's refusal of autotelic music to the songs of birds and whales sounds distinctly like merely another defence of human privilege.

Like Raymond Tallis, Scruton thinks that to admit substantive commonalities between humans and other animals would open the door to what is distinctively human – especially culture – being appropriated by neo–Darwinians. But their defence is misguided, because neo–Darwinians don't own animals, including human animals, even if they appear to think they do. The best defence is the irreducibility of first-person to third-person accounts, and the gulf between science as a particular practice and scientism as a universalist worldview, or crypto-religion.

Personally, perhaps being temperamentally attuned to enchantment, I rarely hear a blackbird or thrush singing without being reminded of solos by the tenor saxophone player, Sonny Rollins.[73] Being supreme improvisers, no tune played or sung by either is ever exactly identical with another, and that uniqueness is key to their enchantment. Richard Mabey, reflecting on nightingale song, has noticed the same thing. 'If I were to try to think of a strictly musical analogy,' he writes, 'maybe it would be improvised jazz, where each new phrase isn't so much consciously worked out, but flows spontaneously and organically from the one before.'[74]

The modern prejudice, in order to minimise the amount of common ground, exaggerates the instinctuality of the nonhuman animal on the one hand and the self-consciousness of the human on the other, but their common ground is more striking. Both artists, avian and human, develop themes and stretch them to break-ing point before returning to their essence, in tones of rich sonority and soaring cadences interrupted by hilarious earthiness; both quote snatches of other songs; both improvise without a net, taking breath-taking chances which somehow work out, and both celebrate the joy of being alive.

The Disenchantment of Music

Let's consider certain ways of thinking about music which, while they have some validity as far as they go, miss its enchantment. One is acoustic science. Music leaves its source as vibrations at frequencies, but it arrives, so to speak, as something that depends on them but is quite different: the qualities we call tones. Then there are anatomy, physiology, and neurology. Sound becomes music thanks to the basilar membrane of the inner ear and its hair cells, the auditory cortex, and thence the rest of the body. Any purely physicalistic understanding of all that, however, falls well short of what is needed; for tones are both produced and heard by a listener, a whole person, not a set of ears plus a brain.

Psychological interpretations of music are, in the end, equally inadequate. As Zuckerkandl put it, in a demanding but rewarding passage that goes directly to the heart of the matter: 'It is not because music expresses or reproduces psychological experiences that we recognise in it the voice of our "within," but because music brings to expression the mode of existence of the world that is of the same nature as my "within," my psyche.'[75] In other words, music doesn't represent anything, including psychological states. Instead, it partakes of, and therefore expresses, the 'inner' dimension of both world *and* self. Hence the philosopher Bryan Magee's initial and enduring experience of music: 'It was as if the inside of things was talking to me.'[76]

Finally, there is neurological and evolutionary theory. After all, doesn't it explain everything, or (we're told) soon will? Certainly there are mounds of books entitled *The Music Instinct, Your Brain on Music* and so on. Let me summarise. There is no overall consensus about music in the scientific community. One school holds with Steven Pinker that it has no evolutionary purpose: 'music could vanish from our species and the rest of our lifestyle would be virtually unchanged'. Or as Pinker puts it, in that pubescent macho style beloved of popular science writers, even when they're professors: 'Music is auditory cheesecake.'[77]

The other school says no, music offers significant evolutionary advantages, serving as an indicator of 'biological and sexual fitness' and thereby attracting potential mates. In this view, 'Music evolved and continues to function as a courtship display, mostly broadcast by young males to attract females.'[78] And/or it promotes cognitive development, another evolutionary benefit. In any case, to quote a typically over-excited journalist, when it comes to our emotional responses to music 'there may be a perfectly respectable evolutionary explanation'.[79] Fancy that! I feel better already.

It's important to note what these two approaches share. The first is simply dismissive: music has no essential value ('cheesecake') because it serves no evolutionary purpose, which is all that really matters. But the second view only departs in upholding the value of music in terms of something else – genetic evolutionary advantage – which is anterior and 'explains' it, and is therefore, once again, more important. That shared assumption not only disrespects the integrity of the musical experience, but it also disenchants it as well; music becomes merely a means to another end, whether a successful or failed one.

So there is a certain element of truth to the evolutionary perspective in live public performances of music (which still excludes listening to music alone at home), and more than an element in some – rock or rave, for example – but there are manifold ways in which music enriches our lives while exceeding any remotely plausible reduction to, say, courtship display. And I want to concentrate on ideas that might be able to extend farther in the direction of where music lives. Which also happens to be where we really live.

What is completely unhelpful is a certain kind of technical analysis that Jankélévitch describes as 'simply a means of not sympathizing, not being touched by Charm, of sundering the covenant made with innocence and naïveté, on which all enchantment depends ...' Such analysis is a way of 'refusing to abandon oneself spontaneously to grace, which is the request the musical Charm is making'. That refusal is characterised by 'the fear of appearing bewitched, the coquetry of refusal, the resolve not to "submit"'.[80] Here is the modernist determination to be the Grown-Up in the room again.

Another musician and theorist, Jon Hassell, puts it this way:

> Current 'new wave' form cultivates the ironic approach (distanced, clever, solipsistic) as the only allowable response. The ironic playpen can be a lot of fun, but it's no substitute for the direct transmission and reception of heartfelt

messages. The coyote's howl is heard with deep feeling (if not approached ironically) because it is felt deeply by a creature who knows only how to be itself and says what it means.

'Music can be like this,' he adds, 'but it's rare.'[81]

The Dangers of Hypercontrol

One of the measures of the power of music to enchant is the way that power has long been feared. Plato's disapproval of unlicensed poets, banned from the ideal republic, extended to music. Only a few of the modes known at his time would be permitted, and only choral music with acceptable words. With instrumental music, he wrote, 'when there are no words, it is very difficult to recognise the meaning or the harmony and rhythm, or to see that any worthy object is imitated by them.'[82]

This disenchanted view of music, concerned above all with its correct use, passed directly on to St Augustine, for whom singing in church was permissible only as long as it inspired feelings of devotion to God. He decided that to find the singing itself more moving than the abstract truth which it is supposed to convey is a grievous sin. The aversion later resurfaced in the Reformation with hostility to musical instruments and even polyphonic singing. Most notoriously, seventeenth-century Puritans banned instruments from church services and suppressed the singing of Christmas carols (although not psalms).

It seems that only some extreme Islamists now worry that music distracts from God. Over the last century, the threat to enchanting music has been mostly secular. It stems from values which partly drive, and are partly driven by, enormously increased technical control over sound, especially the electronic and digital revolution.

There are two kinds of disenchantment at work. One is the commercial homogenisation of popular music for a mass audience, resulting in a dumbed-down Dionysian music that is sometimes vigorous but vulgar. The other is a withering rarefication, the effect of avant-garde intellectualisation of classical music and resulting in Apollonian music that is clever but sterile. Sometimes, the result manages to be both clever and vulgar, but in any case, wild wonder is hard to find.

The touchstone is that every kind of instrument, and (if it's any good, and is played well) each individual instrument, has its own voice, and enchantment finds its way into music when what makes each instrument unique, not only as a kind or even individual but also as played by that particular musician on that occasion, is an integral part of the performance. The competent musician, the instrument, and the idea in the music itself work together to make music, and their relations open further to enchantment.

This is especially likely to happen when genuine improvisation takes place, each musician discovering as they create and creating as they discover – not as an attempt to destroy structures but as a creative and playful weaving, through and among them: aural metaphor, connecting as it crosses the gaps between and within forms – if the music is centre-stage, not background fill – when the exhilaration of life, apprehended as music, connects me to something greater, and I find myself part of it. Then the voice or instrument is suddenly singing not to or about me but is singing, each note birthing the listener into unexpected new life.

Without ruling anything out, that is more likely to happen with acoustic instruments, which have a stronger individuality, not to say eccentricity, including their 'imperfections', than with electronic, computer-generated or pre-programmed sounds, samples and aural cut-and-paste. However, it is certainly possible when a synthesiser, say, is used creatively as an instrument in its own right, rather than in order to produce an imitation of others or a 'synthesis' of them. Also, just on account of the differences between them, the combination of electronic and acoustic instruments often works well.

Digital technology in music – computers, samplers, mixing desks, and so on – is now ubiquitous, and the total control it promises poses a serious threat to enchantment in music. (There is a close parallel here with the danger of virtuosity.) Paradoxically, it discourages *self*-control, so the exercise of digital production and rectification of music is anything but under control, and any restraint in its use must be based on other values and understandings. Why should that be needed at all? Because at a fundamental level, by its very nature, digitalisation is already hostile to enchantment. Every sound is reduced to a binary – either 0 or 1 – that exhausts all the possibilities, so there are no gaps or places between those two, nor outside them, to bridge in an encounter. Compared to analogue, digital sound, even before it gets to music, is already disenchanting.

We have already noted the same problem with digital photography. The technological armoury of the contemporary music editing-suite parallels that of Photoshop, and its deadening effects are the same. There is almost a kind of aesthetic fascism at work, beyond mere sanitisation. We're not just talking about 'cleaning up' the playing; any 'mistakes' can be 'corrected'. Notes are made, not asked, to occur sooner or later, as an 'ideal' recording is assembled from various takes and welded into a performance that never took place. The ultimate opposite of improvisation, it's virtually all safety-net. Who can be surprised if the result is charmless, even lifeless?

Then there is the way computer-driven visual input, as opposed to musical sound, has invaded not only sound-recording but composition itself. Changes are made simply in accordance with visual displays of the number of bars, beats per bar, harmonies and so on, and what these 'should' be. Decibel levels matter more than 'apparent' levels, where the latter term refers to what you actually hear! Haunting this is again the Platonic tradition: complete control over art and ultimately artists, the idea of a piece – not the inner lining of its material and embodied being, but the supposedly pure concept – replacing its sensual reality, and the triumph of vision, with its potential to objectify, over hearing.

We mentioned earlier the sculptor David Nash, and the kind of prior training that enables him to use the gross technology that is a chainsaw with delicacy and responsiveness. Isn't that just what is no longer central to how contemporary musicians learn their trade, in parallel with visual artists who are no longer required to learn how to draw and paint? As Schaeffer says in his 1986 interview, when you stick generations of young musicians, as is happening today, in front of synthesizers – I don't mean the ones for commercial music, but the really precise ones, where you have one control for the frequency, another for the decibels, another for the harmonic spectrum – then you're really in the shit ...[83]

The digital revolution as it affects popular music seems, at the time of writing, to have crested, although its overall dominance is unchanged. After a period of absurdly over-compressed music files, often in order to magnify loudness at the expense of quality, uncompressed files are becoming available and music mastering (encouraged by broadcasting regulations) is mostly avoiding extreme compression. Analogue processing is sometimes incorporated into mastering, acknowledging the desirability of its sound. It can even be sensibly debated now whether well-produced 24-bit digital audio sounds as good as (or better than) LPs and analogue tape.

This evidence of sanity (and with it, the possibility of true enchantment) needs to be sharply tempered by the continuing rule of commercial homogenous pop-pap on the radio and in loops in shops, malls, supermarkets, pubs and bars, restaurants, hotel lobbies, lifts, and people's cars – polluting, invasive, and utterly devoid of personality, the concreteness which is a prerequisite for the magic of enchantment. By the same token, most music videos continue discourage sustained absorption and reflection in every possible way – brevity, jump-cuts, multiple screens, rapid changes of image, and unrelenting speed – and they too are saturated with market values and monocultural messages. Then there is the tinny rubbish leaking out of handheld computers in public urban places, further eating away at any remaining quiet of the commons. And not least, we have to contend with the effect on musical culture of streaming platforms: flattening all songs and tunes into an atomised pseudo-equality devoid of themes, development, and differences of quality. This is no surprise, of course, when the criterion is not the excellence of the music but its profitability; the corruption of art by capital never sleeps.[84] All in all, Ben Franklin's list of existential certainties needs supplementing: now it's death, taxes, and bad music.

The picture at the other end of the elite-popular spectrum is no less disturbing. Regarding a tendency of contemporary recordings, Jean Baudrillard accurately anatomises the

technical delirium of the perfect restitution of music (Bach, Monteverdi, Mozart!) that has never existed, that no one has ever heard, and that was not meant to be heard like this. Moreover, one does not 'hear' it, for the distance that allows one to hear music, at a concert or somewhere else, is abolished ... it is the simulation of a total environment that dispossesses one of even the minimal analytic perception constitutive of music's charm.

Moreover, he adds, such technical perfection expands the criteria for perfection to such an extent that it guarantees perpetual dissatisfaction, since 'exhaustiveness as regards the real becomes forever impossible. The real becomes a vertiginous fantasy of exactitude lost in the infinitesimal.'[85] Indeed, although I also like Hoban's tongue-in-cheek lament:

> What I'm after is that the reproduced sound be more original than the original. The original came and went like everything else; it was no more than a fleeting murmur in a doubting ear … I want nothing less than a sound that will extend rearward in time to replace the sound of which it is a recording, so that nothing is lost. What's the use of holding back any longer? I want to have in reserve a second world that does not pass away.[86]

The pianist Jeremy Denk's initial pleasure in the process of editing recordings of his own concerts was soon replaced by dismay: 'The natural flawed flow of things is vanishing, replaced by this emerging construct. I think about how precious live performance is, and how terrible it is that more and more performances aim to sound like recording rather than the other way around.'[87]

Something strange is going on here. In the case of classical music, control is willing to sacrifice enchantment in a quest for technical perfection, while with popular music, control assists in sacrificing enchantment, through impoverished sound quality, for commercial gain. It's not difficult to imagine a viable middle ground, but it is becoming harder to find. The centre, to coin a phrase, cannot hold. And what is at stake? It is entirely typical of musical enchantment, perhaps especially, that what feels so important is so hard to specify. Let me say it slant, therefore.

> In these last days, maybe,
> of that rogue primate, humanity, what to value?
> What loss to regret?
>
> Many would say: Chartres,
> 'The Last Supper', Principia Mathematica
> or the like.
>
> But for me, it is a woman,
> plaiting her long dark hair, looking out
> through a shuttered window
>
> The kindness – a few coins or
> words, or a look which stops to see –
> of a stranger
>
> And all the vanished moments
> of music, glorious and perishable
> as love.

Notes

1 Laura Barton, *The Guardian* (28.3.08).
2 Jeremy Denk: 'The Flight of the Concord', *The New Yorker* (6.2.12) 24–29: 25.
3 Susan Tomes, *Out of Silence. A Pianist's Yearbook* (Woodbridge: The Boydell Press, 2010): 276.
4 *The Guardian* (26.6.09).
5 Wittgenstein in conversation with Drury in 1949, quoted in James Carl Klagge, *Wittgenstein in Exile* (Cambridge, MA: MIT Press, 2011): 20.
6 Tolkien, *OFS*: 15.
7 Anthony Storr, *Music and the Mind* (London: HarperCollins, 1992): 188.
8 Vikram Seth, *An Equal Music* (London: Phoenix House, 1999): 381.
9 Jeremy Eichler, 'String Theorist', *The New Yorker* (27.8.12) 34–39: 35.
10 *The Globe and Mail* (12.4.1997): D5.
11 Cf. C.S. Lewis, *An Experiment in Criticism* (Cambridge: Cambridge University Press, 2012 [1961]): 24.
12 Malcolm Budd, *Aesthetic Essays* (Oxford: Oxford University Press, 2008): 273.
13 See David Toop, *Ocean of Sound: Aether Talk, Ambient Sound and Imaginary Worlds* (London: Serpents Tail, 1995): 277.
14 Ludwig Wittgenstein, *Lectures and Conversations on Aesthetics, Psychology and Religious Belief*, ed. Cyril Barrett (Oxford: Blackwell, 1966): 29.
15 Richard Taruskin, *Music in the Early Twentieth Century* (Oxford: Oxford University Press, 2010): 155.
16 Victor Zuckerkandl, *Sound and Symbol. Music and the External World*, transl. Willard R. Trask (New York: Pantheon Books, 1956): 145.
17 Oliver Knussen, liner notes to *Takemitsu: Quotation of Dream*, Paul Crossley, Peter Serkin and the London Sinfonia (Deutsche Grammofon, 1998).
18 This is also very much Gregory Bateson's territory in *Steps to an Ecology of Mind* (New York: Ballantine, 1972), e.g. in his discussion of play and metaphor.
19 Antonio Machado, *Times Alone*, transl. Robert Bly (Middletown: Wesleyan University Press, 1983): 153.
20 Iain McGilchrist, *The Matter with Things*, Vol. 1 (London Perspectiva Press, 2022): 586.
21 Stambolian, *Proust*: 176.
22 Iasos in a 1979 documentary, taken here from the liner notes to *Celestial Soul Portrait* (2013).
23 I have drawn on the programme notes for a concert, 'The Music of Marcel Proust', on 22.11.1992 at St John's Smith Square, as well as Merleau-Ponty (see below) and Taruskin, *Music*.
24 Marcel Proust, *Remembrance of Things Past*, vol. 1, transl. C.K. Scott Moncrieff and Terence Kilmartin (London: Penguin, 1983): 228, 231.
25 Merleau-Ponty, *Visible*: 149, 150, 151. See also Matthew Del Nevo, *The Work of Enchantment* (New Brunswick: Transaction Publishers, 2011).
26 *The Irish Times* (22.2.2020).
27 Daniel Levitin, *This is Your Brain on Music* (London: Atlantic Books, 2006): 19.
28 *The TLS* (4.1.2019).
29 Arnold I. Davidson in 'The Charme of Jankélévitch', pp. vii–xii in Jankélévitch, Music Press, 2003): x.
30 Carolyn Abbate, 'Jankélévitch's Singularity', pp. xiii–xx in Jankélévitch, *Music*: xviii.
31 On scientism, see the work of Paul Feyerabend, Tim Ingold, John Gray, Steven Rose and Hilary Rose, Thomas Nagel and Mary Midgley.
32 Jankélévitch, *Music*, 13.
33 Ibid, 14, 19, 20.
34 Ibid, 15, 102.
35 See Ricoeur, *Rule*.
36 Ibid, 102.

37 See 'Vladimir Jankélévitch's Philosophy of Art.' A colloquy convened by Michael Gallope and Brian Kane, Journal of the American Musicological Society 65:1 (Spring 2012) 215–256. A valuable discussion, although too much of it indulges in the exhausted hermeneutics of suspicion and self-important assertions about musicology.

38 Nick Coleman, "Life in mono", *The Guardian* (19.2.08) 7–9.

39 Zuckerkandl: 147. This insight is in complete accord with Merleau-Ponty's later philosophy, of course.

40 *The Penguin Café Orchestra: A History* (London: Editions Penguin Café Ltd., 2001), text by Robert Sandall: 6, 11.

41 'Imaginal': I have borrowed this word and, loosely, concept, from Henri Corbin.

42 Arthur Jeffes and Helen Liebmann quoted in *The Guardian* (25.6.2016).

43 Abate, 'Singularity', xix.

44 *The Guardian* (26.6.09).

45 Ibid.

46 Personal communication.

47 Jankélévitch, *Music*, 66.

48 François Jullien, *Blandness*, 66–67.

49 See my *Enchantment*, 125–26.

50 Yasunari Kawabata, *Snow Country*, transl. Edward G. Seidensticker (London: Penguin Books, 2011).

51 *The Guardian* (16.4.10): 10.

52 David Rothenberg and Marta Ulvaeus (eds), *The Book of Music and Nature: An Anthology of Sounds, Words, Thoughts* (Middletown: Wesleyan University Press, 2001): 41. (This is an excellent collection.)

53 Alex Ross, 'Song of the Earth', *The New Yorker*, 12.5.08, pp. 76–81. See also John Luther Adams, *Winter Music. Composing the North* (Middletown: Wesleyan University Press, 2004).

54 Ibid.

55 Ibid.

56 John Luther Adams, liner notes to "In the White Silence" (2003).

57 John Luther Adams, *The Place Where You Go to Listen: In Search of an Ecology of Music* (Middletown: Wesleyan University Press, 2009): 100.

58 Quoted in Ross, ibid.

59 I have taken this catalogue from Sara Maitland, *A Book of Silence* (London: Granta, 2008) 132.

60 Jankélévitch, Music, 148.

61 Maitland, *Book*, 135. See also Garret Keizer, *The Unwanted Sound of Everything We Want* (New York: Perseus Books Group, 2010) and Malcolm McCullough, *Ambient Commons. Attention in the Age of Embodied Information* (Cambridge MA: The MIT Press, 2013), both excellent. Contrast the blithe and trendy treatment of noise by David Hendy in *Noise: A Human History of Sound and Listening* (London: Profile Books, 2013.) We bet Professor ('I'm with John Cage') Hendy lives in a pleasantly quiet neighbourhood.

62 András Schiff quoted in *The TLS* (8.1.2021) 15.

63 Maitland, *Book*, 278, 279, 27. (David Toop has remarked that Maitland's book is actually more about solitude than silence.)

64 Cf. Adams, *Winter Music*. 140, who says, 'Silence is not the absence of sound. It is the presence of stillness.' I agree, but quietness seems to me even more to the point. See also George Prochnik, *In Pursuit of Silence: Listening for Meaning in a World of Noise* (New York; Doubleday, 2010).

65 David Toop, *Haunted Weather. Music, Silence and Memory* (London: Serpents Tail, 2004): 44. Chris Watson, who recorded two programmes for BBC Radio 4 in Dec. 2002 on quiet and tranquillity, is quoted on p. 53.

66 John Ruskin, *Unto This Last* (London: Cassell & Co., 1907 [1862]): 154.

67 Michel Serres, 'Epilogue: What Hearing Knows', pp. 259–73 in Joshua Landy and Michael Saler (eds), *The Re-Enchantment of the World: Secular Magic in a Rational Age* (Stanford: Stanford University Press, 2009): 267, 259, 272, 271.

68 David Rothenberg, 'Introduction: Does Nature Understand Music?' pp. 1–12 in Rothenberg and Ulvaeus, *Book*: 10, 5, 7.

69 Susan Tomes, *The Guardian* (7.6.08) reviewing David Rothenberg, *Thousand Mile Song: Music in a Sea of Sound* (New York: Basic Books, 2008).

70 Roger Peterson, Guy Mountfort and P.A.D. Hollom, *A Field Guide to the Birds of Britain and Europe*, 4th edn (London: Collins, 1983): 164.

71 Eric Salzman, 'Sweet Singer of the Pine Barrens', pp. 207–214 in Rothenberg and Ulvaeus, *Book*: 212.

72 Roger Scruton, *Understanding Music: Philosophy and Interpretation* (London: Continuum, 2009): 5.

73 Cf. Simon Barnes, who describes Song Thrushes as 'the jazz musicians of suburbia'.

74 Mabey, *Barley Bird*, 63.

75 Zuckerkandl, *Sound*, 370. He asks rhetorically where, then, does it belong, adding the sound advice to beware 'disciplines that implicitly solve this problem merely through their formulation of an initial question' (p.14). Note, again, the resonances with Bateson.

76 Bryan Magee, *Ultimate Questions* (Princeton: Princeton University Press, 2016): 89.

77 Levitin, *Brain*: 215, 214.

78 Levitin, *Brain*, 251, 253.

79 Arminta Wallace, *Irish Times* (20.2.10).

80 Jankélévitch, *Music*, 102.

81 Jon Hassell, in a press release on Fourth World Music (1980).

82 Philip Ball, *The Music Instinct* (London: Vintage Books, 2011): 384.

83 Schaeffer in Rothenberg and Ulvaeus, *Book*: 38. The transcription then adds: '[Laughter]'.

84 See the excellent interview by Rick Beato with Ted Gioia (accessed 27.7.2022; with thanks to Ron Baise): https://www.youtube.com/watch?v=qM4sEl8avug

85 Jean Baudrillard, *Seduction*, transl. Brian Singer (New York: St Martin's Press, 1990): 30.

86 Hoban, *Moment*: 225.

87 Denk, 'The Flight of the Concord', *The New Yorker* (6.2.12) 24–29: 25.

6

MUSIC II

In this chapter we shall explore enchantment first in parts of classical music, then of popular and traditional music. I want to emphasise that I am not trying to be comprehensive, only to follow the golden thread of enchantment, describing and thinking about the instances of musical enchantment I have been lucky enough to experience.

Of course, music cannot be neatly divided into the Apollonian, the Dionysian and the enchanting, leaving us free to concentrate on the last. The order that is the essence of Apollo can enchant, or lead to the threshold of it, by placing one's personal order (and disorder) within a much greater, natural or cosmic order, in almost exactly the way a narrative enchants by allowing one to find oneself within its greater story. And a sympathy obtains between enchantment's delight and Dionysian pleasure: the pleasure of delight, and the delight one takes in pleasure, whether one's own or another's.

Nonetheless, the occasional kinship or similarity of these two modes with enchantment does not make them identical with it, and it seems to me that however subtle and elusive there is a distinctive quality to enchantment, in music no less than elsewhere, that makes it unique.

Classical Music

Much classical music can be fairly characterised as Apollonian, if far from only that. The emphasis is on the order of music and music-as-life, whether in the baroque counterpoint of Bach, sweetened and lightened by his sons and brought to perfection by Haydn and Mozart, or the progressively more extremist and dissonant Romantic and post-Romantic music of modernity. Dissonance in this context is an expressive and structural tool of harmony, not its opposite or absence. More adventuresome audiences enjoy extending their appreciation and grasp of more

DOI: 10.4324/9781003353225-6

challenging kinds of aural order, and hypermodern musical chaos is a kind of tribute to form. If architecture is, as Goethe thought, 'petrified music', the reverse is
also true: there is something architectonic about the structures of music. What varies is not only the forms, however, but crucially the listener's relationship to them.
Let's turn to that.

The violinist Alina Ibragimova defines the job of classical music as 'always trying
to communicate more'. That relationality applies not only to the composer and
the performer but the audience: 'I always feel that everybody is participating in the
concert. We're all gathering together, to listen or to play. It's such a mutual thing.'
And centre-stage is the music itself, performed with passion and dedication, 'when
people just do it because they have such a strong need to do it … it's not about
anything material, money or fame.'[1]

Another violinist, Christian Tetzlaff, has said almost the same thing: 'that's what
the concert situation is about for me, when I'm sitting in the hall and also when I'm
playing myself. It's about communication – I almost want to say "communion." As a
player, you don't really interpret anymore. You listen, together, with the audience.'[2]

There is plenty of what is needful for enchantment in most classical music:
melody, spaces or silences between the tones, presence as manifest in timbre, metaphoric motion. But if, as I suggested, improvisation especially transports, where
does that leave classical music, much of which (since at least the mid-nineteenth
century) is heavily notated? As Susan Tomes observes, musical notation is 'only
a map of the music's landscape, but the journey through the landscape is hardly
delineated by the composer.'[3] Indeed, fully apprehended, any responsive interpretation of a classical work is effectively a new work. The newness is subtle, however
– usually a nuance of tempo, dynamics or the like – and not all listeners are able to
listen on such an exalted plane. Thus in terms of enchantment, the strongly notated
nature of Western classical music puts it at a disadvantage, in this respect, as against
the centrality of improvisation to most jazz and North Indian classical music.

Yet the heavily scripted nature of classical music performance is a fairly recent
development. Bach in his time was famed as an improviser, perhaps even more than
as a composer, and Chopin and Beethoven were renowned improvisers as well. A
member of the audience for a performance by Mozart in Prague on 19 January
1787 recalled that

> we did not know what to admire the more – the extraordinary composition,
> or the extraordinary playing; both together made a total impression on our
> souls that could only be compared to sweet enchantment! But at the end of
> the concert, when Mozart extemporized alone for more than half an hour
> at the fortepiano, raising our delight to the highest degree, our enchantment
> dissolved into loud, overwhelming applause.[4]

In fact, a tradition of improvisation, in which it was generally assumed by composers that musicians would embellish their written parts while something like a
cadenza would be entirely improvised, continued into the late nineteenth century,

and some piano virtuosos improvised entire pieces. The phenomenon of a composer's near-total control over his or her material has thus been true only for a relatively
short period, and there has been a movement in recent years to reintroduce more
embellishment, with improvised cadenzas and ornaments.[5] There are quite strict
limits on how far this can go, however, so there remains a significant difference
between classical music and jazz in this important respect.

Turning to another kind of relationality as a key dynamic, Haydn achieved a
breakthrough with his Opus 20 string quartets which opened the door of chamber
music wider to enchantment.[6] Instead of the first violin always leading the way and
the other instruments following, each instrument now has something of its own to
contribute in what amounts to a vibrant conversation. This model will be taken up
in a looser and more improvised way in chamber jazz.

To my mind, Haydn's chamber music also attains another important kind of
balance, namely between respect for the forms of tradition and community on the
one hand, and unique personal expression on the other, which is near-perfect. This
too contributes to what Patrick O'Brian, apropos Haydn and some of his musical
contemporaries, calls 'the grave happiness of the music'.[7]

In the music of Vivaldi, Telemann and Bach's sons, delightful though it is, form
(whose danger is formulaicity) takes pride of place; in the music of Beethoven, moving though it is, self-expression (whose danger is self-indulgence) begins to dominate. Both emphases, if unchecked by the other, tend to suppress enchantment. I
say this in full awareness, though, that the third movement of Beethoven's late string
quartet Opus 132, for example, is more than any of us deserve. Its enchantment
is transcendent in the immanent way of music, taking us away by taking us home.

Nevertheless, didn't the danger of extravagant emoting become all too apparent
in the subsequent Dionysian Romanticism of Wagner, Strauss, and Mahler? And the
counter-danger of arid Apollonian formalism in the atonal serialism of Schoenberg?
A balance is very important, because holding in tension collective form and personal
content, it indirectly exalts relationship as such, a precondition for enchantment.

Mozart is something of a special case, insofar as his lyricism is so pure, so
already-enchanting, that paradoxically it doesn't leave much work for the imagination to do. If he can be compared to Vermeer, then Beethoven – pulling transcendence, by sheer effort, out of the guts of his being, and ours – is like Rembrandt.
And Haydn? As Jan Zwicky says, 'It's as though Mozart can relieve us of being
human for a while, but Haydn knows being human is all we've got.'[8] But he didn't,
if you'll pardon the expression, make a song-and-dance out of it. The triumph of
Romanticism in the nineteenth century, which did, was so complete that Brahms's
attempt to recover Haydn's balance between classical and romantic sounded to
many dated, even doomed.

Beginning in the late nineteenth century, under intense pressure from democ-
racy, industrialisation and war, classical music fractured, and for many composers,
rather more than for their audiences, the old ways to musical enchantment became
unviable. For some, even valuing and courting wonder in music became suspect.
Some abandoned it, never to return, while others, with varying degrees of success,

found new ways there. Probably the most significant figure in these developments was Richard Wagner. I have already forsworn commenting on Wagner's operas. Something needs to be said about the music for those operas, however.

I could balance the opinion of those for whom Wagner's music is essentially a religious experience against that of others who find it bombastic and manipulative, even bullying. For my part, I agree with Huxley that 'After silence that which comes nearest to expressing the inexpressible is music', and that 'silence is an integral part of all good music.' He continues that 'Compared with Beethoven's or Mozart's, the ceaseless torrent of Wagner's music is very poor in silence. Perhaps that is one of the reasons why it seems so much less significant than theirs. It "says" less because it is always speaking.'[9]

In any case, there are grave problems here respecting enchantment. For example, take Wagner's own conviction that 'What music expresses is eternal, infinite, and ideal; it does not express the passion, love, or longing of such-and-such an individual on such-and-such an occasion, but passion, love, or longing in itself'.[10] No carnal concrete here, just a Platonic Idea 'in itself'; and without the precision of concrete particulars (one might almost say, without incarnation in, and as, a body) you may well have a mystery religion, but no real mystery – not what Mondrian's critic Fairfield Porter called 'the dangerous mystery of fact'. And isn't it always bloodless ideals, particularly those concerned with purity, which lend themselves so easily to bloody causes?

Thomas Mann remarks that Romanticism is not interested in 'the pathos of distance'.[11] That is true, but such a reserved way of putting it could mislead; the Romanticism of which Wagner was an avatar wants to close up distance, to destroy it in a Dionysian unity. 'Have I swallowed Wagner or has Wagner swallowed me?' asks Nicholas Spicer.[12] That is the very definition of false enchantment, of course – wanting to possess or be possessed – and no one who has heard Wagner's music could fail to recognise the accuracy of the description. Finally, step forward Paul Mason, writer and presenter of a documentary on BBC Radio 4. It is entitled 'Wagner: Power, Sex and Revolution': almost a catalogue of issues oblique, if not antipathetic, to enchantment.[13] And I'm sure he's right.

Recovering from his embarrassing Wagnerian *engouement*, Nietzsche realised 'what I really want from music. That it be cheerful and profound like an afternoon in October. That it be individual, frolicsome, tender, a sweet small woman full of beastliness and charm.'[14] I wouldn't want to restrict enchanting music to that, but it's a lot closer to the mark than *Parsifal*. Yet suppose someone says flatly they were genuinely enchanted by it? Then I can only repeat that if so, that person's experience was not itself Wagnerian. Playing a Bach sonata for solo violin, Christian Tetzlaff 'tapered his sound down to a pianissimo so shiveringly soft and guileless that the massive hall appeared to shrink to the size of a chamber.'[15] Now *that's* enchantment.

Some Enchantment in twentieth Century Classical Music

In France, beginning in the early twentieth century, classical composers engaged in a resistance to Wagner in which enchantment figured strongly. Most of it, with the intimacy that favours musical wonder, is chamber music, often for solo piano. Their achievement was to find new ways to innovate and experiment without succumbing to modernism.

The term often used for this music is 'Impressionism', in parallel with the roughly contemporaneous movement in painting, and Claude Debussy is identified as the leading Impressionist composer on the strength of works which invoked, without attempting a quasi-literal reproduction, the experience of nature (hence, 'impressions') that was equally central to the work of Impressionist painters – especially the sea, of which he was passionately fond. Debussy's genius lay in his ability to employ large-scale orchestral effects to that end while finding ways for it to feel delicate and personal. On a smaller scale, his two sets of *Préludes* for solo piano are no less successful.

Debussy's compositions used whole tone and pentatonic scales quite a lot. Their harmonies were modal rather than functional or tonal, when he didn't simply use chords whose sound he liked. They were not atonal in the Viennese School's sense, however – that is, consistently atonal throughout – and that refusal of dogmatism was of a piece with Debussy's artistic philosophy as a whole. 'Works of art make rules,' he once said, 'rules do not make works of art.'

Of his own work (reminding one of Matisse's disavowals), Debussy insisted that 'There is no theory. You only have to listen.' He was also aware of the dynamics of enchantment we have discussed in other contexts. How else could he have described music as 'the silence between the notes', and 'the expression of the movement of the waters, the play of curves described by changing breezes'?[16] In betweenness, play, curves, changing natural phenomena – all these lineaments of enchantment are present in the fluid and sensual sweep of his music.

Maurice Ravel, thirteen years younger, was impressed and influenced by Debussy's early work, but despite being described as a fellow Impressionist, he soon developed in quite a different way. If Debussy's music flows, Ravel's sparkles. His limpid clarity was more carefully crafted and conservative – his favourite musician was Mozart, his least the 'pernicious' Wagner – but at the same time, open-mindedly eclectic: he also acknowledged a debt to Edvard Grieg's lyric pieces for piano and enjoyed contemporary American jazz, while some of his pieces were influenced by Schoenberg. Ravel's praise of the latter comes with a sting in the tail. [17] 'If my music doesn't completely sound like Schoenberg's,' he observed with pointed politeness, 'it's because I am less afraid of the element of charm, which he avoids to the point of asceticism and martyrdom.' (Complemented one time by an incautious well-wisher on his 'lovely music', Schoenberg snapped, 'I don't write lovely music.')[18]

Despite the differences with Debussy, Ravel and he shared important common ground: a quality accompanying the belief – shared with painters valuing enchantment – that in Ravel's words, music 'must be emotional first and intellectual second', and a charm that extends, in his string quartet and some of his works for solo piano, into joy.

One of Ravel's teachers was Gabriel Fauré, whose introspective and restrained chamber works, understatedly passionate and intensely lyrical, are among the most quietly enchanting of his or any time. He left us a larger body of chamber music than the others, including piano trios, quartets, and quintets, sonatas and works for solo piano. The last are crowned by the late *Nocturnes*, with a nod to his beloved Chopin but haunted, like Beethoven's final string quartets, by deafness. These are remarkable for the way they admit darkness without allowing it to overwhelm the light altogether, and they show how a commitment to enchantment can survive, even partly redeem, despair.

Another contemporary figure was the pianist-composer Erik Satie. It's hard to say to what extent Satie's eccentricity was a cultivated persona, but his marginal position vis-à-vis the music establishment of his day coexisted with complete dedication to music. His thunderously quiet, audaciously slow tunes for solo piano (collected as the *Gnossiennes* and *Gymnopédies*) still enchant listeners today. At the time, his deceptively simple and faux-banal work also functioned as Debussy's and Ravel's own anti-Wagnerian conscience, so to speak. Indeed, according to Satie himself, he had 'explained to Debussy the need for us French to prize ourselves away from the Wagnerian adventure, which did not correspond to our natural aspirations, & I explained to him … that we needed to have our own music – with no sauerkraut if possible.'[19] Whether that is true or not, Satie's work itself implied that any sacrifice of charm and delight for pretentious ambition would not escape his derision.

The 'Impressionists' were followed by a younger generation of reluctant admirers, Poulenc, Milhaud, and other members of Le Groupe des Six. Of these, Francis Poulenc especially absorbed the best of Debussy, Ravel, and Satie, and gave it new life in his delightful chamber music for piano and wind instruments. But notwithstanding their individual differences, all these composers produced work that is highly melodic, marrying classical and Romantic domains, giving form to feeling in near-perfect balance, neither sterile nor self-indulgent. They also formed, if not exactly a community, then a network, personally as well as professionally, committed to musical enchantment. Eventually, as we shall see, it extended well beyond early twentieth century France.

Finally, another composer who joined this lineage was the Catalan pianist Federico Mompou, who decided to dedicate himself to composing after hearing Fauré's *Piano Quintet No. 1* in 1909, aged sixteen. Chopin, Debussy and Satie were his strongest influences, and his subtly compelling music for solo piano – the best-known of which is entitled *Música Callada* (Silent Music) – shares the qualities of each of their works while remaining itself.[20] That has something to do with its distinctive sonorities which, in the words of Vladimir Jankélévitch, are 'sedative, calming, serious, vehement, or sometimes mysteriously hammered out and… captivating.'[21] (Somewhere in those resonances is Mompou's grandfather's church-bell factory, very near where he grew up.)

Tōru Takemitsu

The farthest-flung node in the network of twentieth century French-inspired or inflected classical music is the Japanese composer Tōru Takemitsu, whose unmistakably modern music draws on Debussy ('I consider Debussy my teacher') and Messaien, with whom he shared a love of birdsong.[22] But he also appreciated the modal jazz of Miles Davis and Bill Evans, and his initiation into music, in 1944, was hearing a smuggled record of a Parisienne chanteuse, Lucienne Boyer, singing *Parlez-moi d'amour*. Understandably for a fourteen-year-old boy, conscripted into an army supply base in wartime, it made quite an impression, and he soon followed it up with his father's collection of jazz recordings.

Later in life, after some resistance, Takemitsu turned to Japanese traditional music, in which ensembles play without a conductor, the performance being directly modified by the interactions of the players. Still more important, however, was the philosophy of Japanese gardening, with its particular interpretation (in his words) of 'colour, spacing, form' which avoids symmetry and any single order or perspective. Instead, like Far Eastern painting, it favours a metaphoric microcosm of nature as a whole, with a multitude of orientations, as a place through which one can wander.

One of Takemitsu's pieces is 'an imaginary landscape', and another has been described as a walk through 'a sonic garden'.[23] This understanding overlaps with that of Debussy in which the 'most important elements' are, as Takemitsu put it, 'colour, light, and shadow.' Another composition is entitled *Water Music*. In musical terms, this mode translates into the advice he gave a leading interpreter on piano, Noriko Origawa, to concentrate on 'sonority and melody'. The echo with Mompou, reaching back to Debussy, Ravel, and Satie, is unmistakable.

Takemitsu explained his philosophy of music like this:

> What I want to do is not to put sounds in motion towards a goal by controlling them. Rather, I would prefer to set them free, if possible, without controlling them. For me, it would be enough to gather the sounds around me and then gently put them in motion. To move the sounds around the way you drive a car is the worst thing you can do with them.

(Again, imagine what Picasso would have said about this … 'No no, you must seize the steering wheel and make them go where you want!')

A major inspiration for Takemitsu was the concept of *ma*, a uniquely Japanese development of the idea of gaps so important to enchantment.[24] *Ma* are the spaces, intervals or pauses between two or more things of any kind that exist in a continuity, or that occur simultaneously. Takemitsu described *ma* as 'the silence which is not just the absence of sound but a presence as vibrant as sound itself', and remarked that 'I have used few notes, many silences, from my first piece.' The resonance with a Daoist 'void' is clear.

We have also seen the importance of the bridges, connections and meetings across gaps that become realised in metaphor. In Japanese philosophy that which crosses *ma* is called *hashi*: a bridge, for example, or stairs, or chopsticks (bridging plate and mouth), but also any edge or liminal threshold where one world meets another. *Utsori* is then 'the moment when nature is transformed, the passage from one state to another', and *ma* 'the expectant stillness of the moment attending this kind of change'.

Unlike foundational Greek philosophy, in which truth and reality were identified as whatever does not change, in Far Eastern philosophy transience and change itself is fundamental. It is the only thing, so to speak, that doesn't change. It follows that the dynamics of enchantment these terms identify are as culturally central, in this tradition, as they are relatively marginal in the West. But they remain just as central to all our lives, even if largely unrecognised and certainly not widely honoured, because '*Ma* is the place where life is lived'.

Wonderfully, the spaces of *ma* are occupied by *kami*, which we would translate as spirits or gods, or the place and state in which they have their being. The parallel with *Faërie* is exact. A *kami*, to quote Seigow Matsuoka, is 'void of matter but not of body, because it has a definite existence and presence.' And as Roberto Calasso observes, 'A god is never a constant presence.'[25] A *kami* too 'does not abide: its nature is to arrive and then depart.'[26] At such times, the distinctive atmosphere of its coming and going pervades structures. We encounter this coming and going, and their traces, in every field of enchantment.

Modernism in Classical Music

As in visual art, when trying to understand enchantment in music, modernism cannot be avoided. The contrast, and the latter's hostility, are too interesting and instructive. Here too, musical modernism has involved a triumph of theory and ideology over sensuous experience, to the extent that one of its chief movers, Arnold Schoenberg, could say, apparently with a straight face, 'How the music *sounds* is not the point' – as per the sculptor Kapoor's 'It doesn't matter what it looks like'.[27] Such a position has been and often still is treated with reverence instead of the incredulity it deserves. Agenda-free art, where the only concern is the aesthetic integrity of the piece itself, an indispensable requirement for enchantment, is considered by many experts as inferior, something to be scorned or pitied – and all the more so if it proves accessible to many. (After the premiere of his opera *Wozzeck* in Berlin, the arch-modernist Anton Berg was in despair because it had been so well-received; the requisite provocation had failed. He told Adorno, 'if a piece of music nowadays [has] won over the public so immediately, there must be something wrong with it.')[28]

However, the critical victory of musical modernism, assisted by a relatively small elite of composers, conductors, venue directors, and music critics, has been uneven and contested. It was certainly not grounded in universal acclaim. On the contrary, there was and remains considerable resistance among audiences. Attacking modern music that 'few people [are] expected to understand, much less enjoy', Joe Queenan, writing in 2008, described Harrison Birtwhistle's operas as 'harsh and ugly and monotonous and generically apocalyptic', while a 'hundred years after Schoenberg, the public still doesn't like anything after Transfigured Night, and even that is a stretch. The works of the former *wunderkindern* Boulez and Stockhausen have not entered the permanent repertory, and Lutoslawski and Elliott Carter, while respected, are not beloved.'[29] It's the same truth we encountered with modern painting: if you have to 'suspend disbelief', think about it, and convince yourself you like it – as opposed to discovering that you love it as you listen – then any enchantment is already still-born.

Modernist composers have typically reacted by blaming the public for ignorance or incompetence, but it turns out (as Diana Raffman has shown) that even trained musicians literally cannot hear their structures.[30] The only way to escape the negative implications of this for the aesthetic integrity of the music is to take the self-defeating position that it doesn't matter how the music sounds (or the painting looks). And that is indeed how modernism in art retreats from self-importance, via solipsism, into onanism.

These are real problems with modernist music, and the persistent hostility to it by audiences can no longer be dismissed as baseless ignorance, or prejudice unconnected with the music itself, or as if it presents no challenges that weren't present in the music experienced by earlier generations ('Mozart was more difficult than Haydn, Beethoven was more difficult than Mozart', or 'Coleman Hawkins was more difficult than Louis Armstrong, Sonny Rollins was more difficult than Hawkins' – as if this justified anything, or hallowed difficulty as such.)

Furthermore, the ways modernists have persistently associated unpleasantness, ugliness, and gross dissonance with truthfulness is now transparently absurd. It makes no more sense than the opposite, associating all truth with pleasure, beauty, and harmony. Both are dogmatisms, so the one offers no real correction to the other.

For all these reasons, then, I want to press the claim, as I did respecting painting, that there is a significant difference between modern music and modernist. There is a lot of enchanting modern music! Technically speaking, of course, any enchanting art produced in modern times is modern by definition. Beyond that, however, a spirit of adventure and innovation is simply not identical with sweeping away what went before in a peremptory gesture. Examples? For now, of modern musicians, let's say Debussy, Janáček or Messiaen, and in jazz, Monk or Rollins; of modernists, Schoenberg or Berg, and in jazz, Coltrane or Cecil Taylor.

Before we get too happy about enchanting modern music, though, it is under tremendous commercial pressure, with commodity capitalism ramping up technological hyper-control in service of the bottom line. Between the two onslaughts, elite and populist, things can look pretty bad. To quote Jankélévitch, writing in 1961:

> the rapacious need for novelty, so characteristic of the escalating modernist auction, entails the idea that a musical act is a thing, in which case, music is no more than technique, technique alone. And just as technique is the consequence of an indefinite process of perfection – with each automobile or kitchen appliance show ushering in what is new and improved in comparison to last year's – so perpetual progress shall be the law of music. Farther, faster, more powerful! In this arms race, each new music, shattering its predecessor's

records, offers itself as the last thing in modernity; and each musician, forcing predecessors into the category of the unfashionable and outmoded, claims the patent on the invention.[31]

And here is Pierre Schaeffer, the inventor/ discoverer of *musique concrète*, from an interview in 1986 (and I love him for this):

> I must say that I do judge these times to be bad times. We seem to be afflicted by ideologies … [and] technology with which to replace inspiration. If I compare that to jazz for example in its historically fecund period, the extraordinary fruition of American music at the point where the European DoReMi was suddenly seized upon by the blacks for the production of expressive forms; this was sublime. Now if you think that, decades later, this bloated, avaricious and barbarous culture, brutalised by money and machines and advertising, is still living off this precious vein. Well, you have to admit that some periods are simply vile, disgusting, and that this is one of them.[32]

Twelve-Tone Modernism

The impact of Wagner's Dionysian music was enormous. Simply put, and leaving aside Romantic composers who continued in his train, it generated two very different subsequent responses. One was an attempt among French composers, which we have discussed, to recover musical enchantment in new circumstances.[33] The other was severely Apollonian: that of Arnold Schoenberg and the Vienna school of serialist atonalism.

Schoenberg was reacting not only against Wagner's emotive religiosity but also the popular Viennese waltzes of his day, which struck him as unbearably vulgar. (Compared to a great deal of what we hear now, of course, they sound exquisitely refined!) Schoenberg concluded that the entire tonal repertoire was exhausted. As Richard Taruskin comments, 'The bald assertion of tonality's collapse or demise around 1908 is one of the myths of modernism …'[34] The composer decided it should be replaced with a new system, one which imposes seriality on the twelve tones of the chromatic scale, refusing to settle on any key, scale or tonic, and using mathematical means to achieve that end.

The resonance here with Mondrian's rejection of figurative painting in favour of strict abstraction is striking, and no accident. That is not only true of their shared spiritual instrumentalism, the use of art 'as a medium of occult revelation – a representation or even an enactment of an "ascent to a higher and better order."'[35] Like Messiaen's *Quartet for the End of Time*, Schoenberg's most popular work, *Transfigured Night*, is a composition that corresponds to Mondrian's 'transitional' trees and Kandinsky's still-figurative *Improvisations*.

Many have found these works, which are transitional only in terms of their creators' trajectory, not only accessible but enchanting. In this context, it is sad that the flight into pure abstraction in painting and atonal serialism in music continued unchecked, all the more so since the transitional works show just how good they were at semi-representational painting and imaginatively tonal music. (Anton Berg's *Violin Concerto*, another beloved piece by a modernist composer, is also tonal.)

Personally, I don't experience atonal music as liberating but tedious. Perhaps that's because I didn't find tonal music (let alone all of it) problematic in the first place. Be that as it may, Schoenberg's revolutionary programme was always questionable. Tonality in classical music was revitalised by a host of modern but not modernist composers: Debussy, Ravel, Janáček, Messiaen, Britten, and others. Janáček's music is particularly instructive in this context. As Taruskin points out, although unmistakeably modern, his melodic originality 'never took an abstract turn'. 'As a result,' he adds, 'his historical prestige has suffered.'[36]

In relation to enchantment, especially, the destructive effect of imposing a theoretical system on an art, rather than working with it as a partner, is obvious. As Schaeffer puts it, the Vienna school was

> inspired by scientific ideas, by a rigor coming from a discipline which wasn't music but an algebra equation … seeking its discipline – its ordering principles – outside itself, instead of within the source of its inspiration. This coincidence of a music which is debilitated and failing, and a glorious, all-conquering science is what really characterises the twentieth-century condition.[37]

Schaeffer himself originally subscribed to a similar point of view – 'Seeing that no one knew what to do anymore with DoReMi, maybe we had to look outside that' – but adds, poignantly, that 'Unfortunately it took me forty years to conclude that nothing [musical] is possible outside DoReMi.'[38] Even Anton Webern came to the same conclusion. In 1932, he wrote: 'As we gradually gave up tonality, there came the idea: we don't want to repeat, something new must come all the time! It's obvious that this doesn't work, as it destroys comprehensibility.'[39]

The basic problem is that tonal music – which is to say, music – is not itself a system, philosophical or otherwise, in the first place. To assume that what sounds right can be analytically captured and then adjusted in terms of what is and therefore should be right, as defined by a theory, is the classic disenchanted intellectual's arrogant mistake. And as music isn't a theory, it can't be 'corrected' by one. Rather it will depend, as does everything else, in the end, on what cannot be determined or dictated by a system, method or algorithm: judgement, taste, skill, creativity. Or in a word, art.

Caging Music

A friend suggested that the best comment on John Cage would be two or three blank pages. It's certainly tempting, but unlike Cage, who claimed to have nothing to say but was going to say it, I do, and I'm going to say it.

Cage's musical modernism has been highly influential, and not only in music. A student of Schoenberg, Cage once declared that he was faithful to his master's vision, but had gone beyond it.[40] Both composers' primary commitment was to a theory of what music is and should therefore sound like, rather than music as an experience that is both pre- and post-theoretical. Whereas Schoenberg wanted to replace music with a music system, however, Cage's programme was to replace it with pure no-system. In this, he resembled another of his inspirations, equally intellectually driven, Marcel Duchamp, of whom Cage was apparently in awe.[41]

Cage is important to consider for two reasons. One is that as far as enchantment in music is concerned, he was wrong about virtually everything. The second is that he was influentially wrong. This quintessential Apollonian, this 'scary goy' (as Norman O. Brown wickedly put it), was widely hailed as a countercultural guru and his puritanical musical modernism as liberation.[42]

Here are three of Cage's famous aphorisms, or rather imperatives:

> If something is boring after two minutes, try it for four. If still boring, then eight. Then sixteen. Then thirty-two. Eventually one discovers that it is not boring at all.

> The first question I ask myself when something doesn't seem to be beautiful is why do I think it's not beautiful. And very shortly you discover that there is no reason.

> Music is sounds, sounds around us whether we're in or out of concert halls.[43]

The first, about realising that something that sounds boring 'actually' isn't, resonates with a story Cage once told of a Zen master informing a student, after an unsuccessful apprenticeship of three months, then three weeks, that he now had three days in which to attain enlightenment or else commit suicide.[44] Guess what? The student became enlightened on the second day. The implicit menace of Cage's prescription is unmistakable ('Alright, I agree! It's not boring!').

The second prescription hinges on asking yourself why something isn't beautiful and finding there is no reason. In other words, Cage is again urging us to rectify a mistake in our sensual perception and apprehension by engaging in rationalist self-criticism. It's an exercise in disenchanted reason which is invited to direct aesthetic experience, then replace it.

The third takes aim at concert halls. In fact, Cage's whole programme has been summarised as the slogan 'All sounds are music', which translates into an attempt to get us to hear all sounds, including noise, as music, and more generally to experience all life as art. This sounds fine, if a bit fluffy, until you consider it more closely. To begin with, it imposes a duty on limited and imperfect beings which is ultimately impossible to fulfil, and therefore inhumane. In another of Cage's Maoist echoes, along with self-criticism and re-education, it calls for a kind of aesthetic permanent revolution. Jankélévitch, who does understand and value musical enchantment, observes that

To imagine a state of grace that continually refreshed the long droughts of our being would only imagine a chimera. This is something without sense, an unimaginable, almost superhuman idea ... as contradictory as the dream of an eternal celebration, which negates the idea of celebration per se. Because the long working days make possible the very idea of a holiday, and the mediocre, empirical interval makes the blessed instant an escape and a clear victory over an alternative.[45]

All music consists of sounds, but the reverse doesn't hold, because not all sounds are music. Unlike noise – even noise that is deliberately produced – music is a particular kind of sound that results from the corresponding art. I realise, of course, that what counts as music is a result of both sounds 'out there' and 'internal' human perception and judgement, and the same is true of noise. Nonetheless, music and noise both exist as kinds of sound with their own meanings and values. The upshot is that if one ran music together with all sound, as Cage wanted, then since sound as a whole (including noise) is vastly greater, all that would happen is that it would overwhelm music, and you would lose what the latter uniquely offers. I don't think he would have minded (he once admitted that 'The whole pitch aspect of music eludes me'), but we should.[46]

In other words, if you abolish music, you don't turn noise into music but music into more noise. Dissolving music in 'sound effects' thus has the same result as redefining visual art in terms of Duchamp's ready-mades and 'concepts'; art becomes merely banal. And the fact that Cage could contemplate such a grievous loss with equanimity shows the extent to which his vision was ideologically and politically driven. It's a Californian version of the old modernist brutalism: to make an omelette you have to break a few organic eggs. But as someone immortally asked, and as it should always be asked, where's the omelette? Even musically, let alone politically?

I have already mentioned Cage's most famous piece, *4'33"*. It premiered on 29 August 1952, with the 'performer' seated, without playing, at a piano for four minutes and thirty-three seconds. (There are several recordings, which says more about the ability of commodity capitalism to sell you almost anything than it does about the piece itself.) Of course, it's a clever idea. The goal – and there is one, despite Cage's claims to have surrendered intention – is to enable the audience to experience whatever ambient sounds happen to be audible in the room as music. Note that the piece depends on what Cage disavows, namely a difference in the significance of sound, including noise, and of music. The 'silence' of *4'33"* is decisively framed, and its meaning established, by the act of a musician (not someone who can't play the piano) sitting down at a grand piano in a concert hall (not a bar), who then doesn't play anything.

Cage lauded another modernist, Edgard Varèse, for his 'acceptance of all audible phenomena as material proper to music.' This places him, said Cage, in a prominent position vis-à-vis 'present musical necessity.'[47] Behold the iron fist in the Zen/ Dada glove! 'Present musical necessity' indeed.

Of course, it's easy to mock the hush of the contemporary concert hall, the frowns at a persistent cougher and glares when, *horribile dictu*, a mobile phone goes off, and to suggest that all this is somehow inauthentic compared with an audience of lively, noisy dancers, eaters and drinkers, say. But there is something in the phenomenon of an attentive concert audience – one that discourages egotists from doing things that interfere with others fully attending – which is rare and wonderful, even touching. Each such occasion comprises a community which has bothered to turn out and listen, and what is music without listening?[48] Even if, in the most cynical view, the contemporary concert audience developed for reasons of status, class-consciousness and a sectarian version of good taste, it nevertheless provides an opportunity to really listen to live music for those who really want to.

By now, the habit of collectively paying close attention has spread to some non-classical music. Blues, jazz, and folk/ traditional music started life as tiny glows of communal warmth in the night, surrounded by either the dark, dank land, or the hard uncaring city, and eventually made the move from the bar, pub, or dance hall to the concert hall. And yes, both paid a price for doing so in opening the door to elitism, snobbery and the individualism of stars. Yet that move also partly attracted, partly created audiences respecting and honouring the music enough to listen to it as closely as they could: no bad thing! And don't forget that some of those musics also stayed back where they started. It doesn't have to be either/or; there's room for both.

I was present at a concert by Charlie Haden's Quartet West in London in the 1990s which began with the announcement, 'Good evening, ladies and gentlemen. Mr Haden has asked me to make two requests. One, no smoking.' (This was when smoking in clubs, bars and pubs was common.) 'And two, please maintain absolute silence while the band is playing.' Amid the muttering and headshaking around me, I wanted to cheer. Don't the musicians and the music deserve to be listened to? And if you won't give yourself to it, how can it – why should it – give itself to you? And no, you cannot do that if you are busy filming it on your iPhone. I'm told that to a fan who argued, 'But I want to be able to relive my memories of the gig', Jack White, of the band White Stripes, replied, 'What memories? You weren't really there.' (White has also been active in the anti-digital resurgence, limited but a hopeful sign, of vinyl records.)[49]

Incidentally, there is a moment every audience knows when a good piece of music ends which, if it really was good, is one of pure enchantment. It's a very short moment but goes deep, so it feels long. Then applause breaks the spell.

Popular Music

Turning now to popular music, the wrench is not quite as abrupt as one might think; many of the same dynamics of enchantment and issues concerning it are shared. By popular music I mean simply music made for and heard by most people, whether now or in the past. 'Pop music' is a special category within that broader one, signifying popular music that is essentially commercially driven.

Popular music as a whole is a living tradition that no impresario or media company, no matter how powerful, can control. And what a whole! Anglophone popular music, for example, is a mighty confluence of traditional English, Irish, and Scottish songs and tunes feeding into folk, country and ballads alongside black American spirituals and blues, then soul, not to mention Brazilian, Cuban, and West African tributaries, every part of which has its own local and global variants. And throughout the roil of these waters it is often possible to discern the clear, cool, refreshing stream of enchantment.

I've no doubt that in every music, there is potential enchantment for someone. Yet some kinds are openly affined with enchantment, while in others it is simply not a priority. There are often plenty of reasons to like the latter anyway, of course; music can be a good, even great thing without it. Among kinds of popular music, for example, rock-and-roll is famously and rightly associated with hormones, sex, and drugs. Along with the rest of its flamboyantly dysfunctional relatives – metal (of all kinds: thrash, speed, death, etc.), rap, and hip hop, what is now called rhythm-and-blues, punk, grunge, hardcore … – rock is in aid of many things, from getting high or off your face and if possible laid to letting everybody know how angry you are and upsetting as many others who aren't one of your lot as possible. All thoroughly time-honoured Dionysian pursuits.

Another example of Dionysian popular music is soul and old-style rhythm-and-blues. Think of the sheer effort and work-rate of the great soul singer James Brown, say – a wonderful artist, but all that hoarseness, sweat, and agony, literally embodying will and effort, are neither about nor in the service of enchantment. Nor are the sentiments. Now that I've got money, needing luuve is concrete alright, but there isn't much room – or call – for mystery. Its focus is mainly on sexual magic and power (putting a spell on you, my mojo's working, etc.). By the same token, I love a closely-related kind of music – the blues, loud and well-played on electric guitar – but the grin on my face is one of simple pleasure. A solo by Mike Bloomfield is a reason to live. (That said, older acoustic country blues, like the songs of Mississippi John Hurt, can be pure enchantment.)

Another genre of popular music, heavy metal, while clearly exhilarating for some, also leaves little room for wonder. Unsurprisingly, as we learned in 2003, heavy metal, played very loud and repeatedly, was used to torture detainees in Guantanamo Bay, while in the second Iraq war, American soldiers used metal and rap to pump themselves up for fighting. This is music as warfare, under the aegis of Ares. Particular favourites were Metallica, AC/DC, Slayer, and Eminem, featuring such lyrical gems as the repeated invitation to motherfuckers to die. (All credit to the Canadian band Skinny Puppy, though; when they found their music had been used in Guantanamo, they invoiced the US government for musical services.)[50]

With respect to enchantment, rap music, with its aggression and sheer volume, is not radically different. Rap shares some of its relentless anger, sexual desire/ fear and the self-pity of the young male ego, laced with the politics of class and race, with hip hop, although the latter is a distinctly more musical form. Even the verbal inventiveness of rap is hard to enjoy when every word is a weapon.

Earlier, I discussed the endless potential for enchantment of melody and melodic lines. One major stream of popular music which took full advantage of that potential is the Great American Songbook.[51] A stream of glorious songs came out of this golden age, based in Tin Pan Alley in New York, from the 1910s until about the 1960s. In a hybrid of largely black American jazz and European classical music, brilliant lyrics melded with unforgettable melodies by Richard Rodgers and Oscar Hammerstein, Rodgers again with Lorenz Hart, Irving Berlin, George and Ira Gerschwin, Jerome Kern, Cole Porter, Noel Coward, Johnny Mercer, Hoagy Carmichael and latterly Johnny Mandel, as well as Tommy Wolf and Fran Landesman. But golden ages don't last forever, and this one is over. The influence of the Songbook continues in popular music, however, and in the repertoire for chamber jazz, where it still provides many of the standards and ballads for trios and quartets.

There is undeniably a streak of kitsch in American popular music. It is, as Roger Scruton nicely puts it, 'music that has escaped from the paddock of good taste into the open plains of common sentiment.'[52] But what makes common sentiment common is that very few people are untouched by its pains and joys, and that gives the music enormous potential to reach people. It also makes the music itself remarkably sturdy and portable. A tiny example: in *Summer Night* (2001), a Swedish singer with a background in traditional ballads, Lena Willemark, together with Elise Einarsdotter (piano) and Olle Steinholz (bass), takes up songs by Rodgers and Hart, and Carmichael and Mercer, as well as Einarsdotter's originals, and succeeds brilliantly. She does so because her own musical personality, at once forceful and subtle, finds a way to make the songs entirely her own and thereby universal, so to speak. But that universality also had to be there, in the songs, waiting to be realised.

Pop Music

Let's turn to a very different sort of universality, the kind we encountered earlier as the faux enchantment of glamour. In commercial pop music, produced by the correctly named 'music industry', virtually every word is a banality and every note a cliché, usually played electronically and all of it designed, recorded, manipulated, reproduced, and marketed with the maximum of corporate control for the purpose of making a profit. It is the acme of glamour. Of course, the songwriters I just mentioned were perfectly happy to turn a profit too, but their love of their craft and tradition is what really shines through, whereas 'entertainment' has, like all modern industries, become a branch of power-knowledge. This one, like the others, becomes more questionable the more you think about it (which is therefore discouraged). You might think, for example: let me get this straight. Against enormous odds you're actually alive, on the only planet (so far as we know) where that is even possible, and you need to be *entertained*? But yes, sometimes it seems we do.

In any case, it seems to be true that as the perceptive Alex Ross says, 'The old hierarchy of high [art] and low has become a sham; pop is the ruling party.'[53] He is well-placed to know. In recent years, that exemplary magazine *The New Yorker* has carried many essay-reviews of pop music. It sometimes still discusses classical music, more rarely jazz, but now unfailingly pop, and always in earnest, even reverent tones. This strikes me as not only a blatant pitch to a potentially profitable demographic more than a sincere interest, but also an embarrassing sacrifice of its own tradition of dignity in the face of commercial vulgarity: the journalistic equivalent of dad-dancing.

Another example: in May 2011, *The Guardian* published its 'Music Power 100 List', listing 'the 100 most influential people in the industry'. At pole position was the 'crack squad' of 'Team Adele' … It's not Adele's fault, of course, but the language, revolving around 'production', 'market', and 'team', says it all. As Van Morrison once remarked (and you need to hear it in a Belfast accent for full effect), 'Music is spiritual, but the music business is not.' Nor does enchantment merely entertain.

In Britain in recent years, the dominance of popular music (which is to say, most music) by the light entertainment monster was sealed by the popular success of the TV show 'The X Factor'. Criticisms such as Sting's – that it's a kind of karaoke confined within rigid commercial stereotypes, in which competitors 'are either Mariah Carey or Whitney Houston or Boyzone and are not encouraged to create any real unique signature or fingerprint'– are correct but easily shrugged off, because the industry has no interest in wild concrete magic. What it wants is generic reproducibility and the promise of profits that follows. Jon Savage is right: The X Factor was for 'people who aren't passionate about music. And there's always been a huge market for people who weren't passionate about music.'[54]

The same process has of course been taking place in America, and the same truth applies. How else to explain all the vapidly self-absorbed platinum-selling albums and teams of highly paid writers producing lyrics inviting you to shake your posterior, repeated ad nauseam? Garth Cartwright laments that the great era of American popular music is over: 'Since the 1970s an increasingly corporate music industry … has reaped huge profits from peddling endless pap. American music, once so regional and creative and strong and proud, is reduced to just another franchise: McMusic.' Robert Crumb, another authority in his way, agrees: 'The buying and selling of music, what they've done to it, is a disaster on the scale of cutting down the rainforest.'[55]

Inasmuch as the mystery of enchantment requires precision, there is little foothold for it in the few formulaic and homogenous styles of singing and playing that dominate radio, television, social media and corporate spaces, in which 'imperfections' have been eliminated and with them, any individuality, let alone eccentricity, that hasn't been pre-planned, engineered and stylised. Compare this cookie-cutter approach with the phenomenon of timbre, so important to enchantment. Although millions of guitarists play the same kind of instrument, made of wood and metal with six strings, yet you can hear a single chord or a few notes and instantly know it is Jimi Hendrix or Richard Thompson or Jerry Garcia. True, before the end of every concert where he plays electric guitar, Thompson, for example, will have played at least three impossible things (think of Roger Federer's returns). But it is not finally a matter of skill but voice, and thence presence, necessarily unique and therefore potentially universal.

My verdict on pop music could perhaps be extended to much popular music in general, since the distinction is pretty fuzzy. There are two reasons, however, why it doesn't go all the way. One is that the old music industry has become a dinosaur while the internet is evolving into a many-headed corporate monster: the Google-Microsoft-Apple-Facebook-Amazon hydra. Thanks to what remains of the original spirit of the internet, however, a determined as well as talented recording artist whose first concern is creativity rather than profit can still opt for perilous artistic freedom. Thus some independent labels and recording and performing artists are finding ways to survive, giving musical enchantment a tenuous new lease on life. With the derisory royalties currently allowed by the controlling corporations, however, they will need all the alternatives possible.

The other problem with a blanket condemnation of pop music was summed up by Amanda in Noel Coward's *Private Lives*, who remarked that it is 'extraordinary how potent cheap music is'. In other words, there is something so enchanting about music as such that for the right person in the right circumstances, it can survive almost anything. Sometimes, the X factor escapes even 'The X Factor'. This is Cyril Connolly, recalling his time as a boy at St Cyprian's prep school, where Cecil Beaton was a classmate, between 1914 and 1918:

> On Saturday nights, when the school was entertained in the big schoolroom by such talent as the place could offer ... there would be a hush, and Cecil would step forward and sing, 'If you were the only girl in the World and I was the only boy.' His voice was small but true, and when he sang these sentimental songs, imitating Violet Loraine or Beatrice Lillie, the eighty-odd Wulfricians felt there could be no other boy in the world for them, the beetling chaplain forgot hell-fire and masturbation, the Irish drill-sergeant his bayonet practice, the staff refrained from disapproving and for a moment, the whole structure of character and duty tottered and even the principles of hanging on, muddling through, and building empires were called into question.[56]

Music being cheap – inexpensive and, by implication, common – thus need not diminish its power to enchant. I say '*need* not' because much cheap music is rubbish. But the most reliably enchanting melodies from the Songbook tradition, for example, have aged extremely well, and some have become jazz standards which are also proving long-lived. They are deeply loved in both forms by many who know them.

Musically quite simple in their bare bones, their lyrics express sentiments which sometimes appear banal, especially in the cold light of print. That failing also reflects the challenge of trying to capture what notoriously slips through a net of words alone. But sometimes what matters comes through. One of Jesse Winchester's beautifully crafted late songs, sung in that sun-drenched Southern voice, invokes an old do-wop song from his youth. It puzzled the old folks, he says, but in 'those sweet old love songs/ Every word rings true. Sham-a-ling-dong-ding means sweetheart, Sham-a-ling-dang-dong does too.'

Popular Music and Enchantment in the 60s and Now

There was a powerful flowering of collective cultural enchantment in the 1960s, or more exactly, the mid-60s through the early 70s. It was perhaps most obvious in popular music, and its influence remains strong even today. There was a price: British music-hall and French chanson never really recovered, and although the blues prospered as never before, a creative renaissance in jazz between the mid-1950s and the mid-60s came crashing to a halt. But the creativity is undeniable, nonetheless.

Listening again to some of the countercultural music of the 60s, I am struck by two qualities. One, underpinning the sexual and druggy themes, is heavy, menacing, and obviously Dionysian. This was the dominant note among bands, especially rock bands. Think of the Rolling Stones, The Doors, Steppenwolf, Jefferson Airplane, The Velvet Underground, Cream and, slightly later, Led Zeppelin: poster-boy Dionysian sexuality, born to be wild, ten miles high, celebrating acid and smack, relentlessly dark and almost parodically phallic.

Running alongside this note, however, there was something lighter, more subtly intense, often markedly either joyous or sad. That is the sound of enchantment, and if the Dionysian sound dominated much popular music of the time, as did bands, among singer-songwriters enchantment was the theme. Never before or since have they flourished so. It's invidious to name some and not others but of those still sometimes listened to, Bob Dylan, Joni Mitchell, Leonard Cohen, Nick Drake, Phoebe Snow, Neil Young, Richard Thompson, Janis Ian, Jesse Winchester, James Taylor, Paul Simon and Ray Davies (and, slightly later, Rickie Lee Jones, Joan Armatrading and Kate Bush) developed songwriting, rooted in traditional ballads but now with a new individuality, freedom and sophistication, into virtually a new art-form. As Van Morrison, whose album *Astral Weeks* was one musical high-water mark of the time, asked rhetorically in 1985, as per the title of his album that year, 'Didn't I Come to Bring You a Sense of Wonder?'

My own preference, as an enchantment-fixated young man, was always clear. Already in 1969, the Dionysian 60s were going up in flames on the pyre of the Altamont festival to the tune of 'Sympathy for the Devil', but I wasn't there. Instead, I had worked my way up to the front of the stage at Tanglewood, Massachusetts, on a warm summer evening, where I was flying in place, listening with my whole body to Joni Mitchell singing a new song called 'He Played Real Good for Free'. (I listen to her with the same delight now. These things stay with you.)

There were exceptions, of course. Tim Buckley was a notably Dionysian singer-songwriter. (In the interval of his show in a small club in Palo Alto, a quavering voice broke the stunned silence to say, 'Gee, I thought he was a folk singer.') On the other side of the band/sing-songwriter distinction, the Beatles, the Kinks, The Band and the Grateful Dead, among others, offered, as well as sang, enchanting stories.

Another qualification is that geniuses roved, as they will, between any such distinctions: Dylan and Hendrix, perhaps most obviously. (Randy Newman too deserves special mention as a singer-songwriter who has specialised, brilliantly, in disenchantment.) Finally, there was an entire genre, folk-rock or electric folk, in which bands gave old songs new life in ways that rendered their enchantment accessible to contemporary audiences: The Band again, Fairport Convention, Steeleye Span.

Folk-rock continues today in the music of Fleet Foxes, Mumford and Sons, The Low Anthem, Bon Iver and others, and I hear the same wonder. I hear it too in the songs of some new singer-songwriters. But there is no homogeneity here; in each performer, enchantment sings in her or his unique voice, the 'concrete' part of its 'magic'.

None of these new voices of enchantment has been more distinctive than that of Joanna Newsom, and here's a paradox which should alert us to the presence of a truth. Newsom's particular concrete magic is undeniable, whether it appeals to you or not, and her relative success confounds any final despair about the dominance of commercially driven formulaic pop. I don't mean only her singing voice, which matured in later work, but her sensibility and style, both musically and poetically lyrical. (I feel her lyrics bear comparison with Wallace Stevens's poems.)

But Newsom's uniqueness doesn't suppress the felt presence of other unique enchanters; quite the contrary. For me, she evokes two. One is the vibrant intelligence of Joni Mitchell, especially as she was beginning to experiment with jazz, although without her melancholy. (The depth of that melancholy emerges, even without lyrics, in the instrumental versions of Mitchell's songs by the pianists Marc Copland and Fred Hersch.)

The other presence is the Incredible String Band at their best. And I'm sorry to have to say so, but it would be difficult for anyone who didn't hear them, live, to really appreciate the extent of that fragile but powerful best: insistent as only a 'little phrase' of music can be, piercing as a girl's glance, mysterious as a strange taste – and just as hard to describe. I vowed at the outset that I wouldn't quote people simply in order to invoke their authority, but I'll make an exception for Rowan Williams, formerly the Archbishop of Canterbury, and no fool:

> Forget the clichés about psychedelic and hallucinogenic vagueness: this was work of extraordinary clarity and metaphorical rigour … For those of us who fell in love with the ISB, there was a feeling of breathing the air of a very expansive imagination indeed.[57]

One moment in music, only recently become available as a recording, perfectly illustrates the difference between the Dionysian dominance of rock at the time and the quieter, saner note of enchantment. (Saner in the sense that Chesterton specified: 'To be sane is more dramatic than to be mad'. Actually, as he also pointed out, you have to be sane to find 'even a wild poetry in insanity,' whereas the madness of the insane is not even interesting to them.)[58]

On 5 June 1968, the Incredible String Band gave their first concert at the Fillmore East in New York City. It was a single night sandwiched between shows by Jefferson Airplane and The Crazy World of Arthur Brown and, a few days later, Jimi Hendrix and Steppenwolf. The staff, used to an audience of (in the house manager's words) 'Hell's Angels, East Village "Motherfuckers" and off-their-heads rock fans', were unprepared for who arrived. He recalls, 'Our job was to keep on the move all night, patrolling, supervising, and acting as the heavies ... That night, when the doors opened at 7.00, our jaws dropped. A continual stream of quiet, smiling, and happy people walked into the theatre. There was no smoking, no yelling, no garbage on the floors, and most of all, they were extremely polite.'[59]

I was lucky enough to be there, and I still remember the freshness of that night, the sense of amazing luck, even grace, at being present. There were no whoops or shrieks to show how excited one was, only a passionate attention to the music, punctuated with applause to show our appreciation.

Punk rock, in the sharpest possible contrast, is the music of disenchantment. In the mid- to late-70s, it set out to smash the music of the 60s, much of which, it must be admitted, had become decadent and bloated by then. Its success almost destroyed the cultural credibility of singer-songwriters. But it was bracing for a little while.

Another kind of 'music' without any virtue at all that I can find is the schmaltzy, cheesy, kitchy kind of song – sentimentality without sentiment – heard in lifts, bars, and shopping malls. Enchantment relies on relationship and risk, not hammy self-glorification in which nothing is really at stake. Ironically, of course, muzak is often parasitic on genuinely enchanting ballads and standards. But that shouldn't be surprising; the broader parallel with glamour and the enchantment it tries to copy is almost exact. Indeed, many of the most commercially successful songs are now composed by professional teams following pre-set formulae, financed by the label bosses seeking a return on their investment.

Actually, there is a secret affinity between punk and muzak. It was revealed in Sid Vicious's cover of Frank Sinatra's 'My Way', paying the homage that parody always extracts. And Sid and Sinatra were united in their contempt for the 'hippies'. But the ascendency of glamorous but disenchanted popular music-making in the 1970s and 80s, and its enduring impact, may owe most to David Bowie. In his doomed search for an authentic self, each new mask meticulously crafted and controlled, the music was always in service to the glamour of the show, its every detail self-consciously calculated for a desired effect: not to evoke wild wonder but to sell a product, namely himself. Dylan may endlessly reinvent himself, play himself, and go to great lengths to disguise himself, but he is never not himself. Bowie never was.

This commercially driven egotism-without-an-I set the mould for successors from Madonna to Lady Gaga. It also fed neatly into the siren song sung by Thatcher and Reagan, the one that says it's all about *my* needs, desires, success. Still very much with us, that one, as is its underlying emptiness. As Proust says, 'when words are chosen not by our mind pursuing its innermost affinities but by our desire to portray ourselves, then they will represent that desire, not our self.'[60] Then, through no fault of their own, chronically undernourished souls, seeing themselves reflected in Bowie, hail him as one of them. You would think his horrifically despairing finale, *Blackstar*, might make them think again.

Thanks to the dispiriting declension of modernity since the 1980s, wringing from it every last grim and grimy permutation, everyone from or influenced by the 60s who has somehow managed to survive without compromising a basic commitment to peace, love, and understanding is now a radical. (That excludes those who have profited handsomely from the transition from counterculture to cyberculture, led by that grinning pied piper Stewart Brand.) Idealism itself is still as radical as it ever was, if not more so, and so is honouring enchantment, unbiddable, and largely unprofitable.

Songs

Michel Serres is right: 'Language needs music, its essential condition; music has no need of language.'[61] Nevertheless, the art of blending music and words results in something unique that cannot be reduced to either. (Bob Dylan is not 'really' a poet, for example, nor is he trying to be one.)

Many songs by these singer-songwriters, even in their youthful heyday, ached with sadness. Melancholy often shadows enchantment anyway, but in their case, it also coincided with the end of collective cultural enchantment at the time, which was beginning to happen even as it peaked. Dylan, as early as 1963, looking back at his very recent teenaged years, wished in vain that he and his friends could be back together again, and the next year hymned that feeling restless, hungry, and futile in 'One Too Many Mornings'.[62] James Taylor asked plaintively why the song he was singing was so sad, Tim Buckley (in an album entitled *Happy Sad*) recalled the days when love seemed here to stay, and Tim Hardin wondered how to hang on to a dream, while Nick Drake asked painfully, 'I could be/ Here and now/ I would be, I should be/ But how?' and Sandy Denny asked 'Who Know Where the Time Goes?' Joni Mitchell lamented that she really only knew life's illusions.[63] (It took Yeats until the last decade of his life to realise, and record, that 'Players and painted stage took all my love,/ And not those things that they were emblems of.')[64]

Strikingly, all these artists were then in their early to mid-twenties – far too young for serious personal nostalgia, but not too young to have correctly perceived the worm of time at the heart of enchantment, both personally and of the times, even as it blossomed.

Nick Drake epitomises both the promise and the pity of this music. Superbly musical and full, in the words of his biographer, of 'emotional, dark poetry', Drake was left stranded between his awareness that what he was doing was good, even very good, and the fact that it was an utter commercial failure.[65] (More fool the public, then.) Success came far too late: a decade after his death, aged 26, in 1974. He was not a resilient person, and he suffered for it. But without that sensitivity, he could never have written 'Northern Sky', for example – one of the best songs about the enchantment of love ever recorded. It's not a pop song about crushes, 'synthetic creations' (as Laura Barton says) 'padded out with the musical equivalents of sugar and fat and bright blazing E-numbers'.[66] It's about wild, exalted love. Nor would his 'Pink Moon', the musical equivalent of a late Rothko, have been possible. Drake even inspired another enduring song by his friend John Martyn, 'Solid Air', about helplessly watching him vanish into depressive disconnection.

Any account of this music would be incomplete without mentioning Van Morrison, in whose solo work enchantment was, until a few years ago, a central concern. He frames it Romantically – Donne, Yeats, Wordsworth, Coleridge, Blake, Eliot and Whitman, as well as Kahlil Gibran and Omar Khayyam, all appear in his songs – and although later I will distinguish between enchantment and Romanticism, it is true that the Romantic tradition has often carried within itself, and nurtured, enchantment as a value. But Morrison makes it personal, as one must if it is to touch and become real to anyone else. In Greil Marcus's words, Morrison's true sound, when he hits it, 'becomes the active agent: a musical person, with its own mind, its own body.'[67] In other words, a presence.

Morrison's *Astral Weeks*, recorded when he was just 23, is an astonishing work: literate without being literary, musically sophisticated but unpretentious, and effortlessly lyrical. When it appeared in 1968, no one had ever heard anything like it, and despite being hugely influential no one has ever succeeded in doing anything quite like it since (including Van).

'Killing Me Softly with his Song' is remarkable as an enduring song about specifically female musical enchantment.[68] It was written by Norman Gimbel and Charles Fox after Lori Lieberman described to them her experience of listening to Don McClean performing and feeling he was telling her life. (At least, that is how two of the three of them remember it.) Roberta Flack then made it a hit in 1973, singing with Donny Hathaway in mind, and in 1995 it became another success, finding its way to new generations, when the Fugees recorded a hip hop cover featuring Lauren Hill, singing with Wyclef Jean in mind.

Of course, even an artist with a huge capacity for musical enchantment can blow it, or allow other priorities to take over, perhaps. I am thinking of Björk and her album of 2011, *Biophila*, whose music was almost overwhelmed by the accompanying suite of iPad and iPhone apps dedicated to a 'semi-educational' interpretation of the songs, telling you what they mean and even, by implication, how to feel in response. It's a testament to the strength of the songs that anything survived that disenchanting envelope at all.

Finally, nothing about Leonard Cohen? But Cohen was so fluent in wonder, and such a dedicated craftsperson, that the delicately powerful enchantment of some of his songs leaves little to say. I will just mention one key to that phenomenon which Cohen himself mentions. Asked if he works out ideas in his songs, he replied,

> I think ideas are what you want to get rid of. I don't really like songs with ideas. They tend to become slogans … I like to work on a song until those slogans, as wonderful as they are and as wholesome as the ideas they promote are, dissolve into the deeper convictions of the heart.[69]

I want to turn now to two contemporary singer-songwriters in order to illuminate, in a microcosmic way, the complex and subtle relationship of enchantment to the singer-songwriter genre. P.J. Harvey's *Let England Shake* (2010) evokes a land devastated by war, greed and apathy, its point all the more effectively driven home by her fragile feminine singing. The perspective is valuable, even necessary, but I cannot imagine anyone finding this heavy nightmare of history enchanting. (Nor can I imagine England shaking as a result.)

Against Harvey's vision, what could be more insubstantial than Laura Marling's 'Goodbye England (Covered in Snow)', from an album of the same year: 'Winter was on us at the end of my nose/ And I never love England more than when covered in snow'? Indeed, within the song, Marling acknowledges that 'true love is frail and willing to break ... so goodbye old England until next year's snow'. Yet for anyone who loves England, for reasons mysterious even to them and without denying its crimes and failures, it is hard to hear this little dream without a catch in the throat.

Harvey's songs indict nationalism where Marling's evokes the love of the land, among other things. Nationalism and patriotism, as Orwell argued, are not identical, and do not, should not, cancel each other out. Obviously, an enchanted apprehension of a place does not magic away the nightmarish history of that place (even if it is not precisely the same place) – one so light, the other so weighty. But the reverse is also true, and to neglect it would be a kind of self-mutilation. Even – maybe especially – the poor and deprived need enchantment and what it can only give if it isn't given over entirely to the marketplace. But then, so do the powerful. Without it, as Charles Dickens warned the materialistic 'realists' of his time, 'in the day of your triumph, when romance is utterly drive out of your souls, and they and a bare existence stand face to face, Reality will take a wolfish turn, and make an end of you!'[70]

There's something else that makes Marling's song special; and Harvey's, actually. It is a characteristic they share with one from an earlier generation of female singer-songwriters, Joni Mitchell's 'Furry Sings the Blues', from the album that is (alongside *Blue*) her masterpiece: *Hejira* (1976). These songs aren't only about the artist's soul – something that always risks self-indulgence and its disenchantment – even though they do reveal it. Rather, they invoke the concrete magic of moment and place. In the case of this song, in a seamless blend of instrumental and verbal lyricism, it is Beale Street, Memphis, where spirits from the jazz age cluster around the iconic statue of W.C. Handy, dancing and dealing even as the developers move in. And interfused with the musicality is a courage and uncompromising integrity as an artist which reminds me of Karen Blixen.

Dylan

Not surprisingly, Bob Dylan is a special case. Except as an inveterate mould-breaker he doesn't fit easily into the 60s as we usually think of them; he was certainly no hippie, nor was he a political activist for very long. As Joseph Brodsky observes about the poets Mandelstam, Akhmatova and Tsvetaeva, 'They would have become what they became even if none of the historical events that befell Russia in this century had taken place: because they were gifted. Basically, talent doesn't need history.'[71] Indeed, most of Dylan's very best work was done by 1967. Between 1964 and then, he was not so much inspired as possessed, a man on creative fire. Thanks also to his earlier musical apprenticeship, not to forget his bottomless self-belief, the music he recorded then still resounds today.

Dylan's harmonica solo at the end of 'Desolation Row' (for example) blows through my soul as sharp and fresh now as it did forty years ago. But there's nothing like the world's casual reception of what blows you away to remind you that personal enchantment's currency has extremely variable purchase out there. In 1965–66, Dylan released his epic three albums *Bringing It All Back Home*, *Highway 61 Revisited* and *Blonde on Blonde*. By then he had traded the burden of being 'the voice of his generation' for the admiration of his musical peers, including the Beatles and Rolling Stones. But they still outsold him, and the cash tills were ringing louder for Sam the Sham and the Pharoah's 'Wooly Bully', Barry Sadler's 'The Ballad of the Green Berets' and Frank Sinatra's 'Strangers in the Night'. (I still find it personally offensive that the crapulous Rat Pack of Sinatra, Dean Martin and Sammy Davis Jr. kept right on carousing as if nothing had changed. Indeed, only three years later, with typical perversity, Dylan himself started mugging and crooning in *Nashville Skyline*.)

But I want to point out something else. As anyone can attest who has observed him, or has watched Scorsese's documentary *No Direction Home*, Dylan is virtually an incarnation of Hermes: the elusive, inspiring, ambiguous, cunning, liminal, shapeshifting, quicksilver messenger and trickster god, patron of what Keats called 'the chameleon poet', whose unreliable testimony often goes to the heart of what really matters.

It surely matters too that while no one could say Dylan has no ego, from his own point of view 'I don't know who I am most of the time. It doesn't even matter to me … I find the religiosity and the philosophy in the music. I don't find it anywhere else.' Placing the music first, ahead of oneself, is one of the sure-fire signs of an artist trying to work with wonder. Dylan himself has remarked, almost cataloguing enchantment's qualities, that

> The closest I ever got to the sound I hear in my mind was … in the *Blonde on Blonde* album. It's that thin, that wild mercury sound. It's metallic and bright gold, with whatever that conjures up. That's my particular sound.[72]

So Dylan has a complex elective affinity with enchantment. The same characteristic, however, means that he is too complex to be solely so identified. Dylan rarely sings about enchantment, for example. True, 'Mr Tambourine Man' is one of the best songs ever to celebrate the state of mind and world if and when one finds oneself dancing under a sea-encircled sky of diamonds. More often, though, he has excelled at turning the ignoble emotions – contempt, disgust, jealousy, anger, braggadocio, blame, and self-pity – into creative gold. Indeed, judging by his most recent album, it's starting to look like they are what keep him going.

As a mark of his mercurial genius, where a lesser artist might invoke the poignancy of a beloved other ageing, dying or disappearing, Dylan others himself in the same vein. In 'One Too Many Mornings', it's not the scene that starts to fade but his own eyes. The figure of 'Mr Tambourine Man' causes the singer himself to disappear through the mind's smoke-rings. In the extraordinary 'Visions of Johanna', those visions end up taking the place of the singer. (It would have been prohibitively expensive to quote the song, so I can only urge you to look up the lyrics; or, better, listen to it.) And in 'Red River Shore', Dylan concludes that nobody had ever seen him at all except the girl from the Red River Shore – and she is long gone. One of his most powerful songs, this one speaks directly to the enchantment of love and its inevitable loss. (It also testifies to his enduring perversity in leaving it off the album it should have crowned.)

The disenchanted opinion of Dylan's own voice has never changed: 'He can't sing!' That judgement can be contested even in the strict interpretation of singing; at his best, Dylan's vocal style, however unusual, was utterly effective. Now that it sounds as if he has been gargling razorblades, however, has the criticism merit? Not for the enchanted; if anything, the reverse. It is now completely inimitable. Every rasp and snarl, each new intonation in that self-created accent, the ever-increasing vocal strain, opens up new vistas of emotional depth.

Traditional Music

Dylan purportedly once dismissed a journalist's question as to whether he was still a folk musician with the remark that all music is folk music. All popular music, certainly – and that's a lot – is music of and for the people, if not often by them. Singer-songwriters, not least Dylan, keep setting out from and returning to touchstones of traditional music even when the songs are their own. Bands working with enchantment are usually rooted in one form or another of traditional music: The Band (folk and country), The Kinks (music hall), The Grateful Dead (bluegrass and country blues).

There are good reasons why traditional or 'folk' music has more potential for enchantment than commercial pop music. One is simply the musical quality of the best of the songs. Like the best standards from the Great American Songbook, you cannot exhaust them. Play them straight and you may have an interpretation to stand alongside all those that preceded it, but it cannot replace them. Alternatively, the tunes are strong enough to hold improvising; you can bounce off them and play with them, and they bend without breaking.

Another reason is the centrality of narrative. In the next chapter, we shall consider the enchanting potential of storytelling in fiction; here, I'll just note that traditional music is unimaginable without the stories, profoundly human stories of love and loss, life and death, that it tells: 'full,' as Dylan says, 'of legend, myth, Bible, and ghosts'.[73]

Like much jazz, traditional music also benefits from being non-commercial. Enchantment as wonder is about the intrinsic value of what is happening, not amassing money and massaging ego, rendering the music a means to those ends. There is still plenty of room for character! On 22 April 2007, I heard Robin Williamson and John Renbourn at the Half Moon pub in Putney, London. How else could you ever hear a blues, 'Going Down Slow', played on the harp (not mouth organ); a ragtime version of 'What a Friend We Have in Jesus'; a memorable cover of 'Absolutely Sweet Marie'; and a 'Bonny Bunch of Roses' which brought tears to the eyes? Personality and presence, in all its glorious and vulnerable uniqueness, is integral to enchantment.

On another occasion, the evening of 7 February 2013, a friend took me to a concert by John C. Reilly, with members of his bluegrass band, in St Giles in the Fields, Soho, in London. Reilly is a movie-star, but this word-of-mouth event was entirely about the music, keeping the old songs alive. Those traditional American songs, with their roots in British and Irish popular music often as old as the tiny church itself, rang out clear and true as a bell.

That's another reason for the potential enchantment of traditional music: its in-built humility. Self-aggrandisement is harder when the song you are hearing sung by, say, an Englishman, is a love-song from the Appalachians, composed by who knows whom and refined by other unknown artists, with deep roots in Scotland ... and before that? Earlier I mentioned a forty-thousand-year-old bone flute found in Southern Germany, the fingering of which is in a pentatonic scale still found in traditional, folk, blues, rock, and 'world' music ... In short, it's about us, potentially all of us. Michael Donaghy, writing on Irish traditional music, puts it this way:

> A player in such a tradition is expected to improvise, to 'make it new', and the possibilities for expression within the prescribed forms are infinite. But it's considered absurd to violate the conventions of the form, the 'shape' of the dance tune or story, because you leave the community of your audience behind, and you bring the dancers to a standstill. By 'traditional form' I mean the shape of the dance, those verbal and rhythmical schemes shared by the living community which link it to the dead and to generations to come.[74]

For the unknown bearers of music from homes long left behind, whether slaves or emigrants,

> Songs were their souls' currency...
> To be exchanged for other gold,
> Other songs which rang out true and bright
> When flung down
> On the deal boards of their days.

(Thank you, Moya Cannon.)[75]

Thus the currency of traditional music is exchange, not cash for a commodity. Perhaps that is one reason why the songs themselves are so durable, surviving changes of fashion. Walking through the campsite at a folk festival I don't other-wise remember, I once came across four or five young musicians with acoustic instruments entertaining themselves. As I approached, I realised they were singing a traditional song, 'The Lowlands of Holland', a song of love, loss, and the sea, that I had first heard more than twenty years earlier, in 1970, when I was their age, played by Steeleye Span. Martin Carthy, a living embodiment of British traditional music, was a member then, and among them I recognised his daughter Eliza. Hearing that old song given new life, something caught me by the throat and my vision blurred.

Last night I listened to Martin Carthy himself, another twenty years on. He was performing with Dave Swarbrick, a fiddler who plays with a daemonic energy and anarchic elegance, like a drunk man crossing a busy street who somehow never comes to grief. I had last heard Swarbrick in 2007, when the surviving members of Fairport Convention played the songs from *Liege and Lief*, the record that in 1967 gave birth to British folk-rock. Swarbrick stood at one end of the stage with Richard Thompson at the other, and as the guitarist's playing became ever more darkly melancholic his own grew more fiery, in perfect if perilous balance.

Folk-rock – traditional songs, ballads, and tunes played loud on amplified instru-ments – can fairly be said to have been half discovered, half created by Fairport Convention in the song 'A Sailor's Life' from *Unhalfbricking*, released in 1969. For a wildly uncommercial eleven minutes (for which Dylan broke the ground with 'Desolation Row', also at eleven minutes, in 1965), Swarbrick and Thompson duet with each other and Sandy Denny's powerful singing. And when the girl in the song finds out that her sweet William is drowned, her grief is so great that 'her little boat against a rock did run'. Being ourselves each in our own little boat in the great swelling sea, no one listening needs to ask what that means.

At its best, folk-rock is a good demonstration that authenticity can survive tech-nology, find new audiences, and renew its lease on life. (By 'authenticity' I mean the living heart of a tradition, its inner idea and depth. If we discount the over-knowing on one hand and the ignorant on the other, there will be a surprising degree of consensus on what does and doesn't qualify.) This certainly doesn't mean that every technological 'advance', as they like to call it, is good for enchantment. It all depends on the use of the technology concerned, the particular tradition and its condition, and the intention and skill of the performers.

Traditional music has its own especially enchanting instruments, among which the Irish harp is one. That might be on account of its brass strings which reso-nate like tiny church bells (the sound always reminds me of Christmas), but there's also the wonderful repertoire. The compositions of the great late-seventeenth–ear-ly-eighteenth-century Irish harper Turlough O'Carolan, perhaps in particular, pos-sess the dignity of deep feeling expressed in elegant forms, perfectly reconciling Romantic impulse and classical restraint.[76] (Monk's tunes have the same quality.) Why do we assume that dignity must be ponderous, or levity superficial?

Irish traditional music has its geniuses past, like O'Carolan and Seán Ó Riada among others, and present, such as Martin Hayes and Caoimhím Ó Raghallaigh, who fill hushed concert halls. Like Charlie Haden, they have the skill and nerve and *nous* to be able to play slowly, leave spaces, and follow the tune wherever it goes. As Hayes says,

> When I'm playing music, I'm not concerned about style, I'm concerned about this line of melody, and what I might do to support it, to reveal its power or majesty or joy or melancholy … Melody is a universal … There's great freedom in it as long as you honour, completely, the central point, which is the line of melody.[77]

Superb phrasing lets the music breathe in its own freedom. The tunes are old, even when newly made out of older ones, but (as R.S. Thomas says of the blackbird's song) 'fresh always with new tears.'[78] And no one owns them, so enchantment can also reward those who just happen to be present at a pub session, where the artists are unknown outside their own circle and the cost is the price of a drink, on a night when it all takes off.

Whenever I have been transported by this music, part of the enchantment was finding myself in the song, and the song in me. It's a reminder that the old tunes and songs that are sound, the stories with deep roots, have a way of coming to life again, greening after every winter. As George Mackay Brown puts it, in *An Orkney Tapestry*, 'The fiddle, the skull, and the cornstalk yield their full significance only when they are seen in relation to each other.'[79] It's wonderful to be reminded, hearing this music, that one is part, however small, of these cyclical narratives, carried along and renewed along with them. Nor is my verdant metaphor a mere conceit. Human stories are themselves part of the great, compelling and inclusive narrative that is the Earth. They are our version and contribution, and even a glimpse of such continuity awakens its wonder. Jankélévitch says, 'All divine, sublime things that are vouchsafed to human beings in brief glimpses have this same nature, at once dazzling and dubious.'[80]

Notes

1 *The Guardian* (19.10.12).
2 Eichler, 'String Theorist': 39.
3 Susan Tomes, *Beyond the Notes. Journeys with Chamber Music* (Woodbridge: The Boydell Press, 2004): 183.
4 Richard Taruskin, quoted in http://books.google.co.uk/books?id=NmVgkIcGuE oC&pg=PT1636&lpg=PT1636&dq=%22was+literally+an+embellishment+of+the+- soloist%27s%22&source=bl&ots=QTmfLmSCSH&sig=3VFR41HRPdocwWt-gz8Z_ d4vlVk&hl=en&sa=X&ei=y2CtUfemNIzk8gS2uYDAAw&redir_esc=y (accessed 5.6.13; with thanks to Michael Winship).
5 Alex Ross, 'Taking Liberties', *The New Yorker* (31.8.09): 80–81.
6 See concert notes by Richard Wigmore for a concert by the Quator Ebène at the Wigmore Hall, 15.10.2021.
7 Patrick O'Brian, *The Ionian Mission* (HarperCollins, 2003): 41. There is a wonderful poem about Haydn's music by Tomas Tranströmer called 'Allegro'.
8 Jan Zwicky, *Robinson's Crossing* (London Ont.: Brick Books, 2004): 23.
9 Aldous Huxley, *Music at Night and Other Essays* (London: Chatto & Windus, 1932): 19.

10 Storr, *Music*: 145.
11 Nicholas Spice, 'Is Wagner bad for us?', *LRB* (11.4.13) 3–8: 5.
12 Spice, 'Wagne'r: 8.
13 *The Guardian* (25.4.13).
14 *The Basic Writings of Nietzsche*, transl. and ed. Walter Kaufmann (New York: The Modern Library, 1992): 707.
15 Eichler, 'String Theorist': 39.
16 Liner notes to Claude Debussy, *Intégrale de la Musique de Chambre*, Le Quator Talich (Calliope 2003).
17 Roger Nichols, *Ravel* (London: J.M. Dent and Sons, 1977): 133, 156.
18 *The New Yorker* (9.3.2020) 40.
19 Erik Satie, *A Mammal's Notebook: The Writings of Erik Satie*, ed. Ornella Volta and transl. Antony Melville (London: Atlas Press, 2014): 134.
20 See Miquel Desclot, liner notes for Federic Mompou, *Música callada*, Javier Perianes, piano (HMG, 2006).
21 Antonio Iglesias, liner notes to Mompou, *Complete Piano Works* (Brilliant Classics, 2012).
22 For information and following quotations I have drawn on Per F. Broman, liner notes to *Rain Tree: The Complete Solo Piano Music of Tōru Takemitsu*, Noriko Ogawa, piano (Grammofon, 1996) and Leif Hasselgren, liner notes to Tōru Takemitsu, *A String Around Autumn* (BIS Records, 2002).
23 For this and following quotations in this paragraph, Per F. Broman, liner notes to *Chamber Music* by Tōru Takemitsu, Ensemble KAI (BIS Records, 1998).
24 Quotations in this section (including by Seigow Matsuoka) are taken from *Ma: Space-Time in Japan* (New York: Cooper-Hewitt Museum, n.d.). See also Okuyama K., *Notes sur le "Ma"* (Courbevoie: Atelier du Lierre, 2004).
25 Calasso, *Marriage*, 19.
26 *Ma*, n.p.
27 Stephen Toulmin, *Cosmopolis: The Hidden Agenda of Modernity* (Chicago: University of Chicago Press, 1990): 185. (Emphasis in original.)
28 Raymond Geuss, *Outside Ethics* (Princeton: Princeton University Press, 2005): 237, n. 11.
29 Joe Queenan: 'Admit it, you're as bored as I am', *The Guardian* (9.7.08).
30 Diana Raffman, 'Is Twelve-Tone Music Artistically Defective?', *Midwest Studies in Philosophy* XXVII (2003): 69–87.
31 Jankélévitch, *Music*: 108.
32 Rothenberg and Ulvaeus, *Book*: 42.
33 See Rodolphe Bruneau-Boulmier, transl. Charles Johnston, liner notes to Anne Queffélec, *Sati et compagnie* (Mirare 2012), and Taruskin, *Music*: 359.
34 Taruskin, *Music*: 359.
35 Taruskin, *Music*, 339.
36 Taruskin, *Music*, 134, 424, 444.
37 Pierre Schaeffer in pp. 34–43 in Rothenberg Ulvaeus (eds): 36. (He adds perceptively that Pierre Boulez is 'a kind of musical Stalinist', before comparing himself to an anarchist.)
38 Ibid.
39 Storr, *Music*, 171.
40 Michael Hicks, 'John Cage's Studies with Schoenberg', *American Music* 8:2 (Summer, 1990) 125–40: 125, 135.
41 Calvin Tomkins, *Marcel Duchamp: The Afternoon Interviews* (Brooklyn: Badlands Unlimited, 2013): 15.
42 Richard Taruskin, 'The Scary Purity of John Cage', pp. 261–79 in *The Danger of Music and Other Anti-Utopian Essays* (Berkeley: The University of California Press, 2009): 262. A perceptive and hilarious essay.

43 Toop, Ocean: 143, and Toop, Haunted: 59. See also Kyle Gann, *No Such Thing as Silence: John Cage's 4'33"* (Yale University Press, 2010), quoted by Alex Ross, 'Searching for Silence: John Cage's Art of Noise', *The New Yorker* (4.10.10), Bill Fontana in *The Guardian* (16.4.10): 10, and Adams, *Winter Music*: 112.

44 John Cage, *Silence. Lectures and Writings* (London: Marion Boyars, 1978).

45 Jankélévitch, *Music*: 127.

46 Taruskin, *Danger*: 262.

47 Cage, *Silence*: 84.

48 Cf. Scruton, *Understanding*, 12: 'Listening is the heart of all musical cultures'.

49 See http://ohnotheydidnt.livejournal.com/36845709.html (accessed 9.6.13).

50 See Jonathan Pieslak, *Sound Targets: American Soldiers and Music in the Iraq War* (Bloomington: Indiana University Press, 2009).

51 See articles by Terry Teachout, in *Commentary*, 1999–2002. For lyrics and commentary, see Robert Gottlieb and Robert Kimball (eds.), *Reading Lyrics* (New York: Pantheon Books, 2000).

52 Scruton, *Understanding*: 218.

53 Alex Ross, 'The Naysayers: Walter Benjamin, Theodor Adorno, and the critique of pop culture', *The New Yorker* (15.9.2014) 88–94: 94.

54 Sting and Jon Savage: *The Guardian* (14.11.09).

55 Garth Cartwright and Robert Crumb: *The TLS* (12.3.10).

56 Connolly, *Enemies*: 165.

57 Laurence Coupe, *Beat Sound, Beat Vision: The Beat spirit and popular song* (Manchester: Manchester University Press, 2007): 194. This book is very helpful in this area, as is Rob Young, *Electric Eden: Unearthing Britain's Visionary Music* (London: Faber, 2010). For an appreciation of the ISB, see Terry Castle, 'New Music', *Harper's Magazine* (May 2015): 82–3.

58 G.K. Chesterton, *A Motley Wisdom*, ed. Nigel Forde (London: Hodder and Stoughton, 1995); on insanity, Chesterton, *Trifles*: 54.

59 Liner notes to the CD *The Incredible String Band at the Fillmore East*, Hux Records, 2013.

60 Damion Searls, *Marcel Proust and John Ruskin on Reading* (London: Hesperus Press, 2011): 36.

61 Serres, *Senses*, 123.

62 'Bob Dylan's Dream', from *The Freewheelin' Bob Dylan* (1963), and 'One Too Many Mornings', from *The Times They Are A-Changin'* (1964).

63 'Both Sides, Now', from *Clouds* (1969).

64 From 'The Circus Animals' Desertion', pp. 394–95 in W.B. Yeats, *The Poems*, ed. Daniel Albright (London: Everyman's Library, 1992): 394.

65 Gorm Henrik Rasmussen, *Pink Moon: A Story about Nick Drake*, transl. Bent Sørensen (London: Rocket 88, 2012): 88.

66 *The Guardian* (24.11.06).

67 *The Guardian* (5.6.10).

68 See Rick Beyer, *The Greatest Music Stories Never Told* (New York: A&E/ HarperCollins, 2011): 178–79.

69 *The Guardian* (20.01.2012): 11.

70 From *Hard Times* (1854).

71 Robert B. Silvers (ed.), *The Company They Kept*, vol. 2 (New York: New York Review of Books, 2011): 112.

72 Jonathan Cott, ed., *Dylan on Dylan: The Essential Interviews* (London: Hodder & Stoughton, 2006): 204, xi.

73 https://bob-dylan.org.uk/archives/14153 (accessed 21.6.2022).

74 *The TLS* (14.8.09): 23.

75 Moya Cannon, 'Carrying the Songs', from her collection of the same name (Manchester: Carcanet, 2007): 14.

76 See the novel *Carolan's Farewell* by Charles Foran (Toronto: HarperCollins, 2005). An excellent contemporary interpreter of O'Carolan's tunes and composer of his own was Micheal O'Súilleabháin.

77 *The Irish Times* (22.2.20).

78 R.S. Thomas, *Collected Poems 1945–1990* (London: Phoenix, 2000): 85.

79 George Mackay Brown, *An Orkney Tapestry* (London: Victor Gollancz, 1972): 140.

80 Jankélévitch, *Music*: 127.

7

FICTION I

Writer and reader share a covenant. Without the writer, there's nothing to read. But without the reader, the words cannot come to life outside the author's own head. What Edna O'Brien calls 'the private transaction between unknown reader and unknown author', in privacy and silence, is crucial.[1] Written words are thus a pushmipullyu: writing at one end and reading at the other.

Although much younger than either painting or music, printed words are an equally powerful source of wonder, and maybe even stranger. For one thing, the enchantment we have already encountered is essentially a nonverbal experience, as most of the other arts confirm. This time, however, words are of the essence. In which case, they surely carry one over into that place where they no longer matter. Maybe we should say, with the Daoist philosopher Zhuang Zi, show me someone who has gone beyond words, so I can speak with them![2]

I struggled with what to call the next two chapters. Writing? But reading is just as important. Story, or narrative? But that is not confined to words, as we have seen; indeed, it's not even confined to art. Literature? But G.K. Chesterton was right: 'Literature is a luxury; fiction is a necessity.'[3] Fiction, then. But the experience of enchantment in reading or hearing words is not confined to novels, say. Here is Cyril Connolly, writing in 1944, on encountering the words of Sainte-Beuve, who lived in the first half of the nineteenth century:

> Intense emotion, a mixture of relief and despair, at reading Sainte-Beuve's notebook Mes Poisons, and discovering "This is me" ... How deeply moving to listen to such a voice from the past which in the present becomes an inspiration! I feel like a cringing cur kicked about in a crowd, which, running down an alley, finds there silence, an apprehension of revelation, and then, round a corner, comes suddenly upon a huge dark doggy statue, a canine colossus from another age, lending him courage and wishing him well.[4]

DOI: 10.4324/9781003353225-7

A textbook case, so to say, of finding oneself in the story. And doubled for me many years later, at 3 o'clock in the afternoon of 15 August 2011 in unlovely King Street, Hammersmith, when I read Connolly's words and with the same emotion, discovered myself in them in turn. As Alan Bennett's Hector says in *The History Boys*,

> The best moments in reading are when you come across something – a thought, a feeling, a way of looking at things – which you had thought special and particular to you. And now, here it is, set down by someone else, a person you have never met, someone even who is long dead. And it is as if a hand has come out, and taken yours.

The nearly seventy intervening years between Connolly's experience and mine, like the seventy years plus separating him and Sainte-Beuve, were mere linear time, dissolved without residue in the moment of enchantment.

Such enchantment is thus not restricted to what we call fiction. Still, I find it hard to shake the impression that stories about imaginary people, places, and/or worlds are the purest kind. Although all writing, in an unavoidable way, is fictive. Certainly any recreation of a world can only be successfully written, or understood, with the imagination of both parties engaged; and it tells a story. That is obviously true of novels concerning partly-imagined characters in a place that still exists – Proust's Paris, say – but it applies equally to autobiography, history and geography, and so-called travel writing and nature writing. (These genre labels have all the utility and charm of a plastic bag, which is to say, some and none respectively.)

Even scholarly works of history require imagination to make the connections between known facts, tease out underlying patterns and infer meanings, and appreciate them. The same point is only more obviously true of autobiographical accounts. Karl Ove Knausgaard, the Norwegian literary diarist, claims to hate stories: 'Just the thought of a fabricated character in a fabricated plot made me feel nauseous.'[5] I'm sure it did. (Compare Gollum, upon tasting a sacramentally wholesome Elven-cake: '"Ach! No!" he spluttered. "You try to choke poor Sméagol. Dust and ashes, he can't eat that …"')[6] But could anyone be so simple-minded as to believe that their account of their own life, no matter how accurate and detailed, is not also fabricated? Or that that aspect is not crucial to its literary success? Certainly not Knausgaard.

The pervasiveness of narrative imagination in factual accounts can also be reversed: in order to succeed, fiction must take account in turn of ordinary disenchanted reason and reality. And in order to be able to do that, one must be able to clearly distinguish between them. Unlike his modernist critics, nervously defending the fortress of reality against the insidious immorality of fantasy, Tolkien himself was clear about the difference, and not having any doubts about ordinary reality, he could wholeheartedly explore fantasy without recourse to irony or other virtue-signalling devices.

Thus he stressed that fantasy is 'a rational not an irrational activity'. Indeed, 'The keener and clearer the reason, the better fantasy will it make … For creative

Fantasy is founded on a recognition of fact, but not a slavery to it.' If it was impossible to distinguish between frogs and men, for example, 'fairy-stories about frog-kings would not have arisen.'[7] As we have already found, difference is a pre-condition of connection. In W.H. Auden's words, 'for there to be one there must first be two.'[8]

This point is essential to enchantment, because the heart of the imagination at work is metaphor. To meet with Achilles who is also a lion, or the king who is also a frog, is potentially a moment of enchantment, and in that moment, to realise something important and true. Metaphoric imagination, in connecting, both creates and discovers. In so doing, it apprehends something new and significant.

To various degrees, writers have always known this – the exhilaration, even intoxication, which keeps their bum on a chair while the rest of life goes by. Enheduanna, a Sumerian high priestess in the second millennium BCE, left us an impassioned celebration of writing. She compares it to 'giving birth, creating life, conceiving the world.'[9] So the writer, whether man or woman, takes on the role of the cosmogonic maternal female and, no matter how tiny the extent, is creator not only of words but worlds.

This work cannot be done by simile, using the apparently innocuous word 'like' to chain metaphor within safe limits. Freya Stark, for example, writes: 'Outside our bay but quite near, the ruffle of the wind continued. One could see but not hear it making a noise, running its fingers through the blue and tangling it in waves.'[10] She doesn't say that the wind ruffled the water *like* fingers – a move which would instantly reduce the true immediacy of experience, and thus betray what is actually being described.

Or take a situation described by Bruno Schulz:

> The girls sat perfectly still, the lamp smoked, the piece of material under the needle of the sewing machine had long since slipped to the floor, and the machine ran empty, stitching only the black, starless cloth unwinding from the bale of winter darkness outside the window.[11]

Its glittering reality, and the seriousness and depths of that reality, can only be plumbed by full-blown metaphor. It wasn't merely *as if* the machine was stitching a cloth of winter darkness from outside. And this is consistent with Schulz's succinct definition of the ideal of fiction, when not disenchanted by logical correctness, as 'a renewal of life through the power of delight.'[12]

We should also be wary of allegory, a device used to try to control meaning by restricting and literalising it as this or that one only. A reader should be free to find/create new and personal ones. Nor should we confuse metaphor with mere fancy or confabulation which, like surrealism, invents without finding out anything new. That is why Antonio Machado writes that 'Dream study has not yet produced anything of importance in poetry. The poems written while we are awake, even those less successful, are more original and more beautiful, and sometimes more wild than those made from our dreams.'[13]

Karen Blixen nicely summed up the implications of this process for the writer. A poet and a friend, she says, were discussing imaginative fiction and normal daily reality.

> The friend held that to a poet the two must be one, and that therefore his existence must be mysteriously happy. The poet contradicted him. A poet's mission in life, he said, was to make others confound fiction with reality in order to render them, for an hour, mysteriously happy. But he himself must, more carefully than the crowd, hold the two apart.[14]

For the reader too, a relationship between 'reality' and 'imagination' requires a distinction between them in the first place, a gap that can be crossed. Then it becomes possible to experience being in the room where you are writing or reading, yet also in the story, and finding yourself there – a self you hadn't met before but whom you instantly recognise, a self who hadn't existed before but now does, complete with a past and even memories! This was my experience of enchantment while reading *Peer Gynt*, mentioned earlier, when I found I was (as well as merely was not) the character in the story I was reading. I don't believe it is particularly unusual.

Reading and Deep Reading

On reading I take my stand, alongside countless readers, with Jorge Luis Borges:

> I think of reading a book as no less of an experience than travelling or falling in love. I think that reading Berkeley or Shaw or Emerson, those are quite as real experiences as seeing London … Many people are apt to think of real life on the one side, that means toothache, headache, travelling and so on, and then on the other side, you have imaginary life and fancy and that means the arts. But I don't think that distinction holds water. I think that everything is a part of life.[15]

Reading, particularly narrative fiction, is a truly extraordinary phenomenon; much more so than the internet, say. When one reads, an entire and definite world, composed of particular places and populated with distinctive persons, springs into existence in one's mind and, since one's mind is part of it, in the world. Francis Spufford recalls the moment when he first learned to read: 'the furze of black marks between the covers of *The Hobbit* grew lucid, and released a dragon.'[16] In any intelligent apprehension, these worlds and their inhabitants are fully real in the experience of the reader, dragons and all. As Russell Hoban has God say (in the course of a conversation), 'Whatever exists is real'.[17] (If dragons don't exist, how can we think and talk about them in a non-random way?)

As lived experience, there is simply no fundamental difference between 'is' and 'seems', for every 'seems' is itself an experience, and therefore another version and instance of 'is'.[18] So, in Paul Feyerabend's words, 'There is no other way out: we either call gods and quarks equally real, but tied to different circumstances, or we altogether cease talking about the 'reality' of things and use more complex ordering schemes instead.'[19] And fiction in particular teaches us that there are different kinds of real, but not degrees. (Hence my preference for the word 'imaginal' over 'imaginary', the former meaning stuff that can make you stop and laugh or cry, even if you can't point to it in the room.)

Compared with reading, a visual representation of fictional reality edges dangerously close to literal-minded facsimile, and all the more so as it tries to be 'exact', as with the greater part of films and video games. With theatre, no one present is completely unaware that the actors are not literally the people they are portraying, so the play is at least tensive; the actors are and are not those people. But I suspect that as enchantment, even plays cannot compete with the subtlety, range, and power of reading. For one thing, they too impose a single visual form, whereas literature is, in Tolkien's words, 'at once more universal and more poignantly particular', each hearer or reader supplying their own unique exemplar in their imagination.[20]

To repeat Proust, every reader is the reader of himself.[21] Yet Paul Ricoeur is also right: 'As a reader, I find myself only by losing myself.'[22] There is no contradiction here, because reading isn't only about the person engaging. Its self-discovery takes place through encountering a strange other as also oneself, and simultaneously realising the strange otherness of one's own self. 'What the poet is searching for', as Machado so aptly puts it – and what the attentive reader finds – 'is not the fundamental I, but the deep you.'[23] For above all, reading is an encounter between the reader and an imaginal world, created by the writer, and brought to life by a reader's quickening touch of participation. But once it has happened, that world and its personalities acquire their own agency, their own dynamics and imperatives; so the whole experience is animistic and relational. Since the other party in any real relationship cannot be wholly controlled, it resonates with unbiddable wildness. And that gap between the reader's self and the writer's and characters' otherness, when it is crossed by realising their metaphoric equivalence, gives birth to literary enchantment.

David Sexton describes the process thus:

> When you read, in silence, you can achieve a mysterious form of communion with the writer. You can hear his voice, the voice of the absent and the dead, speaking not just to you but through you. It is then both your own voice and that of another. The writer has inhabited you ...[24]

With these conditions in place, fiction can be a portal opening onto enchantment as generously as any art. Indeed, we might agree with the philosopher José Ortega y Gasset (and I do) that 'a novel that lacks this glorious and unique magic is a poor novel whatever other virtues it may possess ... freeing us from our own self and generously bestowing upon us the gift of transmigration.'[25] I would only add that the mythic provenance of such a gift, in its strongest and purest form, is Hermes.

Reading is therefore best undertaken with all the seriousness of play and for its own sake, rather than for any other reason – even self-improvement, or extending the range of empathy, or strengthening the moral fibre of civil society, although any of these might be a result. As Scott Black says, 'reading is an art as well as a skill, and all arts are perfected in spaces poached from necessity.'[26]

So let's call it 'fiction' after all: the enactment, in words, of metaphor as it creatively animates the entire natural world, including human nature. That is the proper context for fiction, and indeed all art. It is far from a purely human affair. As I mentioned earlier, nature proceeds, in Wallace Stevens's words, 'not [by] identity but resemblance' – in other words, not unity but relationships, bridging differences – and 'Because this is so in nature, it is so in metaphor'.[27] It follows, as he adds, that 'The body is the great poem.'[28] (Although that surely makes the Earth a greater poem still.)

Like all deep truths, the fictive metaphoricity of more-than-human nature is reversible. 'Words for me,' insists Fernando Pessoa, 'are tangible bodies, visible sirens, incarnate sensualities.'[29] Relating to words this way – words *being* this way – is surely inherent in reading whenever it exceeds mere information. The enchantment of reading qualifies as embodied and emplaced because it not only requires sight but, less prosaically, is never very far from hearing words spoken. (Although hearing the words in that way must follow from reading them, not lead or replace it.)

In addition, the avatars one becomes, almost shamanistically, through reading about them, are themselves embodied and emplaced in their own worlds. When you read, therefore, psychic analogues of all the senses are vicariously engaged, plus the additional sense of self-and-other as it develops through narrative time. No matter how different the senses, strange the bodies, or alien the places, there are never none at all; and if we cannot relate to them through our own, if only to go beyond our own, then what we read is meaningless.

I would even speculate that the moments of enchantment deep reading affords are identical with those experienced by the authors. Maybe part of their mind exclaims in wonder at what they have just written, while the reader, even many years later, is another witness to its birth. After all, literal time and space matter little in this domain where, as Marina Tsvetaeva says, 'Reading is complicity is the creative process.'[30]

Enemies of Deep Reading

That leaves reading's much-hyped contemporary elaborations – cyberspace and the internet, email, texting, and tweeting – as literature's noisy new brats. Cue gloomy prognostications about the future of reading, deep in particular. And if by that we mean slow, considered, and potentially life-changing reading, based on the ability to be alone with a book, and thence its author, concentrating on it, thinking with it and following where it goes – not 'sharing' it, reposting it, leaving a comment on it, or even thinking about any of those things instead of what you are reading – then those fears are well-founded.[31] We are increasingly sacrificing depth for a restless, nervy, superficial breadth: a 'tyranny of the virtual', in Will Self's words.[32]

The mode of reading encouraged by the Web and social media involves jumping repeatedly from one link to the next, skittering along the surface and never following a train of thought for long. As Jonathan Franzen says, 'Distraction pours through every portal, especially through the internet. And most of what pours through is meaningless noise. To be able to hear what's really happening in the world, you have to be able to block out 99% …'[33]

Information, of which digital information is now the paradigm, matters, but it is no substitute for the meaning uniquely supplied by narrative, any more than is knowledge for the wisdom of what to do with it. Ironically, for all the claims of being networked, the internet also promotes narcissism and, although one is never properly alone either, isolation. When was it decided that lived bodily reality (sometimes contemptuously known to cybernerds – our charming modern Gnostics – as 'meatspace') was optional? Or that virtual reality is more real than actual reality, of which the former is a tiny subset?

This is only one of the dark paradoxes that attend the internet. To an unprecedented extent, it has made knowledge available. As part of the same process, however, it also supplies an almost infinite reservoir of 'evidence' for any view whatsoever. Most grievously, far from increasing our intelligence the internet, by offering itself as an anonymous collective substitute for actual thinking, has made it easier to be stupid and vicious on a massive scale.

What then will become of deep reading in the age of Facebook, Twitter, Myspace, LinkedIn, Friendster, TikTok, Instagram, Tumblr, Pinster, Flickr, WhatsApp, and Snapchat?[34] All of them are deliberately designed, with a combination of exquisite skill and ethics-free venality, to grab and keep our attention. That the result is a flattening and shortening of the ability to follow a thread, to concentrate and to remember is hardly a surprise, and that that amounts to a grievous cultural loss goes without saying. I pity those who will miss out on reading, properly so-called, as a result. But it is unlikely to die out altogether, even if it increasingly disappears from collective view.

Personally, I am moving in the opposite direction: an old barnacle-encrusted whale, leaving behind the millions of sprats splashing in the shallows, giggling at the latest meme, and descending past the schools of journalists at mid-depth, with their earnest blogs and vlogs and weblogs, headed further down, deeper and darker, to where the really toothsome stuff awaits. (The *bona robas*, as Leigh Fermor liked to say, teasing the strait-laced.) I am utterly alone there yet in superlative company, as, from within the pages, characters, places, and moments come to life in my mind. I revel, begrudging not a moment, in *Middlemarch, Parade's End, The Alexandria Quartet, Stalingrad, A Glastonbury Romance*, the Aubrey-Maturin novels … When they're as good as these, the longer the better! (I just chanced upon Patrick O'Brian's description of it: 'right deep swimming in a book'.)[35] Then there's afterwards, when, as Virginia Woolf says, some 'consecration descends' from reading the great works of literature 'which we return to life, feeling it more keenly and understanding it more deeply than before.'[36]

At further risk to my intellectual street-cred, electronic reading is part of the same disenchanting process, because it impoverishes the concrete experience of reading. A book is not merely an idea in relation to which its form is secondary. In addition to its form and style, each book has its own look, heft and even smell which enters into the experience of reading it, and long afterwards can still evoke that reading simply by being noticed, picked up, handled, and dipped into; but an e-reader remains an identical glass-and-metal slab no matter what the content. It has minimal personality and therefore presence.

The very concept of 'content' is another piece of starveling Platonism. Words aren't merely 'on' a page any more than a soul is 'in' a body. When deep reading is taking place – the kind that opens a door on enchantment – the words and the pages they are printed on, the book containing them, the person reading the book and the place where it is happening all together make up that door. Nothing is inessential, and the act of deciding that this part is while that one isn't is already to start disenchanting it.

In short, an e-book, a mere tool for reading, is the disenchanted ghost of a book. Well, it's still voluntary, you might say. But we are all being hustled along in this direction, like it or not. The Google Books Library Project is steaming ahead with 'converting' all books ever published into a 'universal library' based on the principle of universal digitalisation, or in the words of Kevin Kelly, one of its prophets, 'the migration of all we know into universal form of digital bits', culminating in 'one very, very, very large single text: the world's only book.'[37] The aura of gee-whiz idealism and breathless geekery cannot disguise the true nature of this project and its soft imperialism: we will establish a universal way of not only knowing but living in which wisdom ('all we know') has been reduced to information ('text'), and there will be no other source ('the world's only book'). We can't say we haven't been warned. In the words of a Latin proverb, beware the man of a single book – even if it is a very long book.

Closer to home, I have just seen a prospectus on the 'vision' for the current British Library Extension Project. It's the future alright. Under the banner of becoming 'open, creative and innovative' – not to forget 'sustainable' and 'accessible' – the empire of knowledge-as-power will rule triumphant, rendering it ever-increasingly difficult to even distinguish between knowledge and power, as anything they cannot encompass and appropriate is expelled: true freedom of thought, non-instrumental creativity, inherent mystery, and wisdom that transcends mere information. I can hardly wait.

This programme doesn't only exist at high levels. In November 2009, Camden council in north London issued a report laying out its vision of the future of libraries. It read, in part: 'The People work stream sits alongside service visioning, ICT [information and communications technology], procurement, spatial strategy, pilot RFID [radio frequency identification], enabled library and communications work streams.'[38] And in this steaming pile of barely literate jargon, all without even a mention of books or reading as such but flushed with technophilia, the future of public libraries is the one thing that does seem fairly clear.

Meanwhile, whatever can't fit onto the screen of a smartphone is steadily dropping by the wayside. The transition to a principally electronic culture will take another decade or two, and may never be entirely complete, but many books of a kind hitherto widely valued are already in danger of becoming vestigial relics ('What, read a whole book?'). And in a cunningly self-protective way, that includes books which explain why.

It is thus extremely easy to overlook that the opposite end of the relevant scale is not merely moderate electronic consumption – reducing your Facebook time, say, or driving a Prius – but rather sometimes, at least, spending time in the company of effectively eternal things: what Yeats delineates when he asks that 'for portions of the year/ May [I] handle nothing and set eyes on nothing/ But what the great and passionate have used/ Throughout so many varying centuries'.[39] What would those things be? They include at least the Sun, Moon, and stars; fire and flame, earth, and the Earth, clean air, and pure water; green and growing things; fellow-creatures, including, but far from only, fellow-humans, again including, but far from only, loved ones; shelter; food (not food-like substances) and drink; and art.

Here is an index of sanity, and the relative lack of concession to obvious utility does not invalidate its truth. We may only be able to dip in and out of such relationships and way of life, but it would be a disaster for us to forget them altogether. It already is.

Deep reading is an indefeasibly private process. As Joseph Brodsky insists, 'A novel or a poem is not a monologue but a conversation of a writer with a reader, a conversation … that is very private – excluding all others …'[40] (This description surely applies equally to essays.) As such, it is connected in a fundamental way with a certain kind of self – the one who maintains a room behind the public shop, off-limits to everyone else, to use Montaigne's homely metaphor – and as the one declines, it's hard not see the other doing so in tandem.[41] But I guess such reading and such selves were never all that common in the first place, were they?

I believe they will survive, although in keeping with many other features of contemporary society it may retreat to the keep of a relatively privileged few, as in medieval and feudal times. Whether that would be a good or bad thing depends on the alternatives, doesn't it? Some may be still worse. Being removed from the danger of corruption by large-scale public movements may be a blessing; sometimes, not to be noticed is a good thing. In any case, it will remain true that the ultimate opposite of someone reading – not surfing or skimming or collaborating, but really reading – is a mob; and in this respect, a cyber-mob is no improvement.

Children's Literature

This topic is an obvious, almost unavoidable choice. We nearly all start reading as a child, and the worlds of wonder one enters then are at least as compelling as any later literary experience.[42] Edward Blishen is right that 'In childhood one reads as if having one's fortune told.'[43] (Here again is an affinity between enchantment as fate and the word as spell.) So let me draw on my own experiences again. After all, if the wonder isn't real to me, how can I communicate it to you?

Thanks to a well-read Anglophile mother, I grew up nourished on the cream of late Victorian, Edwardian, and more recent children's books. I needed little encouragement and read whenever and wherever I could, including under the covers with a flashlight and, when that was taken away, by the crack of light falling through the doorframe onto my bed, line by line. Thus, while one part of me was negotiating the challenges of growing up in the Canadian mid-west, a distinctly non-enchanted environment, another was living in various imaginal parts of England – the Forest, the Riverbank, the ancient ruins of Cair Paravel, the Shire – in a condition of life-saving wonder. Let's look into some of them.

I won't dwell long on A.A. Milne's *Winnie-the-Pooh* books for fear of making my more sensitive readers fwow up.[44] What I notice now is the dry humour of the writing, and the complete range of temperaments: phlegmatic (Pooh), sanguine (Piglet), choleric (Tigger and Rabbit) and melancholic (Eeyore, archetypally so). Most of all, I am struck by how self-contained is this world, an Ashdown Forest forever incorruptible even if oneself, the reader, cannot stay there forever. (In the other one, the one laid out on maps of Sussex, the government is considering fracking licences as I write.) Equally, it's a world in which – unlike, say, Winnipeg in the 1950s – wonder is possible and permitted, not ignored or derided.

As is often the way with enchantment, literary or otherwise, this one showed up again in an unexpected time and place. Many years later, not long before his death, I was keeping the poet John Heath-Stubbs company. He was telling me about an insider's report he had had of the consultations for the next Poet-Laureate, that when his name was mentioned it was generally agreed that 'Oh no, no, not Heath-Stubbs, he won't do at all'. I commented, 'How like them' – quoting, as he would have known, Eeyore – to which he replied, a smile lighting up his wintry face, 'Quite'.

I still love Kenneth Grahame's *Wind in the Willows*. Unlike Milne's Forest, Graham's world includes in it an unsafe place – the Wild Wood – although, in a nice touch, Badger, a pivotal character, lives in its heart. Actually, there are two such dangerous places, the other being 'the Wide World'. And since they are contained in and by the story, it is all the stronger. But Toad threatens to drive a motorcar through the lot and unleash the wrath of both: the plebeian stoats, weasels and ferrets, on the one hand, and powerful arbitrary authorities like the police and judiciary on the other.

I would add that the account of Toad's travails as 'a helpless prisoner in the remotest dungeon of the best-guarded keep of the stoutest castle in all the length and breadth of Merry England' had me laughing helplessly.[45] I'm not sure I fully appreciated the joke as a child. But I did feel the pull of an enchanted place – *Faërie*, in a word – which, for that very reason, is permanently under threat. As indeed all wild woods everywhere now are.

That Grahame himself knew exactly what he was doing was shown when he was asked, in that cleverly disenchanted way that so misses the point, whether Toad, being able to drive a car and commandeer a train, was the size of a 'real' toad or of a man. (This is just the sort of question Winnicott criticised as destructive: 'Is it real or imaginary?') Both and neither, Grahame replied: Toad was train-sized, and the train was Toad-sized.[46]

I was bored by E. Nesbit's *Railway Children* but loved her tales of adventures with the Psammead, at once waspish and marvellous. I followed with horrified fascination the Queen of Babylon's misadventures in London – a place itself already legendary for me – as she liberated her belongings from the British Museum, and I segued from her to C.S. Lewis's White Witch, Queen Jadis, as easily as he clearly did. (Unlike Lewis, I found George MacDonald's fairy tales mostly strange and unsettling. Nor could I make much of *The Water Babies*, although I do remember the odd but vivid sensation of what it was like to be one.)

I also lived quite a while in Narnia. The quiet enchantment of the wardrobe in an English country-house, opening onto a lamppost shining in the midst of a snowy forest at night in another land, is among the strongest and purest in all literature. It is all the more regrettable, then, that the final book, *The Last Battle*, Lewis the storyteller takes second place to Lewis the Christian apologist, and allegory drives out narrative enchantment. I found myself shut out, disenchanted, and baffled. As Spufford (himself a practising Anglican) says in his book on his own childhood reading, 'I thought I already had a place that would remain forever rich and full, not because it had passed into eternity, but because the story had said it was so.'[47] (Aslan as Christ more-or-less went over my head. What mattered was the story.)

Oddly enough, many years later another children's writer, Philip Pullman, repeated the same betrayal.[48] Obsessed with (as he sees it) Lewis's misogyny, racism, and religiosity, and determined to counter his baleful influence, Pullman ended up mirroring him. The wonderful storytelling in *His Dark Materials*, starting with another child hiding in another recognisably English wardrobe, is gradually over-taken by his determination to be another Grown Up telling his readers what he thinks they need to know.

The problem isn't secularism and atheism as such, any more than it is Christianity as such; it's didacticism, which is the death of story and with it, most enchantment. The affines of allegory, in which only one true meaning is allowed, aren't restricted to the One True God; they also include dogmatic atheism, whose adherents know – beyond any doubt, *mirabile dictu* – that there is no God, and scientism, with its strident monopoly of truth.

Michael Oakeshott has ably defended the distinctiveness of art from its frequent reduction either to practical considerations of personal usefulness and social func-tion or to scientific truth, whether directly or indirectly. He points out that the idiom of art is delight in images which 'do not belong to a universe of discourse in which "fact" and "not-fact" can be distinguished: they are fictions … And on this account, also, they are neither illusions nor make-believe images, nor are they images made in an activity of pretending; for illusion, make-believe and pretence are all impossible without a reference to "fact".'[49]

Pullman thus engages in a double misunderstanding. He considers fantasy, including his own, as 'not-fact', and therefore inferior to fact (and all the more so scientific fact), when it is fiction, and therefore neither. And he confuses not-fact with illusion, when the two are not at all identical; as Oakeshott says, 'illusion is mistaking "fact" for "not-fact", or "not-fact" for "fact".'

Relatedly, Pullman harps on about the writer's duty to be 'realistic'. But separating Will and Lyra forever, for example, isn't any more realistic than letting them be together would be. Both are narratives, and free choices by the author, and neither are determined by 'the facts'!

It seems unkind to add (but I shall, in the unlikely event you haven't noticed it) that Pullman's repeated paeans to so-called realism fly directly in the face of his actual writing, which includes talking bears, visible animal souls, flying witches, and other fantasy staples. He sees something important about Lewis but simply doesn't understand Tolkien, but that doesn't stop him from attacking the latter for failing to be what Tolkien never wanted to be – a realistic writer – while simultaneously praising the epic literary form for addressing 'large and public matters', such as 'the return of a king'. How is it possible to take such muddle-headed simple-mindedness seriously?

Ursula Le Guin rightly calls out another strand of the suspicion of literature which foregrounds enchantment, namely 'a deep puritanical distrust of fantasy'. Fantasy, to such people, is escapism:

> They confuse fantasy, which … is a universal and essential faculty of the human mind, with infantilism and pathological regression … as if evil were a problem, something that can be solved, that has an answer … That is escapism, that posing evil as a 'problem', instead of what it is: all the pain and suffering and waste and loss and injustice we will meet all our lives long, and must face and cope with over and over and over, and admit, and live with, in order to live human lives at all.[50]

I don't think I would re-read the Narnia books now. But I would, and have, *The Hobbit*. Tolkien's Middle-earth cannot really be compared with Lewis's Narnia – Faërie is not a competition – but it is different in two respects that probably, in the long run, make it more durably enchanting. One is its extraordinary internal consistency, which gives rise to a powerful sense of place. Lewis's pen struggled to keep up with the inventiveness of his imagination, and the resulting inconsistencies – classical Greek fauns alongside Father Christmas, say – never gave him pause, although they dismayed Tolkien. The other difference is the latter's determination, on account of living, as he recognised, in a largely post-Christian world, not to proselytise. But I'll save Middle-earth for later.

There are other enchanting children's books which feature enchantment itself. Two sparkling instances I only discovered later in life are Frances Hodgson Burnett's *The Secret Garden* and Elisabeth Goudge's *The Little White Horse*. (The Christianity of the latter is in, not added to, the story.)

I'm also well aware that some are by American authors. These include Maurice Sendak's *Where the Wild Things Are* (wild, note), E.B. White's *Charlotte's Web* (although gloominess keeps breaking through), and Frank L. Baum's *Wizard of Oz* books, especially the later ones. And one of the best, which found its way to me at exactly the right time, is Norton Juster's *The Phantom Tollbooth*. Michael Chabon is worth quoting here:

> The book appeared in my life as mysteriously as the titular tollbooth itself, brought to our house one night as a gift for me by some old friend of my father's whom I had never met before, and never saw again. Maybe all wondrous books appear in our lives the way Milo's tollbooth appears, as inexplicable gift, cast up by some curious chance that comes to feel, after we have finished and fallen in love with the book, like the workings of a secret purpose.[51]

Finally, there are the tales of Michael Ende. *The NeverEnding Story* – made into a film its author loathed – is a story about the enchantment of stories, and about nihilism ('the Nothing') which is eating up 'Fantasia', where they live, and where the reader who inhabits the stories goes. The parallel with Tolkien's *Faërie* is precise, not necessarily due to any direct influence but to the nature of the beast. Furthermore, Bastian, the principal protagonist, finds himself as a character in the book he is reading. Indeed, his participation is crucial, because he is co-creating the story within it as he reads, so the outcome will depend on whatever he does next …

Michael Ende's other outstanding book is *Momo*. Here, grey men in suits are taking over the world and turning it into a machine for greater productivity. They realise that children have both tremendous powers of imagination and an unmatched ability to live in the present. (Far from being mutually antagonistic, these two abilities go hand-in-hand.) That makes children the 'the raw material of the future,' a resource that must be captured and put to 'productive work'.[52] So the grey men convince adults, even parents, to legislate and enforce the conversion of free time and daydreaming into the instrumental training they call 'education'.

Isn't this precisely what is happening in contemporary Western and Western-influenced society? (English children are the most unhappy in Europe and the most subject to stressfully premature lessons and testing, which the current minister of education therefore proposes to increase.) Yet the applicability grows organically out of Ende's story, never imposed on it, nor on the reader.

Good children's literature persists, and despite the ever-encroaching demands from fools of education ministers, single-minded industry leaders and neurotically over-ambitious parents, many children are still occasionally allowed to be enchanted. Even literary professionals cast a largely indulgent eye over this bit of their domain, perhaps because they are secure in the knowledge that these readers or listeners will soon have to leave childish things (as they see it) behind. Maybe, privately, they also remember, and even miss it.

From our perspective here, however, growing up entails moving through and beyond such scepticism, what Ricoeur calls 'the hermeneutics of suspicion': the analysis of literature that reduces it to the power-play of interests, usually those of gender, class, race, and/or nationalism.[53] Disenchantment is now the default position of contemporary criticism, both in print and in the lecture-hall: 'keeping one's distance from a work of art' (as Rita Felski writes) 'in order to place it within an explanatory frame, whether drawn from politics, psychoanalysis, or philosophy.'[54]

As Lewis warned half a century ago, 'so fully armed determination not to be taken in' mitigates 'the surrender needed for the reception of good work.' We must engage with a book fully, let it work on us and risk being taken in if we are to get anything from it. To learn nothing new, to 'meet only ourselves,' as Lewis says, is surely a worse risk.[55] In which case, critics and teachers who are compulsively critical are actually examples of arrested development, and that is what they are encouraging. True maturity comes with a 'second naïveté', recovering the ability to play and the capacity for wonder.

Mary Poppins

Within the family of enchanting children's literature that of P.L. Travers deserves its own treatment, because she was particularly concerned with, and aware of, wonder. Mary Poppins is at once a force of nature and a spiritual being of indeterminate sort (angel? Daemon? Deva?). In both respects she is completely unbiddable, a barely-self-controlled cyclone of wild enchantment temporarily resident in 17 Cherry Tree Lane, Kensington. She treads a path perpetually liable to both startling irruptions of enchantment into conventional reality and equally outrageous bare-faced denials of enchanted reality. (It's difficult not to imagine that the same wasn't true of her creator, who was a friend of W.B. Yeats and AE, the Irish 'mystic'.)

In *Mary Poppins in the Park*, we are faced with the kind of tensive truth which demands that a choice not be made: 'Which are children in the story: the Princes, or Jane and Michael?'[56] That is, are the London children reading a story about three princes in a fairy tale, or are the princes reading a story about two children in London? And the more the story comes to life for its readers, the more impossible it becomes to know for sure.

In *Mary Poppins in Cherry Tree Lane*, there is a Proustian moment of metaphoric realisation – of being here-but-also-elsewhere, being this-person-but-also-another. When the very grown-up Mr Banks encounters the Bird Woman, whom he knew but has forgotten from his childhood, he 'stopped dead in his tracks ...' (That in itself is a common sign of enchantment.)

> Suddenly, [he] was flooded with a sense of being somewhere else. And, also, of being someone else who was, at the same time, himself. White-collared and velvet-suited, he was standing tip-toe in button-up boots, his nose just reaching a glass-topped counter

– the sweets shop where the Bird Woman, already ancient, was regarding him with amusement.[57]

In *Mary Poppins Opens the Door*, when a policeman sternly demands 'an Explanation', Mr Twigley gives 'a gleeful cackle. "You've come to the wrong place, Officer dear! I've never yet made an Explanation. And what's more ... I don't believe in 'em!'"[58] In the cause of resisting unnecessary disenchantment, especially of the kind that fetishises causality, nor do I. And we are in good company: Nietzsche, for example, and Wittgenstein ('Our disease is that of wanting to explain').[59]

Elsewhere in the same story, Travers gives this moving account of liminal liberation – almost eschataological, except it happens repeatedly – when the old year dies on the first stroke of midnight, while the new year isn't born until the last stroke sounds:

> And in between – while the other ten strokes are sounding – there lies the secret Crack ... The eternal opposites meet and kiss ... The stars bend down and touch the earth ... Night and day meet here, so do the poles. The East leans over towards the West and the circle is complete. This is the time and place, my darlings – the only time and the only place – where everybody lives happily ever after.

As I have been at pains to emphasise throughout this account, without the crack – in short, without liminality – there can be no experience of unity, transcendence or wonder. But that gap in turn presupposes relative distinct and therefore different states or conditions which are not themselves liminal or enchanted.

I have also praised the enchanting power of reflection as a doubling (or in the case of paintings of trees or clouds already reflected in water, tripling) of metaphoricity. In the same story, Mary Poppins has promised to stay '"till the door opens."' And as she spoke, she gazed thoughtfully at the door of the Nursery.' When Jane complains that the door is always opening, 'Mary Poppins glares at her. "'I meant the Other Door."'

One evening, from their nursery room, the Banks children are watching, with a sudden sense of foreboding, the reflection of their room on the wall of the house next door where, 'on the outer side of the window, another Nursery glimmered'; and in that room, they see Mary Poppins moving towards the door and opening it, not onto a wall but 'field on field of sky, and the dark spreading night.' And through it she goes, leaving them watching a shooting star (which is Mary Poppins leaving): 'Away through the sky streaked the shining spark, cleaving a path through the darkness. And as they watched it, every heart was filled with a sudden sweetness.'[60] That sweetness is the very taste of enchantment.

Fairy Tales

Tolkien held that 'If fairy-story as a kind is worth reading at all it is worthy to be written for and read by adults. They will, of course, put more in and get more out than children can.'[61] And if intelligence, taste and/or education are supposed to be a bar, how to explain Auden, his staunch and lifelong defender? Or Louis MacNeice, one of the finest poets and critics of his generation and beyond, who affirmed that

> Real fairy stories always meant much to me as a person, even when I was at a public school where to admit this meant losing face. Contrary to what many people say even now, a fairy story ... is a much more solid affair than the average naturalistic novel, whose hooks go little deeper than a gossip column.[62]

The significance of fairy tales extends well beyond their ostensible remit as reading matter for children. To quote the philosopher Alasdair MacIntyre,

> It is through hearing stories about wicked stepmothers, lost children, good but misguided kings, wolves that suckle twin boys, youngest sons who receive no inheritance but must make their own way in the world and eldest sons who waste their inheritance on riotous living and go into exile to live with the swine, that children learn or mislearn both what a child is and what a parent is, what the cast of characters may be in the drama into which they have been born and what the ways of the world are.

The deeper still truth is that 'there is no way to give us an understanding of any society, including our own, except through the stock of stories which constitute its initial dramatic resources. Mythology, in its original sense, is at the heart of things.'[63]

Turning to some literary instances, the presence of irony is a pretty dependable sign of the absence of enchantment, even when that is apparently the subject-matter. For example, Sylvia Townsend Warner's *Kingdoms of Elfin* (1977) treats fairies with an irony which succeeds mainly in demonstrating her own cleverness while flattering the knowingness of the reader. Hope Mirrlees's *Lud-in-the-Mist* provides an interesting contrast. First published in 1926 by this inner member of the Bloomsbury circle, it sparkles with deft and dry humour; but by taking *Faërie* seriously, it also enchants.

Susanna Clarke's *Jonathan Strange and Mr Norrell* (2004), set in a counterfactual nineteenth-century England where public magic works, can indeed enchant, on account of skilfully providing a well-constructed narrative in which you can find and/or lose yourself. That hardly marks it out from many other books, however, and its focus is on the power of magic and the glamour of power. Most magic, and all ceremonial or occultist magic, is hopelessly entangled with power (even when the power sought is over oneself). As such, it accords with Tolkien's definition of magic: 'not an art but a technique; its desire is power in this world, domination of things and wills'.[64]

Of other work where we could say the subject is Faërie itself, Randolph Stowe's *Girl Green as Elderflower* (1980), John Crowley's *Little, Big* (1981) and several of Ursula Le Guin's stories stand out. (Le Guin is equally insightful on magic.) Blessedly absent is any self-referential or meta-level irony, signalling that the author is an Adult who knows this is just a story and he is letting the reader in on the joke, but really, we are only pretending that these things happened, and so tediously on.

John Bayley notes astutely of Angela Carter that 'whatever spirited arabesques and feats of descriptive imagination Carter may perform she always comes to rest in the right ideological position.'[65] Her short story *The Company of Wolves* (1979), which led to Neil Jordan's film of 1984, uses a fairy tale to foreground something else which is valued more highly, thus turning the tale itself into a means to deliver a message: in this case, a psychoanalytical and feminist perspective on adolescence. That's fine as far as it goes, and those perspectives have a lot to offer, but fairy tales are nothing if not more-than-human; it is one of their strengths to be able to include not only humans but other animals and spirits (or if you prefer, non-ordinary experiences of more-than-human agency).

Despite the impoverishment of confining the meaning of fairy tales to the human mind alone – as if all other beings and the rest of the world, seen and unseen, were a mere backdrop – psychologising is still popular among the literary intelligentsia. Hilary Mantel recently stated that 'The journey into the wood is part of the journey of the psyche from birth through death to rebirth.'[66] How flattering to our human self-importance! Terry Pratchett, in contrast, also treats elves, dwarves and other personae and motifs drawn from fairy tales ironically but he does so with affectionate respect, in the course of advancing a tolerant and inclusive humanism which is open to non-anthropocentric enchantment.

Harry Potter Fails to Cast Spell Over Professor Richard Dawkins

That was the headline in *The Daily Telegraph* on 25 October 2008. Dawkins's concerns over the 'pernicious effect' on children of reading what he described as 'anti-scientific' fairy tales and 'mythical thinking' resulted in *The Magic of Reality: or How We Know What's Really True* (2011). Like a good monist, Dawkins cannot see anything non-scientific as other than anti-scientific, and like the religious fundamentalists he attacks but mirrors, he is never in any doubt as to what is really true. But ultimate truth is not the province of true science.

Thus we are lectured on why it is impossible, on account of the laws of physics and chemistry, for a fairy godmother to turn a pumpkin into a coach ... Well, useful to get that learnt. And such mean-spirited and cloth-eared literalism would need little discussion, except that as an attitude it long predated Dawkins and will, unfortunately, survive him.

Henri Michaux eloquently puts the opposite case:

> Forever disposed towards the unbelievable, disposed to believe it, to accept the extraordinary (in his eyes so plausible) ... the child, despite the new obstacles, is more open than he ever will be again; he lives among miracles, among miracles of every kind, and would like them explained, quite openly, with miraculous explanations which will not depress his soul but uplift it and fill it full.[67]

Actually, this point, suitably developed, applies just as much to adults. Chesterton tells of struggling through modern literary novels (*Suburban Sue: A Tale of Psychology*, and also *Psychological Sue: A Tale of Suburbia*) before turning with indecent relief to a copy of *Grimm's Fairy Tales*, opening the pages to one entitled 'The Dragon's Grandmother'. 'That at least was reasonable, that at least was true ... [a] touch of ordinary human reality ...'[68] While we have to be trained to perceive the self as insane and the world as boring or meaningless, our ineradicably natural mode is just the reverse: the self is, or can and should be, essentially healthy, while the world is actually wild, dangerous and full of marvels.

Auden mocked those who wanted to clean up fairy tales and turn them to good account as 'the Association of Positivist Parents, the League for the Promotion of Worthwhile Leisure, the Cooperative Camp of Prudent Progressives.'[69] I would like to propose Dawkins as President-for-Life, but if he declines then Jack Zipes, the Marxist literary scholar, would do. For a fairy tale 'counterworld' that teaches us to be independently-minded critics of the status quo, even if that would be a very good thing, is another kind of usefulness, another form of disenchanted power-knowledge intent on putting enchantment to work, when its true value is not as a counterworld but *another* world, albeit in this one.[70]

Not to be outdone, evolutionary psychologists are also busy at work, arguing that stories matter because they make us fitter for the struggles of life.[71] Strange, isn't it, how something always only seems to matter because it's useful for something else, something more important? Mary Midgley is surely right (as she so often is): the idea that we are rational and realistic, and therefore mythless – not only that we are free of myths, but that we don't need any – is the dominant myth of our times.[72] And I'm afraid 'our' fairy tale is one in which the magician renders everything invisible that isn't useful, convenient or profitable.

Bruno Bettelheim pioneered this sort of redemptive project in *The Uses of Enchantment* (1976), and I'm sure that fairy tales can accomplish therapeutic services.[73] The point is, however, that fairy tales, and all creative fiction, can only have whatever positive effects they may, of any kind, if they are left alone, free to act in the reader's mind and life however they will. And any adequate theory of them will also start from there.

What of the hugely successful Harry Potter stories? They ticked enough of the right narrative boxes to enchant many readers – and I'm sorry, but given the indifferent quality of much of J.K. Rowling's writing, the disenchanted metaphor seems right … except that she does tell a good story. But her interest lies almost entirely with magic – that is, power, both secular and supernatural – and the psychology of growing up. And she is very perceptive about both things.

Enchantment itself, however, is not an important value in her books. As A.S. Byatt notes, 'Rowling's world has no place for the numinous'. Where the animism proper to enchantment is open to the wild and more-than-human world, the concerns of Harry and his friends and enemies are strictly human-centred. What matters about the high-tech wizardry, phallic wands and all, is not its intrinsic wonder but instrumental power – what it can do, for you – and in this, Rowling is fully in tune with the technological fetishism of our age. Byatt rightly contrasts her work with the 'compensating seriousness' of Susan Cooper, Alan Garner, and Ursula K. Le Guin. As she adds, 'There's nothing wrong with this, but it has little to do with the shiver of awe we feel looking through Keats's "magic casements, opening on the foam/ Of perilous seas, in faery lands forlorn."'[74]

Yet it could be said that Harry Potter is a modern fairy-story. So I would like to try for a richer and deeper sense of what qualifies as a fairy-story or fairy tale by adopting an excellent term suggested by Alice Kane, a Canadian storyteller: 'wondertales'. She describes wondertales as 'those longish fairy tales that have elements in them sometimes of myth, at other times of simple folktale, and always of enchantment.'[75]

Literary Modernism

The fate of storytelling in modern fiction is strange. Readers cannot get enough of it, but many critics turn up their noses at it. Sound familiar? It should, because modernism is at work in the literary world as much as in visual art and music. Lorna Sage, for example, still speaks for many critics when she defends the uncompromisingly modernist and persistently unpopular writer Christina Brooke-Rose by maintaining that her voice 'has seemed more distant and characterless than in fact it is' ...[76]

Just to remind you, by 'modernism' I mean neither modern, as an historical period, nor a certain cool, sceptical temperament that is not itself a problem and has always been around. I mean precisely an 'ism': a worldview or ideology, often passionately but not always consciously held, which features a belief in the 'right' and ability of humanity to entirely determine its own fate (rather than, say, God, or nature). As a corollary, modernists usually profess secularism and materialism, since these seem to hold out the promise of mastery. They also have a touching confidence in the ability of reason – and relatedly modern science and technology, conceived as the highest kind of reason – to determine reality or the truth. And often, despite much evidence to the contrary, in efficient administration as its practical expression.

These strands coalesce into a narrative of Progress and its enemies that bears a significant debt to Christian eschatology, including an emphasis on the virtuous saved and the wicked who are damned. Chief among those enemies are 'superstition', 'myth' and 'tradition'. 'Nostalgia' is a sin too. This outlook gives rise to the secular equivalents of infidels, apostates, and heretics.

Literary modernism began in the first decade of the last century. Its chief practitioners such as James Joyce and Virginia Woolf, and in poetry Ezra Pound and T.S. Eliot, took storytelling to its limits and often beyond. Its exponents today are more likely to be critics or academic scholars than writers, but they retain a persistent problem with straight story. Why? Because the highest form of truth for modernists is theoretical explanation and information: in a word, *logos*.

Once again, this goes back to Plato, who never forgave Homer for his or her popular stories (mere myth and opinion), well-told (misleading rhetoric and sophistry), and a lack of interest in universal truth modelled on mathematics, physics and astronomy, uniting in cosmology. The upshot is that for modernists, storytelling, despite its popularity, is something of an embarrassment. Indeed, the very fact that it is so popular seems to prove the point: it is obviously best suited to the uneducated masses, who don't know any better. This leaves much of the literary establishment painted into its own tasteful, right-thinking corner, whose occupancy it signals through a superior tone and knowing irony.[77]

Another effect is to drive primary storytelling into what is patronisingly called, with the acquiescence (for quite other reasons) of the publishing industry, 'genre fiction'. There are still 'literary' writers who know how to tell a good story, of course: Donna Tartt, John Le Carré, Anne Tyler, Larry McMurtry, Barbara Kingsolver, George Saunders, William Boyd, and Sebastian Faulks, among many others. Not to mention the incontestably modern, but not therefore modernist, Bohumil Hrabal and José Saramago. Nonetheless, many readers who want story above all must now look for it in children's literature, romance, Western, crime thriller, spy fiction, comedy, horror novel, detective story, and fantasy.

Such an attitude was anatomised by Walter Benjamin, in a prescient essay entitled 'The Storyteller', published in 1936, in which he lamented that

> the art of storytelling is coming to an end. Less and less frequently do we encounter people with an ability to tell a tale properly. More and more often there is embarrassment all around when the wish to hear a story is expressed … The art of storytelling is reaching its end because the epic side of truth, wisdom, is dying out … A great storyteller will always be rooted in the people, primarily in a milieu of craftsmen … The fairy tale, which to this day is the first tutor of children because it was the first tutor of mankind, secretly lives on in the story.[78]

No wonder, then, that Tolkien has been one of the chief butts of modernist hostility.[79] He not only believed that 'the "fairy-story" is really an adult genre, and one for which a starving audience exists', but demonstrated the truth of that belief beyond any doubt. In so doing, as the redoubtable Tom Shippey says, he 'challenged the very authority of the literati, and this will never be forgiven'.[80] Another perceptive critic notes of Tolkien's tale that its 'perfectly sincere, perfectly impossible narrative' throws into sharp relief the poverty of both postmodern irony and strict realism.[81] It is also one of the reasons for his books' success: far from what the term 'fantasy' usually conveys, that is just the kind of truth we sometimes encounter in our lives.

Consider another example, Italo Calvino's fine tale *The Baron in the Trees* (1957), about the life and love of a young man in Liguria who ascends into the trees and decides never to set foot on the ground again. *The Baron* enchants because it tells a good story full of wonder, and tells it straight. From that perspective, anyone who remembers it will have found trying to read his later *If on a Winter's Night a Traveller* (1979) a painful experience, like encountering a once fine figure of a man who has succumbed to a terrible wasting disease: hypermodernitis, as it might be. Its acute self-consciousness, archly knowing voice and shattered story do not subvert or transcend an authorial self, with all its particularities and therefore limitations, as I suppose Calvino hoped; they merely withhold one. And without such concreteness, no 'magic' is possible.

Most versions of modernism valorise deep and serious concerns and demand their prominence in art. Bayley suggests that

> The reader today has become conditioned, partly by academic critics, to look in Melville and Conrad [say] for the larger issues and deeper significance, rather than enjoying the play of life, the humour, and detail of the performance. Yet surface is what matters in good fiction …

Bayley goes on to say that most readers will ultimately find Melville on the crew of the Pequod more absorbing than Ahab's 'parabolic significance'. And he rightly praises the novels of Patrick O'Brian, saying that 'he has contrived to invent a new world that is almost entirely, in this sense, surfaces, and all the better for it.'[82]

Yet much as I admire Bayley's craftspersonlike criticism, I think this misstates the issue. It accepts at their word the pompous proponents of depth – by which they mean general 'underlying' truth – and their arrogation of all important meaning; and that acceptance licences the equation of surfaces with superficiality, triviality, and deception. Whereas thanks to the effect of concrete magic, in art no less than the rest of life, true depth exists nowhere else than in, and as, so-called surfaces and details. By 'true depth' I mean that of life itself. We do not experience life in the abstract, let alone in some supposedly pure state or mode of being; indeed, being the necessarily limited creatures we are, we cannot. As Nietzsche asserted, 'The "apparent" world is the only one: the "real" world has just been *lied* [about] …'[83]

So by cultivating and working with surfaces and details, writers like O'Brian are only doing openly and deliberately what all artists must do, and what those who think that there are messages which exist separately from mediums do badly. As Wittgenstein says, you can't 'speak of the meaning of a work of art, say a particular piece of music, as if the meaning was something that could be separated from the work itself.' And the work itself is precisely its concreteness, in which inheres its magic, if any. In the words of the poet Vernon Watkins, it is 'an exact mystery'.[84]

Narrative

What is narrative? Trying to define it, I came up with 'discursive patterns, unfolding through imaginative time, which give rise to metaphorical meaning'.[85] But what does this exclude – a scientific report? A mathematical theorem? So rather than go there, whence return is doubtful, let's concentrate on how narrative enchants.

Its power has already emerged in this book as a key dynamic of enchantment, captured in the meaning of the word itself: to be in a song. It is also the principal means through which our own selves are created with a past and therefore possible futures, a definite character and therefore fate, whatever that turns out to be. ('Character is fate', says Heraclitus.)[86] And collective social and historical identities involve the same process writ large. 'We make fiction,' as Hoban says, 'because we are fiction.'[87] Our selves are fictions we maintain through the stories we tell about ourselves and each other.

In this connection, it is a pleasure to be able to quote a creative scientist, Antonio Damasio. His work, incidentally, is a good instance of the truth that when a scientist is being creative and insightful beyond the strictures of their own discipline, it is because however scientific the material they are engaged in the mode of the humanities, where truth is metaphoric, and metaphor tells the truth. (His conclusion below is a quotation from T.S. Eliot.)

> The story contained in the images of core consciousness is not told by some clever homunculus. Nor is the story really told by you as a self, because the core you is only born as the story is told. You exist as a mental being when primordial stories are being told and only then: as long as primordial stories are being told, and only then. You are the music while the music lasts.[88]

We have already discussed narrative in relation to both music and painting in terms of lines, both visual and melodic. Storylines work the same sort of way: you partly follow and partly create them, making the path as you walk it, creating the world (although it is potentially already there) as you read your way into it. I'm not sure if all narratives are journeys but all journeys, both 'inner' and 'outer', whether Odysseus's, Marcel's or Bilbo's, are certainly narratives.

Furthermore, narrative journeys are impossible without places to come from and go or return to. That reconnects us with the matter of *Faërie* as the place where one finds oneself when one is enchanted, and when the world is. Hence the particularly enchanting power of long stories, well-told, about worlds in which one can lose one's dusty quotidian self and find another one, internally related but not identical, whether in Middle-earth, Blandings, Ankh-Morpork, Combray or on the high seas during the Napoleonic wars. (A welcome recent discovery, for me, was Miklós Bánffy's superb trilogy *The Writing on the Wall*, which conducts us into Hungarian Transylvania at the start of the last century.)

The lineaments of true enchantment are all discernible in place-based narratives. Proust insists that true paradises, those that enchant, are ones we have lost. His, in late-nineteenth-century Paris and Normandy, was already disappearing even as he wrote it into literary immortality. Another, the Shire, is modelled on a Warwickshire village at the time of Queen Victoria's Diamond Jubilee in 1897 – at the very latest, another victim of the Great War. But when Evelyn Waugh said, 'Mr Wodehouse's idyllic world can never stale', he pointed to the same truth.[89] Even assuming, generously, that anything quite like Blandings and the Drones Club, nominally of the first decade of the twentieth century, ever existed in the first place, Wodehouse's world – as he himself wrote in 1974 – 'was always a small world … And now it is not even small, it is non-existent. It has gone with the wind and is one with Nineveh and Tyre.'[90] To this list we could add Terry Pratchett's Discworld, whose creator comically emphasises its literal non-existence as a flat disc supported by four elephants on the back of a great turtle flying through space.

The question of whether the remembered paradise is 'real' or 'imaginary' is misleading, since it obscures the shared desire to save it in the transmuted form of art. Consider, for example, Gavin Maxwell's belovèd *Ring of Bright Water* (1960). 'Camusfeàrna' named a recognisably particular Scottish coastal setting, and Maxwell himself was clearly a magnet for tragedy and disaster, but against that sombre background the enchantment of his otters and their humans, although doomed, shone all the brighter.

Another lost and therefore true paradise is Corfu in the late 1930s, as portrayed in Gerald Durrell's *My Family and Other Animals*. Simon Barnes recalls his realisation

> that this wasn't a book at all, in the normal sense of the term: it was a letter addressed to me personally, written with a deep, intimate knowledge of the sort of person I was and the sort of things I liked.

And as he adds, 'I don't think this is a unique experience, either. It's that kind of book.'[91] It has also been noticed by other writers. Osip Mandelstam describes a poem as a message in a bottle which, upon being found by a stranger years later, turns out to be addressed to its finder. This experience is a kind of enchantment I call 'address', and it can happen both in art and life outside art. It especially tends to happen with divination.[92]

Another instance is David Thomson's *Woodbrook* (1974), a poignant evocation of his time as a young man in County Roscommon in the 1930s and 40s, tutoring the children of an Anglo-Irish family. His love of Phoebe, one of his charges, of Woodbrook, the house and farm, and of the West of Ireland can hardly be separated, but in the end, ineluctably and painfully, he lost all three. Indeed, whether due to personal or historical changes, all three lost themselves, so to speak. (Mind you, Thomson's diffidence and passivity can be infuriating; sometimes I wanted to slap him. But maybe they too were fated.)

Patrick O'Brian's Aubrey-Maturin novels constitute a masterclass in non-modern storytelling which, like all the best teaching, remains implicit in the story itself. Over the course of twenty books, one comes to live into the Earth's seas and lands, in their wildness, interleaved with several different human cultures, ours yet not ours, all leaving plenty of gaps for enchantment to cross. Through the character of the physician and natural philosopher Stephen Maturin – multi-ethnic, complex, introverted and dark – O'Brian's account escapes the confines of Hornblower, and in so doing the character of Jack Aubrey – who loves life, and whose desire to continue living therefore includes ensuring his ship can fire three broadsides to every two of the enemy – comes splendidly, often comically, into his own.

Exactly as per the etymological meaning of enchantment – in a song – Jan Morris writes of the books constituting a world 'of which ... we have ourselves become citizens', while Peter Hitchins avers that 'the reader soon feels he she is taking part in them'. And there is not only the honour and delight of being able to inhabit another world, one which offers more purchase to enchantment by being both like and unlike the present one; there are the new relationships it affords. I feel an odd but enduring kinship with Stephen Maturin in particular, no less than if I could shake him by the hand. He has joined the company of my life.

These stories offer one other additional insight. O'Brian had to create characters whose lives, while supremely meaningful to themselves and others they knew, had left no trace in the historical record; to posterity, they had become invisible. Isn't that the case for most of us? Or indeed all, given enough of those great disenchant-ers, time and space. One day Shakespeare and Beethoven will be unknown, and Jesus, even if there are still any knowers. Yet – and this is the point – that should not be taken to imply that our lives have no meaning to us and each other, or that their enchantment cannot be true. Our lives are whole cloth of which ephemerality is the warp, wonder the woof, and neither is more important or real than the other.

One could extend this list of literary paradises, although not indefinitely. They comprise highly developed, detailed, and self-consistent worlds. Which world a reader favours depends on taste and temperament. Some of Wodehouse's more eminent contemporary admirers profess atheism, for example, which bars them from a Middle-earth whose religious dimension, although unmentioned in the text itself, their keen noses can detect. Pratchett, despite being a master of comic prose approaching Wodehouse, is felt to be too common for the patrician reader, and conversely, the stoutly plebeian reader will not often venture into Mme Verdurin's salon, let alone that of the Duchess de Guermantes. The mode of involvement, however, and the ensuing literary enchantment, is common to all.

Enchantment and the Modern Novel

To get an idea of the odd relationship between fiction as a whole and literary enchantment, let me list a few modern authors and works where it strongly figures, including some mention of the critical response. Briefly – since we shall shortly go into a few instances in depth – I would suggest the following.

Herman Melville's *Moby-Dick*, a mighty epic as unique as the white whale itself, is an unmatched account of false enchantment. Ahab, himself in the grip of his monomania, wants above all to possess and destroy the whale. As so often, those who seek not shared delight but total control are themselves completely controlled by their desire.

James Joyce's *Dubliners* are deceptively slight and enchanting stories that have been overshadowed by his subsequent turn to modernism, first in *Ulysses*, and then the epically unreadable *Finnegan's Wake*.

Joseph Conrad's *Heart of Darkness* is storytelling at its finest. The entire novel is framed as a story told aloud by the narrator Marlow to some fellow sailors, passing the time aboard a boat at night, liminally moored just offshore.

Marcel Proust's *In Search of Lost Time* takes the form of a quest and can be seen as, among other things, a profound meditation on enchantment, its loss, and its recovery. Its famous *moments bienheureux* are embedded in story of the discovery – which it not only tells but enacts – of how to live in a way that, while spurning obsession or fetishisation, nonetheless takes them as lodestars. In terms of reception it occupies an undisputed place in the literary canon, yet its exact status as a modern novel remains somewhat ambiguous. It certainly never spawned a 'school'.

Alain-Fournier's *Le Grand Meulnes* is a paradigmatic story of young, enchanted love, its loss, and the tragic failure of efforts to recover it by main force. It is usu-ally thought of as a one-off, sealed by its author's tragically early death, but that is somewhat misleading. Les Sablonnières – the mysterious old château, complete with compelling young woman, which haunts Augustin Meulnes – is, in effect, indistinguishable from David Thomson's Woodbrook, for example, and both fall within the demesne of *Faërie*. Once left, it cannot easily be found again; but sooner or later, leave it you must.

Close kin is a short story by H.G. Wells, *The Door in the Wall* (1911), which also concerns what the narrator explicitly calls 'an enchanted garden', much bigger than the tiny patch of disenchanted West Kensington that it occupies. The central character, an otherwise successful man of the world, wanders into it as a child, and, of course, out again; and searching for it compulsively, years later, leads to his death. Or did he find it again? We on the outside cannot finally say.

John Cowper Powys's baggy monster *A Glastonbury Romance* is eloquently concerned with both the wonder of enchantment and the power of magic. It seems to have been considered eccentric almost from publication. (I suspect that in most important respects, Russell Hoban is the Cowper Powys *de nos jours*.)

Giuseppe Tomasi di Lampedusa's final story, 'The Siren', which we shall discuss later, may be the purest portrait in literature of the enchantment of erotic love at its most savage and tender.

Gabriel García Márquez's *One Hundred Years of Solitude* mixes the marvellous with the quotidian in a way that came to be called 'magic realism'. That category assumes a radical difference between the two, however, which his own characters don't share. In other words, unlike Márquez himself, the classification assumes the characters are naïve or childish for accepting enchantment as real.

Ursula Le Guin's *Earthsea* books and other novels address both wonder and magic as power, and as gendered, and do so with sensitivity and depth. They are widely read and respected, often loved, but that hasn't stopped some critics from tacitly marginalising them as science fiction and/or fantasy.

John Crowley's *Little, Big* is a wonderfully rich tale with enchantment at its heart, but its identification as fantasy has kept it (despite support from Harold Bloom) penned in that critical stall. The contrast with Mark Helprin's *Winter's Tale* is instructive; despite significant thematic similarities, the latter was successfully marketed, and therefore acclaimed, as a literary novel. (*Winter's Tale* also qualifies as both enchanting and about enchantment, but I won't argue the case here.)

The fiction of Karen Blixen, Russell Hoban, and Mikhail Bulgakov all takes enchantment as one of its principal subjects. So too does J.R.R. Tolkien's *The Lord of the Rings*. We shall come to them. But most literary criticism has shown enormous resistance to admitting this fantasy, epic, romance, or whatever it is into the category of literature at all.

Now these authors may or may not be novelists, but they are certainly storytellers. As a few members show, the difference between 'proper' fiction and storytelling is not neat. The work of Conrad, early Joyce and Proust counts as both, and the last author may be the greatest storyteller of all. That doesn't alter the peculiarity of the list, however, and its oblique relationship to the critical literary canon. It shows the awkward, uneasy place in modern literature of literary enchantment. As

I've said, most strongly narrative work that can't simply be ignored is shunted into genre fiction.

Among novels that tend to dominate the literary A-lists, enchantment does not require, even tends to avoid, work that prominently features the virtuosically hyper-ambitious (David Mitchell), knowingly clever (Thomas Pynchon), topically dystopian (Margaret Atwood), obsessed with violence and misery (Roberto Bolano), compulsively transgressive (Brett Easton Ellis), self-consciously gargantuan (David Foster Wallace) and, of course, violently disenchanted as a point of principle (Martin Amis).

To pick a recent example, even an admiring reviewer called the prose of Sayaka Murata's *Convenience Store Woman* (2016) 'flat and unsparing as a fluorescent light', with the emotional bandwidth of, yes, a convenience store. In a follow-up novel, *Earthlings*, relentless Apollonian banality finally tips predictably into Dionysian murder and cannibalism. Then there are Sally Rooney's novels, extremely successful despite, or because of, their dispiriting banality, elevating unjustified self-absorption to almost heroic levels. The same cannot be said of Jonathan Franzen's work, though. There are certainly exceptions.

There is a discernible difference between wilful creation in the service of the artist and his or her vision, and artistic co-creation in the service of a value or ideal that lies outside the artist's control and is felt to be worthy of respect, even reverence, in its own right, resulting in the attitude Al Alvarez describes as 'self-awareness and self-denial – modesty, even'.[93] Critics go for the former approach surprisingly often. Not long ago, a reviewer described the effect of some short stories as 'like a spade to the face.'[94] This was supposed to be a good thing.

There is often a strongly political – or at least, politicised – dimension to literary modernism. An instance is the immediate fate of Giuseppe Tomasi di Lampedusa's *The Leopard*. Steeped in enchantment in ways inseparable from its storytelling, it is now a universally recognised masterpiece (well over a million copies sold in 121 editions and 23 languages). Yet he died in 1957 having failed to find a publisher. It was rejected – and upon posthumous publication, initially attacked – as insufficiently politically progressive, left-wing and 'committed'. Nor was it either socially realistic or experimentally avant-garde. This was the same ideological modernism that led André Gide to reject Proust's manuscript (which, to his credit, he later admitted deeply regretting).

It is no surprise that philistine commercialism has no time for wild enchantment, but the puritanical Left supplies another significant component of modernist hostility to artistic enchantment. Sometimes we even find the two conspiring. It's happening now with the obsessive focus on gender/ sex and sexual orientation (but not, significantly, class), which the corporate sector is perfectly happy to commodify and sell to you as an 'identity'.

Another distinguishing mark of the disenchanted modern novel is its emphasis on psychology. I don't mean the academic discipline but a conception, felt as much as thought, of the human mind as a thing that is significantly separate from the world and even the body. Isn't this present from Cervantes on? *Don Quixote* leans heavily on the difference, both tragic and comic, between things as they supposedly are (a windmill) and as the Don perceives them (a giant). Such is the epistemological conundrum haunting the Western imagination for at least half a millennium, and it has steadily gathered pace and momentum: how do we know that what we perceive is real? How can we be sure? Is there anything really there at all, or are we actually sealed up inside our individual minds? It has simultaneously helped give rise to modern science and, at the same time, seriously impoverished our lives – as if ways of thinking could replace ways of living, and as if believing, or not believing, was more important than what we actually do.

Around the end of the nineteenth century and the start of the twentieth, this orientation crystallised into literary modernism – a development that coincided almost exactly with the founding of psychoanalysis and academic psychology. Since then, storytelling and psychology have worked at cross-purposes in the novel. To an extent that varies from book to book, what remains of story continues to enchant while its psychology, privatising life experience, and tacitly ceding everything else to scientific materialism, disenchants. (That was Weber's point about the disenchantment that follows from splitting concrete magic into 'subjective' and 'objective'.)

Hence the contrast with wondertales, in which psychology is either absent or minimal, although not character, with which we now confuse it. The difference is this: character – qualities of temperament, and their particular combinations that make up personalities – is more-than-human, present throughout the world, and we participate in it alongside everyone else. But in psychology, humans alone supposedly own personality, while everything else, including nonhumans, become objects. Indeed, subjectivity is now only permitted in our heads, and that too is always in danger of being reduced to just another object. If that ever happened, the disenchantment of the world would be almost complete.

Story, Voice, Presence

Narrative itself can enchant, which puts storytelling to the fore with wondertales as its oldest and purest form. That leaves a problem, however, because it obliges us to admit fiction by authors like Dan Brown, J.K. Rowling and many others, which fails on most counts except the ability to tell a story (especially plot). I think we should ask for something more. What further dynamic of fiction might be at work in a deeper and more delicate delight?

In a little book with considerable heft, *The Writer's Voice*, Al Alvarez argues that good writing is 'not even about storytelling … Imaginative literature is about listening to a voice … an undeniable presence in your head, and still very much alive, no matter how long ago the words were spoken …' (He could have been talking about Connolly's experience of St Beuve, 'still very much alive', or mine of Connolly.) Alvarez goes on to describe voice as 'the vehicle by which a writer expresses his aliveness', although I would rather say that voice, when there is one, is not merely a vehicle but itself partakes of the aliveness which it expresses.[95]

I have already suggested that a unique and unmistakable voice, in its concreteness, is a key to artistic enchantment. In another passage which resonates with accounts of other kinds of artists working with enchantment, Alvarez maintains that

> To create voices in the reader's head, images in the mind's eye, imaginary presences with lives of their own is an intricate and subtle skill that requires self-awareness and self-denial – modesty, even – as well as a craftsman's fascination with the work as something with a life of its own, independent of its maker and his noisy ego.

As Michael Longley said, 'You take your poems seriously, but you don't take yourself seriously. What the muse hates more than anything else is self-importance.'[96]

Is this the answer, then? Certainly it's an important one, but what if the voice is distinctive but has no story to tell? Or even deliberately refrains from saying anything in particular, as a point of modernist principle similar to that which drove Calvino from story and story from him? John Ashbery, whose self-consciously clever and deliberately 'difficult' poetry radiates disenchantment, is one example.

In Chapter 2, I said that what unites the poles of subjective and objective, and thereby prevents the descent into disenchantment when either one is emphasised at the other's expense, is presence. And what is the effect of an effective voice but, as Alvarez says, 'an undeniable presence'? That is, you find yourself in the presence of someone, another unique subject and agent, and no less so for being scientifically implausible, technically non-material, or simply spooky. This doesn't only happen to readers, of course; writers too find 'their' characters taking on lives of their own. In both cases, then, voice may be what links narrative and presence, with the last the most powerful of the three.

But doesn't the enchantment, or at least its quality, depend on who is present? If the mythic pantheon of classical deities symbolises all possible presences, it's not hard to think of a few whose effect, however powerful, is not altogether enchanting and sometimes far from it: Apollo, Dionysus, Ares, Artemis … So my best shot at specifying a dynamic to produce literary enchantment falls short in the end. Of course! It's wild, and there are no guarantees. Worse still, for those who want to tame it and ride it to glory, there is no method.

In contemporary music, we found two drivers of disenchantment working to the same end: the populist drive for technological mastery, a prerequisite for commercial success, and the intellectual drive for control of the musical agenda. The parallel in literary culture is close. We have just been discussing the academic and critical disenchantment of story, so let's turn to its commercial counterpart.

Books abound promising to explain the mystery of story, giving you the key to unlocking its potential and making you the famous and well-paid master of a pet art. For instance, following Robert McKee and Christopher Booker, there is John Yorke's *Into the Woods. A Five Act Journey into Story* (2013). To clothe his analysis as itself a story was a clever conceit but look, as ever, at the language. It's not organic, arboreal, or otherwise, but relentlessly mechanical. Yorke's quest is to find the 'story engine', the 'universal story structure' of 'all narrative', the structure that is 'the root of character, dialogue, theme, genre, everything', whereby 'you can theoretically import any problem into the story machine and resolve it'.[97] Dressed up in smart casual complete with a MacBook Pro, this is just a reboot of an old programme, Platonic *logos*. It is not predicated on a love of mythic story, as it pretends, except insofar as that can be disenchanted, controlled, and sold in the marketplace.

A related problem attends the flourishing business of courses and workshops in vocational creative writing. Attending to prescribed and proscribed techniques for writing (for a while, you weren't supposed to use the past tense), in conjunction with either a fearful or inflamed adherence to a politically 'progressive' agenda, leads to relentless sameness. It is not fertile ground for the wild enchantment that attends art.

Despite the fact that creativity itself cannot, by definition, be taught, I'm sure in that in such courses one can learn valuable things about the craft of writing. That is not to be underestimated, since without craft the creativity isn't much use. What is worrying is the extent to which the main thing that students are actually, if inadmissibly, learning is how to succeed at taking, and/or teaching, such a course. In other words, they are being encouraged, in the name of writing, to do something else. This is invariably the case where method or methodology is the chief preoccupation; you end up learning *how* to do something, rather than learning to *do* it.

Students are thereby inducted into a world of institutionalised and professionalised writing, now rendered merely technical. The 'rationalisation and intellectualisation' that Weber blamed for disenchantment – in this case, the professionalisation of literary creativity and its canalisation into institutionally-approved content and styles – has found a burgeoning new market. Even 'transgression', of the right sort – scrupulously avoiding anything which could attract the dreaded suffix '-phobic' – is carefully coached. The resulting orthodoxy is as hostile to genuine creativity, literary or otherwise, as any other kind.

The fact is that however infuriatingly archaic and unfair it may be, enchantment favours the amateur: the person doing it mainly if not entirely for the love of doing it, without much thought of gain thereby. That pursuit, as Simon Leys says, 'embodies an exquisite inexpertness beyond the reach of the professionals' virtuosity.'[98]

It's usually not difficult to detect 'creative writing', especially fiction; it has a self-conscious, earnest sameness about it. And that quality extends directly to what gets published, since publishing houses choose many of their authors from the creative writing stable, not least among their friends and colleagues. Rilke maintains that 'A work of art is good if it has arisen out of necessity'– that is, the inner necessity of the particular work itself to be done.[99] The artist's work is then to discover and develop the style it needs. Rilke doesn't mean someone's psychological or social need for 'self-expression', or to 'be an artist', or to be a 'success'.

But vocational creative writing opens its arms to many with nothing burning to say, equips them with an armoury of ways to say it and, for some, opens the doors to being published. Sharing the drive for institutional control, it is increasingly tied to the incestuous circle of elite publishers, editors, agents, critics and star authors which is as powerful as it ever was before the internet supposedly got rid of gate-keepers, and lately has been joined (particularly where the 'young adult' market is concerned) by the joyless custodians, enlightened insofar as is commercially convenient, of correctness.

The social conscience of this collective is adaptable; currently, LBGTQ+ sells. And that's alright, but not when those with other concerns, and especially no concerns outside the stories themselves, are shut out. I know many fine authors excluded from the circles of current literary power who are now forced to self-publish, and whose excellent stories will therefore never see a published review or the inside of a bookshop.

Of course, writing outside the system – any system – will survive, even if it doesn't flourish, thanks to (in Clay Ramsay's words) 'the striving, unworkshopped, unprizewinning literary humanity down on C Deck'.[100] It is to them and their equivalents in other fields of art that this book is really dedicated.

In Chapter 8 I would like to turn to some examples of enchanting modern writing in more detail. Which ones, though? The range of possibilities is overwhelming, so I will concentrate on those where the subject-matter itself, importantly if not entirely, is also enchantment. This strategy is somewhat arbitrary, but it seems to me that for readers who care about it, the enchantment in such cases could be doubled. Our concern too is double: what we can learn about literary art in relation to enchantment, and what we can learn about enchantment from the art.

Notes

1. Edna O'Brien: 'The Magic and Mystery of a Story', *The Guardian Weekly* (27.5.16): 37.
2. Chuang Tzu, *The Tao of Nature*, transl. Martin Palmer (London: Penguin Books, 2010): 54. (I have altered the translation slightly. And the Anglicised name is now spelled Zhuang Zi.)
3. John Gross (ed.), *The Oxford Book of Essays* (Oxford: Oxford University Press, 1992): 372–73.
4. Connolly, *Grave*: 58–59. Cf. Stefan Zweig on the experience of discovering Montaigne's essays: 'Four centuries have gone up in smoke: it is not the Seigneur de Montaigne who is speaking to me ... nor even a writer, but a friend who has come, to counsel and disclose himself.' From his *Montaigne*, transl. Will Stone (London: Pushkin Press, 2015): 52–53.
5. *The New Yorker* (5.1.2015): 70.
6. Tolkien, *TLotR*, 622.
7. Tolkien, 'On Fairy-Stories': 45, 51. Cf. Iain McGilchrist, *The Matter with Things: Our Brains, Our Delusions and the Unmaking of the World*, vol. 1 (London: Perspectiva, 2021): 767–68.
8. Auden, *Prose* VI: 343.
9. Stefan Zweig, *The World of Yesterday: Memoirs of a European*, transl. Anthea Bell (London: Pushkin Press, 2014 [1942]): 406.
10. John Julius Norwich (ed.), *Christmas Crackers* (Harmondsworth: Penguin Books, 1980): 59.
11. Kenneth Gross (ed.), *On Dolls* (London: Notting Hill Editions, 2012): 68.
12. Bayley, *Power*: 389.

13 Machado, *Times*: 77.

14 Isak Dinesen [Karen Blixen], *Carnival: Entertainments and Posthumous Tales* (Chicago: University of Chicago Press, 1977): 175.

15 William H. Gass, *Fiction and the Figures of Life* (Boston: Nonpareil Books, 1971): 123–24. (Note the resonance with Wittgenstein's 'Life is the world.')

16 Francis Spufford, *The Child that Books Built* (London: Faber and Faber, 2002): 4. Spufford's book is one of the best about reading I have ever read, after Proust and Ruskin.

17 Hoban, *Moment*: 185.

18 'When it comes to experience, you can't open up the is/seems gap.' Galen Strawson, 'Real Naturalism', *LRB* (26.9.13) pp. 28–30: 29. Cf. Thomas Nagel, 'What is it Like to be a Bat?' (1974), who asks rhetorically, 'does it make sense…to ask what my experiences are really like, as opposed to how they appear to me?'

19 Paul Feyerabend, *Farewell to Reason* (London: Verso, 1987): 89.

20 Tolkien, *OFS*: 71, 48.

21 Stambolian, *Proust*: 210.

22 Paul Ricoeur, *From Text to Action: Essays in Hermeneutics II*, transl. Kathleen Blamey and John B. Thompson (Evanston: Northwestern University Press, 1991): 88. (Thanks to Laurence Coupe.)

23 Machado, *Times*: 149.

24 *The Guardian* (19.5.1995).

25 José Ortega y Gasset: 'Notes on the Novel' (1925), *The Dehumanization of Art and Other Essays on Art, Culture, and Literature*, transl. Helene Weyl (Princeton: Princeton University Press, 1968): 91.

26 Scott Black: 'Reading Adventures', *English Language Notes* 51.2 (Fall/Winter 2013) 25–44: 36. This excellent essay (to which I also owe the Ortega y Gasset quotation that follows) belongs with Rita Felski, *Uses of Literature* (Oxford: Blackwell, 2008) as rare instances of academic literary criticism which understands and respects enchantment.

27 Stevens, *Angel*: 73. That is an insight whose details and implications Gregory Bateson, among others, spent his entire professional life working out.

28 Stevens, *Collected*: 908.

29 Fernando Pessoa, *The Book of Disquiet*, transl. Richard Zenith (London: Penguin, 2002): 224.

30 Joseph Brodsky, *Less Than One: Selected Essays* (London: Penguin, 1986): 179.

31 For an early and cogent warning, see Mark Helprin, *Digital Barbarism: A Writer's Manifesto* (New York: HarperCollins, 2009).

32 Will Self, 'The Printed Word in Peril', *Harper's Magazine* (Oct. 2018): 23–31.

33 *The Guardian* (3.10.15).

34 See, among many other books and articles, Nicholas Carr, *The Shallows: How the Internet Is Changing the Way We Think, Read and Remember* (New York: W.W. Norton, 2008), the research of Anne Mangan (University of Stavanger) and Virginia Clinton (University of North Dakota), Will Self, 'The Printed Word in Peril', *Harper's Magazine* (Pct. 2018) 23–31 and Mark McGurl, *Everything and Less: The Novel in the Age of the Internet* (London: Verso, 2021).

35 Patrick O'Brian, *The Yellow Admiral* (London: HarperCollins, 2003): 42.

36 Virginia Woolf, *Genius and Ink: Virginia Woolf on How to Read* (London: TLS Books, 2018): 47. She also recommends checking one's opinions by 'reading and reading again the masterpieces of the past' (115).

37 Roberto Calasso, *The Art of the Publisher*, transl. Richard Dixon (London: Penguin, 2015): 43.

38 *The Guardian* (14.11.2009).

39 W.B. Yeats, *The Poems*, ed. Daniel Albright (London: Everyman's Library, 1992): 212.

40 Joseph Brodsky, *On Grief and Reason: Essays* (London: Penguin, 1995): 44.

41 See my essay 'A Room at the Back', pp. 175–79 in *Analog Sea Review* 3 (2020); for a longer version, see http://www.patrickcurry.co.uk/papers/On%20Solitude.pdf

42 See Humphrey Carpenter, *Secret Gardens: The Golden Age of Children's Literature* (Boston: Houghton Mifflin, 1985); Alison Lurie, *Don't Tell the Grown Ups: The Subversive Power of Children's Literature* (London: Back Bay Books, 19989 [1990]); and David R. Loy and Linda Goodhew, *The Dharma of Dragons and Daemons* (Boston: Wisdom Publications, 2004).

43 Edward Blishen: 'Town, Bad: Country, Good', pp. 15–24 in Richard Mabey, with Susan Clifford and Angela King (eds), *Second Nature* (London: Jonathan Cape, 1984): 19. (A superlative collection of essays.)

44 From Dorothy Parker, of course.

45 Kenneth Grahame, *The Wind in the Willows* (New York: Charles Scribner's and Sons, 1960): 117.

46 Kenneth Grahame, *The Annotated Wind in the Willows*, ed. Annie Gauger (New York: W.W. Norton and Co., 2009): lxiv–lxv.

47 Spufford, *Child*: 106. See also Laura Miller's reflections in *The Magician's Book: A Skeptic's Adventures in Narnia* (New York: Little, Brown and Co., 2008).

48 See my 'The Third Road: Faërie in Hypermodernity', pp. 468–78 in Graham Harvey (ed.), *The Handbook of Contemporary Animism* (Durham: Acumen, 2013).

49 Michael Oakeshott, 'The Voice of Poetry in the Conversation of Mankind', pp. 488–541 in idem, *Rationalism in Politics and Other Essays* (Indianapolis: Liberty Fund, 1991 [1959]): 519–20.

50 Ursula Le Guin, *The Language of the Night: Essays on Fantasy and Science Fiction*, rev. edn (London: The Women's Press, 1989): 58, 59.

51 Michael Chabon, 'On "The Phantom Tollbooth"', *NYRB* (11.5.01).

52 Michael Ende, *Momo* (London: Penguin, 1986), first published in English as *The Grey Gentlemen* (London: Burke Books, 1974): 55.

53 'Hermeneutics of suspicion' – and 'second naïveté' – Paul Ricoeur, *The Symbolism of Evil*, transl. Emerson Buchanan (Boston: Beacon Press, 1967): 351–52. See also Edith Cobb, *The Ecology of Imagination in Childhood* (Putnam: Spring Publications, 1998).

54 Felski, *Uses*: 57.

55 Lewis, *Experiment*: 127–28, 85.

56 Travers, *Mary Poppins in the Park*: 168.

57 Travers, *Mary Poppins in Cherry Tree Lane*: 70.

58 Travers, *Mary Poppins Opens the Door*: 57.

59 Ludwig Wittgenstein, *Remarks on the Foundations of Mathematics*, transl. G.E.M. Anscombe, ed. G.H. von Wright and Rush Rhees (Oxford: Blackwell, 1956), Part IV, §31. Cf. Wittgenstein, *Philosophical Investigations*: 40e.

60 Travers, *Door*: 209, 35, 248–50, 254.

61 Tolkien, *OFS*: 58.

62 Bruno Bettelheim, *The Uses of Enchantment: The Meaning and Importance of Fairy Tales* (Harmonsworth: Penguin, 1978): 23.

63 Alasdair MacIntyre, *After Virtue* (London: Duckworth, 1985): 216.

64 Tolkien, *OFS*: 49–50.

65 Bayley, *Power*: 519.

66 Hilary Mantel, 'Wicked parents in fairytales', *Guardian* booklet on fairy tales (10.10.09).

67 Henri Michaux, *Spaced, Displaced*, transl. David and Helen Constantine (Newcastle upon Tyne: Bloodaxe, 1992): 17, 19. See also Spufford's *Child*.

68 Chesterton, *Trifles*: 53.

69 In a review in 1944 of a new edition of Grimm's fairy tales.

70 Most recently in Jack Zipes, *The Irresistible Fairy Tale: The Cultural and Social History of a Genre* (Princeton: Princeton University Press, 2012).

71 E.g., Brian Boyd, *On the Origin of Stories: Evolution, Cognition, and Fiction* (Cambridge MA: Harvard University Press, 2009).

72 Mary Midgley, *The Myths We Live By* (London: Routledge, 2003).

73 A recent variation is by Joan Acocella, in 'Once Upon a Time', *The New Yorker* (23.7.12): fairy tales reconcile us to reality. (Doesn't that just make you want to read some right away?)

74 A.S. Byatt: 'Harry Potter and the Childish Adult', *The New York Times* (7.7.03).

75 Alice Kane, *The Dreamer Awakes*, ed. Sean Kane (Peterborough: Broadview Press, 1995): 169.

76 *TLS* (12.8.94). It's not irrelevant that Brooke-Rose was another strident critic of Tolkien.

77 See virtually any issue of the *LRB* or the *NYRB*.

78 Walter Benjamin: 'The Storyteller', pp. 83–109 in *Illuminations*, ed. Hannah Arendt (New York: Schocken Books, 1969): 87, 101, 102. See also Bill Buford, 'The Seductions of Storytelling' in *The New Yorker* (24.6 & 1.7.96). Buford points out that in the authoritative *New Princeton Encyclopedia of Poetry and Poetics* (1388 pp.), at the time he was writing, there is no entry for 'story'.

79 See my essay 'The Critical Response to Tolkien's Fiction', pp. 369–388 in Stuart D. Lee (ed.), *A Companion to J.R.R. Tolkien* (Oxford: Wiley Blackwell, 2014), reprinted in my *Deep Roots in a Time of Frost: Essays on Tolkien* (Zurich: Walking Tree Books, 2014), pp. 197–226, and forthcoming in a revised edition of the former.

80 Tom Shippey, *J.R.R. Tolkien, Author of the Century* (London: HarperCollins, 2000): xxxiv. Cf. Charles Stephens, *Shakespeare's Island. Essays on Creativity* (Edinburgh: Polygon, 1994): 'The colossal success of *The Lord of the Rings* is a precise index of the collapse of "modernist" literature in the 1960s' (p. 84).

81 Brian Attebery, *Strategies of Fantasy* (Bloomington: University of Indiana Press, 1992) 46.

82 John Bayley, 'In Which We Serve', pp. 357–366 in Patrick O'Brian, *The Ionian Mission* (London: HarperCollins, 2003): 365.

83 Friedrich Nietzsche: *Twilight of the Idols*, transl. Duncan Large (Oxford: Oxford University Press, 1998): 17.

84 Vernon Watkins, *An Exact Mystery – The Poetic Life of Vernon Watkins* (N.p.: The Choir Press, 2020). With thanks to Xavier Curry.

85 From my 'Radical Metaphor: or Why Place, Nature and Narrative are Each Other but aren't Themselves', pp. 35–38 in *EarthLines* 6 (August 2013): 36.

86 Chapter 5, § 69.

87 Hoban, *Moment*: 146.

88 Antonio Damasio, *The Feeling of What Happens* (London: Vintage, 2000): 191. With thanks to Hans Kortekaas.

89 Quoted on the back cover of virtually every one of Wodehouse's books.

90 P.G. Wodehouse, *Joy in the Morning* (London: Herbert Jenkins Ltd., 1974): 1.

91 Simon Barnes, 'Paradise Regained', pp. 14–20 in *Slightly Foxed* no. 44 (Winter 2014): 15.

92 See my *Enchantment*: 22–23.

93 Al Alvarez, *The Writer's Voice* (London: Bloomsbury, 2005): 15.

94 Chris Power reviewing Kevin Barry in *The Guardian* (28.04.12).

95 Alvarez, *Voice*: 21.

96 *The Irish Times* (27.3.10).

97 John Yorke, *Into the Woods. A Five Act Journey into Story* (London: Penguin, 2013): x, xii, xviii, 72–73, 204. (The inevitable failure to encompass narrative as necessarily wild also results in such gems as 'We are all identical – yet we are all different' [p. 124].)

98 Leys, *Hall*: 57.

99 *Analog Sea Review* 3 (2020) 21.

100 Personal communication.

8

FICTION II

Lampedusa's Siren

In Giuseppe Tomasi di Lampedusa's short story 'The Siren', Rosario La Ciura, a 24-year-old future professor of classics, meets Ligeia, a Siren, in the sea off the coast of Sicily. The following observations will make more sense if you have read it, of course, but fundamentally this is a powerful account of Aphroditic enchantment, one that is itself enchanting in a rawly poignant way. It must be admitted, however, that its perspective is strongly male. Not wholly or exclusively – it is quite possible to imagine a story about a young woman falling in love with a merman, with similar consequences – but rather, I think, in the emphasis on the concrete magic of their sex as 'the highest state of spiritual ecstasy together with the most basic form of physical pleasure …'[1]

The 'male wound' (which I have discussed elsewhere) describes the traumatic separation from, and denial of, the maternal female that is required for men's early psychosexual development.[2] For them, therefore, sex with a woman often carries a peculiar charge. As Edward Hoagland says in his painfully honest essay on men, ageing and sex, 'we don't speak of "dirty old women." They don't covet pretty men at their bedside, or cross the River Styx joking of blondes, having a different concept of dignity.'[3] And since to deny the female is also to implicitly deny embodiment and thence the greatest and most mysterious maternal matrix of all, the Earth, it is not surprising that when sex is experienced as congress with, to quote the Professor, 'an animal – and at the same time an Immortal', it is explosively powerful, and even redemptive.[4] It is also as good an instance as any (or better) of concrete magic, upstream of any firm distinction between physical and spiritual.

The story possesses additional torque insofar as the principal pursuits of Rosario are thinking, reading, and writing: activities which tend to take one further away from conscious embodiment, and all the more so when pursued as a career. If such a

DOI: 10.4324/9781003353225-8

man still harbours any desire (conscious or unconscious) to reconnect with the fundamentals of life, then an encounter with a Ligeia – lascivious, but 'to me the wisest of Mothers' – can hardly avoid being momentous. 'She was entirely uncultivated, knew no wisdom and dismissed any moral restriction with scorn – nevertheless, she was part of the source from which all culture, all learning, all morality springs …'[5]

I can also confirm that the course of such encounters, and the fate of those involved, is decided in their first moment. In 'The Siren', that is the moment when Rosario beholds Ligeia's face as she appears over the side of his boat, her smile expressing 'a kind of animal joie de vivre, an almost godlike happiness'. By the time he had experienced her fragrance, 'a bewitching marine aroma, youthful and euphoric', and her voice, 'slightly guttural and thick, with innumerable overtones', it was all over bar the shouting, shortly to follow.[6] (With unmatched perspicuity, Adriana Cavarero delineates how the female figure whose 'animal innocence that holds on to life without reflection' throws into stark relief our long-standing masculinist philosophies of death, culminating in scientism and most recently transhumanism.)[7]

A momentous encounter, then: potentially healing but perilous, because there is no room for the 'domestic' here, no human middle to mediate between animal and divine and offer a sustainable, liveable connection. But wouldn't that mean the death – slow, to be sure, but ineluctable – of enchantment anyway? Yes, but it might leave behind a life, or lives, in which that enchantment is still part of the whole. Whereas for Professor Rosario, it framed his entire subsequent life, or occupied it, unapproachable by any other part. So was he finally a tragic figure, or blessed? As so often with enchantments, it is impossible to say. Even, sometimes, for the persons themselves.

Mikhail Bulgakov and Stories Within Stories

Bulgakov's masterpiece, *The Master and Margarita*, was first published posthumously, after it was smuggled out of the Soviet Union. It recounts the events of the spring of 1929, when the Devil and his retinue took up residence in Soviet atheist Moscow. Margarita, Bulgakov's unforgettable female protagonist, is 'the true hero of the novel', to quote Arpad Szakolczai.[8] Invited to be the queen of the ball, the principal event in the annual diabolic social calendar, she accepts, and in performing her duties acquires the occult powers she needs to release her lover, the Master, a writer who has been imprisoned in a psychiatric hospital. (Margarita's exhilarating ride on a broomstick among the apartment-blocks of Moscow at night is not easily forgotten.)

Within this story, however, unfolds another that the Master is writing. This one concerns the relationship between Yeshua Ha-Notsri, acclaimed as the Messiah, and Pontius Pilate, the fifth Procurator of Judea, and its episodes erupt into the main narrative with astonishing clarity and sense of time and place, not least the descriptions of contemporary Jerusalem. A two-thousand-year-plus gap vanishes as if one was reading an eye-witness account of events unfolding in real time. It has the visionary intensity not of a dream or hallucination, but of reality when it is most fully realised.

Perhaps the most powerful moment of enchantment, however, comes as the two stories meet when the Master intervenes to change the fate of the 'real' Pontius Pilate. And, of course, Bulgakov himself is implicated through the writing the story that contains all the others. That fact, and the reader's awareness of it, adds another character and level – a caged writer and playwright, completely at the mercy of Stalin, in 1939 – to mingle with both the story he is writing about the Devil, the Master, Margarita and various Moscovites a decade earlier, and the story inside that story of Jeshua and Pontius Pilate, from the year 33. Plus, arguably, the story of the contemporary reader.

This creative confusion of levels or worlds that are normally kept distinct and apart is a key dynamic of enchantment. Normally: that is, within the bounds of what is considered, when we are disenchanted, to be possible. It works in the same way as encounters when perspectives meet, and gaps are bridged. So it is understandable that when different story-worlds are skilfully brought together, as Bulgakov does, the response can be powerfully enchanting. (It helps, of course, that one of them is fundamental to the cultural history and self-understanding of the entire 'Western' world.)

René Magritte virtually based his lifework on the same principle, but there are many other instances in literature. One is Flann O'Brien's precocious novel *At Swim-Two-Birds* (1939), in which the characters in author Dermot Trellis's book, dissatisfied with their allotted roles, conspire to drug him, take control of the story's plot and rewrite their own roles. Eventually Trellis is tried and condemned by his own creations, and is about to die a painful death when a housemaid uses the pages of the manuscript telling this story to start a fire, and all of them go up in smoke … So there are four levels here – O'Brien's story about the unnamed narrator, the narrator's story about Trellis, Trellis's story, and the story written by his characters about themselves when they assume lives independently of their creator – which collide to wonderful effect.

In *The French Lieutenant's Woman*, John Fowles boldly drew on this dynamic when, as the author, he enters the Victorian railway carriage occupied by his principal character, Charles, and sits down nearby to observe him, to the latter's discomfiture. A bit flashy, perhaps, but I well remember my astonishment and delight. The novel has long been classed as postmodern, and not without reason, but in the experience of the reader, as we have seen in other contexts, the nature of such moments of enchantment isn't modern at all, whether post- or pre-. It's non-modern.

More recently, in S.M. Saumarez's *The Akashic Record*, set in a drowned future London (complete with photographs!), a group of young adults is rehearsing a puppet-show of *Faust* – which it was, long before Goethe – until, in a moment of pure wonder, their own stories and that of the show meet and merge.[9]

Another example comes from a television play, the finest in a decade that in Britain was the high point of the form: Dennis Potter's *The Singing Detective* (1986). The principal character, Philip Marlow, is a detective-story writer who has been hospitalised for his crippling psoriatic arthropathy. Marlow is named after Raymond Chandler's famous fictional detective. At the same time, signalled by the fact that they suffer from the same disease, Marlow is also Potter himself. Towards the end of the story, the writer Marlow, semi-delirious, encounters his own creation, a detective also named Philip Marlow, in the hospital ward, and narrowly misses being shot by him. The moment Potter's 'real' fictional character meets his doubly fictional character is one of wonder for the author-character and viewer alike.

However, the ultimate and most tantalising possibility of artistic enchantment and its power to re-arrange reality occurs when that work enters directly into primary reality. This is given to very few to experience, and fewer still to create, but only omniscience could rule out the possibility. Yeats recalls reading of a Japanese artist,

> an animal painter so remarkable that the horses he had painted upon a temple wall had slipped down after dark and trampled the neighbours' fields of rice. Somebody had come into the temple in the early morning, had been startled by a shower of water drops, had looked up and seen painted horses still wet from the dew-covered fields, but now 'trembling into stillness'.[10]

But I said Bulgakov was concerned with enchantment. In his case, it takes the form of the selfless love between Margarita and the Master which saves both of them, passing even the tests of Satan himself, the master of this world – including his incarnation in Bulgakov's world as undisputed arbiter of life and death, Stalin. Call it a romantic conclusion if you want, but I'm against rationing hope. In any case, it cannot be denied that the possibility of enchanted love surviving even the black magic of power was close to Bulgakov's heart.[11]

Russell Hoban and the Punch and Pooty Show

You may have noticed quotations from Russell Hoban elsewhere in this book. Enchantment was one of his principal concerns, and he was a reflective as well as creative writer. It figures strongly, for example, in *Kleinzeit*, an animistic tale set in modern London in which anything – Underground (the London metro), Hospital, the Thames, Death, and A4 yellow paper – can turn out to have a voice, a message, and an agenda. It's a very funny book, not as the opposite of serious but of not funny.

Hoban develops this theme further in *The Medusa Frequency*, told through and around the tale of Orpheus and Eurydice. Living in London, Herman, the central character, is repeatedly confronted with the head of Orpheus, all singing if not all dancing. One night in a flat in Eel Brook Common, Fulham, with his lover asleep in bed and the District Line trains rumbling past, he goes to the kitchen and opens the fridge. There were three cans

> of beer, most of a salami, a mouldering of old cheeses, half a tub of margarine, half a jar of marmalade, half a pint of milk and the head of Orpheus.

Loss! it said. That's what she was to me, you know: she was the loss of her even when she was apparently the finding of her. And I was the same to her, I was to her the loss of me … From the moment that I tasted the honey of Eurydice I tasted also the honey of the loss of her … From the very first moment that beauty appears to us it is passing, passing, not to be held.

There is no need to stress the resonances, not only with enchantment as transfigured normality but the theme of loss, the absence haunting presence. But when Orpheus's and Herman's conversation is interrupted by the arrival of his companion, he shuts the fridge and returns to bed. When he re-opens it the next morning, he finds only 'an exhausted looking cabbage.'[12]

The book Hoban will chiefly be remembered for is *Riddley Walker*. One of a kind, it follows the fortunes of its eponymous character in a blasted south-east England many years in the future, after a nuclear holocaust has left only the barest rudiments of artistic culture intact. It is told in the argot of the time by Riddley Walker as he negotiates the powers of the day, principally the Ardship of Cambry (the Archbishop of Canterbury), the Pry Mincer (Prime Minister) and their hevvies (no translation needed). People have been left with a deep suspicion of experts and authorities, exemplified in the detested figure of 'Mr Clevver'. Their leaders, however, are secretly in a race to rediscover how to pull apart the 'little shining man' and unleash 'the One Big One' again … Of course. But what they stumble upon is the secret of the One Little One, that is, gunpowder. The Bomb will take longer but not, one feels, forever.

As he struggles to survive in the shifting sands of alliances and betrayals, Riddley gradually realises that 'Power dint go a way. It ben and it wer and it wud be. It wer there and drawing. Power wantit you to come to it with Power. Power wantit what ever cud happen to happen.' (Tolkien noticed the same thing, which he called 'the most widespread assumption of our time, that whatever could happen must happen'.) Riddley also discovers that he 'dint care who wer doin it. Every body juicying for Power 1 way or a nother nor I dint want no part of it no mor.' He was after something else, which comes from 'jus letting your self be where it is. Its tuning in to the worl its leaving your self behynt and letting your self be…' And what do you find if you succeed in tuning in to the world of your precise circumstances? Its inner lining and depth: in Riddley's words, 'The idear in the hart of every thing', or in Hoban puts it, speaking directly, 'the moment under the moment'.[13]

The chief tool of ideological domination in this society is a travelling puppet-show that recapitulates, invariantly and quasi-religiously, the story of the One Big One, the events that led up to it, and the result. But in a charcoal dig, Riddley finds the preserved puppets of a Punch and Judy show, and with their help he spontaneously recreates the show in all its salty humour and vigorous humanity. This new show is not a state-sanctioned instrument of propaganda, nor is it 'religious'; it tells a story, semi-ritualistically but creatively, for its own sake. He decides to take it on the road. 'Ready to cry ready to dy ready for any thing is how I come to it now. In fear and tremmering only not running a way.' (Here is 'fearless receptivity' again.)

'Not to lern no body nothing' – no method, no system, or programme – 'I cant even lern my oan self all I can do is try not to get in front of whats coming. Jus try to keap out of the way of it.'[14]

As the book ends, it is apparent that Riddley's show is the start of something new but enduring. No one has seen anything like it before, and the impact is widely felt. Some members of the audience have trouble with the boundaries between 'real people' and 'characters' – a common sign of enchantment at work – sometimes with hilarious consequences. In one early performance, at the point where Punch, with violence in mind, is trying to get hold of Pooty's baby, 'No sooner does Punch get his hans on that Babby nor in comes a big hairy han which it grabs Punch and my han inside Punch.' It's Easyer, a hevvy, and he yells at Punch, "You littl crookit barset I tol you not to try nothing here!"'[15]

I won't belabour the connections. Not only is Hoban's tale compelling and potentially enchanting but its ultimate concern, like Bulgakov's, is the survival, in a brutal and hostile world ruled by power, of enchantment itself. In the one as love, the other as art.

Karen Blixen: Feast and Famine

Karen Blixen was a true storyteller – a member, in her own words, of that 'ancient, idle, wild and useless tribe' with its roots in the oral tradition, itself going back to the originary poet-philosopher-seers.[16] It is not surprising that she spoke of her stories as having a bodily or instinctual source, almost like dance. I am reminded of a more recent member of the same tribe who was asked, 'Do you think of yourself primarily as a singer or a poet?' and answered, less flippantly than it appeared, 'I think of myself more as a song and dance man, you know?'[17]

Alongside many other artists, Dylan would also find it easy to sympathise with Blixen's complaint that

> People are always asking me what is the significance of this or that in the tales – 'What does this symbolise? What does that stand for?' and I always have a difficult time making them believe that I intend everything as it's stated. It would be terrible if the explanation of the work were outside the work itself.[18]

It would, indeed, be fatally disenchanting.

Blixen's commitment to story was absolute. One of her short stories, 'The Cardinal's First Tale,' explicitly compares the novel and the story to the detriment of the former, especially when a novelist is ready to sacrifice story to character. The 'divine' art of story will suffer nothing else to take pride of place, because 'to its human characters there is salvation in nothing else in the universe ... For within our whole universe the story only has authority to answer that cry of heart of its characters, that one cry of heart of each of them: "Who am I?"'[19] I recently found an affirmation of the same truth in an unexpected place, the work of Alasdair

MacIntyre: 'I can only answer the question "What am I to do?" if I can answer the prior question "Of what story or stories do I find myself a part?"'[20]

She wrote luminous short stories, full of a sadness that is 'blessed and without bitterness' – in the words of Tolkien, whose work shares the same Northern air – but still very sad for all that.[21] Blixen is best-known, however, for *Out of Africa*, a poignant memoir of her years in Kenya in the 1930s. (Please forget the shameless Hollywood film.) It begins, 'I had a farm in Africa ...' and an awareness of existential fragility underlies everything that follows. Africa became Blixen's paradise because it was, finally, a lost one. (She made no serious attempt to return years later when she could have, knowing that her Africa was gone anyway.) In the end, when she was forced by financial ruin to leave, she realised, in words I quoted earlier, that 'It was not I who was going away, I did not have it in my power to leave Africa, but it was the country that was slowly and gravely withdrawing from me, like the sea in ebb-tide.'[22]

In a later memoir she describes the disenchanting effects of colonial administration, even when well-meant. From the native African point of view, it involved

> transforming, to them, Rite into Routine. What by now most of all they feared from our hands was boredom, and on being taken into hospital they may well have felt that they were in good earnest being taken to die from boredom.

She also contrasts, in a way that chimes with what we have found elsewhere, 'the world of day ... the domain of organising and regulating universal powers' with the world of imagination.[23]

To die of boredom is not as fanciful as it may sound. Taking its contrary as not excitement but meaningfulness, a vibrant plenitude of self-sufficient meaning, then the flat, grey sterility of boredom is one of the termini of disenchantment, and I for one have no difficulty imagining that it could be lethal. For tiny intimations, one needs no more than daytime TV, or interminable online forms, or the crushing banality of mobile telephone conversations in public – trivial, to be sure, but now imagine no escape ...

Uncompromisingly championing the imagination attracted criticism. It is, Blixen wrote, 'a misunderstanding when I am time after time accused of escapism, of not being prepared to 'involve myself' or of having lived and continuing to live in an ivory tower'. Her accusers must have known, having read *Out of Africa*, that she had come to writing late, and that behind it lay almost twenty years of active life and death. 'Is it not the case,' she asks shrewdly, 'that they themselves, in their consideration of the book, remain on a purely aesthetic plane, in a kind of critical ivory tower?'[24]

Blixen's commitment to storytelling was rooted in creative enchantment as a way of life. For her, not only the work quietly waits to be realised, but so too does your self, which is your destiny: the idea, as she put it, that God had when he made you. A proud person 'is conscious of the idea, and aspires to realise it.' (She was a firm believer in pagan pride as against Christian self-abnegation.)[25]

Babette's Feast is one of Blixen's short stories.[26] It was turned into a film, directed by Gabriel Axel, which retained all of the story's integrity and enchantment. So it can be done! (The same is true, by the way, of John Huston's film of Joyce's short story *The Dead*, which Blixen had read and admired.)

The story is a meditation on enchantment, art, and life. Babette is former head chef of the Café Anglais who has had to flee Paris for her involvement in revolutionary politics. She takes refuge in Berlevaag, a tiny, poor and pious community in Danish Jutland, becoming the housekeeper for a pair of spinster sisters, Martine and Philippa, in the local Lutheran sect. When she wins the French lottery, she spends the entire proceeds on a meal – as prepared by her, a once-in-a-lifetime experience – for the members of the congregation. Tragicomically, they resolve not to be impressed by its sensual, worldly delights, but the enchantment of the food, wine and occasion is so strong that their faith in God and each other is renewed, although they have no idea why.

Food is the sacrament of Babette's artistic creation. One guest, General Loewenhielm, recognises a dish from a meal at the Café Anglais, many years before – *Cailles en Sarcophage* – and recalls his dinner companion then telling him it had been invented by the chef, "'a person known all over Paris as the greatest culinary genius of the age, and – most surprisingly – a woman!'" Indeed, his companion had continued (virtually defining enchantment),

> this woman is now turning a dinner at the Café Anglais into a kind of love affair – into a love affair of the noble and romantic category in which one no longer distinguishes between bodily and spiritual appetite or satiety.

Of what happened that evening,

> None of the guests later on had any clear remembrance … They only knew that the rooms had been filled with a heavenly light, as if a number of small halos had blended into one glorious radiance. Taciturn old people received the gift of tongues; ears that had for years been almost deaf were opened to it. Time itself merged into eternity. Long after midnight the windows of the house shone like gold, and golden song flowed out into the winter air.

Leaving, the old Brothers and Sisters stumble, hand in hand, out into the snow and under the stars, and "'Bless you, bless you, bless you,' like an echo of the harmony of the spheres rang out on all sides.' Then, locking the door, the two sisters remember Babette, who has had no share of the wonderful evening. 'So they went into the kitchen, and Martine said to Babette: "It was quite a nice dinner, Babette."' (Like Hoban, Blixen has a nice comic touch.)

The sisters are horrified to discover that Babette has spent all her money on the meal, but she asserts that being a great artist, she shall never be poor. Philippa can only reply, in tears, 'In Paradise you will be the great artist that God meant you to be… Ah, how you will enchant the angels!' Which is kind, to be sure, but Babette is already that artist in *this* world, as the extraordinary meal she had just prepared showed. And the sisters were there! Shall we laugh, or cry?

Concrete magic is present in this story as the enchantment of that humble but precious thing, food, when prepared with love and skill, that feeds both body and spirit and is infused with the spiritual mystery inherent in the material. But Blixen's own twist at the end reminds us that enchantment will always be the stone that the builders reject, the road less travelled, the neglected stepdaughter. The congregation are not among the movers and shakers of this world, of course, but they are the servants, however humble, of a religion that is. Capitalism is simply the latest and most 'successful' such overarching human institution. And what is perceived in such a frame as useless, not to mention idle and wild, will inevitably be ignored or neglected, when not actually suppressed. Our faith, those of us who love enchantment, is that it will survive, nonetheless. And I guess that is how it might.

Patrick Leigh Fermor's Twice-Born Journey

Let's cast our net a little wider. I mentioned earlier the fictive dimension of even what is technically non-fiction, such as 'travel-writing'. A classic instance is surely Patrick Leigh Fermor's account of his journey as a young man across old Central Europe, in the decade before the Second World War broke and swept much of it away forever.[27] Actually, there are two journeys, each distinct but entwined: the original one, undertaken (mostly) on foot, and its brilliant recreation, many years later. And the gap between the two, together with its brilliant bridge of words, provides his account's fundamental opening to enchantment.

Leigh Fermor was aware of it – at the time, intermittently, and long afterwards, intensely. Not only was his trip attended by fateful serendipities – not for nothing is the first book entitled *A Time of Gifts* – but 'I felt preternaturally light', and things 'shed a golden radiance' or came together in 'a luminous moment'.[28] At the same time, he is never very far from 'a sudden sharp intimation, like a warning tap on the shoulder, of the fleetingness of everything'.[29]

His writing is shot through with wonder, both in the extraordinary places and people he encounters – farms, monasteries, cathedrals, castles, mountains, forests, the rivers that supplied the fluid backbone of his journey, and all their denizens – and in the pellucid prose in which he seeks, with such success, to 'reconstruct' these lost worlds. Of course some of them, to some degree, still exist; but not as they did then. So it is never far from loss.

Contemplating the devastating effects of a huge concrete hydro-electric dam across the Danube between Romania and Yugoslavia, putting underwater one of the iconic landscapes of his journey, he notes sombrely that 'in everything but economics, the damage is irreparable … myths, lost voices, history, and hearsay have all been put to rout, leaving nothing but this valley of the shadow.'[30]

Indeed, it strikes me that to even a reasonably well-educated mind at the start of the twenty-first century, the places that Leigh Fermor describes are now so exotic, not to say fantastic, and so vanished, that to all intents and purposes they may as well be scenes from Tolkien's epic. Where the latter is mythmaking informed by history and autobiography, the former is autobiography and history in the act of becoming myth. I'm not saying there is no difference, but it is not a radical one. And both accounts are elegiac, suffused with an awareness of existential transience.[31]

Consider what Leigh Fermor gives us as the fruits of his journey of many leagues (his word) through the vanished Holy Roman, Ottoman, and Habsburg Empires to the Iron Gates, the Black Sea and Constantinople: old country-houses, in parts castle, monastery, and farm, with their 'pinnacles, pediments, baroque gables, ogees, lancets, mullions, steep slate roofs, towers with flags flying and flights of covered stairs ending in colonnades', where the author spends hectic days followed by long dinners and a smoke with various of their unwittingly doomed aristocracies, while now 'the memory of those aromatic fumes still enclouds the last night and the last house on the Great Plain'; the tumultuous confabulation of old market-towns, much of it still late-mediaeval, helplessly awaiting Bomber Command; Romanesque and Gothic cathedrals, their interior depths even vaster than the flying buttresses, arches, and spires; Mitteleuropa itself, perpetually at the mercy of 'assailants from the East, with the Huns as their dread vanguard'; and endless battlegrounds, here where the Emperor Charlemagne subdued the Avars, there where Nicholas, Count of Salm threw back the Turks, and everywhere the paladins of Christendom, haburgeoned, jambed and casqued, in pitched battle with the paynim hosts of Islam. There is a carved ivory horn from 'the oliphant of Lehel' and the thousand-year-old crown of St. Stephen, together with its mace-like sceptre, orb, armlets, and sword of state.[32]

Upon entering a forest in the Carpathian uplands,

> there, all at once, lay a space like an enormous room: a long, enclosed clearing where beech trees sprang up like gigantic pillars flinging out vaults of tangled and interlocking boughs. Grey in shadow, their smooth trunks were flecked with silver where the sunbeams spilt their way through an infinity of leaves and scattered blurred discs of light over the bark and the muscular spread of the roots...[33]

Where exactly would we draw a firm line here between history and mythicity, or even between Middle Europe and Middle-earth (including that particular forest and Fangorn)?[34] I don't see this suggestion as anything outrageous. Isn't it our common fate? At the risk of banality (but that's one part of 'common') I once found myself, a few years ago, in a museum with an exhibition about the 1960s, and there, in a temperature- and light-controlled glass case, were about thirty of my LPs, ones I had owned in my teenaged years: Hendrix, Cream, Dylan, and so on. For a moment I felt, 'What are my records doing in there?' Personal experience had become social history; indeed, not only that, but for the younger people looking on and discussing them in whispers, mythology. If you think I'm exaggerating, live a little longer, and watch it happen!

It's not surprising, then, that the whole of Leigh Fermor's account has an Elvish gleam whose traces remain long after one has finished reading, like the glowing phosphorescent traces of passing dolphins in the Aegean night-sea he loved, imperceptibly dissolving in the mind.

Enchantment in Middle-Earth

With good reason, the essays and letters of J.R.R. Tolkien have been among our chief guides to enchantment.[35] His own wondertale, *The Lord of the Rings*, was published in 1955–56 after the young Rayner Unwin told his father, proprietor of George Allen and Unwin, that he thought it was a work of genius so they should indeed publish it, although it might cost them as much as a thousand pounds. Sir Stanley responded, 'If you think this to be a work of genius, then you may lose [us] a thousand pounds.' (Now *that's* publishing.)

In the event, to both Unwins' and Tolkien's own amazement, it became a huge success in the late 1960s, and by now it has sold at least two hundred million copies. Together with his earlier children's book *The Hobbit*, *The Lord of the Rings* has almost certainly enchanted more people, and enchanted many of them more deeply, than any other book in the last century. To the despair of the professional literati, with their inveterate snobbery, it has topped almost every poll to date of Anglophone readers as their favourite or most important book.[36] Add the fact that it is so fabulously fictive, overflowing with imaginal beings, places and events but not a single lawyer, serial murderer or even sex, and it can hardly be avoided. And that's fine, because it will sharpen and deepen many of the issues in this chapter and beyond.

Once again there is a personal dimension here that may speak to others. When I first read *The Lord of the Rings* at sixteen, I fell into it the way one falls in love, and was so taken aback at finding myself at the end, appendices and all, that I could only start again from the beginning. It wasn't like falling into a dream, though; more like waking up. When I read, 'All that is gold does not glitter,/ Not all those who wander are lost;/ The old that is strong does not wither,/ Deep roots are not reached by the frost', it hit me like a splash of cold water. I raised my head to breath keen air and see unconquered mountains stretching out of sight, and for more than a year I was living less in America, where I just happened to be, than in Middle-earth, more real to me. What do I mean by 'real'? Meaningful, compelling, intrinsically valuable: in other words, enchanting. As Paul Feyerabend puts it, '"real" is what plays an important role in the kind of life one wants to live.'[37]

In the subsequent fifty-odd years, returning to *The Lord of the Rings* many times I have yet to exhaust it, or to come out of it without feeling renewed. But I only mention this because my experience is not unusual; on the contrary, it is typical of countless readers. Not for heavyweight support but illumination, let me quote David Foster Wallace: 'In dark times, the definition of good art would seem to be art that locates and applies CPR to those elements of what's human and magical that still live and glow despite the times' darkness'.[38]

The critic Roger Shattuck touches on something important, too. Great books, he says, allow readers to achieve their own personal experience more fully and directly. 'This sense, this secret, is what allows certain people to live life at all times as an adventure … Literature is one of the keys.'[39] And appreciating *The Lord of the Rings*, not uncritically but post-critically, could almost be a test of the seasoned naïveté needed to apprehend this truth.

Enchantment prefers strong stories, but it is not the exclusive preserve of any one genre, not even fantasy. Mervyn Peake's *Gormenghast*, for example, is pure Gothic; *Faërie* is nowhere to be found. Similarly, to lump George R.R. Martin's *Game of Thrones* alongside *The Lord of the Rings* as 'fantasy' is true only in the thinnest and most banal sense, like saying that Francis Bacon and Samuel Palmer, say, were both painters. Martin's stories concentrate relentlessly on the opposite of enchantment in all respects: violence, cruelty, misogyny and power (political, ethnic, sexual). It fascinates some of us and can even enchant as skilful narrative. However, we are apparently also supposed to respect it as more 'real'. But are wonder, delight and kindness any less real than squalid power-ploys? And why exactly is nihilism truer than Tolkien's qualified affirmation of life?

I should add, in case any reader is tempted to judge Tolkien's books by the films, please don't. They have their moments, but for the most part what is good in them is not original, and what is original is not good. The result is like nothing so much as an indifferent videogame (which is even truer of the subsequent films of *The Hobbit*). In the end, knowing both the books and the films, I can only agree with Christopher Tolkien, J.R.R.'s son and literary executor, that 'They eviscerated the book by making it an action movie for young people aged 15 to 25.' He adds bitterly that 'Tolkien has become a monster, devoured by his own popularity and absorbed into the absurdity of our time. The chasm between the beauty and seriousness of the work, and what it has become, has overwhelmed me. The commercialisation has reduced the aesthetic and philosophical impact of the creation to nothing.'[40] Still, I cannot entirely endorse that last point. I have met people who watched the films, often without having read the books, and were moved by something there. And the books survive.

In my view, there are several dimensions of enchantment at work here. The first and broadest results purely from the power of narrative. Tolkien was a superb storyteller (as Peter Jackson's clumsy meddling only confirms), always mindful that in the words of another master storyteller, Robert Louis Stevenson, 'It is not character but incident that woos us out of our reserve': 'The right kind of thing should fall out in the right kind of place; the right kind of thing should follow; and … all the circumstances in a tale answer one to another like notes in music.'[41] Plus this particular story, *The Lord of the Rings*, was carefully crafted by a powerful mythopoeic imagination informed by exceptional linguistic and historical erudition.

Readers tacitly recognise Middle-earth towards the end of the Third Age as their world. It is one in which human communities (the Shire), the living natural world (Middle-earth itself), and ultimate spiritual values (the Sea) are all under severest threat, and the source of the threat is pathological modernity.[42] Mordor, the greatest power of all, is the only modern state in Middle-earth. It has a centralised political and bureaucratic system, an industrial economy, an unrivalled military apparatus, and an aggressively imperialistic foreign policy. As a result, readers thus not only find their own fears and hopes addressed by the story, but they also find themselves in it as well, reading on to find out what will happen to them next.

Do I need to add that this is a world which is still open to enchantment? Middle-earth, unlike our world, has never been modernised. Apart from Mordor, there are no nation-states, no capitalism, and no technoscience. Community solidarities are strong, the air is clean, the earth rich and the water pure, and there is an underlying sense (despite the lack of formal religion, which Tolkien deliberately excluded) of a cosmic dimension to life. Tolkien thus shows us a world in which these things still matter as much as anything else. In other words, it is radically non-modern. Yet we recognise it, so it seems we have not entirely forgotten it after all. And this world is what stands in jeopardy as the story opens, and hangs in the balance almost throughout.

Does it survive? Yes, but only just. Things might easily have gone the other way, and in the end the Ring of Power is destroyed only by Gollum's unforeseen inter-vention, just when Frodo was about to claim and thus perpetuate it. In other words, the outcome is a result of ethics and effort, but finally grace – something which can never be counted upon, is not a method and cannot be tested, improved, applied or taught. And even so, the cost has been high, nearly ruinous. Théoden asks Gandalf, rhetorically, "however the fortune of war shall go, may it not so end that much that was fair and wonderful may pass forever out of Middle-earth?"[43]

Vital to the enchantment of *The Lord of the Rings* is its vibrant sense of place. Middle-earth in all its aspects, from geology and botany to weather and astron-omy, is made up of places of extraordinary richness, variety and reality. As Dwayne Thorpe says, 'Tolkien's readers all have the same impression: they have walked or ridden every inch of Middle-earth in all its weathers.'[44] His passionate love of trees, woods and forests in particular makes them unforgettable, and to this day his imag-inal ones and the 'real' ones I encounter invoke each other.[45] For that matter, the Alps remind me of the Misty Mountains even more than the reverse. (As Tony Blair does of the quisling wizard Saruman, although Blair succumbed much more quickly to the glamour of power.)

This sort of storytelling is very old, which is why it can be so fresh. The anthro-pologist Keith Basso, in his book *Wisdom Sits in Places*, says that 'unless Apache lis-teners are able to picture a physical setting for narrated events – unless, as one of my consultants said, "your mind can travel to that place and really see it" – the events themselves will be difficult to imagine.' The reason is not only that everything that happens does so somewhere, but that the location of an event 'is an integral aspect of the event itself.'[46] When I was reading *The Lord of the Rings* to my young daugh-ter, she asked, 'How is it I can see everything he's describing? How does he do that?' But this is an experience which is quite normal with good storytelling; indeed, it is only rare in the case of strictly 'realistic' fiction.

Thus, as a whole and in all its parts, whether mountains, forests, rivers, coun-tryside, or cities, Middle-earth is itself one of the principal characters of the book. Every one of them is unique; there are no generic spaces, only particular places with their own personality and agency. The same is true of Kenya in Blixen's book,

Hoban's London, Proust's Paris and Combray, and Bulgakov's Jerusalem, as well as the other place-based narratives I have mentioned.

Middle-earth thus returns us, through the enchantment of its storytelling, to animism: a sense of all nature as potentially alive, and our fellow-beings, human or otherwise, as subjects, agents, and ultimately equals.[47] It's a thoroughly non-modern awareness, and despite our training we have never entirely lost it; except in the most hardened cases, it requires only an awakening touch to come to life again. Indeed, I believe that indigenous enchantment itself is never dead but merely overlaid (often thickly, it is true), waiting to be rediscovered. In the right circumstances, the trip between the ancient oral culture that is our common birth right and who we are now can be very short.

Lucien Lévy-Bruhl noticed this. When we hear or read fairy stories, he writes, we are often transported back 'into the world of our ancient forefathers. And there we find in the full flower of life, vividly before us, the mysterious, "fluid" world of the primal myths. No matter how far removed we thought we had been from the mentality which in the first place produced them, the spectacle captivates us at once, and holds us fast.'[48] But Tolkien's work doesn't cast a spell; it awakens readers from the deadening spell of modernism. It is a call to *live*. That is why re-reading becomes, for many, a kind of semi-annual ritual of renewal. It's not because they can't remember what happens next. As George Stambolian says, with characteristic acuity, 'as with any great work, familiarity does not destroy the element of surprise. The reader expects, and takes delight in, the unexpected.'[49]

Another dimension stems from Tolkien's own relationship with enchantment. It is the lesson he put into his tale ('if', he says, 'one may speak of lessons that don't lecture'),[50] that no matter how wonderful and precious, enchantment will not, cannot, stay. And without it, the disenchanted 'grey and leafless world' must simply be endured. It is impossible to say how many readers, consciously or otherwise, recognise this final truth, but it is one that critics have almost completely missed. Or did it offend their belief in human Progress, ever onward and upward? In any case, far from it being simply a sentimental or soothing book, there is a deep and unassuageable sadness at the heart of *The Lord of the Rings*.

To understand why, we need to appreciate that Tolkien's Elves are unique in modern literature. Neither silly nor pretty, like the fairies of Shakespeare or Peter Pan, they are

> a race high and beautiful, the older Children of the world ... who now are gone: the People of the Great Journey, the People of the Stars. They were tall, fair of skin and grey-eyed, though their locks were dark ... their voices had more melodies than any mortal voice that now is heard. [51]

In *The Lord of the Rings*, the Elves specifically symbolise enchantment; indeed, they embody as well as practise it. The Elven land of Lothlórien is 'the heart of Elvendom on earth', and Sam's halting response to it – 'I feel as if I was inside a song, if you take my meaning' – is the etymological definition of enchantment.[52]

But ultimately it is doomed, and so too are the lives in Middle-earth of all the chief Elvish characters, who must either pass over the Sea forever, or 'dwindle to a rustic folk of dell and cave, slowly to forget and to be forgotten', or else, in Arwen's case, to stay and die like mortals. ('A Part of the Tale of Aragorn and Arwen' is irredeemably bleak. Before Aragorn dies, he predicts their reunion 'beyond the circles of the world', but Arwen clearly doesn't believe him and goes to her death, not long afterwards, unconsoled.)

Tolkien is clear that the Elves, whose dominion passed long ago, dwell now elsewhere if anywhere. In more than a thousand pages, Tolkien allows himself only one hint that it is still possible to encounter one, when he describes Galadriel as seen by Frodo: 'Already she seemed to him, as by men of later days Elves still at times are seen: present and yet remote, a living vision of that which has already been left far behind by the flowing streams of Time.'[53] (This is exactly how starlight, the kind Elves love most, works. One is seeing the light in the present, but the light that one sees is ancient.) Yet the present sense of Elves, or persons very like them, is hard to shake. Montaigne, for example, describes 'those divine, supernatural and extraordinary beauties which can sometimes be seen shining among us like stars beneath a bodily and earthly veil.'[54]

However, the Elves and Elvishness also symbolise, in Tolkien's words, 'certain aspects of Men and their talents and desires'.[55] It is thus our own capacity for enchantment that is passing away. Of course, if Sauron wins the War of the Ring, he will destroy enchantment; if not necessarily his goal, which would be the result. As with those of Bulgakov and Hoban, this story thus includes the same dance between enchantment and power-knowledge that we have found in other arts. In this case it emphasises the difference between them. As Tolkien points out in a letter, Galadriel reproves the hobbits for 'their confused use of the same word ['magic'] for both the devices and operations of the Enemy, and for those of the Elves ... the Elves are there (in my tales) to demonstrate the difference.'[56] Their so-called magic is art in the service of enchantment, whereas Sauron is 'the Lord of magic and machines'. (Those two words share the same root in Proto-Indo-European: *magh, 'to have power'.) The One Ring is both a *magic* ring and a ring of *power* because those are one and the same.

Tolkien's particular twist, however, is that even if Sauron loses the war – the best possible outcome – enchantment will fade anyway. The way Tolkien works this is to link, counter-intuitively, the One Ring of Power with the Three Elvish Rings. Their only power is to protect, preserve, and sustain. Nonetheless, as Elrond says, 'when the One has gone, the Three will fail, and many fair things will fade and be forgotten.'[57]

One reason is that their role was primarily to resist Sauron, so his fall took with it most of their raison d'être. They have no place in the succeeding age, 'the Age of Men'. (How depressingly disenchanted that sounds! Even allowing for the fact that Tolkien thereby included women, as per the linguistic convention of his day – no Dwarves, or Ents, let alone Elves?) More fundamentally, as Verlyn Flieger points out,

> there is a concealed sting in Lórien's beauty. Its timelessness is not the un-
> spoiled perfection it seems. Rather, that very perfection is its flaw. It is a
> cautionary picture, closer in kind to the Ring than we'd like to think, shown
> to us in all its beauty to test if we can let it go. *The Lord of the Rings* is, among
> other things, a story about the ability to let go. The Ring is the obvious ex-
> ample … The timeless beauty of Lórien is the deeper example.[58]

This truth is one we have repeatedly encountered in relation to enchantment. I
have already described it as the absence that attends presence, and said that the
ability to let go, to refrain from trying to own or hang on to it, is a prerequisite for
enchantment. (Easy to say!)

Jan Zwicky gives us another perspective. She counterposes 'the technological', all manipulation and control, with 'the lyric', which resonates closely with
enchantment. As human beings we cannot live long at or through either pole. Our
tool-using capacities rule out permanent lyricism, while our affinity with wordless
joy rules out a completely technological mode, at least without self-mutilation.
To put it another way, we are not Elves, so we can visit *Faërie*, but we cannot stay
there. That is what makes lyric enchantment so poignant. (There are a few people,
it seems, whose sadness lies in not being able to become cyborgs, robots, or some
other kind of machine. I pity their sorrow, but their desire even more.)

But there is a third mode, which Zwicky calls 'the domestic', that allows the
lyric to come and go, and permits practical use as distinct from exploitation. 'The
domestic accepts the essential tension between the desire for lyric enchantment and
the compelling capacity for technology. In this acceptance, it mediates'.[59] And what
are the hobbits, and the corresponding aspects of humans, if not domestic? Doesn't
the whole book end with Sam – its final hero – returning home to wife and child,
evening meal and fire?

That is one of the things that the critics object to most ('cosy', 'nostalgic', etc.).
They don't seem to realise that this is all Tolkien can offer as a bulwark against the
howling void: courage in a tight spot, a fierce love of what is small, insignificant
and useless, and a bittersweet appreciation of the enchantments of embodied life
and, however briefly, of being alive. Which is why the final quality and 'lesson' of
Tolkien's work is not escape or transcendence or even enchantment but what he
calls 'a sadness that [is] yet blessed and without bitterness'.[60] Tolkien saw this as the
best thing that could be saved from the existential wreck, the only 'triumph' really
on offer.

Isn't this what we also found with Bonnard, and Vermeer, and the quiet fire of
chamber music, both classical and jazz, the sweet pain of Joni Mitchell's songs and
the work of Blixen and other storytellers and poets who found themselves in *Faërie*
but had to leave, or were left by it? Not to mention the non-dogmatic humanism
of authors such as Montaigne, Goethe and William James, and more recently Freya
Stark and Jan Morris, who championed these values. It is also what Proust's great
work seeks: a life that makes room for, and honours, the moments of enchantment
which give it meaning but do not exhaust it. So this truth is about far more than

Tolkien, or even fiction. What we are finding is pointers to a way of life that isn't itself enchantment but, because it has learned (or is learning) to let it go, can make it welcome.

Beyond that, on this side of the grave, there is only, in Tolkien's fine phrase, 'hope without guarantees'.[61] Though it is bitter to receive, as Arwen found, death in his fictional world was ultimately the gift of God to humans; and accepting it, personally, is the ultimate instance of letting go. With touching chutzpa, Blixen declares, after the manner of Jacob with the angel, 'My life, I will not let you go except you bless me, but then I will let you go.'[62] This is not the modernists' death as shameful failure or meaningless interruption, but as what completes life.

And of course, any attempt to finally escape death can only fail ignominiously. But Tolkien goes further, and in one of his invocations of old truths with uncannily current relevance, he insists that trying to literally live forever – whether as a cyborg, uploaded software, cryogenic zombie or some other post-humanist fantasy – can only result in the hideous parody of immortality he calls 'endless serial living'. Someone who indefinitely postpones death ends by both craving and fearing it. They become, in fact, a Ringwraith. For it is precisely the uniqueness and therefore vulnerability of what enchants that allows it to do so at all. Not a supposedly universal immortality but personal perishability is what gives our lives their savour. That is why Tolkien has the immortal Elves call death 'a gift'. We all die, but we don't all die the same way.[63] Who honours life stands a chance, at least, of dying with dignity.

Herman Melville maintains that 'To produce a mighty book, you must choose a mighty theme.' Despite the places where its author's skill fell short of his vision (a failing of which he was well aware), *The Lord of the Rings* is a mighty book. More importantly, we might ask who the fantasists and escapists are. Not the storytellers! In art, as in love, the movement starts with delight but exceeds it. Wonder brings wisdom in its train.

Notes

1 Giuseppe Tomasi di Lampedusa, 'The Siren', pp. 83–126 in *Childhood Memories and Other Stories*, transl. Stephen Parkin (London: Alma Classics, 2013): 118.

2 See Curry, *Enchantment*: 34, 38, 115.

3 Edward Hoagland, *Sex and the River Styx* (White River Junction: Chelsea Green Publishing, 2010): 225.

4 Lampedusa, *Siren*: 120.

5 Lampedusa, *Siren*: 123, 121.

6 Lampedusa, *Siren*: 116, 117.

7 Adriana Cavarero, *In Spite of Plato. A feminist rewriting of ancient philosophy*, transl. Serena Anderlini-D'Onofrio and Áine O'Healy (Cambridge: Polity Press, 1996).

8 On Bulgakov, see Szakolczai, *Liminality*, chapter 10 for, e.g. the discernment of 'three different storylines' (p. 184) and the quotation here regarding Margarita (p. 192).

9 S.M. Saumarez, *The Akashic Record* (Kibworth Beauchamp: Matador, 2014).

10 W.B. Yeats, *Poems*: xxvi.

11 I am passing over his other assertion, expressed in the book as 'Manuscripts don't burn', because it is so unsatisfactory. However understandable a hope, manuscripts do burn. They are, and have been, irretrievably destroyed, lost, and forgotten. It might work as 'Ideas can't be destroyed' but even that is debatable, as well as sententious.

12 Hoban, *Medusa*: 68, 75.

13 Russell Hoban, *Riddley Walker* (London: Jonathan Cape, 1980): 150, 164, 191, 156.

14 Hoban, *Riddley*: 199.

15 Hoban, *Riddley*: 213. There is a clear literary precedent for the incidence of Punch and Easyer in *Don Quixote* Part 2, Chapter 6; thanks to Clay Ramsay.

16 Judith Thurman, *Isak Dinesen: The Life of a Storyteller* (New York: St Martin's Press, 1982): 348, 265. On Blixen, in addition to work referenced below see Szakolczai, *Permanent Liminality*, Chapter 8; e.g. 'Blixen was primarily not a novel-writer, but a storyteller …' (p. 159).

17 Bob Dylan, interviewed at a press conference at KQED, San Francisco, Dec. 1965.

18 Donald Hannah, *Isak Dinesen and Karen Blixen: The Mask and the Reality* (London: Putnam and Co., 1971: 137.

19 Isak Dinesen [Karen Blixen], *Last Tales* (London: Penguin, 1986 [1957]): 26.

20 MacIntyre, *Virtue*: 216.

21 Tolkien, *TLotR*: 1029.

22 Blixen, *Africa*: 284.

23 Karen Blixen, *Shadows on the Grass* (Harmondsworth: Penguin, 1984 [1960]): 79, 87.

24 Frantz Leander Hansen, *The Aristocratic Universe of Karen Blixen: Destiny and the Denial of Fate*, transl. Gaye Kynoch (Brighton: Sussex Academic Press, 2003): 133).

25 Hannah, *Dinesen*: 122.

26 All quotations from 'Babette's Feast', pp. 19–59 in Isak Dinesen [Karen Blixen], *Anecdotes of Destiny* (New York: Vintage Books, 1993 [1953].

27 Patrick Leigh Fermor's trilogy concerning this journey comprise *A Time of Gifts* (London: John Murray, 1977), *Between the Woods and the Water* (London: John Murray, 1986) and *The Broken Road: From the Iron Gates to Mount Athos*, ed. Colin Thubron and Artemis Cooper (London: John Murray, 2011). The last, being essentially unfinished, is much the least satisfactory.

28 Fermor, *Gifts*: 21, 49, 358.

29 Fermor, *Broken*: 43.

30 Fermor, *Between*: 278–79.

31 Tolkien provocatively remarks that 'History often resembles "Myth", because they are both ultimately of the same stuff' (OFS: 31). I think he is correct but it's not a claim I want to pursue here.

32 Quotations in this paragraph are from (respectively) Fermor, *Between*: 5, 81, 85, 51, 55, 259–60.

33 Fermor, *Between*: 200.

34 It's also true that there is a great deal of 'actual' history in Tolkien's fiction. See, for example, Tom Shippey, 'Goths and Romans in Tolkien's Imagination', pp. 19–32 in Helen Conrad-O'Briain and Gerard Hynes (eds), *Tolkien: The Forest and the City* (Dublin: Four Courts Press, 2013).

35 I think the best single book remains Shippey, *Tolkien*. But for Tolkien and enchantment, see Verlyn Flieger and Douglas A. Anderson (eds), *Tolkien on Fairy-stories* (London: HarperCollins, 2008) and my *Deep Roots in a Time of Frost: Essays on Tolkien* (Zurich: Walking Tree Books, 2014).

36 On Tolkien and the critics, see my 'Critical Reception, Lee, *Companion*, reprinted in my *Deep Roots*. Most recently, in 2022, 'The Big Jubilee Read' circumvented the problem of actual readers' preferences by appointing a panel of literary professionals to choose what they should like; needless to say, the result excluded Tolkien.

37 Paul Feyerabend, *Conquest of Abundance. A Tale of Abstraction versus the Richness of Being* (Chicago: University of Chicago Press, 1999): 248.

38 This quotation is all over the internet, e.g. https://www.goodreads.com/quotes/49274-if-what-s-always-distinguished-bad-writing--flat-characters-a-narrative-world

39 Roger Shattuck, *Proust's Binoculars: A Study of Memory, Time, and Recognition in A la recherche du temps perdu* (London: Chatto & Windus, 1964): 134.

40 https://wrongplanet.net/forums/viewtopic.php?t=211993 (accessed 26.6.2022). The original article was published in *Le Monde* on 9 July 2012.

41 Robert Louis Stevenson, *The Lantern-Bearers and other essays*, ed. Jeremy Treglown (London: Chatto and Windus, 1988): 179, 175. (With thanks to Scott Black.)

42 It is no coincidence that in repeated polls of British readers in the late 1990s, all of which *TlotR* topped, it was often followed by another book deeply worried about the trajectory of modernity, Orwell's *1984*.

43 J.R.R. Tolkien, *TLotR*: 550.

44 See Curry, *Defending*: 40. Lawrence Durrell once astutely remarked, 'What makes "big" books is surely as much to do with their site as their characters and incidents.' From his essay on 'Landscape and Character', pp. 156–63 in *Spirit of Place. Mediterranean Writings* (London: Faber and Faber, 1971): 163.

45 The case of Sara Maitland, in *Gossip from the Forest* (London: Granta: 2012), is not unusual but it is particularly sad. It's not just the ease with which she rejects the work of arguably the greatest modern writer of fairy tales and literary defender of trees and forests in a book on just that subject, nor the spiteful glee she shows in doing so. It's that she is indulging in just the sort of masculinist monomania that any feminist (female or male) ought to resist and dispute. There are an insufficient number of women characters in *TlotR*, so that, it seems, is that.

46 Keith H. Basso, *Wisdom Sits in Places. Landscape and Language Among the Western Apache* (Albuquerque: University of New Mexico Press, 1996): 86, 87.

47 As I maintained in *Defending*.

48 Lucien Lévy-Bruhl: *Primitive Mentality: The Mythic World of the Australia and Papuan Natives*, transl. Brian Elliott (St Lucia: University of Queensland Press, 1983): 257. Lucien Lévy-Bruhl's concept of 'participation', influential but widely misunderstood, is directly relevant to the experience of enchantment. For example, he warns against 'taking for granted that things are given first and that afterwards they enter into participations... Participation enters into the very constitution of these things. Without [it], they would not be given in experience: they would not exist.' (*The Notebooks on Primitive Mentality*, transl. P. Rivière (Oxford: Basil Blackwell, 1975): 179–80.) For a promising new restatement and development, see forthcoming work by Anthony Thorley. (I would add that the common charge levelled against Lévy-Bruhl of racism is simply ignorant.)

49 Stambolian, *Proust*, 248.

50 Tolkien, *OFS*, 43.

51 Tolkien, *TlotR*: 1137.

52 Tolkien, *TlotR*: 351.

53 Tolkien, *TlotR*: 373.

54 M.A. Screech, *Montaigne and Melancholy: The Wisdom of the Essays*, rev. edn (Lanham: Rowman and Littlefield, 2000): 145.

55 Tolkien, *Letters*: 189, and cf. 176.

56 Tolkien, *Letters*: 146.

57 Tolkien, *TlotR*: 269.

58 Verlyn Flieger, *A Question of Time: J.R.R. Tolkien's Road to Faërie* (Kent State University Press, 1997): 112.

59 Zwicky, *Lyric*: 138.

60 Tolkien, *TlotR*: 1029. Michael D.C. Drout argues this point in an insightful essay, 'The tower and the ruin: the past in J.R.R. Tolkien's works', pp. 175–90 in O'Briain and Hynes, *Tolkien*: 77–78.

61 Tolkien, *Letters*: 237.

62 Blixen, *Africa*: 276.

63 From Miroslav Holub, in his poem 'The Dead', quoted on p. 316 of Seamus Heaney's brilliant exploration of the issue in 'Joy or Night: Last Things in the Poetry of W.B. Yeats and Philip Larkin', pp. 316–331 in Seamus Heaney, *Finders Keepers. Selected Prose 1971–2001* (London: Faber and Faber, 2002).

9

POETRY

Poetry is a kind of fiction where story, stripped to essentials, stands out with the bare beauty of a tree in winter, and metaphor is its sap. For that reason, it may be the most concentratedly enchanting kind, the purest possible distillation of enchantment in words, like the sweetest honey or the strongest good wine. Indeed, as Connolly says, to stand out, poetry 'must be a double distillation of life that goes deeper than prose. It must be brandy as compared to wine, otherwise consumers will get their poetry from short stories and novels.'[1] Maybe that's the reason why so many people cannot bring themselves to read it: they can't hold their poetry, and must turn to something weaker. Or else they are understandably warned off by signs of privilege, especially higher education.[2]

Now if this chapter were an historical survey of enchantment in English poetry, it would have to put the Romantic poets of the late eighteenth and early nineteenth centuries – Wordsworth, Coleridge, Shelley, and Keats – centre-stage. But it's not, so I'll exercise my right to outrageously omit them except to note three things. One, wonder was indeed consciously central to their poetry, and many of the poems that resulted still stand as among the most enchanting ever written. Two, they insisted on the validity of the truths and realities which the poetic imagination, open to wonder, could reveal (a stance they shared with their great contemporary, Goethe). And three, notwithstanding what I've just said, Romanticism as a broad cultural movement eventually succumbed, perhaps inevitably, to the disenchanted environment in which it found itself.

The intellectual provenance of that disenchantment was, and remains today, Platonic-Pauline-Cartesian. As we have seen, it consisted of a violent split between matter and spirit or mind, extended philosophically by Kant and Hegel but rejected, with great effort and at great cost, by Nietzsche. And as Romanticism gradually enlisted on the 'subjective' side, its radical potential weakened, leaving William Blake, for example – its most uncompromising poetic exemplar – as merely

DOI: 10.4324/9781003353225-9

an eccentric voice in the metropolitan wilderness. But not entirely; for as I well remember from my first encounters with them, the poems themselves, read with an open heart and mind, still carry the thrill of true enchantment.

The potential of poetry to enchant being wild, it can show up in unexpected places with no regard for consistency. Elsewhere I have rightly counted Ezra Pound as a modernist, but his two-line poem 'In a Station of the Metro' breaks through into non-modern wonder:

> The apparition of these faces in the crowd;
> Petals on a wet, black bough.

Its genesis was seeing faces – 'suddenly a beautiful face, and then another and another, and then a beautiful child's face, and then another beautiful woman' – as he emerged from a train in La Concorde station in Paris. It took him nearly two years and a series of ever-shorter drafts to arrive at this scintilla of deep feeling. Its formal resemblance to a haiku is less important than the *mono no aware* – intense pathos at fleeting beauty – with which it overflows.

If they give it even a moment's thought, the movers and shakers of this world, philistine partisans of power-knowledge and rational self-interest, have long considered poetry absurd, irrelevant and frivolous. Coming from them such an assessment, although it doesn't guarantee enchantment, is a promising sign. If poetry was something they liked and pushed, it would be more alarming. For example, on 25 November 2008, the British government issued this stirring statement:

> The time has come to begin the search for a new Poet Laureate, the first for the 21st century. Culture Secretary Andy Burnham today announced that preparations for the appointment are underway, with the Department for Culture, Media, and Sport consulting widely in the poetry sector.

(Maybe you didn't know there was a poetry sector.)

On the whole, though, the governing consensus has long been that poetry is of no use. That is something for which we should be glad, even though it's a long descent from classical times, when 'the seer, the poet and the philosopher [were] originally identical, a shaman-like figure, and in the course of Greek intellectual history gradually differentiating into the separate figures of *mantis*, *poietes*, and *sophiste-philosophos* ...' (Those are the words of the classicist Professor J.S. Morrison, formerly President of Wolfson College, Oxford, so they count as a sober assessment.)[3]

In our dark times, it is enough to realise and appreciate poetry as Michael Oakeshott described it: 'a sort of truancy, a dream within the dream of life, a wild-flower planted among our wheat.'[4] And for the finely tuned, the words of a poet may still carry the hidden weight of a seer-philosopher. With the great ones like Yeats, Dickinson, and Rilke, you'd have to be deaf or dead not to hear it.

Yeats's poem 'The Circus Animals' Desertion', finished not long before he died, recounts the vanity of all his life's poetic images. They had sustained him until now and performed reliably, but they have deserted him in old age, until 'Maybe at last being but a broken man/ I must be satisfied with my heart'.[5] Those images were celestial (the circus animals also signify the zodiac) and archetypal, drawn from the realm of Ideas. But newly chastened – 'Mind grows young and body old', as he says in another poem[6] – Yeats realises that although complete in themselves, they only become real for us in the mire of earthly and bodily human life. 'Magic' in the sense of wonder requires its concrete pole. Not a fantasy of complete and eternal bliss, but the imperfect, impermanent, actual thing which is all we can have. As Merleau-Ponty says, 'what enables us to center our existence is what also prevents us from centering it completely …'[7]

For some this resolution is shocking, especially on the part of a lifelong adherent like Yeats. Why? Another poet-seer-philosopher, Homer, scandalised Plato and his subsequent followers, including the Church Fathers, in the same sort of way. Homer portrayed gods, spirits and humans as able, on occasion, to interact directly, and such mythic egalitarianism was offensive to the hierarchical acolytes of pure spirit. Yeat's *volte-face* is not as strange as it might appear, however, for although passionately interested in Platonism, as well as astrology and the occult, his relationship with them was ultimately strategic. When philosophical system reached the point of disenchantment, he put it instead – as per Hermes' artistic ruthlessness – into the service of poetic enchantment, and refused to countenance the reverse. (This cunning move was one that Ted Hughes was unable to make, leaving his occultism and astrology adjuncts to his poetry, instead of nourishing it.)

Contemporary enchanting poetry now has powerful internal enemies, or rather, false friends. As we found with music, they gather at two opposing ends of a spectrum, one populist, and the other elite. The former is performance or slam poetry – a fine thing in its way, no doubt, but its noisy bravado and willingness to sacrifice complexity in pursuit of a large audience means that it has little room for the quiet depths required for, and encouraged by, poetic wonder. Really engaging with a poem surely requires not a crowd but an encounter – in this case, the solitary, intensely private, and personal encounter of deep reading. As Stephen Spender points out, 'a poem is written by one person writing for one person reading or listening – however many readers or listeners there may be.'[8]

The other danger is academic poetry: over-institutionalised, thick with official assessments, grants, and patrons of particular schools with preferred styles. As Mark Edmundson says, 'Poetry is now something of a business.'[9] That is never good for enchantment. As part of the same development, there are also schools of literary and cultural theorists, just down the hall, to be negotiated: not other poets but critics, with considerable cultural power. And part of the exercise of that power is soft censorship in line with the identity politics entrenched in much of the academy, which are allowed to take precedence over the internal criteria that arise when, as Seamus Heaney says, 'The poetic art is credited with an authority of its own.'[10]

'These strictures,' as Edmundson adds, 'are instalments in the war of philosophy against poetry' (a war first declared by Plato).[11] And then there are some poets themselves who are happy to open the gates of poetry to the enemies of *mythos* and enchantment. It comes as no surprise that John Ashbery, for example, was strongly influenced by John Cage, nor that he was fascinated by surrealism and Dada.[12] John Bayley, describing Larkin's work, wrote that 'the interior of his poetry, like a Vermeer interior, is both wholly accessible and completely mysterious.'[13] Larkin was indisputably a modern poet, but the literary modernists have succeeded in reversing both terms, producing poems that are both wholly opaque and completely banal.

It is easy, in what amount (god help us) to poetry wars, to lose sight of what is fundamental. Adam Zagajewski points directly at it: 'To defend poetry means to defend a fundamental gift of human nature, that is, our capacity ... to experience astonishment and to stop still in that astonishment for an extended moment or two.'[14]

There is a *via media* in terms of 'style' that is a royal road to poetic enchantment, as well as for song lyrics. In close parallel to enchanting painting and music, it points, suggests, evokes. In so doing, it avoids both literalism – the highly-structured realism that Wallace Stevens nailed as 'a corruption of reality'[15]– and formless abstraction lacking all (or as many as possible) empirical referents. In the one, there is too little for the imagination to do; in the other, too much.

Heaney was a poet who always tried to be accessible to those willing to pay attention but sacrificed none of his poetic integrity in doing so. (The same could be said of Mary Oliver, Adam Zagajewski, Paul Durcan, Czeslaw Milosz, Tomas Tranströmer, R.S. Thomas, Wisława Szymborska, Richard Wilbur, and C.K. Williams, among many others.) This ability has nothing to do with modernists using demotic discourse deliberately and therefore self-consciously, often ironically and, most offensive trait of all, patronisingly.

Auden is ambiguously placed in this context. He manfully struggled, with mixed success, against his own disenchanting modernist virtuosity. In this struggle, Hardy and Frost helped keep Auden honest.

Many of Heaney's poems concern wonder, finding it in the extraordinariness of the ordinary. His commitment is evident from his insistence that with all due respect to social and historical formations, ultimately 'The soul exceeds its circumstances'.[16] (Earlier we noted the same of Dylan and the 60s.)

One poem, 'Lightenings', addresses the issue almost directly.[17] The monks of an Irish cloister are at prayer when a big ship appeared above them in the air, its anchor hooking into the alter rails. Then a man climbs down the rope and struggles to release it. '"This man can't bear our life down here and will drown,"'

> The abbot said, "unless we help him." So
> They did, the freed ship sailed, and the man climbed back
> Out of the marvellous as he had known it.

Note the reversal at the end; having apprehended this airy ship as a wonder, we are left with our world as enchanted by virtue of having seen it through the sailor's eyes. Hermes conducts us along the rope connecting the marvellous with the quotidian and back again: enchantment doubled!

Power's dismissal of poetry is, of course, correct in its way. But something that cannot be used can still have effects. That is why Shelley's boast about poets as the 'unacknowledged legislators of the world' and Auden's counter-lament that 'poetry makes nothing happen' are equally unsatisfactory, both being half-truths.[18] Art can have effects in the primary world, but those effects can't be successfully planned or managed. Even to set out to change things using art is to leave enchantment for power-knowledge, which is something quite else. Relatedly, the assertion famously made by Adorno, although later retracted, that 'To write poetry' – and by impli- cation, to make any art – 'after Auschwitz is barbaric' is as one-sidedly wrong, not to say fatuous, as the belief that art could ever prevent such things.[19] The 'power' of imaginative literature, as opposed to a tract, is rather to enchant. Granted that, however, poetry can indeed change lives. As Louis MacNeice puts it, 'a poem is a personal utterance, but this does not disprove the possibility of a poetic truth ...'[20]

I think this is part of the point Robert Frost was making when he said that a poem 'begins in delight and ends in wisdom', before adding that 'The figure is the same as for love.'[21] Why so? Because art and love share a heartland ruled by wonder, not will. Delight is, of course, one of the modes of enchantment. But note the direction: from delight to wisdom, not the other way around.

There certainly is wisdom to be had, if you get there from delight. Reading Yeats or Leonard Cohen or Grevel Lindop on the joys and sorrows of being a man, for example, I experience deep recognition. Reading the poems of Nuala Ni Dhomhnaill or Sharon Olds, however, I learn, as the latter says, 'to love what I do not own' – a point which resonates strongly with Tolkien's definition of enchantment as a love of the other as other.[22] I feel lucky and honoured to be led in this way across the gulf that divides and connects men and women, into the presence of the mystery of female desire and sex- uality, and maternal love. (The work of George Eliot, Margaret Lawrence, and Ursula Le Guin affects me in the same sort of way. And poetry is, after all, a kind of fiction.)

Then there are poems that touch on the mystery of being at all, which men and women share alike. When Tomas Tranströmer writes, 'He who has gone furthest has a long way to go', or 'the emptiness turns its face to us'/ and whispers/ "I am not empty, I am open", what is there to add? What he calls 'the great enigma' is gently laid bare for all those who haven't forgotten, or have remembered, how to think with their hearts and feel with their minds.[23] Some might even learn to do so upon reading his words.

Asked in an interview about being described as a mystic or religious poet, Tranströmer replied:

> Very pretentious words, mystic, and so on. Naturally, I feel reserved about their use, but you could at least say that I respond to reality in such a way that I look on existence as a great mystery and that at times, at certain moments, this mystery carries a strong charge, so that it does have a religious character, and it is often in such a context that I write. So these poems are all the time pointing towards a greater context, one that is incomprehensible to our nor- mal everyday reason. Although it begins in something concrete.

Echoing what I mentioned earlier about humility as opposed to self-importance, Tranströmer has also written perhaps the best description I have ever read of poetic creativity:

> Fantastic to feel how my poem grows
> while I myself shrink.
> It grows, it takes my place.
> It pushes me aside.
> It throws me out of the nest.
> The poem is ready.[24]

It would be difficult to improve on that account. Nonetheless, I have something to add. It could perhaps be seen as a response, however tentative, to the question: where is a work of art before it's been realised? I have made much of the absence implicit in presence, but it seems that in artistic creation a strange inversion takes place: the work is already present even though it is still absent. Which, since it is both at once, is again metaphor at work. I learned this from a poem that I once wrote:

> I live with this:
> the work is not yet done –
> is far from done – yet somewhere,
> in another place
> or country,
> *it already exists*: luminous,
> polished, perfect
>
> Speaking to me softly while it waits,
> in the dark,
> to be done

For good reason, there are probably more poets quoted throughout this book than any other kind of occupation. That isn't just because I happen to like poetry, or essays by poets. Schooled in perceiving and expressing the essentials of human life, poets are well-placed to see and say such things clearly. So it's absurd to pick only one more to mention here, but I can't afford to be afraid of being absurd, so I will close with Edward Thomas. He is usually classed as a 'nature poet' and he was that, incomparably so. On the other hand, it would make equal sense to call him a 'culture poet'. The point is, his poems are some of the most darkly enchanting in the English language.

After years of jobbing journalism, Thomas finally found the confidence to devote himself to writing poems, largely thanks to the moral support of Robert Frost. In the years 1915–16, he wrote more than 140. Then, at thirty-eight years old, he voluntarily enlisted. Not long afterwards, despite his age, he insisted, over

the objections of his commanding officer, on being moved to the Front. F
on 9 April 1917, pierced by a fragment of shell.[25]

What I'm about to quote is not intended to replace his poems but to throw
on them, their author, and the nature, in both senses, of poetic wonder. The last
pages of Thomas's diary contain these notes. (In their raw intensity, they resonate
with those of Alain-Fournier, encountering his fate, in the form of Yvonne de
Quiérecourt, in Paris. The Frenchman had died three years earlier in the same war.)

The light of the new moon and every star

And no more singing for the bird …

I never understood quite what was meant by God

The morning chill and clear hurts my skin while it delights my mind.

Neuville in early morning with its flat straight crest with trees and houses –
the beauty of this silent empty scene of no inhabitants and hid troops, but
don't know why I could have cried and didn't.

And a slip of paper on which is written in pencil:

Where any turn may lead to Heaven

Or any corner may hide Hell

Roads shining like river up hill after rain.

I hesitate to add anything for fear of gilding the lily, but let me just point to the signs of
enchantment: the light of moon and stars – an ordinary, even ugly place transformed
by, and into, beauty – a shining river running up, not down, a hill – the engagement
of the senses, and emotions – and the irrelevance, at best, of 'God'. [26] (Why the last?
Because 'what they mean by God' is typically universal, amounting to everything and
anything. As such, He is entirely abstract and without any concrete magic. The gods,
in their luminous and irreconcilable particularity, suffer from no such handicap.)

In 'How Poetry Comes To Me', another poet, Gary Snyder, turns to the question beloved of interviewers: where does a poem come from? (Michael Longley
once replied, 'If I knew, I'd go there.') Snyder's poetic response was this:

It comes blundering over
Boulders at night, it stays
Frightened outside the
Range of my campfire
I go to meet it at the
Edge of the light[27]

Elsewhere, he remarks that 'Certain people are clear, and break the rules because they want to know. They also understand there's a price to pay, and won't complain.'[28] I have no doubt that Thomas was one of those people. He was determined to go to that place – the place where poetic enchantment comes from – and he passed beyond the edge of the light in search of it. And he was not going to complain. But with that too short treatment, we leave poetry. It's inexhaustibly lovely, dark, and deep, but like the poet, we too have miles to go before we sleep.

Notes

1 Connolly, *Enemies*: 108.
2 More than a whiff of that about *Poems That Make Grown Men Cry* (2014), even though many of the poems are of course wonderful.
3 J.S. Morrison, 'The Classical World', pp. 87–114 in Michael Loewe and Carmen Blacker (eds), *Oracles and Divination* (Boulder: Shambhala, 1981): 95. Cf. Sir Philip Sidney in his *Defence of Poesy* (1595): 'Among the Romans a Poet was called Vates, which is as much as a Diviner …'
4 Oakeshott, *Poetry*: 541.
5 Yeats, *Poems*: 395.
6 'Margot'.
7 Jack Reynolds, *Merleau-Ponty and Derrida: Intertwining Embodiment and Alterity* (Athens OH: Ohio UP, 2004): 18.
8 Robert B. Silvers (ed.), *The Company They Kept*, vol. 2 (New York: New York Review of Books, 2011) 51.
9 Edmundson: 'Poetry Slam': 65. See also Dana Goia's excellent article 'Can Poetry Matter?', published in *The Atlantic* in May 1991 and incorporated into his book of the same title published in 2002 by Graywolf Press.
10 Seamus Heaney, *The Government of the Tongue* (London: Faber and Faber, 1988) 92.
11 Edmundson: 'Poetry Slam': 66.
12 See Claude Rawson, 'Bards, Boardrooms, and Blackboards: John Ashbery, Wallace Stevens, and the Academicization of Poetry,' pp. 181–191 in Vereen Bell and Laurence Lerner (eds), *On Modern Poetry. Essays Presented to Donald Davie* (Nashville: Vanderbilt University Press, 1988): 185.
13 John Bayley: 'The Last Romantic', *LRB* (5.5.1983).
14 Jan Zwicky, *Wisdom and Metaphor* (Kentville: Gaspereau Press, 2003): 108.
15 Stevens, *Collected*: 906.
16 Seamus Perry, 'We did and we didn't', *LRB* (6.5.2021): 21–24.
17 Wes Davis (ed.), An Anthology of Modern Irish Poetry (Cambridge, MA: The Belknapp Press, 2010): 347–48.
18 In the poem 'In Memory of W.B. Yeats'.
19 See Mark Glanville, 'The man who wrote poetry after Auschwitz', *TLS* (20.11.2020) 19–20: 19.
20 MacNeice, *Poetry*: 184.
21 Robert Frost, preface to his *Collected Poems* (1939).
22 Sharon Olds, *Selected Poems* (London: Cape, 2005): 21. I am not suggesting that female desire etc. exhausts their poetry, by the way.
23 The quotations in this section are from Tomas Tranströmer, *The Great Enigma. New Collected Poems*, transl. Robin Fulton (New York: New Directions Publishing, 2006): 73, 191, 230 xiv–xv, 79.
24 Tomas Tranströmer, *The Great Enigma. New Collected Poems*, transl. Robin Fulton (New York: New Directions Publishing, 2006): 79, xiv–xv.
25 See letter by Jean Moorcroft Wilson in the *TLS* (13.11.2015).

26 Edward Thomas, *Collected Poems*, ed. R. George Thomas (London: Faber & Faber, 2004): 171, 172. I also benefited from 'The Dark Earth and the Light Sky', a play by Nick Dear in 2013 at the Almeida Theatre.

27 Gary Snyder, *No Nature. New and Selected Poems* (New York: Pantheon Books, 1992): 361.

28 Gary Snyder, *The Practice of the Wild* (Berkeley: Counterpoint: 1990): 176.

10
CONCLUSION

This book has addressed wonder in, and as, painting, music, and fiction. I have explored, defended, and tried to understand that experience. It has arisen out of my own values, concerns, and realisations respecting art, often when I am enchanted by it. My experience is not so unusual; art is something than can even, and for many people does, make life worth living. For my part, I feel about art the way you might about someone who saved your life. And maybe it has.

But in the same way as a musician might love playing or a painter painting, I also love thinking. So unsurprisingly, one of the things I like thinking about is art. And to adapt slightly a remark by Wittgenstein, I think with my keyboard, because my head often knows nothing of what my hands are typing.[1] (Indeed, those are often the best bits.)

I have tried to do this as well as I can, of course. I have even offered a theory of sorts, concerning enchantment in art as centred on the senses, fully engaged, working together with the imagination apprehending the lining and depth of the work's sensuous reality. I have suggested that in both its creation and apprehension, the activity of art is grounded in our nature as Earthlings which, by implication, is best understood through a non-scientific naturalism. ('Non-scientific' because it is essentially first-person – whether singular or plural – as distinct from the third-person perspective to which natural science remains committed, and therefore also the social sciences which model themselves on it.)[2]

I have also noticed two extremes hostile to enchantment which I describe as Apollonian (hyper-separate power-over) and Dionysian (orgasmic unity). These two enemies of enchantment – artistic no less than in any other context – tend to extrude two institutionalised practices. One is high theory, the 'rationalisation and intellectualisation' decried by Weber, mainly but not entirely in universities and among modernist critics. The second consists of those wanting not to correct our emotional responses to art but to exaggerate, vulgarise and exploit them: in short, the moneymen. And these two, as we have seen, are not above collaborating.

DOI: 10.4324/9781003353225-10

But none of this is meant to be an 'explanation' of artistic wonder, rather a way to think about it which respects the phenomenon and perhaps even deepens it. And I have offered it in the spirit of a blackbird trying out a new variation of his song, or a sapling rooting itself in unfamiliar ground; that's what we do.

It has been far from a solo effort, however. The entire book has been conducted in dialogue with others, some living, some technically dead. One, although a late-comer here, is the philosopher Michael Oakeshott, in an essay (written in 1959) called 'The Voice of Poetry in the Conversation of Mankind'. 'Poetry' here is essentially a placeholder for all enchanting art, whose effect he calls 'delight' – one of the modes of enchantment I named at the beginning.

Here is his defence of just such a project as mine (the nicely judged understatement of which makes one aware of the brassy stridency of so much contemporary discourse).

> [A]nyone fond of reflection who has found delight in listening to the voice of poetry is unprotected against the inclination to meditate upon the nature of that delight, and if he gives way to the impulse to put his meditations in order, he is only doing his best to understand the quality of the voice and its relationship to other voices. And if that best is good enough, he may say something worthwhile on behalf of poetry.[3]

Oakeshott distinguishes delight from two other modes. One is 'practical activity' – of necessity, the dominant one for humans and other animals, arising from the need to survive. This, he says, is 'a struggle from which the practical self cannot escape and in which victory is impossible because desire can never be satisfied [and] every attainment is recognised to be imperfect'. He insists that 'poetic' activity has no role in this struggle, no part to play for good or ill. To heed the voice of poetry and experience its delight is thus 'to enjoy, not a victory, but a momentary release, a brief enchantment.'[4]

The other mode is the pursuit of scientific knowledge and its attendant rationalism. This too has its own validity and interest, but not as a universal template for human endeavour. To repeat Oakeshott, 'there is nothing sacrosanct about practical enterprise … or scientific inquiry that "escape" from them is to be deplored.'[5]

Now, we can qualify his sober conclusion – the moments of enchantment are, as I have said, short but deep, and they can be life-changing – but there is little doubt that it is fundamentally sound. I have already emphasised, after Tolkien, that stays in *Faërie* for us mortals are necessarily limited, which is what gives enchantment its frequent emotional tone of poignancy. From this truth Oakeshott infers that 'there is no *via contemplativa*; there are only moments of contemplative activity abstracted and rescued from the flow of curiosity and contrivance. Poetry is a sort of truancy, a dream within the dream of life, a wild flower planted among our wheat.'[6]

I have no wish to disturb the enchantment of these words, themselves almost poetry. Nevertheless, I will work around them to arrive at a somewhat wilder and more open place. And I can take my lead from Oakeshott himself, who lets slip that beyond 'a brief enchantment,' attending to poetic delight is 'perhaps, obliquely … to enjoy something more. Having an ear ready for the voice of poetry is to be disposed to choose delight rather than pleasure or virtue or knowledge, a disposition which will reflect itself in practical life in an affection for its intimations …'[7] (Disposed, or doomed? It can be hard to tell the difference.)

Cue, then, what he had almost denied but what I want to affirm: the possibility indeed of a way of life in which – although not itself enchanted, or only intermittently so – enchantment is central. And I am not merely including art in that category. I have tried to show that the activity of art is, at heart, at one with the activity of life itself; or, as Wittgenstein would say, the world. Putting it at the centre of one's life, therefore, is to honour enchantment itself.

Such a way of life is indeed one which is 'disposed to choose delight' and therefore remain open to it. This is the attitude Frey Stark terms 'fearless receptivity'. And since enchantment is wild, and the enchanting other is and/or comes alive in the encounter, I have identified this way of life as the central principle of animism. (The technical inanimacy of most artwork is, in this context, unimportant.)

It is also associated with what Zwicky's 'domestic', distinct from but open to lyrical enchantment, as well as to our endemic instrumentalism, technological and otherwise. It is central to the humane humanism of Montaigne: earthy but receptive to the spiritual, reflexively sceptical and therefore hostile to all forms of dogmatism (including, these days, scientism). That is also Oakeshott's own tradition, including his central metaphor of the human project as a conversation between very different voices. And it is a fair description of Proust's narrator Marcel's painstaking lifelong project of a life constructed around, but not reducible to, moments of enchantment (*moments bienhereux*) which are partly discovered and partly re-created through art.[8]

I have already argued that such moments both reveal and help us realise truths of a very important kind: the intrinsic value, beyond all calculation, of what or who enchants. That is why Marcel says (in words which themselves have the taste of verity) that when they occur, 'we feel in ourselves the joy of rediscovering what is real'.[9]

In addition to its more strictly personal dimension – or perhaps it would be better to say, extending it – such rediscovery has literally vital implications for the most serious crisis now facing us all: anthropogenic ecocide. Without sufficiently widespread personal experience of the intrinsic value of the natural world, and the love that that entails, even the most enlightened political and economic policies and the most comprehensive scientific research will fail. Can't art help us to realise this, if we allow it to? We have already seen that the activity of art participates in that of life itself, through their shared relational, metaphoric, liminal creativity and its concrete magic. By the same token, isn't art – and all the more so enchanting art – potentially a celebration of life?

Karen Blixen records that the Kikuyu held their *ngomas*, their dances, 'only during the time of the full moon. When the moon did her best, they did theirs. With the landscape bathing and swimming in gentle powerful light from the sky, to the great illumination over Africa they added their little red-hot glow.'[10] This seems to me a perfect metaphor for human culture, pre-eminently art. All we do is borrow, shape and re-present what nature (including our own) gives us, adding our hot little glow to the great performance of more-than-human life. As Polixenes says in *The Winter's Tale*, 'art, which you say adds to nature, is an art that nature makes…'[11]

It is also a valid question whether a life without the experience of enchantment, and without realising the profound relationality and interdependence of which it is a lineament, is fully human, or fully alive. Tolkien, as we have seen, thought not, averring that it is 'as necessary for the health and complete functioning of the Human as is sunlight for physical life'.[12] Czeslaw Milosz, with all the authority of someone writing amid the smoking ruins of Warsaw in 1945, insists that 'It's madness to live without joy.'[13]

Indeed, I would say that to live, and especially to try to live, without wonder is deeply unnatural. Concrete magic is only possible for embodied beings, and the other side of that truth is that while we live it is always possible. And despite being cordoned off as 'cultural', and therefore supposedly reserved for humans alone, enchantment is thoroughly natural in a non-reductive, first-person sense. Why? Because we are fully natural and ecological beings, whose nature happens to include culture. As Gregory Bateson kept pointing out, the way people work creatively, including thinking creatively, and how nature works are one and the same. And that is where the activity of art itself, both creation and apprehension, takes place.

By the same token, enchantment, at least in its deep and radical form, cannot finally be charged as frivolous. It is merely fluffy or negligible only in the necrotic single vision – no other voices or values allowed – in which power is all that counts. The servants of power (usually but not only capital) are supremely indifferent to enchanting art, when not actually hostile; and as we have seen, that includes those who seek to merely use it for their own ends, whether propaganda or profit. Perhaps the art itself can be said to survive, in the loosest sense, but its enchantment cannot.

But enchanting art has ostensible admirers who also do it no favours. The problem follows from pursuing an agenda in which art is enlisted and demanded to assist or illustrate. Instead of poetic imagining allowed to be itself, untrammelled by our egoistic demands and expectations, and thereby perhaps to show us something new, art is pressed into the service of what is already believed and held to be all-important. Thus even the most passionate and progressive causes, if they mine art for moral instruction, political consciousness-raising, or ideological support, cannot but disenchant it.

Another problematic friend is the psychological interpretation of art as symbols, usually of psychic or mythic archetypes. That dimension can be acknowledged, of course, and up to a point even enhance appreciation. But if the art slips into servitude, then this too is a kind of mining in support of a theory, a usage in the service of a prior commitment.

In short, both the creator of enchanting art and the one who apprehends it as such give pride of place neither to power nor knowledge but to delight, the delight to which use-less and price-less beauty gives rise. Not even soft power in a good cause, although that has its place, nor even profound wisdom, although that may come unbidden, but simply for its own sake.

The point, then, is not that enchantment has no benefits. It is rather that its wonder being wild, these cannot be counted upon, managed, or predicted; so upon pain of potentially terminal domestication, they cannot form any part of a defence of enchantment, artistic, or otherwise. The enchantment of art must be allowed to stand on its own terms: a unique and precious voice in the human conversation which needs, and indeed will bear, no further justification.

Notes

1 Ludwig Wittgenstein, *Culture and Value*, rev. edn, ed. G.H. von Wright (Oxford: Blackwell, 1998): 24e.
2 See Thomas Nagel, *Mind and Cosmos: Why the Materialist Neo-Darwinian Conception of Nature is Almost Certainly False* (New York: Oxford University Press, 2012).]
3 Oakeshott, 'Voice': 494–95.
4 Ibid: 540.
5 Ibid: 540.
6 Ibid: 541.
7 Ibid: 540.
8 See especially Stambolian, *Encounter*.
9 Proust, *Remembrance*, vol. 3: 913.
10 Blixen, *Africa*: 162.
11 Shakespeare, *The Winter's Tale*, Act 4, Scene 4.
12 Tolkien, *Smith*: 101.
13 Czeslaw Milosz, *Selected and Last Poems 1931–2004* (Penguin 2014): 41.

INDEX

Page numbers followed by n indicate notes.

1960s, the 73, 74, 153, 212; music of 156–59
Abbate, Carolyn 119, 122
Abstract art (painting) 34, 54–8, 63, 71, 73,
    80, 83, 85, 93–7, 100, 103, 106, 147–48
Adams, John Luther 2, 124, 127
Adnan, Etel 16, 108
Adorno, T.W. 30, 98, 145, 227
Agit-prop (political art) 2
Alain-Fournier 193–94, 229
Albion Band, The 1, 120
Alvarez, Al 195, 196–97
Amis, Martin 195
Aphrodite 11, 60, 61, 66, 69, 98, 111, 112
Apollonian mode 9, 80, 95, 131, 138, 140,
    147, 149, 195, 232
Armatrading, Joan 156
Armstrong, Louis 146
Art as use-less 23–4, 28, 208
Art for art's sake 25–6
Art Nouveau 73, 74
Art market, the 95, 103–05, 109n52
Ashbery, John 197, 226
Atonalism 14, 32, 35, 140, 142, 147, 148
Atwood, Margaret 2, 195
Aubrey, Jack 192
Auden, W.H. ix, 6, 9, 101, 172, 184, 187,
    226, 227
Augustine, St 131
Avery, Milton 95

Bacon, Francis (painter) 80, 93, 103, 104, 214

Bacon, Francis (philosopher) 96
Baggins, Bilbo 191
Bailey, David 76
Ball, Philip 118
Band, The 156, 157, 163
Bánffy, Miklós 191
Bardot, Brigitte 78
Barnes, Simon 137n73, 192
Barton, Laura 111, 160
Bashō, Matsuo 16
Basso, Keith 215
Bateson, Gregory ix, 12, 15, 56, 200n27, 235
Bataille, Georges 100
Baudrillard, Jean 133
Baum, Frank L. 181
Bayley, John 185, 189–90, 226
Béart, Emmanuelle 69–70
Beatles, The 156, 162
Beaton, Cecil 155
Beauty 3, 11, 12, 20, 26, 54, 59, 67–72, 85,
    96, 98, 100, 119, 207, 218, 224, 235
Beethoven, Ludwig 29, 50, 139, 140, 141,
    143, 146, 193
Benjamin, Walter 12, 20–1, 189
Berg, Anton 145
Bergotte 66
Berger, John 21, 34
Berlin, Irving 153
Bernstein, Jay 32
Bettelheim, Bruno 187
Birtwhistle, Harrison 145

Björk 160
Black, Scott 175
Blair, Tony 215
Blake, William 19, 84, 160, 223–24
Blishen, Edward 178
Blixen, Karen 17, 161, 173, 194, 208–11, 215, 218, 219, 220n16, 234
Bloomfield, Mike 152
Bohr, Neils 13
Bolano, Roberto 195
Bonnard, Pierre 52, 54, 59–64, 65, 66, 71, 75, 76, 77, 84, 86, 93, 107, 116, 218
Borges, Jorge Luis 173
Botticelli, Sandro 69, 72
Boulez, Pierre 145, 167n37
Bowie, David 158–59
Boyd, William 96, 189
Brahms, Johannes 114, 140
Braque, Georges 93, 94
Brecht, Bertold 2, 34
British Library, The 177
Brodsky, Joseph viii, 77, 161–62, 178
Brook, Peter 18
Brooke-Rose, Christina 188
Brown, Dan 196
Brown, James 152
Brown, Mackay George 108, 166
Brown, Norman O. 149
Buber, Martin 17
Buckley, Tim 156
Bulgakov, Mikhail 194, 204–06, 208, 216, 217
Burke, Kenneth 11
Burnett, Frances Hodgson 181
Burnham, Andy 224
Bush, Kate 156
Byatt, A.S. 187

Cage, John 14, 34, 68, 103, 123, 148–50, 226
Calder, Alexander 74
Calasso, Roberto 145
Calligraphy 84, 103
Calvino, Italo 189, 197
Cannon, Moya 164
Capra, Frank 40–1
Caracci, Annibale 48
Carmichael, Hoagy 153
Carrington, Leonora 101
Carter, Angela 185
Carthy, Eliza 165
Carthy, Martin 165
Cartier-Bresson, Henri 59, 62, 77, 78, 79, 81

Cartwright, Garth 154
Cavarero, Adriana 204
Cave art 4–5, 37–9
Celan, Paul 12
Cervantes, Miguel de 195–96
Cézanne, Paul 53, 70, 93–4, 96, 99, 102
Chabon, Michael 182
Chamberlain, Lesley 20, 47n120
Chaplin, Victoria 24, 42
Chapman, Dinos 105
Charme 119–20
Cheng, François 72, 84, 85
Cheng, Li 81
Chesterton, G.K. 16, 157, 170, 186
Chinese landscape painting 1, 75–6, 80–85
Chomet, Sylvain 41
Chopin, Frédéric 114, 139, 143
Christianity 15, 32, 180, 188, 209
Circus 42, 74
Clarke, Brian 73, 74
Clarke, Susanna 185
Cohen, Leonard 156, 160, 227
Coleridge, Samuel Taylor 160, 223
Colour 53–4, 55, 59–61, 64–7, 75, 76, 81, 86, 95–6, 98, 100
Coltrane, John 34, 146
Connolly, Cyril 3, 23, 155, 170–71, 196, 223
Conrad, Joseph 27–8, 34, 190, 193, 194
Concrete magic 4, 15–7, 18, 19, 33, 34, 50, 115, 196, 203, 211, 229, 235; and art 17–8, 50, 53, 72, 77, 80, 81, 102, 115, 118, 125, 154, 157, 161, 190, 234
Copland, Marc 157
Coward, Noel 153, 155
Craig-Martin, Michael 102
Crafts 26–8, 103, 189, 197
Cream 156, 212
Crowley, John 16, 185, 194
Crumb, Robert 154
Cubism 83, 93–4, 97, 99
Cunningham, Bill 78

Dada 24, 100, 150, 226
Dalí, Salvador 100–01
Dao, the 72, 83, 144
Damasio, Antonio 190–91
Davies, Ray 156
Davis, Miles 144
Dawkins, Richard 186–87
Dean, Tacita 79
Debussy, Claude 34, 142, 143, 144, 146, 148
Delaunay, Robert 94
Denk, Jeremy 111–12, 134
Denny, Sandy 159, 165

Derrida, Jacques 68
Dhomhnaill, Nuala Ni 227
Dickens, Charles 161
Dickinson, Emily 224
Dionysian mode 9, 39, 80, 95, 114, 131, 138, 140, 141, 147, 152, 156–57, 195, 232
Discworld 191
Disenchantment 10, 15, 22, 24, 26, 28–31, 33, 53, 58, 64, 82, 93–4, 95, 97, 101, 105, 114, 182–83, 196, 197–98, 209, 223; in music 129–31, 158, 161
Disney 41, 47n123
Domestic, the 59, 204, 218, 234
Donaghy, Michael 164
Doors, The 156
Drake, Nick 156, 159–60
Duchamp, Marcel 34, 74, 100, 101–04, 149, 150
Duffy, Brian 79
Durrell, Gerald 192
Durrell, Laurence 5, 18–9, 221n44
Dylan, Bob 2, 24, 49, 156, 158, 159, 161–63, 165, 208, 226

Earth, the 11, 30, 33, 36, 37, 66, 69, 73, 81, 92, 95, 166, 175, 178, 203, 214–16, 232
Ecocide 5, 234
Edmundson, Mark 225, 230n9
Elderfield, John 60
Eliot, George 227
Eliot, T.S. 3, 114, 160, 188, 191
Eluard, Paul 121
Elves, the 16, 17, 186, 216–19
Empson, William 99
Enchantment, nature of 1–6, 8–31; false 9, 29, 96, 119, 141, 193
Ende, Michael 182
Enheduanna 172
Ernst, Max 101
Esterly, David 27
Evans, Bill 34, 144
Evolutionary psychology 5, 28–9, 130, 187
Explanation 17, 101, 107, 130, 183–84, 186, 188, 208, 233

Faërie 13, 14, 17, 52, 58, 61, 112, 121, 145, 179, 181, 182, 185, 191, 194, 214, 218, 233
Fairport Convention 157, 165
Fairweather, Ian 57
Fairy tales and wondertales 41, 172, 180, 183, 184–87, 189, 201n73, 216, 220n35

Fantasy literature 41, 171–72, 180–81, 189, 194, 214
Fauré, Gabriel 116, 120, 143
Fearless receptivity 30, 78, 207, 234
Felski, Rita 183, 200n26
Fermor, Patrick Leigh 176, 211–13
Feyerabend, Paul 135n31, 173–74, 213
Fiction *see* stories
Figurative art (painting) 51, 55–8, 60, 71, 72–4, 76, 85, 93, 94, 96, 99–100, 106, 147
Film (movies) 40–3, 174, 185, 209, 210, 214
Fink, Bob 113
Flack, Roberta 160
Flam, Jack 54–5, 92
Flieger, Verlyn 217–18, 220n35
Fontana, Bill 124
Fowles, John 205
Francesca, Piero della 71
Frankenthaler, Helen 95
Franzen, Jonathan 176, 195
Freud, Lucien 69
Fuller, Peter 21
Fung, Bettina 76

Gablik, Suzi 26
Gaps 9, 13–4, 22, 42–3, 57, 58, 77, 82, 85, 98, 101, 115, 122–24, 126, 131, 132, 144, 173–74, 184, 192, 205, 211
Garcia, Jerry 116, 154
Gasset, José Ortega y 174
Gaudi, Antoní 73
Gide, André 23, 195
Gift, enchantment as a 12, 22, 25, 27–8, 29, 64, 78, 112, 182, 211, 219, 226
Glamour 29–30, 41, 153, 158
Glier, Mike 56, 87n33
Gnosticism 103, 176
Goethe, Wolfgang von 55–6, 64–5, 139, 205, 218, 223
Goldsworthy, Andy 68, 81
Gollum 171, 215
Gompertz, Will 103–04
Google Books Library Project 177
Goya, Francisco 69, 105
Grahame, Kenneth 179–80
Grateful Dead, The 156, 163
Great American Songbook, The 153, 155, 163
Greenberg, Clement 63, 72, 97
Grieg, Edvard 142
Guthrie, Tyrone 18
Gynt, Peer 1, 173

Hammershøi, Vilhelm 71
Haden, Charlie 151, 165

Harry Potter stories, the 186–87
Harvey, P.J. 161
Hassell, Jon 130–31
Haydn, Joseph 138, 140, 146, 166n7
Haye, Jonathan 85
Hayes, Martin 117–18, 165–66
Heaney, Seamus 3, 225, 226
Heavy metal music 152
Helprin, Mark 194, 200n31
Hendrix, Jimi 2, 154, 156, 158, 212
Hepburn, R.W. 10, 43n7
Hepworth, Barbara 34, 53
Heraclitus 107, 190
Herbert, Zbigniew 37
Hermes 10–2, 37, 69, 112, 162, 225, 226
Hersch, Fred 157
Hill, Lauren 160
Hirst, Damian 47n115, 53, 64, 97, 103–04, 109n48
Hitchins, Ivon 106–08
Hoban, Russell 12, 14, 23, 38, 134, 173, 190, 194, 206–08, 210, 216, 217
Hockney, David 34, 56, 74, 84
Hodgkinson, Howard 75
Homer 3, 188, 225
Horkheimer, Max 98
Human nature 2, 11, 28, 36, 175, 226
Hundertwasser, Friedensreich 73, 97–8
Huxley, Aldous 141

Iasos 116
Ibragimova, Alina 139
Imaginal, the 14, 56, 121, 136n41, 174, 179, 213, 215
Imagination, the 30–1, 43, 56–8, 74, 75, 100, 123–24, 140, 171–74, 182, 209, 214, 223, 226, 232
Impressionism (in painting) 49, 50, 59, 63–4, 76, 81
Impressionism (in music) 142, 143
Improvisation 53, 56, 121–22, 131–32, 139
In between, the 14, 31, 56–8, 71, 85, 97, 100, 142, 184
Incredible String Band, The 157–58
Indiana, Gary 35
Internet, the *see* social media

Jackson, Peter 214
James, Clive 48
James, William 10, 17, 29, 60, 218
Janáček, Leoš 146, 148
Jankélévitch, Vladimir 16, 119–20, 122, 126, 130, 136n37, 143, 146–47, 149–50, 166

Jeffes, Arthur 121
Josipovici, Gabriel 57, 61, 71, 93, 103
Joyce, James 34, 124, 188, 193, 194, 210
Jullien, François 69, 83, 84, 90n149, 123
Jung, Carl 108
Juster, Norton 181–82

Kami 145
Kandinsky, Wassily 33, 54, 57, 73, 94, 99–100, 103, 147
Kane, Alice 187–88
Kapoor, Anish 21, 45n54, 145
Kawabata, Yasunari 86n13, 99, 124
Keats, John 30, 67, 162, 187, 223
Kelly, Kevin 177
Kent, Sarah 35, 46n109
Kermit the Frog 43
Kertész, André 77
Kiff, Ken 63–4, 67, 75, 76
Kinks, The 156
Klein, Yves 67, 94
Knausgaard, Karl Ove 171
Koons, Jeff 101, 104
Koudelka, Josef 77
Kravis, Judy 11
Kuan, Fan 8, 82
Kundera, Milan 25, 33

Lacan, Jacques 35
Lambirth, Andrew 75
Lampedusa, Giuseppe Tomasi di 194, 195, 203–04
Lancrenon, Sylvie 69
Land art 68, 81, 90n153
Landscape painting, Chinese 1, 75–6, 80–85
Larkin, Philip 35, 226
Lawrence, D.H. 26
Lawrence, Margaret 227
Le Corbusier 32–3, 105
Le Guin, Ursula 36, 181, 185, 187, 194, 227
Lee, Laurie 27
Lessing, Doris 11, 100
Leys, Simon 68, 198
Lévy-Bruhl, Lucien 11, 216, 221n48
Lewis, C.S. 4, 13–4, 126, 180–81, 183
Liminality 4, 6n10, 11, 15, 16, 115, 184
Lindop, Grevel 227
Linklater, Richard 40
Little phrase, the 116–18, 157
Literature, children's 178–83
Logos 10, 11, 34, 188, 198
London Review of Books 202n77
Longley, Michael 18, 197, 229

Love, enchantment as 6, 8, 9, 10, 15, 19, 27, 28, 29, 118, 119, 159–60, 161, 163, 182, 192–4, 206, 208, 210, 213, 219, 227
Lyric, the 218, 234

Ma 144–45
Mabey, Richard 129
Machado, Antonio 115, 172, 174
MacIntyre, Alasdair 185, 208–09
MacNeice, Louis 6, 26, 32, 184, 227
Magee, Bryan 129, 137n76
Magritte, René 60, 100–1, 109n35, 109n38, 109n40, 205
Maitland, Sara 221n45
Male gaze, the 69–70
Malevich, Kazimir 94, 96
Mandelstam, Osip 162, 192
Manet, Édouard 70
Mann, Sally 78
Mann, Thomas 141
Marc, Franz 73, 99
Marcus, Greil 160
Marinetti, Filippo 126
Marling, Laura 161
Márquez, Gabriel García 194
Martin, George R.R. 214
Martyn, John 160
Mason, Raymond 70, 77
Matar, Hisham 48
Matisse, Henri 34, 50, 52–6, 58–63, 65, 67, 72–6, 85–6, 92, 94, 95–6, 99, 106, 116, 142
Matsuoka, Seigow 145
Maturin, Stephen 176, 192
Maxwell, Gavin 191–92
McGilchrist, Iain 116, 199n7
Megamachine, the 28–9, 45n81, 108
Méligny, Marthe de 59–60
Melville, Herman 190, 193, 219
Merleau-Ponty, Maurice 15, 30–1, 94–5, 117, 120, 123, 136n39, 225
Messiaen, Olivier 127, 146, 147, 148
Metaphor, as such 2–3, 4–5, 6n9, 12–3, 15, 28, 44n19, 56, 166; in art 2, 11, 13–4, 38, 43, 234–35; in fiction 172, 174–75, 183–84, 190–91; in music 119–22, 131–32, 139, 144, 157; in painting 51, 54, 56, 57, 58, 71, 75, 82, 84–5, 97–8, 100, 101; in poetry 223, 228
Michelangelo 53
Michaux, Henri 186
Midgley, Mary 135n31, 187
Milne, A.A. 179

Milosz, Czeslaw 226, 235
Mirrlees, Hope 185
Miura, Isao 35, 76
Mitchell, Joni 156, 157, 159, 161, 218
Miyazaki, Hayao 41
Modernism 31–4, 46n97; in art generally 21, 26, 29, 34–7, 46n105; in music 142–51; in painting 52, 62, 72–4, 90n153, 93, 96, 98, 101, 105; literary 188–90, 193, 195, 196, 216
Modernity 4, 15, 16, 24, 29, 33, 46n97, 108, 126, 138, 159, 214, 221n42
Modigliani, Amedeo 69
Moments bienhereux 234
Mompou, Federico 143, 144
Mondrian, Piet 33, 54, 56, 57, 60, 71, 73, 80, 94–5, 96–9, 100, 103, 141, 147
Monet, Claude 14, 29, 49–52, 53, 54, 56, 59, 60, 74, 75–6, 82, 86, 93–4, 99, 101, 102, 106, 116
Monism 4, 15, 33, 186
Monk, Thelonious 34
Montaigne, Michel de 80, 178, 199n4, 217, 218, 234
Montale, Eugenio 35
Moriyama, Daido 64, 79, 81
Morris, Jan 192, 218
Morris, William 3, 26
Morrison, Van 154, 156, 160
Movies *see* film
Mozart, Wolfgang Amadeus 116, 133, 138, 139, 140, 141, 142
Murata, Sayaka 195
Music 111–34; classical 138–51; popular 151–63; traditional or folk 163–66
Mūthos 10, 34
Mythicity 112

Nagel, Thomas 128, 135n31, 200n18
Narnia 180
Narrative 8, 14, 19, 51, 74, 75, 82, 84, 97, 118–19, 138, 163, 166, 161, 173, 175, 176, 180, 185, 187, 188, 189, 190–95, 196–98, 214, 216
Nash, David 78
Nature 5, 10, 11, 12, 15, 16, 28, 33; in fiction 175, 216, 229, 232, 235; in/ and music 127–29, 142, 144–45; in painting 54–5, 58, 73, 80–82, 84, 85
Naturalism 15, 33, 200n18, 232
Nesbit, E. 180
Neurophysiology 15, 17, 65
Newman, Barnett 68
Newsom, Joanna 157

New Yorker, The 153–54, 201n73
Nietzsche, Friedrich 5, 39, 107, 141, 184, 190, 223
Noise 113, 125–27, 136n61, 136n64, 149, 150
Novel, the 171, 174, 178, 184, 186; and enchantment 193–96, 205, 208, 220n16
Nude, the 60, 69–70, 80

Oakeshott, Michael 36, 67, 101, 180–81, 224, 233–34
O'Brian, Patrick 140, 176, 190, 192
O'Brien, Flann 205
O'Carolan, Turlough 165, 169n76
O'Donoghue, Hughie 75
Olds, Sharon 227
O'Neill, Terry 77
Opera 3, 5, 39, 114, 141, 145
Ó Raghallaigh, Caoimhím 165
Ó Riada, Seán 165
Origawa, Noriko 144
Ortega y Gasset, José 174
Orwell, George 161, 221n42

Palmer, Samuel 104, 214
Paradises, literary lost 62, 191–93
Paradox 11, 13, 18, 23, 50, 57, 116, 157, 176
Parker, Charlie 34, 35, 123
Peer Gynt 1, 173
Penguin Café Orchestra, The 121
Perspective, in art 83–4, 93
Pessoa, Fernando 23, 175
Phenomenology, Goethean 55–6
Photography 64, 76–9
Picasso, Pablo 2, 34, 35, 37, 52, 53, 58, 62–3, 92–3, 94, 96, 100, 103
Pinker, Steven 130
Place 1, 4, 9–10, 12, 16–7, 30, 36, 40, 58, 71, 77, 107, 111, 112, 120–21, 125, 144–45, 161, 171, 177, 179, 181, 184, 191, 215–16, 230
Plato and Platonism 10, 15, 20, 21, 33, 50, 94–9, 103, 120, 131, 132, 141, 177, 188, 198, 219n7, 223, 225
Play 39, 58, 73, 115, 122, 131, 135n18, 175, 183
Plumwood, Val 45n83, 61
Poetry and enchantment 223–30
Polixenes 235
Pollock, Jackson 94–5, 100, 103
Poppins, Mary 183–84
Porter, Fairfield 96–7, 141
Potter, Dennis 205–6

Potter, Harry 187–88
Poulenc, Francis 143
Pound, Ezra 34, 188, 224
Powys, John Cowper 194
Pratchett, Terry 186, 191, 193
Proust, Marcel 1, 19, 23, 40, 51, 54, 59, 62, 66, 71, 116–17, 158, 171, 174, 183, 191, 193, 194, 195, 216, 218–19, 234
Psychedelic art 73, 74
Psychology 15, 17, 32, 35, 113, 115, 186, 187, 195–96
Publishing industry, the 198–99, 213
Pullman, Philip 180–81
Puppetry 42–3, 205, 207–08

Queenan, Joe 145–46

Ramsay, Clay 199
Raphael 71
Rauschenberg, Robert 23, 94
Ravel, Maurice 142–43
Reading, deep 173–78, 225
Redon, Odilon 59, 95
Reitz, Edgar 40
Relationality and encounter 9, 18, 31, 35, 36, 48, 79, 84, 85, 94, 101, 102, 106, 112, 115, 117, 118, 119, 132, 139, 140, 174, 204, 205, 206, 211, 215, 217, 224, 225, 229, 234, 235
Renbourn, John 164
Renoir, Pierre-Auguste 53, 59
Richter, Gerhard 70–1
Ricoeur, Paul 6n9, 44n19, 174, 182, 201n53
Rilke, Rainer Maria 198, 224
Ringwraiths 30, 219
Rock music 130, 152, 156, 157, 158, 164, 165
Rodgers, Richard 153
Rollins, Sonny 34, 129, 146
Romanticism 74, 140, 141, 160, 223–24
Rooney, Sally 195
Ross, Alex 124, 153
Rothenberg, David 127–28
Rothko, Marc 80, 94, 95–6, 160
Rowling, J.K. 187–88, 196
Ruskin, John 3, 21, 28, 56, 105, 107–08, 127

Saatchi, Charles 104
Sainte-Beuve, Augustin 170–71
Saint-Saëns, Camille 116
Santayana, George 23
Satie, Erik 143, 144
Saumarez, S.M. 205

Savage, Jon 154
Savall, Jordi 112, 122
Saville, Jenny 69
Scarry, Elaine 52, 53, 65, 68–9
Schaeffer, Pierre 124, 132–33, 147, 148, 167n37
Schiff, András 126
Schoenberg, Arnold 34, 97, 99, 140, 142, 145, 146, 147–49
Schjeldahl, Peter 63, 102, 104
Schulz, Bruno 172
Scruton, Roger 128–29, 153, 168n48
Sehnsucht 17
Self, Will 176
Sendak, Maurice 181
Serialism, twelve-tone *see* atonalism
Serres, Michel 63, 127, 159
Seurat, Georges 50, 53
Sewell, Brian 37
Sex, and enchantment 11, 25, 61, 68–70, 77, 78, 98–9, 156, 203–04, 227
Sexton, David 174
Shakespeare, William 3, 50, 193, 216
Shapiro, David 99
Shattuck, Roger 213–14
Shelley, Percy Bysshe 22, 223, 227
Shippey, Tom 189, 220n34, 220n35
Simons, Jonathan 22
Smith, Ali 48, 94
Snyder, Gary 229–30
Social media and the internet 22, 81, 154, 155, 173, 175–78, 199, 200n34
Spender, Stephen 225
Spufford, Francis 173, 180, 200n16
St Clair, Kassia 65
Stambolian, George 216
Stark, Freya 30, 80, 172, 218
Steeleye Span 157, 165
Stevens, Wallace 4, 5, 10, 30, 34, 66, 85, 100, 157, 226
Stevenson, Robert Louis 214
Stowe, Randolph 185
Sullivan, Michael 80–2
Supernaturalism 5, 15, 33, 187, 217
Surrealism 24, 54, 83, 100–01, 172, 226
Surt, George 27
Suzuki, Shunryu 18
Swarbrick, Dave 117, 165
Swann, Charles 116–17
Szakolczai, Arpad 6n10, 11, 16, 204

Tallis, Raymond 129
Takemitsu, Tōru 115, 127, 143–45, 167n22
Tanizaki, Jun'ichirō 53

Taruskin, Richard 31, 114, 147, 148, 167n42
Tensive truth 4, 14, 34, 43, 52, 57, 60, 83, 97, 120, 174, 183
Tetzlaff, Christian 113, 139, 141
Theosophy 98, 99
Thierrée, Jean-Baptiste 42
Thierrée, Victoria 42
Third thing, the 4, 38, 57–8, 85, 115
Thomas, Edward 228–30
Thomas, R.S. 166, 226
Thomson, David 192
Thompson, Richard 154, 156, 165
Tolkien, Christopher 214
Tolkien, J.R.R. 6, 9, 17, 27, 31, 36, 52, 83, 112, 171, 174, 181, 182, 184, 185, 189, 194, 202n79, 207, 209, 211–12, 213–19, 220n35, 220n36, 221n45, 227, 233, 235
Tomes, Susan 112, 119, 139
Toop, David 127, 136n63
Toro, Guillermo del 41–2
Transhumanism 46n90, 204
'Transport', musical 1, 19, 121–22, 166
Tranströmer, Tomas 166n7, 226, 227
Tsvetaeva, Marina 175
Turner, J.M.W. 81, 85, 107–08

Van Gelder, Leslie 38, 47n116
Van Gogh, Vincent 59, 66, 94, 97
Varèse, Edgard 150
Vermeer, Johannes 16, 48, 59, 62, 66, 70, 71, 140, 218, 226
Vuillard, Edouard 59, 61, 64

Wagner, Richard 21, 39–40, 97, 114, 126, 140–41, 142–43, 147
Wallace, David Foster 195, 213
Warhol, Andy 74, 103, 104, 109n47
Warner, Sylvia Townsend 185
Watkins, Nicholas 60
Watson, Chris 127
Way of life, the enchantment of art as a 5, 55, 59, 74, 209, 219, 233–36
Waugh, Evelyn 191
Weber, Max 4, 10, 15, 22, 24, 28, 33, 50, 100, 115–16, 196, 198, 232
Whistler, James 22
White, E.B. 181
Wildness 22–5, 102, 174
Williams, C.K. 23, 226
Williams, Rowan 157
Williamson, Robin 157–58, 164
Wilson, Edmund 36

Winnicott, D.W. 13, 27, 57–8, 115–16, 179–80
Winship, Eleanor 122
Winship, John 76
Winterson, Jeanette 28
Wittgenstein, Ludwig 5, 15, 30, 52–3, 96, 105, 112, 113, 114, 184, 190, 232, 234
Wodehouse, P.G. 191, 193
Wondertales *see* Fairy tales
Woodman, Delia 76
Woolf, Virginia 34, 36, 176, 188, 200n36
Woolridge, Shane 12
Woon, Wendy 93
Wordsworth, William 160, 223
Worlds, literary 191

Wou-ki, Zao 85–6

Xi, Guo 81, 82
X Factor, The 154

Yeats, W.B. 19, 159, 160, 178, 183, 206, 222n63, 224–25, 227
Yorke, John 197–98, 202n97

Zagajewski, Adam 33, 71–3, 226
Zan, Ni 1, 81
Zhuang Zi 45n67, 170
Zipes, Jack 187
Zuckerkandl, Victor 115, 121, 129, 136n39, 137n75
Zwicky, Jan 14, 17, 59, 83, 140, 218, 234